Cognitive-Experiential Theory

Cognitive-Experiential Theory

An Integrative Theory of Personality

Seymour Epstein

OXFORD
UNIVERSITY PRESS

OXFORD
UNIVERSITY PRESS

Oxford University Press is a department of the University of Oxford.
It furthers the University's objective of excellence in research, scholarship,
and education by publishing worldwide.

Oxford New York
Auckland Cape Town Dar es Salaam Hong Kong Karachi
Kuala Lumpur Madrid Melbourne Mexico City Nairobi
New Delhi Shanghai Taipei Toronto

With offices in
Argentina Austria Brazil Chile Czech Republic France Greece
Guatemala Hungary Italy Japan Poland Portugal Singapore
South Korea Switzerland Thailand Turkey Ukraine Vietnam

Published in the United States of America by
Oxford University Press
198 Madison Avenue, New York, NY 10016

First issued as an Oxford University Press paperback, 2016

Library of Congress Cataloging-in-Publication Data
Epstein, Seymour.
Cognitive-experiental theory : an integrative theory of personality / Seymour Epstein.
pages cm
Includes bibliographical references and index.
ISBN 978-0-19-992755-5 (hardcover); 978-0-19-049324-0 (paperback)
1. Cognitive-experiential psychotherapy. 2. Personality. I. Title.
RC489.C62E67 2013
616.89′14—dc23
2013028669

To my wife, Alice

CONTENTS

ACKNOWLEDGMENTS

I wish to express my appreciation to the following individuals who read several chapters in my book and made extremely helpful comments: Icek Aizen, Rachel Aizen, Alice Epstein, Scott Barry Kaufman, George Levinger, and Nancy Link. Martha Epstein was helpful in getting references. Particularly appreciated are the contributions by Ed O'Brien, an unidentified reviewer, and Everett Waters, who read and commented on the entire book. Waters and the unidentified reviewer made general comments about each chapter. O'Brien went even further by reviewing each of the chapters in meticulous detail. O'Brien also made an unusual contribution by assigning several chapters for critical review by members of his graduate classes in clinical psychology. The book is greatly improved by the comments from all of these sources.

INTRODUCTION

Can a theory of personality be constructed that coherently integrates the most important insights from the classic theories of personality? Allport (1965) thought that it could be done, but it would take the kind of investment in resources and effort that had been required to construct the atomic bomb. He added that it would be worth the investment. Others believe that such integration is impossible because of irreconcilable differences in the theories (e.g., Wood & Joseph, 2007).

ALLPORT'S CHALLENGE

Following a failed attempt to understand a case history from the vantage point of several classic personality theories, Allport (1965) concluded that although all had something to contribute, none could provide a satisfactory explanation of the whole person. He believed that such an explanation would require a synthesis of the best contributions of all the theories: "Yet the challenge remains: if there is truth in all, to what extent and in what direction, is each approach most valid? Eclecticism in personality theory is no doubt necessary, but it is a task for the future to blend the approaches so that a *systematic* eclecticism, a true synthesis of theories, will emerge" (p. 211).

A RESPONSE TO ALLPORT'S CHALLENGE

I introduced a global theory of personality (Epstein, 1973) several years after Allport's challenge. I believe my theory goes a long way toward responding to his challenge. The theory, which I referred to as cognitive-experiential self-theory (CEST), more recently shortened to cognitive-experiential theory (CET), is the subject matter of this book. If there is any attribute that best describes the theory, it is that it is highly integrative.

Readers will likely detect in CET aspects of several other theories with which they are familiar, including Freud's (1933) psychoanalytic theory and its various alternatives, including Carl Jung's (1968) analytical psychology, Alfred Adler's (1959) individual psychology, Karen Horney's (1950) personality theory, and John Bowlby's (1969) object relations theory. Nonpsychoanalytic theories that made significant contributions to CET include Dollard and Miller's (1950) stimulus-response learning theory, Skinner's (1974) intraindividual learning theory, Carl Rogers's (1951) and George Kelly's (1955) phenomenological theories, and the views of modern cognitive scientists about unconscious processing. It may seem from such a variety of influences that I selected the most impressive aspects of each theory and attempted to find a way to integrate them into a coherent framework. However, this is not the way that CET became integrative; it did so not by initial design, but by coherently expanding from a foundation based on a few basic assumptions.

That CET turned out to be highly integrative surprised me as much as anyone. I first became aware that it might be integrative when people from different theoretical orientations told me when I presented CET at invited lectures that my views were compatible with their own. It followed that if my theory were both coherent and compatible with a variety of other theories, it must be integrative.

EVOLUTION OF THE THEORY FROM A FEW BASIC ASSUMPTIONS

Like Allport, I believed that each of the classic personality theories had something to offer, but that each lacked important insights provided by others. As a result, I did not feel comfortable adopting any of the theories as my own because none provided me with a satisfactory framework for understanding people and for guiding my research and psychotherapy. As a result, for many years, I remained in an unresolved state, seeking a theoretical framework with which I could feel comfortable.

The "Light Bulb" Insight That Launched Cognitive-Experiential Theory

I can recall the occasion when I had a sudden flash of insight that provided the foundation for the theory I was to work on for the rest of my career. I had been pondering Carl Roger's (1951) view of a self-concept that has both agentic and growth properties. I knew that William James (1910) and Gordon Allport (1961) had dismissed such properties of the self as unscientific and that others had ridiculed the idea of an agentic self as a "ghost in the machine" or as a homunculus that pulled the strings that controlled the larger person. The trouble with such a self, they said, is that explaining the behavior of the ghost or the homunculus was no less daunting than explaining the behavior of the real person. James and later Allport recommended that such a self be banished from psychology. The only scientifically viable view of the self, they said, was as an object of belief. They noted that people have beliefs about themselves that importantly influence their thoughts, feelings, and behavior, and that it is therefore important to understand such beliefs, which can be studied scientifically, like any other beliefs. Thus, although there was no argument about the importance of the self as an object of belief, the same could not be said for the self as an agent of behavior.

Although I could not, at first, see how a self that presumably has agentic and growth properties could be conceptualized in a scientifically defensible manner, I found the idea intriguing and was not yet willing to abandon it. I therefore pondered Rogers's belief about the self-concept to see if I could find a way to reconceptualize it in a more acceptable manner. According to Rogers, his clients in therapy were absorbed with finding their true, authentic selves, which he said they often accomplished when provided with unconditional positive regard. He further noted that when his clients found what they regarded as their authentic selves, they became more accepting of themselves and of others. They also reported that it made them feel for the first time that their feelings and conscious beliefs were harmonious. Rogers believed that people's newly discovered authentic selves consisted of beliefs previously held outside of awareness that had been derived directly from their own experience, as contrasted with beliefs they had introjected from others, particularly from those they wished to please, such as their parents. As I contemplated how such a position could be scientifically articulated, I had a "light bulb" insight in which everything fell into place. The insight was that the self-concept is not simply a conscious concept of the self, as Rogers believed, nor even multiple concepts about the self. Rather, it was an organized implicit theory about the self that had been automatically acquired from lived experience, and it was necessary for adapting to everyday life.

Note what is accomplished by the simple transformation of a conscious self-concept into an implicit self-theory. It provides an answer to the question of how Rogers's views about a self with agentic and growth properties could be articulated in a scientifically acceptable manner because these properties are inherent in all scientific theories. Thus, scientific theories are agentic in the sense that they direct the behavior of the scientists who hold them, and they grow through their interaction with data. In a similar manner, implicit self-theories direct the behavior of people in their everyday lives, and they grow through their interaction with the data of experience. As will be seen, this initial insight of viewing the self-concept as an implicit theory about the self that was automatically acquired from experience provided the foundation on which CET was constructed.

The Development of the Theory

According to CET, everyone, like it or not, constructs an implicit self-theory because such a theory is necessary for adaptive behavior in human society. It is assumed that everyone has implicit beliefs automatically derived from experience that influence how they think and feel about themselves. Moreover such beliefs are organized into a hierarchical, implicit, dynamic structure referred to as the *experiential system* that influences people's feelings and behavior and biases their conscious thinking.

Important as such self-beliefs are, they are insufficient for adequately directing people's reactions in the real world. To do so, it is also necessary to have implicit beliefs about other people, the impersonal world, and the interactions among these three kinds of beliefs. In other words, people need an overall theory of reality with subtheories about the self, others, the impersonal world, and their interactions. Moreover, if people have implicit beliefs acquired directly from experience and explicit beliefs introjected from others, they must have two views about reality, one implicit, which is based on direct experience, and another that is explicit and introjected from others.

Note how the theory developed with a momentum of its own from the realization that a self with agentic and growth properties can be explained in a scientifically acceptable manner. It was through a continuous process of such extrapolation from previous generalizations to new generalizations that the theory continued to develop. Expressed otherwise, as each question was answered, it raised other questions, which, when answered, raised yet other questions. It was through this process that the theory expanded. Although this process explains the expansion of the theory, it was not the only reason the theory became integrative.

Integration Promoted by the Founding Insight

The foundation of CET is the assumption that people automatically construct an implicit theory of reality that includes subtheories concerning the self, others, the impersonal world, and their interactions. This foundation turned out to be well suited for assimilating a wide variety of information that integrated two traditions in psychology that usually were treated in isolation from each other. One is the predominant *nomothetic approach* in psychology, according to which behavior is regarded from the perspective of an objective observer. The other is the *idiographic view,* in which behavior is viewed through the eyes of an individual. By assuming that every person develops a unique theory of reality that is determined by that person's experiences in living, CET operates within the idiographic tradition. However, CET accepts this view only within limits. Unlike the position of phenomenologists, it does not assume that each person's behavior varies along unique dimensions. Rather, consistent with a nomothetic approach, CET assumes that people's most important beliefs vary along common dimensions. For example, it is assumed in CET that all people have certain basic beliefs that can be identified and measured. By being built on a foundation that is compatible with both a nomothetic and an idiographic approach, CET is able to assimilate a wide variety of divergent material. For example, it can assimilate insights from phenomenologists such as Carl Rogers and George Kelly (1955) with those from objectivists, such as learning theorists, psychoanalysts, and cognitive scientists.

SOURCES OF INTEGRATION

As noted previously, CET did not become integrative by design but as a byproduct of other influences. Among these influences are the nature of the founding insight about the self as an implicit theory, which has already been discussed; an intimate familiarity with the major theories of personality; and an openness to a variety of other sources of influence.

Integration Promoted by an Intimate Familiarity with the Classic Personality Theories

An important source of information for developing my theory was my knowledge of the major personality theories and most of the minor ones. I was intimately familiar with such theories from having taught graduate and undergraduate courses on theories of personality for many years. Thus, when questions arose in the development of my theory that required answers, resolutions provided by some of the classic theories readily came to mind. I could then decide which, if any, could be coherently assimilated into my own theory. A good example of this was provided by how I decided on the basic human needs or motives. I knew that, according to learning theory as well as early psychoanalytic theory, it was assumed that the one most basic motive is to behave according to the hedonic principle, the desire to experience pleasure and to avoid pain. This concept is embedded in learning theorists' conception of reinforcement and in the emphasis in early Freudian theory on a pleasure principle. For phenomenologists, such as Lecky (1951), Snygg and Combs (1949), and Rogers (1951), the most fundamental need is to maintain the stability and coherence of people's conceptual systems. As support for their position, individuals throughout history have endured great suffering, including torture, rather than renounce their beliefs.

For Maslow (1970), the most important psychological need is the need for security. According to Bowlby (1969) and other object-relations theorists, the most fundamental need is for relatedness. They note that there is nothing more important to a child than being cared for and that children will not develop normally—and may even die—if only their physical needs are attended to. Allport (1937) and Kohut (1971) believed that the most fundamental need is to maintain self-esteem. Each of these theorists provided compelling arguments for why the need they proposed is the most fundamental need of all. How can one choose among them? The position adopted by CET is that all these theorists are both correct and incorrect. They are correct because the need they proposed is in fact capable of dominating all the other needs, and they are incorrect for not recognizing that the needs proposed by others can dominate the need they proposed. Accordingly, it is assumed in CET that there are the following five basic needs: the need to behave according to the hedonic principle, the need to maintain the coherence and stability of people's conceptual systems, the need for security, the need for relatedness, and the need for self-esteem.

Openess to a Wide Variety of Information

A further reason for CET developing into a highly integrative personality theory was my lack of commitment to any available theory of personality and my openness to a variety of views. As noted previously I, like Allport, believed that all the classic personality theories contained valuable insights about human nature, but none was sufficient by itself. Accordingly, I was receptive to whatever any theory could provide for answering the questions that arose during the development of CET. Sometimes I could adopt other views, and, at other times, I could adapt them to make them coherent with CET. An example of such an adaptation was my incorporation of a modified version of Jung's use of the term "complex" to refer to a constellation of attitudes, feelings, and behavioral tendencies focused on a particular kind of figure, such as a mother figure. According to Jung, a complex has a nucleus and peripheral representations. He states that a complex draws relevant material to it like a magnet draws iron filings to it. For example, according to Jung, a person with a mother complex is unusually sensitive and reactive to any stimuli that are associated with mother figures. I found these ideas compatible with mine on the influence of cognitive-affective networks. Accordingly, by considering complexes as cognitive-affective networks without including Jung's extraneous baggage that was unacceptable to me, such as his view that complexes are influenced by unconscious memories from people's racial past history, I was able coherently to include the idea of complexes in CET as particularly influential cognitive-affective networks based on people's personal history.

In summary, I believe it was for all the reasons cited here that CET became a highly integrative and global personality theory, not by intent, but by extrapolating according to a variety of influences.

HOW GLOBAL IS COGNITIVE-EXPERIENTIAL THEORY?

There is good reason to believe that CET is comparable in scope to psychoanalytic theory, which is the most comprehensive personality theory there is. Cognitive-experiential theory can compete with the scope of psychoanalytic theory because it is sufficiently similar to allow it to capture its explanatory power. More specifically, it endorses many of the same phenomena as psychoanalysis does, including, most importantly, the ubiquitous influence of unconscious processing. Thus, it can explain almost everything that psychoanalytic theory attempts to explain by adapting many psychoanalytic principles and concepts that are not dependent on Freud's views about the operating principles of unconscious processing. Cognitive-experiential theory can therefore explain in a scientifically more defensible manner than psychoanalysis the operation of unconscious processing by proposing an adaptive unconscious that is consistent with evolutionary principles in place of the Freudian maladaptive unconscious that is inconsistent with evolutionary principles.

A further consideration is that CET can borrow freely from personality theories other than psychoanalytic theories. Moreover, it is able to introduce completely new ideas that are unrelated to both psychoanalytic and other theories. The result is that, because of its openness to a wide variety of sources of influence combined with the conceptualization of an adaptive unconscious mind, CET is able to extend its reach in a scientifically acceptable manner beyond that of psychoanalytic theory.

THE NATURE OF INTEGRATION IN COGNITIVE-EXPERIENTIAL THEORY

Cognitive-experiential theory integrates important aspects of self-theory, learning theory, cognitive science, psychoanalytic theory, and emotions theory.

- *Integration of Self-Theory.* Self-theory and, relatedly, phenomenological theory are integrated in CET by the assumption that people's beliefs about themselves are a fundamental aspect of their adjustment. Self-theory originally played such a central role in my theory that I labeled it cognitive-experiential self-theory (CEST). Since it no longer is so central, I have changed its name to cognitive-experiential theory (CET). According to self-theory and CET, what people believe is a major determinant of how they interpret events, behave, and feel. However, unlike in Rogers's theory, in which the self-concept exists only at a conscious level, in CET, it exists at both implicit and explicit levels. A further major difference is that, in CET, more importance is given to beliefs about other people, the inanimate world, and the interactions among these beliefs than in self-theory. Moreover, in CET, the three kinds of implicit beliefs are organized into an overall theory of reality.

- *Integration of Learning Theory.* Learning theory plays a critically important role in CET because the content of the experiential system consists of implicit beliefs that were automatically acquired by associative learning. Such learning is assumed to operate according to the same principles in humans as in higher order animals that used it successfully to adapt to their environments over millions of years of evolution. Cognitive-experiential theory differs from learning theory by its emphasis on and identification of the attributes of associative learning that go beyond identifying its operating principles. Most importantly, CET is primarily concerned with the learning of schemas, or internal representations, including implicit beliefs, whereas learning theory emphasizes the learning of behavioral responses.

  Cognitive-experiential theory also extends learning theory by including a concept of preadaptation, according to which adaptations, as in associative learning, that evolved for one purpose, such as learning from experience, are used for other purposes, such as reacting to entirely new situations. This assumption considerably expands the explanatory power of associative learning. For example, it can account for phenomena that are of particular interest for dual-process theories, such as implicit learning and unconscious pattern recognition that cannot be explained by learning from past experience.
- *Integration of Cognitive Science.* Important aspects of cognitive science are included in CET through its emphasis on the influence of schemas and its views on the storage and retrieval of information. As in cognitive science, unconscious processing in CET is regarded as the default mode. However, unlike in cognitive science, such processing is attributed in CET to the operation of an experiential system. Cognitive-experiential theory also differs from cognitive science in its greater emphasis on emotions.
- *Integration of Psychoanalytic Theory.* Aspects of psychoanalytic theory are assimilated in CET by adaptations of unconscious processing, psychodynamics, and transference. Cognitive-experiential theory differs from psychoanalytic theory in its substitution of an adaptive unconscious system represented by the operation of the experiential system for the Freudian maladaptive unconscious system. Moreover, CET differs from the view in psychoanalysis that all information acquired after the prelanguage years that was not repressed would be conscious. According to CET, unconscious processing is the default mode because it is more efficient than conscious processing. Cognitive-experiential theory differs from psychoanalytic theory in its treatment of psychodynamics by proposing several basic needs and their interaction in place of the Freudian assumption, in the later version of his theory, that there are two basic needs: the pleasure principle and the death instinct. Transference is

regarded in CET in a more general way than how it is viewed in psychoanalysis. It is attributed in CET to stimulus generalization regarding all significant relationships and not just in regard to parental figures.

- *Integration of Emotions Theory.* Emotions theory is included in CET by the importance attributed to affect as a source of motivation, of reinforcement, and of increasing activation across networks. I use the word "affect" to refer to the pleasant or unpleasant feeling of an emotion. Affect is also considered in CET to provide a royal road to the identification of the important schemas in people's implicit theories of reality. Affect in CET is also regarded as playing a critical role in establishing a sufficiently accurate model of the world with which nonhuman higher order species can cope. However, although it does the same in humans, it also can have an opposite effect in humans because of its biasing influence on their rational thinking. This, of course, assimilates two opposite views on the influence of affect on the establishment of a form of "truth."

REFERENCES

Adler, A. (1959). *The practice and theory of individual psychology*. Totowa, NJ: Little Field Adams.

Allport, G. (1937). *Personality: A psychological interpretation.* New York: Holt, Rinehart, & Winston.

Allport, G. (1961). *Pattern and growth in personality.* New York: Holt, Rinehart, & Winston.

Allport, G. (1965). *Letters from Jenny*. New York: Harcourt, Brace, & World.

Bowlby, J. (1969). *Attachment and loss. Vol. I: Attachment*. New York: Basic Books.

Dollard, J., & Miller, N. E. (1950). *Personality and psychotherapy: An analysis of learning, thinking, and culture.* New York: McGraw-Hill.

Epstein, S. (1973). The self-concept revisited or a theory of a theory. *American Psychologist, 28*, 404–416.

Freud, S. (1933). *New introductory lectures. Vol. 22 of The Standard Edition*. London: Hogarth Press.

Horney, K. (1950). *Neurosis and human growth*. New York: W. W. Norton.

James, W. (1910). *Psychology: The briefer course*. New York: Holt.

Jung, C. (1968). *Analytical psychology: Its theory and practice*. (The Tavistock Lectures.) New York: Pantheon Press (Random House).

Kelly, G. A. (1955). *The psychology of personal constructs. Vols. 1 & 2*. New York: W. W. Norton.

Kohut, H. (1971). *The analysis of the self.* New York: International Universities Press.

Lecky, P. (1951). *Self-consistency: A theory of Personality*. Fort Myers Beach, FL: Island Press.

Maslow, A. H. (1970). *Motivation and personality* (2nd ed.). New York: Harper & Row.

Rogers, C. (1951). *Client-centered therapy*. Boston: Houghton Mifflin.

Skinner, B. F. (1974). *About behaviorism*. New York: Knopf.

Snygg, D., & Coombs, A. W. (1949). *Individual behavior*. New York: Harper & Brothers.

Wood, A., & Joseph, S. (2007). Grand theories of personality cannot be integrated. *American Psychologist, 62*, 57–58.

PART ONE

The Theory

CHAPTER 1

The Basic Theory: Two Systems

The theory on which this book is based is called cognitive-experiential theory (CET). The most fundamental assumption of the theory is that humans operate with two information processing systems, an "experiential system," which automatically learns from experience, and a "rational system," which is a verbal reasoning system. The experiential system of humans is the same system with which higher order animals have successfully adapted to their environments over millions of years of evolution, although it is probably more advanced in humans because of their larger brains. There are two fundamental components of the system: content and process. The content of the experiential system consists of implicit beliefs that were automatically acquired by associative learning. I use beliefs in the same way as schemas, as simply cognitive representations. The implicit beliefs do not exist as isolated representations but are assumed to be organized into an implicit theory of reality that determines how higher order animals and people represent themselves, others, and the impersonal world. The experiential system operates by well-established principles of associative learning. Often, outside of their awareness, the experiential system influences people's interpretations of events, feelings, behavior, and even their conscious thinking. Thus, to understand a person, it is necessary not only to understand the content in the person's experiential system but also to understand the operating rules and attributes of experiential processing in general.

Although the experiential system influences behavior primarily by the implicit beliefs that were acquired by automatically learning from past experience, it also influences behavior in completely new situations. This can be attributed to a process referred to as *preadaptation*, according to which an adaptive process that evolved to serve a particular function, such as learning from experience, is available for use for other purposes, such as responding to entirely new situations. Thus, the experiential system responds to all situations according to the principles and attributes of experiential processing in a manner that is rapid, automatic, primarily nonverbal, holistic, minimally demanding of cognitive resources, and normally outside of awareness. This can account for the kind of intuition that is exhibited in the implicit learning of completely new material and the unconscious detection of new patterns.

The rational system operates according to a person's understanding of logic and the consideration of evidence. In contrast to the experiential system, the rational system governs the operation of people's explicit theories of reality. Unlike the experiential system, the rational system is uniquely human because it requires the use of grammatical language.

In this chapter, I compare the operating principles and attributes of the experiential and rational systems. If the reader remains skeptical about people processing information with two different systems, in the next chapter, I present evidence from everyday life to convince the reader that people do, in fact, process information in ways that are consistent with my proposal of an experiential and a rational system.

The theory presented here was introduced many years ago (Epstein, 1973) and further developed in several articles over the next two decades. Following a particularly influential article on CET in the *American Psychologist* (Epstein, 1994), a plethora of near-clones of CET appeared in which the authors claimed that their theories were original based mainly on using either of two procedures, namely misrepresenting CET or applying the principles of CET to the content of their own psychological discipline, such as social psychology or cognitive psychology (e.g., Kahneman, 2003; Sloman, 1996; Smith & DeCoster, 2000; Strack & Deutsch, 2004). Nevertheless, the near-clones differ from CET in two important ways. One way in which they differ is that their theories are much narrower in scope and less detailed than CET. For example, the authors list many fewer attributes of experiential processing than the 14 attributes in CET. Also, CET is the only modern dual-process theory that provides an overall theory of personality and measures of individual differences in experiential and rational processing. The second important way in which the near-clones differ from CET is in their assumption of what they regard as the most fundamental attribute of the experiential system, as indicated by the name they confer to their equivalent systems. For example, they identify their experiential-like system as a "peripheral system" (Petty & Cacioppo, 1986; Petty & Wegener, 1999), an "associative system" (Sloman, 1996; Smith & DeCoster, 2000), an "implicit system" (Johnson-Laird, 1983), an "impulsive system" (Strack & Deutsch, 2004), a "tacit system" (Hogarth, 2001), a "heuristic system" (Chaiken, 1980; Chen & Chaiken, 1999), and a completely noncommittal "System 1" (Kahneman, 2003; Stanovich & West, 2000). None of these identifies the essence of experiential processing in the manner that the automatic, associative, learning system of CET does by accounting for nearly all of the 14 attributes of experiential processing. Also, the idea of an adaptive automatic, associative learning system that humans share with other higher order animals makes good sense from an evolutionary perspective.

In this chapter, I compare the operating principles and attributes of the experiential and rational systems of CET. As helpful background information, I first present two other unconscious processing systems: the views of Freud and of cognitive scientists.

THE UNCONSCIOUS OF FREUDIAN THEORY AND OF COGNITIVE SCIENCE

The tooth, claw, and phallic unconscious of Freudian theory and the kinder, gentler cognitive unconscious of cognitive science could hardly be farther apart. As each has its advantages and disadvantages, it raises the question of whether it is possible to provide a synthesis that includes their advantages without their disadvantages. This is accomplished in CET, not by conscious design but by extrapolating from basic assumptions in CET.

What Is Right with the Freudian Unconscious

Freud's views of the unconscious mind are among the most influential ideas of the twentieth century. Psychological disorders and human irrationality before Freud were attributed to physical anomalies or to possession by evil spirits. Thus, psychotic symptoms were attributed to evil spirits or to unidentified malfunctions of the brain and nervous system. In contrast, Freud placed the study of maladaptive behavior squarely in the domain of the behavioral sciences, and, more specifically, in the field of psychology. The result was that maladaptive behavior could be explained by the same kinds of scientific principles that had been successfully applied to other phenomena. According to Freud, people are irrational because their attempts to think rationally are subverted by the influence of their unconscious mind, which operates by nonrational rules that he believed he was able to identify. In addition to providing an explanation of human irrationality, Freud provided explanations of dreams, mental disorders, the psychopathology of everyday life, religion, humor, creativity, slips of the tongue, human development, and individual differences in personality. Although the scope of these contributions is most impressive, their value depends, of course, on their validity, which, as will be seen, there is good reason to doubt.

Not only did Freud recognize the importance of the unconscious mind, he believed he had uncovered the secrets of how it operates by his observation of his patients' and his own dreams. He identified the operating principles that he believed governed the content of dreams and that provided the key for unlocking the secrets of their meaning. The operating principles he believed involved association, condensation, displacement, and symbolic representation. Of all the accomplishments in his long and productive life, he said the one he was most proud of was uncovering the secrets of the unconscious mind, which he believed he was able to accomplish by his investigation of dreams. In a foreword to a later edition of his book, *The Interpretation of Dreams* (Freud, 1900/1950; foreword 1931), Freud stated that his understanding of the operation of the unconscious mind by studying dreams was "the most valuable of all the discoveries it has been my good fortune to make. Insight such as this falls to one's lot but once in a lifetime." Impressive enough, assuming his understanding of the operation of the unconscious mind is correct. But is it?

On the positive side, Freud was undoubtedly correct in his emphasis on the importance of the unconscious mind, a view that is consistent with the thinking of modern cognitive scientists. However, as will be seen, he was wrong in a critically important way: he had the wrong unconscious. According to CET (Epstein, 1999), the unconscious processing that Freud observed was the degraded operation of the experiential system that occurs in the altered state of consciousness produced by sleep.

What Is Wrong with the Freudian Unconscious

A critical flaw in Freud's view of the operation of the unconscious mind is that it is indefensible from an evolutionary perspective. A waking person behaving according to the principles of dream formation, which Freud refers to as the primary process, would be psychotic and unable to survive unaided. Such a person would experience wishfulfillment of ungratified needs by having gratifying fantasies rather than by taking adaptive action. Thus, people starving from hunger would die with smiles on their faces while imagining they were enjoying their favorite foods instead of doing something to obtain food.

Freud, of course, recognized that it was necessary to bring reality-oriented behavior into the picture. His solution was to introduce a system that operated by what he referred to as the "secondary process." In contrast to the primary process, which is motivated by the pleasure principle, the secondary process is motivated by the reality principle, which promotes problem solving by logical and realistic reasoning.

The trouble with the solution of a secondary process motivated by the reality principle is that it operates primarily through the use of grammatical language. Thus, Freud is unable to account for the adaptive behavior of nonhuman animals that have no grammatical language. It is noteworthy in this respect that Freud never refers to animal behavior in his discussions of adaptation. In addition, Freud's theory of the nature of unconscious processing is inconsistent with evolutionary principles in another way. According to Freud, the unconscious mind is the foundation of all mental activity. He considered it to be analogous to the unseen part of a vast iceberg that supports a small observable conscious peak. From an evolutionary perspective, it makes little sense that the very foundation of the human mind would be maladaptive.

Freud's theory of the unconscious mind is untenable for yet a third reason. He believed that all mental activity after the acquisition of speech would be conscious if it were not repressed (i.e., blocked by anticipatory anxiety). That is, for Freud, conscious, explicit information processing, which is possible only after speech has been acquired, is the natural condition, and unconscious processing is a special condition produced by repression. This is opposite to the view of cognitive scientists (see reviews in Ellis & Hunt, 1993; Reber, 1993) who believe that unconscious processing is the natural, default condition because it is much more efficient for directing everyday behavior than conscious reasoning. Moreover, their position is supported by considerable research, as well as by logic.

In summary, as appealing as the explanatory power of Freud's conceptualization of the operation of the unconscious mind appears to be, it suffers from the critical flaw that his view of how it operates is scientifically indefensible. This is not to deny the value of the contribution he made by drawing attention to the importance of the unconscious mind. It will be shown that when the experiential system of CET is substituted for Freud's conceptualization of the unconscious mind, the impressive scope of Freud's psychoanalytic theory can be retained in a scientifically defensible manner.

What Is Right with the Cognitive Unconscious

Unconscious processing in modern cognitive science is viewed as a "kinder, gentler" form of processing outside of awareness than the Freudian view of unconscious processing. Cognition is assumed by cognitive scientists to be primarily unconscious not because of repression but because it is the natural, default state of everyday information processing. Operating automatically and without requiring awareness, unconscious processing is less demanding of cognitive resources than conscious reasoning. Unlike the properties of the Freudian maladaptive unconscious that were inferred from dreams, the properties of the cognitive unconscious were derived from logical considerations and research. Because the cognitive unconscious processes information in a way that is adaptive, it is compatible with evolutionary theory. It can explain much human decision making in everyday life, and it is supported by a great deal of laboratory research.

What Is Wrong with the Cognitive Unconscious

In marked contrast to the Freudian unconscious, the cognitive unconscious is a relatively bland form of information processing that does not provide a three-dimensional view of full-blooded human beings who experience emotions intensely and often disruptively, together with their cognitions. A person with only a cognitive unconscious mind would be like the Tin Man in the Wizard of Oz who has a brain but no heart, or like a robot with a computer in its head that can processes information but has no feelings that can direct its behavior. Thus, the problem with the cognitive unconscious, unlike the problem with the Freudian unconscious, is one of limitation rather than invalidity. Although cognitive psychologists have begun to devote serious attention to the influence of emotions and affect on cognition and behavior, the extent to which they consider the influence of the intense emotions that people regularly experience in their everyday lives is minimal when compared to their emphasis on the influence of the much milder emotions and affect that can be acceptably administered in laboratory research; this has led to inappropriate generalizations. For example, based on research with induced mild negative affect, it has been concluded that negative affect promotes realistic thinking, whereas in research that examined much stronger negative affect in real life, it was found to be related to unrealistic, maladaptive thinking (Epstein, 2011).

THE POSITION OF COGNITIVE-EXPERIENTIAL THEORY

The Experiential System

An integration of the cognitive unconscious and the Freudian unconscious can be obtained by replacing them with the experiential system of CET. This, in effect, makes the cognitive unconscious emotionally driven. Once the assumption is made that the cognitive unconscious is emotionally driven, it overcomes the limitations of the relatively bland unconscious of cognitive science.

As a result of being emotionally driven, the experiential system of CET shares many of the features of the psychoanalytic unconscious. According to both positions, the unconscious mind operates in a manner that is hedonistic, associative, impulsive, emotional, and rapid. Moreover, the rational system of CET and the ego of psychoanalysis are highly similar because both operate by the reality principle in a manner that is conscious, primarily verbal, deliberative, and logical. The similarities in the two processing systems may lead to the view that the experiential and rational systems of CET correspond to the id and the ego of psychoanalysis. This would be incorrect because although the rational system and the ego are similar, the experiential system and the id are different in the following ways: (1) the experiential system is a self-contained adaptive system, whereas the id is adaptive only in conjunction with its control by the ego; (2) the experiential system operates by well-established rules of associative learning for connecting stimuli, responses, and outcomes, whereas the id is a cauldron of seething instinctual drives that simply strive for expression; (3) the experiential system operates adaptively by learning from experience, whereas the id is incapable of learning anything; (4) improvement in therapy according to CET ultimately requires adaptive changes in the experiential system, whereas improvement in therapy according to Freud requires insight into maladaptive unconscious processing and the replacement of the influence by the id with control by the ego; and (5) the experiential system can account for primary processing, which is the way unconscious processing operates according to Freud, whereas primary processing cannot account for the experiential system. According to CET, as previously noted, Freud's primary process thinking can be understood according to CET as a degraded form of experiential processing in the altered state of consciousness produced by sleep (Epstein, 1999).

As previously noted, the experiential system is an automatic, associative learning system. There are three kinds of such learning: classical conditioning, operant conditioning, and observational learning, all of which operate by the same principles and have similar attributes. The principles include contiguity, association generalization, and reinforcement. The three kinds of learning comprise a system not only because they learn according to the same principles and have similar attributes, but also because they serve a common primary purpose, which is to promote adaptation by establishing a working model of the environment and one's behavior in it. This raises the question of whether the assumption of an organized experiential system is defensible considering that its components differ in important ways, including in anatomical location. Such a system with semi-independent components can be compared to a transportation system that includes travel by land, sea, and air. Although the different means of transportation operate in different ways and in different locations, they contribute in a semi-organized manner to the same purpose, namely, getting from one place to another.

Through classical conditioning, human and nonhuman animals learn about relations between stimuli with each other and with outcomes. Through instrumental conditioning, they learn about relations among stimuli, responses, and the outcomes that follow from their responses. Through observational learning, they vicariously accomplish both of these other kinds of learning. Through these automatic learning processes, human and nonhuman animals construct a working model of their environment (or, in the language of CET, a theory of reality), which has allowed both humans and nonhuman animals to adapt successfully to their environments.

The Rational System

Before discussing the rational system, a caveat is in order about the use of the word "rational" in CET. According to Webster's Third New International

Dictionary (Merriam-Webster Editorial Staff, 1966), the word "rational" has two meanings. In one, it refers to sensible or reasonable behavior, and, in the other, it refers to reasoning according to logical principles. It is used in CET in the latter sense and has no implications about whether rational reasoning is a superior mode of processing information in a particular situation. Logical reasoning is not always the best way to solve a problem. The reasoning can be flawed, based on incorrect premises, or not suited to a problem that requires holistic impressions rather than analytical analysis. Moreover, even if it is accurate, in addition to being logical, deliberative processing may be too inefficient and demanding of cognitive resources to be practical in many situations. In sum, it cannot be assumed that rational processing is always superior to experiential processing.

The rational system is an inferential system that operates according to a person's understanding of logical reasoning, which is largely, but not entirely, culturally transmitted. The capacity for the use of complex language and, relatedly, complex logical inference is an inherent function of the human brain. Because CET has nothing new to say about rational processing and because the rules of logical reasoning are well established, little attention will be given to it other than to compare it to experiential processing. However, there is one exception: CET has a great deal to say about the biasing influence of the experiential system on people's logical reasoning, which is regarded in CET as a major source of human irrationality, despite their capacity for logical reasoning.

If you want to understand how the rational system operates, observe how people reason as they attempt to solve problems by using logic and evaluating evidence. They are likely to think of possibilities, which may be generated by the experiential system, and find some more acceptable than others. They make logical inferences that go beyond the immediate facts, and they then seek evidence that supports some ideas more than others. They also try to be internally consistent and not contradict themselves.

The situation is much more difficult for observing the operation of the experiential system because it operates automatically and normally outside of awareness. Most people are unaware that they even have an experiential system, let alone being aware of its manner of operation.

Comparison of the Two Systems: The Second Light Bulb Experience

At first, I was only aware of the operating principles of the two systems. For the experiential system, the operating principles correspond to the rules that govern automatic, associative learning from experience and, for the rational system, they are the rules that govern logical reasoning and the consideration of evidence.

In an article in which I introduced the foundation of CET (Epstein, 1973), I assumed that people have self-theories that consist of implicit beliefs learned automatically from experience that are usually adaptive, are organized in a manner that is differentiated and integrated, and are intimately associated with affect. In addition to descriptive beliefs, they also have motivational beliefs. It will be recalled that in the first light-bulb experience it had occurred to me that if the self-concept were transferred into an implicit self-theory the concept would be scientifically defensible. Only in a second "light bulb" experience did I become aware that the experiential system has important additional attributes.

One day, as I was surfacing television programs that I could watch while doing my morning exercises, a program caught my attention that consisted of exchanges between two rapists and an audience of women. A psychologist directed the program, with the aim of keeping the discussions focused and productive. At one point, a woman asked one of the rapists how he selected his victims. She particularly wanted to know if they were more sexually attractive than his partner. The rapist replied that his partner was more attractive than any of the women he raped. The motivation for his last rape, he said, was a feeling of rage at all women that suddenly swept over him. It was the victim's misfortune that she happened to be the first one available. Another woman asked the rapist how he felt after he raped women. Did he feel pleased with himself for having obtained sexual gratification? "No, lady," he said. "As I saw the woman weeping, I felt deeply ashamed about what I had done. I felt like I was a beast that was out of control. I even hoped I would get caught." Another woman yelled at him, "You are just saying that now; you are lying to try to get our sympathy. If you could feel compassion for her after the rape, you wouldn't have done it in the first place! You are an uncivilized brute, and you will probably do it again when you are released. You ought to be kept locked up forever and the key thrown away." Other women became increasingly angry. One yelled, "You are worse than a murderer. You ought to get a death sentence. That's the only way to be sure you will never do it again."

At this point, the psychologist interceded. He asked the women to consider what a reasonable punishment would be. He noted that if the punishment for rape were a death sentence, it would encourage rapists to murder their victims so they would not be able to bear witness. One of the women, in an emotional outburst directed at the psychologist, said, "You intellectualize everything. You feel sorry for the rapists and have no compassion for the women who were the victims. Where is your humanity?" I marveled at the exchange because it was as if the psychologist and the women were speaking different languages. The primary source of their difference, it seemed to me, was that the women were intensely emotional whereas the psychologist was reasoning in a calm, deliberative manner. I began taking notes on the different ways in which the parties were communicating. I found that thinking in an intense emotional state fostered gross overgeneralization, holistic rather than analytical processing, wish-fulfillment rather than realistic thinking, all-or-none categorical thinking, concrete thinking, and personalized thinking, such as when a woman said to the psychologist, "I am sure you wouldn't be so dispassionate if your wife were raped." Other salient features were that the responses in an emotional state were rapid, impulsive, and unequivocal rather than nuanced. When I was through taking notes, I had a list of the attributes of experiential and rational processing that has hardly changed in the many years since those observations.

Table 1.1 presents the most recent comparison of the attributes of the two systems.

Table 1.1. COMPARISON OF THE ATTRIBUTES OF EXPERIENTIAL AND RATIONAL PROCESSING

Experiential System	Rational System
1. Solves problems in living by what was automatically learned from experience	1. Solves problems by conscious reasoning
2. Nonverbal: Encodes information often in images	2. Verbal: encodes information in abstract symbols, including words and numbers
3. Motivated by hedonic principle: Pursues what feels good and avoids what feels bad	3. Motivated by reality principle: by what is regarded as logical and accurate
4. Emotional	4. Affect-free
5. Associative connections between stimuli, responses, & outcomes	5. Cause-&-effect relations among stimuli, responses, & outcomes
6. Behavior mediated by automatic representations of events and feelings	6. Behavior mediated by conscious appraisal of events
7. Holistic	7. Analytic
8. Effortless & minimally demanding of cognitive resources	8. Effortful & demanding of cognitive resources
9. Rapid processing: Oriented toward immediate action; impulsive	9. Slower processing & capable of long-delayed action
10. Resistant to change: Changes with repetitive or intense experience	10. Changes more readily: Can change with speed of Thought
11. More crudely differentiated: Broad generalization gradient; categorical thinking	11. More highly nuanced and differentiated
12. More crudely integrated: Context-specific; organized by cognitive-affective networks	12. More highly integrated: Organized by context-general principles
13. Experienced passively and Preconsciously: We are seized by our emotions & ego-alien thoughts	13. Experienced actively and consciously: Reasoning considered under conscious control
14. Self-evidently valid: Experiencing is believing	14. Requires validation by logic and evidence

Discussion of the Attributes of the Two Processing Systems

The experiential system is an associative learning system, whereas the rational system is primarily a verbal reasoning system. The most fundamental distinction between the two systems is that the experiential system is an automatic, associative learning system, whereas the rational system is primarily a verbal reasoning system. Almost all the other differences between the two systems follow from this distinction. For example, automatic associative learning can explain why the master motive of the experiential system operates according to the hedonic principle because reinforcement by affect is necessary for almost all, and arguably all, associative learning. Because the experiential system of humans is basically the same system with which nonhuman animals process information, it follows that it must be a nonverbal system that represents events holistically, concretely, and often in images. In like manner, nearly all the other attributes in Table 1.1 can be attributed to the experiential system being an automatic, nonverbal processing system that humans share with other animals.

As the essence of the rational system is that it is primarily a verbal reasoning system, it explains why the master motive of the rational system operates by the reality principle because the purpose of reasoning is to obtain logical and accurate solutions to problems. Through the use of verbal reasoning, humans are able to analyze events and objects into their components, to have a long time perspective, to think at a high level of abstraction, to make highly nuanced distinctions, and to question the validity of their impressions, as well as to behave according to almost all the other attributes of the rational system listed in Table 1.1.

It should be noted that the assumption that the rational system is a reasoning system and the experiential system is an automatic learning system is not meant to imply that the rational system cannot learn from experience and that the experiential system can not reason. However, each does so in a different and more limited way than the other. For example, in contrast to the automatic learning of the experiential system, the rational system can learn from experience by logical inference. That is, it learns by reasoning about experience, rather than automatically from experience. As for reasoning by the experiential system, although it obviously cannot reason with the use of language, it can reason in a limited way through the use of imagery. Thus, it can imagine alternatives and select the image that is accompanied by the most favorable or least distressing feelings. This, of course, is a form of trial and error, but, because it is carried out mentally, it can be considered a form of reasoning.

The experiential system encodes information primarily in images, whereas the rational system operates by the use of grammatical language. Among the most important distinctions between the two systems is that the experiential system encodes information primarily nonverbally, whereas the rational system does so primarily verbally. The ability to use complex grammatical language places human beings in an entirely different category from all other species. Although other species exhibit rudimentary forms of reasoning and arguably even rudimentary language (which would indicate, according to CET, that they have a primitive rational system), their use of language in communicating and reasoning is primitive compared to its use by humans. Thus, humans can uniquely communicate across great distances, accumulate information over generations, and reason at a very high level of abstraction. The importance of accumulating knowledge over generations and distant locations cannot be overstated. Not very long ago, flying through the air was little more than a magical dream. With the invention of the airplane, it became a reality. This was followed within a few generations by an impressive increase in the speed, range, and carrying capacity of aircraft. Within the span of a few more generations, people flew to the moon and, soon after, their rockets will likely fly to more remote planets. It is because grammatical language provides the human species with such a tremendous advantage over all other species that it is assumed in CET to be the most critical dividing point between the experiential and the rational system and, relatedly, between human and nonhuman information processing.

The experiential system as a nonverbal system is particularly responsive to nonverbal communication, such as presentations of information in the form of pictures. In contrast, the rational system is uniquely responsive to information presented in the form of oral and written verbal communication. However, it is important to recognize that there is no clear dividing line that allows for the assignment of all nonverbal communication to the experiential system and all verbal communication to the rational system because pictures can be used to provide analytical information, as in maps, graphs, icons, and diagrams in anatomy books, and language can be used to evoke images, as in poems, myths, fairy tales, short stories, and novels.

Metaphors are particularly interesting because they provide a link between the two processing systems. Although presented in words, they engage the experiential system by evoking images, associations, and emotions that make the information they present more engaging and comprehensible than the same information presented in prose. For example, consider the following two statements. "Ralph was extremely angry," and "Ralph's anger knew no bounds. He yelled and gestured and became a raging lion." They both contain the same abstract information, but the second one evokes associations, images, and feelings. Prototypes are also of special interest because they indicate how the experiential system can generalize and reason abstractly by using concrete images to represent broad categories. Thus, an image of a sparrow can represent birds in general.

The master motive of the experiential system operates by the hedonic principle, whereas the master motive of the rational system operates by the reality principle. Master motives of the two systems are the hedonic principle for the experiential system and the reality principle for the rational system. It will be recalled that the women who reacted to the rapists in the example previously presented behaved primarily according to the hedonic principle because it made them feel good to think of the rapists being permanently incarcerated or given a death sentence so they would never be able to rape again. In contrast, the psychologist responded mainly in terms of the reality principle when he noted that it would be counterproductive to have a death sentence for rapists, who would then be motivated to murder their victims.

It may appear from this example that the reality principle is always more adaptive than the hedonic principle. Although this is often the case, the picture is not as simple as it may seem, for the hedonic principle is highly adaptive in its own way. As previously noted, the hedonic principle is an important source of realistic behavior because it plays a critical role in the construction of an implicit theory of reality through reinforcement. Thus, like nonhuman higher order animals that have only an experiential system, humans are able to construct a sufficiently accurate working model of their environment to which they can successfully adapt. Because humans also have a rational system, they therefore have two routes for establishing "truth": a primarily inferential reasoning path in their rational system and a primarily empirical path mediated by feelings in their experiential system.

The hedonic principle is an extremely important influence on behavior as it affects almost everything a person does. People want to feel good and not to feel bad, and they will go to great lengths to behave accordingly, including engaging in behavior that they know is unwise according to their conscious reasoning. Examples include abusing drugs, eating unhealthy food that tastes good, engaging in unsafe sex, and engaging in sexual escapades that can destroy career and family life. An example of the hedonic principle having a positive influence is when it leads someone to follow their heart in an activity in which the person is good at and enjoys.

The hedonic principle is a mixed blessing not only because it is a source of maladaptive as well as adaptive learning, but also because of its influence in biasing the operation of the rational system. For example, the hedonic principle biases conscious reasoning in part by rationalization, in which people attribute to their rational thinking what was primarily determined by their experiential system, and they do so in a manner that provides them with the most favorable interpretation they can think of that is within conscious acceptable limits.

The experiential system is intimately associated with affect, whereas the rational system is affect-free. It follows from the assumption that the experiential system is an automatic learning system that affect is critically important because of its role in reinforcement. Thus, without affect, there would be no automatic learning and therefore no experiential system. The opposite side of the coin is that it is assumed that the greater the affective reinforcement, the greater the strength of a learned response, as indicated by its resistance to extinction and its spread of activation to associated cognitive-affective networks.

The importance of the role of affect in experiential processing is also indicated by emotions providing a royal road to the schemas in people's implicit theories of reality. It is assumed that the stronger an emotion is associated with a belief, the more important the belief is in a person's implicit theory of reality. Thus, in a woman who says her intelligence is more important to her than her appearance but who exhibits greater pride when complimented on her beauty than when praised for her intelligence or greater distress when the former is slighted than when the latter is slighted, the more likely it is that her appearance is more important to her than her intelligence in her experiential system, despite the opposite view in her rational system.

The question may be raised as to whether all schemas in the experiential system are affectively charged. As all schemas in the experiential system are assumed in CET to have been acquired through affective reinforcement, they are all assumed to be emotionally charged. However, the emotional charge may be so slight as to simply reflect the undetected affect that accompanies any degree of assimilation, recognition, or predictability. That is, the reinforcement need not be through the presentation of an extrinsic reward or punishment, but can be inherent in a task by itself. For example, in a task of implicit learning, the learning in itself may be rewarding. In other words, simply making connections in a task may be reinforcing. At any rate, whether there is any learning at all without reinforcement is of no practical significance for the issues of interest in CET—which is not to deny that this issue is theoretically important for those with other interests, such as those with a particular interest in implicit learning and implicit memory.

Although the rational system is assumed to solve problems through affect-free reasoning, people can nevertheless be passionately involved in intellectual endeavors. However, when this occurs, it is assumed in CET that the affect is contributed by the experiential system. As an example, consider whether performance on a mathematics problem falls completely within the realm of the rational system. A person's response to a mathematics problem is obviously influenced by his or her past history of success and failure with mathematics. Thus, a person with a favorable history concerning mathematics may approach the problem with confidence, whereas another with an opposite history may be discouraged at the outset. It may therefore be concluded that the feelings a person has about mathematics are contributed to by the experiential system, despite the topic appearing to be completely in the realm of the rational system. According to CET, such behavior indicates how people can have strong emotions related to intellectual pursuits despite the rational system being an affect- free system.

Associative connections in the experiential system versus cause-and-effect relations in the rational system. The experiential system associates stimuli, responses, and outcomes with each other according to their contiguity in time and space and their contingent reinforcement. If A immediately precedes B and occurs at no other time, the experiential system behaves as if it believes that A causes B. It is beyond its capacity to understand cause-and-effect relations in the way that the rational system can recognize that A and B may have a causal relation to each other even if they do not occur close together. If a person is observed to have planted a bomb that explodes two hours later, a human jury would find him guilty for causing the explosion even if he were 50 miles away when the explosion occurred. A dog, however, would consider him innocent. Conversely, if a dog saw a cat in the immediate vicinity of the bomb just before it exploded, it might automatically behave with terror at the sight of the cat, as if it believed the cat caused the explosion.

How maladaptive, then, is the experiential system, considering that it is incapable of comprehending cause-and-effect relations? Not very, says Rescorla (1988), as in almost all situations in the natural world, the associative connections work out very much as they do in a cause-and-affect analysis. Thus, often, when A immediately precedes B, it is because A caused B. Of course, nonhuman animals did not evolve to cope with the complexity of human technology, which is why the dog in the previous example failed to get the cause-and-effect relation correct when a bomb was set off by remote control. Under most circumstances, a dog's behavior is highly adaptive. Thus, when a dog keeps checking a location where a rabbit was last seen, it is behaving adaptively because it is a likely location for finding a rabbit.

Humans, because of the rapidity of the experiential system, initially tend to react associatively in their thinking about cause-and-effect relations, but they subsequently often correct their inappropriate interpretations by the intervention of their rational system, as demonstrated in the following incident. No sooner had an acquaintance of mine plugged a toaster she had just retrieved from a repair shop into an electric socket when all the lights in her kitchen went out. She assumed the toaster was the cause. She then noticed that all the lights in her apartment were out, and she assumed she had triggered the operation of the main circuit breaker. When she looked out of her window she saw that the lights in all the houses across the streets were out. For a moment, she thought she had caused that too. Her thinking became more realistic when she heard a report on the radio that a widespread blackout had occurred in the entire city.

In this example, the misinterpretation of a cause-and-effect relation was amusing, but in other cases it can have serious consequences. Such misinterpretations can be highly compelling because they are the result of the very fundamental information processing of the experiential system and may be more common than is generally recognized. The reason that people are normally unaware of its prevalence is that associative processing usually operates outside of awareness and people are very good at rationalizing, so the reasons they give for their behavior are often accepted as valid. Such associative thinking and subsequent rationalization can result in poor business decisions, as well as in problems in interpersonal relationships. An unfortunate example of the latter is a teacher who unconsciously associates one of her pupils with a favored sibling of whom she was envious and resentful. The teacher is then inappropriately critical of a pupil in her class who reminds her of her sibling, which causes the child to rebel. This confirms to the teacher that she was right to regard the child as troublesome, which serves to justify and maintain her destructive behavior toward the child. The same kinds of unconscious cause-and-effect misattributions with destructive consequences occur in many other situations, including relationships between spouses, between parents and their children, and between employers and employees. The best antidote for such behavior is to be aware of one's biases and to control them according to the understanding provided by the rational system.

Behavior is mediated in the experiential system by feelings, whereas in the rational system it is mediated by conscious appraisals. According to CET, behavior is mediated in the experiential system by feelings, which can vary from full-blown emotions to "vibes," which refer to subtle feelings that are of such low intensity and salience that they are often unnoticed. It is because of the unidentified influence of vibes on conscious thought and behavior that they are regarded in CET as having special importance for irrational thinking and maladaptive behavior. However, vibes can also be a source of adaptive behavior. People may have a vague feeling that a certain course of action is right or wrong and act on it despite being unable to explain why. The behavior may turn out to be adaptive because the feeling is based on the outcomes of unidentified past similar experiences. In other words, the person was automatically extrapolating empirically from past relevant events. According to CET, this explanation can account for favorable decisions that are commonly attributed to intuition, in which a person makes a correct decision without being able to articulate the thinking that led to the decision.

When people attempt to solve problems by the use of their rational system, they reason according to their understanding of logic and the consideration of evidence. Emotions are not supposed to play any role in such reasoning. Yet, if it is true, as assumed in CET, that feelings routinely influence processing in the experiential system, which then biases conscious processing in the rational system, it follows that people's attempts to reason logically and objectively are often compromised by feelings activated by memories outside of their awareness of past relevant experiences. This has important implications for being able to reason objectively and accurately. It means that people can not reason objectively by attempting to dismiss their feelings because the feelings will then continue to influence them outside of awareness. The only solution, according to CET, is for people to become aware of their vibes and automatic thoughts so that they can compensate for their influence and reason in an objective, unbiased manner.

Holistic processing occurs in the experiential system versus analytical processing in the rational system. Holistic processing refers to reacting to something in its entirety, to getting an overall impression of an object or event or of a group of objects or events, which is the way your experiential system processes information. The opposite of holistic is analytic, which refers to breaking things down into their components, and this is the way the rational system often attempts to solve problems. Consider the difference between seeing a picture of a human face and reading a verbal description of it. You can take in the picture at a glance, whereas you have to read about each feature separately. The former representation is holistic, and the latter is analytic. The analytic procedure in this case is obviously more effortful and time consuming, and it is likely to be less accurate because it responds to reduced information. As another example, consider how long it takes to read a book compared to seeing a movie about the book. It is obviously much more efficient to present the story holistically in the form of sequences of scenes than to present descriptions of the components of the scenes.

In the examples so far cited, a holistic representation was superior to an analytical procedure, but this is not always the case. A fundamental aspect of scientific procedure is that it analyzes objects and events into their components, as illustrated in the atomic chart in chemistry. With a limited number of elements, an extremely large number of compounds can be generated, including almost all known substances on earth, which is most remarkable. As if that were not enough, identifying the elements in compounds contributes to an understanding of the compounds themselves, including the elements that can be extracted from them and combined with each other to form new compounds. Further, general laws can be formulated that allow predictions to be made about the interactions of the elements in a variety of conditions, including, for example, the effect of temperature and pressure on chemical reactions. Not surprisingly, such analytical thinking has played a critical role in humankind's unique accomplishments.

Effortless, automatic processing in the experiential system occurs in contrast to the deliberative processing that is more demanding of cognitive resources in the rational system. As the experiential system is minimally demanding of cognitive resources and highly efficient in directing everyday behavior, operating primarily in the experiential mode is the default condition in most situations. However, its efficiency is sometimes gained at a significant cost. As demonstrated by research on heuristic processing (e.g., Kahneman, Slovic, & Tversky, 1982), which is a simplified way of thinking that is characteristic of processing in the experiential mode, such processing can be a source of serious errors. The research on heuristics is extensive, but, for now, it will suffice to note that although experiential processing is highly efficient in most everyday situations, it is prone to certain kinds of errors. As an example, the experiential system is more responsive to the frequencies of numerators and tends to ignore the frequencies of denominators in small ratios. Thus, people treat 10:100 as more likely to occur than 1:10 (e.g., Denes-Raj & Epstein, 1994; Tversky & Kahneman, 1991), which can be attributed to a numerator frequency bias while ignoring the relation indicated by the ratio. However, an opposite effect is exhibited in response to larger ratios (e.g., 9:10 vs. 90:100), in which case people treat as more probable the ratio expressed in small numbers (e.g., 9:10), which is attributed to a small numbers effect that apparently overrides the frequency effect (Pacini & Epstein, 1999a). Both of these effects can be explained by the concretive processing of the experiential system: frequencies are more concrete than ratios because they do not require a consideration of relations between numbers, and small numbers are more concrete than larger numbers because they are easier to visualize. Such concrete thinking can result in serious errors in decision making in certain situations, such as when investing in the stock market and estimating the probability of diseases.

At first consideration, it may seem that the effortful processing of the rational system is bound to be more effective than the effortless, automatic processing of the experiential system. However, the situation is not so simple because the rational system also has its costs. As previously noted, the rational system is much less efficient for directing everyday behavior than is the experiential system because it is slower and more demanding of cognitive resources. Moreover, it operates by rules that are inappropriate for solving certain kinds of problems, such as situations that cannot be analyzed into their components but must be responded to holistically, as when appreciating the beauty of a sunset. Another cost is that awareness can sometimes interfere with the automatic operation of the experiential system. Wilson and his co-workers (Wilson, Dunn, Kraft, & Lisle, 1989) reported that those participants in their research who analyzed the reasons for their attitudes were less able to predict their later behavior than were participants who were not asked to analyze the reasons for their attitudes. In another study, Wilson and co-workers (Wilson, Lisle, Schooler, Hodges, Klaaren, & L Fleur, 1993) found that students who analyzed their preferences for posters before bringing one home were less satisfied with them after two weeks than were those who selected a poster based on their feelings. Wilson and Schooler (1991) also found that students who thought carefully about their preference for various jams performed more poorly when judged against expert opinion than did students who made more holistic judgments. They also found that spontaneous preferences for college courses better predicted the judgments of experts than did preferences based on detailed, analytic evaluations. In a study by Yanko and Epstein (1999), young children exhibited an intuitive understanding of ratios expressed in small numbers in a game of chance but lost this ability when asked to give the reasons for their choices. These same studies, as well as others, indicate that there are a variety of problems that can better be solved by holistic judgments than by deliberative, logical information processing (e.g., Dijksterhuis, 2004; Reber, 1993; Wilson, 2002).

Outcome-oriented processing in the experiential system occurs in contrast to process-oriented processing in the rational system. The experiential system is particularly responsive to the outcome of responses, but it makes no distinction between whether the outcomes were accidentally or intentionally produced. In contrast, the rational system takes into account intentions independent of outcomes. As people mature, they give higher priority to their rational than to their experiential processing. Thus, a young child is likely to judge behavior solely by its outcome, whereas an older child is more likely to take into account whether the outcome was intended. However, even adults, despite knowing it is irrational, often behave experientially to outcomes. For example, people are more likely to reward a messenger who brings them good news than one who brings them bad news despite knowing that the messenger is not responsible for the message. In research that examined people's reactions to arbitrary outcomes, most people indicated they would feel guilty for unfortunate outcomes that they unintentionally caused (Epstein et al., 1992). When they were asked how a completely logical person would react, most said that such a person would not feel guilty for accidental outcomes. This research indicates that people tend to react experientially in an outcome-oriented manner even when they know better in their rational system. Of further interest, it was found that some participants believed it was logical to feel responsible for accidental outcomes, thereby demonstrating how the experiential system can bias the operation of the rational system.

Rapid processing, short time perspective, and action orientation in the experiential system occurs in contrast to slower processing, longer time perspective, and greater ability to delay action and control behavioral impulses in the rational system. Because nonhuman animals have only an experiential system, they have a very limited time perspective. Only to a limited extent can they understand noncontiguous relations, delay action, and prepare for the future. This informs us that the same must be true for the operation of the experiential system of humans. Such abilities are greatly enhanced in humans by their use of language.

Because the experiential system responds more rapidly than the rational system, it is almost always the initiator of sequential interactions between the two processing systems. The rational system may subsequently operate as a corrective system. This is illustrated in research on the fundamental attribution error or correspondence bias. Gilbert and Malone (1995) found that people first attributed behavior to the attributes of an actor and only after reflection took the situation into account. As this latter step was suppressed under cognitive load, it indicates that the initial reaction was based on experiential processing and the subsequent reaction on processing in the rational mode. A common example in everyday life is the experiential system instigating an impulsive response, such as telling off one's boss, and the rational system rejecting it as unwise. The ability of humans to delay responses as a result of having a rational system gives them a great advantage over other species in controlling behavioral impulses and emotional reactions, which is extremely important in engaging in high levels of abstraction.

Because of their different time perspectives, the two processing systems can be a source of conflict between immediate and delayed gratification. An example is a conflict about dieting, in which an immediate desire for gratification conflicts with a longer term motivation to lose weight for health reasons.

The experiential system is resistant to change in comparison to the rational system, which can change with the speed of thought. Change in the experiential system usually requires many trials or fewer more emotionally intense trials. If the intensity is extreme enough, even one-trial learning can occur, as in the response to a single traumatic event such as a rape or a battle experience. By contrast, changes in the rational system can occur with the speed of thought, without requiring extreme events. Simply inform a person how to solve a simple mathematics problem and the person can immediately solve it.

The difference between the rapidity of changing behavior in the two systems is of particular importance in understanding the different reactions of patients in psychotherapy to insight and to intellectual understanding. Thus, intellectual information can provide immediate understanding in the rational system, yet have little or no effect on the experiential system. Providing lasting change in the experiential system often requires a working-through process in which the understanding is verified in emotionally significant experiences in real life. For example, a person traumatized by flying in a thunderstorm in which the aircraft was tossed about may, despite understanding that this is an unusual experience unlikely to be repeated, develop a fear of flying which is overcome only after many uneventful flights.

The experiential system is less differentiated and nuanced than the rational system. The experiential system reacts more categorically than the rational system. This can readily be observed when people are highly emotional and therefore functioning primarily in the mode of the experiential system. People under such circumstances tend to make all-or-none judgments, to overgeneralize, and to eschew qualification. For example, they view people as either completely good or completely bad, as completely agreeing or disagreeing with them, or as always or never behaving in a certain way. They make statements, such as "There you go again, always thinking of yourself and never of me." The categorical thinking of the experiential system can be advantageous in times of crises when immediate action is required and there is no time for deliberation or qualification. However, it can be a source of stereotyping, prejudice, and oversimplification.

In contrast, the rational system, with the aid of language, is far more discriminating than the experiential system because language helps people to distance themselves from their emotions, make important distinctions, and note subtle nuances.

The experiential system is less integrated and coherently organized than the rational system. Although the experiential system is an organized, adaptive system, it is less coherent than the rational system. This follows from its situation-specific encoding and retrieval of information, and from its generalization on a perceptual rather than a conceptual basis. In contrast, the rational system is able to organize information in broad, cross-situational abstract categories. The influence of emotions on the organization of the experiential system is another limiting factor in the coherence of the experiential system. Emotions can be viewed as cognitive-affective modules that organize information in particular ways. Thus, the activation of an emotion produces a shift in the organization of a person's experiential system in which the activated emotion functions as the nucleus of a cognitive-affective network. An angry person views the world from the perspective of someone who has been wronged and who has ill will toward a perceived antagonist. Compare this cognitive-affective belief with that of a person experiencing a different emotion, such as depression, in which the focus is on the self as helpless and hopeless. The focus in depression tends to be on failings in the self and not, as in anger, on failings in others. It is apparent that the personality of someone in a state of depression is very different from the personality of the same person in a state of anger. It follows that the organization of personality varies with the emotion that a person is experiencing and, to that extent, it is not unified. The rational system, as an affect-free system, is inherently more unified as it does not include the equivalent of emotional modules. Accordingly, on this basis alone, the rational system is a more unified operating system than the experiential system.

Another important reason that the rational system is more coherent than the experiential system is that the rational system is conceptually organized whereas the experiential system is organized around specific experiences. There is obviously greater coherence among schemas that include broad cross-situational generalizations than among schemas based primarily on situation-specific representations. In research in which participants were asked to respond to vignettes from two perspectives, an experiential perspective (e.g., how most people would respond in the situations described) and a rational perspective (e.g., how a completely rational person would respond), their responses were more situation-specific from an experiential perspective and more cross-situationally general from a rational perspective (Epstein et al., 1992).

People passively experience the automatic thoughts, feelings, and behavioral tendencies generated by their experiential system as outside of their control, whereas they experience the thoughts in their rational systems as under their conscious control. Although people are usually aware of their emotions, they are normally unaware of the preconscious interpretations they make that instigate those emotions. As a result, they feel seized by their emotions rather than in control of them. In like manner, they consider ego-alien thoughts that arise unbidden in their minds as outside their control. In contrast to believing that emotions and unbidden thoughts just happen to them and that there is nothing they can do about having them, people consider themselves to be in control of their conscious thoughts because they believe they can decide what to think and they can dismiss such thoughts at will.

There is a folk song that states that people can imprison your body, but your thoughts always remain free. I suspect most people would agree with this view regarding their conscious, voluntary thoughts but not their automatic, unbidden, and unwanted thoughts and emotions. This raises the question of whether people do, in fact, have free will with regard to controlling their conscious thoughts but not their automatic, preconscious, or unconscious thoughts. Some would argue that there is no free will, that all thoughts are determined, and that the belief that one is in control of some thoughts is an illusion. Although the question about whether there is free will may not be answerable when framed in terms of the presence or absence of absolute free will, it is answerable when framed in terms of the relative degree of free will between automatic and deliberative thoughts. Certainly, people believe they have greater free will in controlling their conscious, deliberative thoughts than in controlling their automatic, unbidden, and unwanted thoughts. As an example, consider the inability of people to control their phobias compared to their ability to control a conscious decision to go to one movie or another. At the very least, the difference in these kinds of beliefs has important real-life consequences regarding feelings and behavior that are anything but illusory. Thus, people are willing to invest a great deal of effort and expense to eliminate unwanted, intrusive thoughts such as those that occur in phobias and compulsions.

Beliefs in the experiential system seem self-evidently valid, whereas beliefs in the rational system require verification by logic and evidence. There is nothing more compelling than experiencing something, particularly if it elicits strong emotions. As previously noted, although such behavior is highly adaptive when the experiential system is the only processing system, as it is in nonhuman animals, it can be maladaptive in humans by overriding the better judgment that may be available to them in their rational system (Denes-Raj & Epstein, 1994). Thus, it is important, when possible, to verify experiential with rational processing.

A Comment on the Combined Influence of the Two Systems

So far, I have discussed the operation of the two systems separately. However, it is important to recognize that they operate in parallel and are bidirectionally interactive. Thus, operating more rapidly, the experiential system usually instigates an interaction between the two systems. On its part, the rational system can influence the experiential system by the associations it elicits. Both systems are assumed to contribute to all behavior along a dimension varying from a negligible contribution to almost the sole contribution. Their relative influence is assumed to vary as a function of the person and the situation. Some people are more experiential and others are more rational, and some situations, such as romantic relationships, are processed primarily experientially whereas others, such as solving mathematics problems, are processed more rationally.

Summary of the Operating Rules and Attributes of the Two Systems

It is assumed in CET that people process information with two systems, an automatic, primarily nonverbal associative learning system that humans share with other animals and a primarily verbal reasoning system that is unique to the human species. The former is referred to as an "experiential system" because it adapts by empirically learning from experience, and the latter is referred to as a "rational system" because it solves problems by reasoning. The experiential system contains subsystems of classical conditioning, operant conditioning, and observational learning, all of which involve automatic learning from experience, direct or vicarious. To understand the experiential system, it is necessary to understand both its operating rules and attributes. Its operating rules include contiguity, association, reinforcement, and generalization. Its attributes are summarized in Table 1.1. Its major strength is that it is a highly efficient system for directing everyday behavior.

The rational system solves problems and guides behavior by conscious reasoning and the consideration of evidence. It is responsible for humankind's' unique accomplishments, but it is too burdensome and slow for directing everyday behavior. Neither system is generally superior to the other because each has its advantages and disadvantages, and both are necessary for functioning adequately as a human being.

REFERENCES

Chaiken, S. (1980). Heuristic versus systematic information processing and the use of source versus message cues in persuasion. (1980). *Journal of Personality and Social Psychology*, *39*, 752–766.

Chen, S., & Chaiken, S. (1999). The heuristic-systematic model in its broader context. In S. Chaiken & Y. Trobe (Eds.), *Dual-process theories in social psychology* (pp. 73–96). New York: Guilford Press.

Denes-Raj, V., & Epstein, S. (1994). Conflict between experiential and rational processing: When people behave against their better judgment. *Journal of Personality and Social Psychology*, *66*, 819–829.

Dijksterhuis, A. (2004). Think different: The merits of unconscious thought in preference development and decision-making. *Journal of Personality and Social Psychology*, *87*, 586–598.

Ellis, H. C., & Hunt, R. R. (1993). *Fundamental of cognitive psychology*. Madison, WI: Brown & Benchmark.

Epstein, S. (1973). The self-concept revisited or a theory of a theory. *American Psychologist, 28*, 404–416.

Epstein. S. (1994). Integration of the cognitive and the psychoanalytic unconscious. *American Psychologist, 49*, 709–724.

Epstein, S. (1999). The interpretation of dreams from the perspective of cognitive-experiential self-theory. In J. A. Singer & P. Salovey (Eds.), *At play in the fields of consciousness: Essays in honor of Jerome L. Singer* (pp. 59–82). Mahway, NJ: Lawrence Erlbaum Associates, Inc.

Epstein, S. (2011). The influence of valence and intensity of affect on intuitive processing. In M. Sinclair (Ed.), *Handbook of intuition research.* Cheltenham, UK: Edward Elgar Publishing. 37–51.

Epstein, S., Lipson, A., Holstein, C., & Huh, E. (1992). Irrational reactions to negative outcomes: Evidence of two conceptual systems. *Journal of Personality and Social Psychology, 62*, 328–339.

Freud, S. (1900/1950). *The interpretation of dreams*. Translated by A. A. Brill. New York: Modern Library.

Gilbert, D. T., & Malone, P. S. (1995). The correspondence bias. *Psychologi3 al Bulletin, 117*, 21–38.

Hogarth, R. M. (2001). *Educating intuition.* Chicago: University of Chicago Press.

Johnson-Laird, P. N. (1983). *Mental models*. Cambridge, MA: Harvard University Press.

Kahneman, D. (2003). A perspective on judgment and choice. Mapping bounded rationality. *American Psychologist, 58*, 697–720.

Kahneman, D., Slovic, P., & Tversky, A. (1982). *Judgement under uncertainty: Heuristics and biases.* New York: Cambridge University Press.

Merriam-Webster Editorial Staff. (1966). *Webster's third new international dictionary.* Springfield, MA: G. & C. Merriam Co.

Pacini, R., & Epstein, S. (1999a). The interaction of three facets of concrete thinking in a game of chance. *Thinking and Reasoning, 5*, 303–325.

Pacini, R. & Epstein, S. (1999b). The relation of rational and experiential information processing styles to personality, basic beliefs, and the ratio-bias phenomenon. *Journal of Personality and Social Psychology, 76*, 972–987.

Petty, R. E., & Cacioppo, J. T. (1986). *Communication and persuasion: Central and peripheral routes to attitude change*. New York: Springer-Verlag.

Petty, R. E., & Wegener, D. T. (1999). The elaboration-likelihood model: Current status and controversies. In S. Chaiken & Y. Trope (Eds.), *Dual-process theories in social psychology* (pp. 41–72). New York: Guilford Press.

Reber, A. S. (1993). *Implicit learning and tacit knowledge*. New York: Oxford University Press.

Rescorla, R. A. (1988). Pavlovian conditioning: It's not what you think it is. *American Psychologist, 43*, 151–160.

Sloman, S. A. (1996). The empirical case for two systems of reasoning. *Psychological Bulletin, 119*, 3–22.

Smith, E. R., & DeCoster, J. (2000). Dual-process models in social and cognitive psychology: Conceptual integration and links to underlying memory systems. *Personality and Social Psychology Review, 4*, 108–131.

Stanovich, K. E. & West, R. F. (2000). Individual differences in reasoning: Implications for the rationality debate. *Behavioral and Brain Sciences, 23*, 645–665.

Strack, F., & Deutch, R. (2004). Reflective and impulsive determinants of social behavior. *Personality and Social Psychology Review*, *8*, 220–247.
Tversky, A., & Kahneman, D. (1991). Evidential impact of base rates. In D. Kahneman, P. Slovic, & A. Tversky (Eds.), *Judgment under uncertainty: Heuristics and biases* (pp. 153–160). New York: Cambridge University Press.
Wilson, T. D. (2002). *Strangers to ourselves: Discovering the adaptive unconscious.* Cambridge, MA: Harvard University Press.
Wilson, T. D., Dunn, D. S., Kraft, D., & Lisle, D. J. (1989). Introspection, attitude change, and attitude-behavior consistency: The disruptive effects of explaining why we feel the way we do. In L. Berkowitz (Ed.), *Advances in experimental social psychology*. Vol. 22. San Diego, CA: Academic Press, 287–343.
Wilson, T. D., Lisle, D. J., Schooler, J. W., Hodges, D., Klaaren, D. J., & LaFleur, S. J. (1993). Introspecting about reasons can reduce post-choice satisfaction. *Personality and Social Psychology Bulletin*, *19*, 331–339.
Wilson, T. D., & Schooler, J. W. (1991). Thinking too much: Introspection can reduce the quality of preferences and decisions. *Journal of Personality and Social Psychology*, *60*, 181–192.
Yanko, J., & Epstein, S. (1999). *The interference of providing reasons for their judgments on children's understanding of simple ratios.* (Analyzed, unpublished data).

CHAPTER 2
Evidence in Everyday Life of Two Modes of Information Processing

There is abundant evidence in everyday life that people process information in two ways. Examples include conflicts between the heart and the head; the difference between practical and intellectual intelligence; the greater appeal and ease of comprehension of pictures, concrete examples, and narratives than of abstract information; the difference between intrusive, unwanted, uncontrollable thoughts and controllable, conscious thoughts; the irrational superstitions people have in contrast to their otherwise rational thinking; the influence of emotions on thinking; the influence of thinking on emotions; and the nearly ubiquitous belief in religion throughout history in almost all societies.

CONFLICT BETWEEN THE HEART AND THE HEAD

People refer to conflicts between the heart and the head, which suggests that they are aware of two different ways of thinking—one associated with feelings, represented by the heart, and the other associated with intellect, represented by the head. A good example of this conundrum is when a young woman reports she cannot decide between two suitors because one is more serious and trustworthy and the other is more enjoyable to be with but somewhat frivolous. Both have proposed to her, and she faces the dilemma of whom to choose. She clearly has a conflict between the head and the heart. The existence of a conflict between them is consistent with the two processing systems proposed in cognitive-experiential theory (CET).

TWO KINDS OF INTELLIGENCE

The two different ways of processing information is demonstrated by the existence of two different kinds of intelligence, intellectual and practical. A widespread anomaly in human behavior is why "smart people think dumb." It is not unusual for people with high IQs doing poorly in everyday life, whereas others of average intellect may do exceptionally well. What do the latter but not the former have? A reasonable likelihood is that they have practical intelligence.

Robert Sternberg (1985) has done a great deal of research on practical intelligence compared to intellectual intelligence (Wagner & Sternberg, 1986). He has found that people with very ordinary IQs often demonstrate remarkable practical intelligence and that people with superior IQs may lack practical ability. Does this mean that there is an inverse relation between the two kinds of intelligence? This apparently is not the case. Rather, the two kinds of intelligence have been found to be independent of each other (e.g., Epstein & Meier, 1989; Sternberg, 1985; Wagner & Sternberg, 1986). It is only because people think that those with high IQs should have more practical intelligence than others and find this may not be so that they mistakenly conclude that there is an inverse relation between the two kinds of intelligence.

The existence of two kinds of intelligence is consistent with the assumption in CET that there are two kinds of information processing, rational and experiential. Because primacy of experiential information processing is the default condition for regulating daily behavior, its ability to do so effectively is demonstrated by practical intelligence. The efficacy of rational information processing, conversely, is demonstrated by intellectual intelligence.

THE DIFFERENCE BETWEEN INSIGHT AND INTELLECTUAL KNOWLEDGE

It is widely recognized in psychotherapy that there are important differences between intellectual knowledge and insight. Information obtained from textbooks and lectures is of a different quality from information acquired from experience. Experientially derived knowledge, as previously noted, is often more compelling than intellectual knowledge. According to most therapists, experientially acquired information is more likely to influence behavior than is intellectual knowledge (e.g., Brewin, 1989; Fazio & Zanna, 1981; Shiffrin & Schneider, 1977).

Psychotherapists widely regard personally meaningful experience in or out of psychotherapy as more effective in changing maladaptive feelings and behavior than intellectual information. If intellectual information could change deeply rooted behavioral patterns, psychotherapy would be a much simpler and more rapid process. All that a therapist would have to do is to observe the ways in which a client is thinking or behaving in maladaptive ways and then impart this information to the client and indicate adaptive ways to respond. In practice, such behavior on the part of a therapist is likely either to produce resistance in therapy, including antagonism toward the therapist, or a glib acceptance of the explanation without any improvement in feeling, or behavior.

To be effective, insight, according to CET, must be meaningfully related to personal experience. It is of considerable theoretical as well as practical interest that such insight in psychotherapy can change behavior and feelings in the same way that emotionally significant experiences in real life can. Does this mean that intellectual information is of no value in psychotherapy? Intellectual information can be useful when it identifies problems that have to be resolved and indicates experientially appropriate procedures for resolving the problems. There is also some benefit to be gained from identifying problems in terms of reducing inappropriate generalization and increasing control.

In conclusion, the difference between intellectual knowledge and insight in the conduct of psychotherapy is consistent with the assumption in CET that there are two processing systems, rational and experiential.

THE APPEAL AND INFLUENCE OF PICTURES

According to CET, the experiential system is primarily a nonverbal system that often represents information in the form of images. This can explain why pictures are more appealing, easier to comprehend, and easier to remember than the equivalent information presented in words (Paivio, 2007). It is for these reasons that many pictures are often included in introductory textbooks. At a time before the printing press, it was a common practice for merchants to remember accounts by associating them with images, such as imagining accounts in different rooms of a house (Paivio, 2007). By imagining different rooms, a merchant could then recall the accounts assigned to a room. Similar visualization techniques, such as associating names with images, are still used. People can also improve their recall of information if they represent the information in the form of an image, no matter how fanciful. I am not very good at remembering names, particularly unusual ones, so I needed all the help I could obtain in remembering that the name of a student in our psychology department was Arelis. She is an attractive, friendly person, and quick to laughter. I visualized her standing next to a trellis on which there was a climbing rose in bloom. Thereafter, if I did not immediately recall her name, I imagined her standing next to a trellis with roses on it. The term "trellis" was sufficiently close to Arelis for me to recall her name when I imagined this scene. The image of flowers on it also helped because I thought of her as an attractive person. Notice that two features of the experiential system were involved in this example, representation by imagery and connection by association.

Pictures are often also a more efficient and compelling way of presenting information than words, thus the statement that a picture is worth a thousand words. Consider how many words it would take to describe a picture that you can recognize at a glance or how long it would take to see a movie compared to reading a book about it. Pictures, of course, are more similar to real experience than are words, which is another reason why pictures communicate more effectively with the experiential system than do words.

As a practical application of the greater appeal and comprehension of pictures than of words, advertisers have learned through trial and error, focus groups, and intuition to apply this principle to increase the appeal of their messages. Advertising agencies and their clients have been willing to bet great sums of money when promoting cigarette smoking that the visual appeal of their messages to the experiential system will prevail over the verbal messages that smoking endangers one's life. More recently, the surgeon general changed these messages by including graphic images, such as a picture of a diseased lung. People have testified on TV that such images have been much more effective in motivating them to give up smoking than the previous verbal messages. Advertisers often combine associations and visual representations of attractive people or scenes with smoking. In an informal tabulation of the content of several cigarette advertisements, I found that the content included a wide variety of appealing scenarios, including beautiful nature scenes, happy social events, attractive people, and, most ironically, vigorous, virile people, brimming with health. The associations may make no sense to the rational system, but communicate effectively with the experiential system.

THE APPEAL AND INFLUENCE OF CONCRETE EXAMPLES

As with pictures, the use of concrete examples is an effective way to increase the interest, comprehension, and appeal of messages. People normally perform more effectively when a problem is presented in a concrete version than when it is presented in an abstract version (e.g., Donovan & Epstein, 1997; Epstein, Denes-Raj, & Pacini, 1995). We conducted a study on the comparative difficulty of solving a conjunction problem presented in concrete and abstract versions (Donovan & Epstein, 1997). The solution to conjunction problems requires an understanding of one of the simplest rules in probability theory, the conjunction rule. According to the conjunction rule, the probability of the occurrence of two events is lower than the occurrence of either one of them. In an abstract version of the conjunction problem, participants had to rank-order the likelihood that "A," a likely event, "B," an unlikely event, and both "A" and "B" would occur. In a concrete version, participants rank-ordered the likelihood of winning a lottery with a very low probability of winning, of winning a lottery with a higher probability of winning, and of winning both lotteries. A response that both events are more likely than either one of the events was scored as a conjunction error (CE). Not surprisingly, participants made a much lower number of CEs in solving the concrete rather than the abstract version of the problem. We have found in other research that presenting a concrete version of a problem first was helpful in solving a subsequent abstract version of the problem. This was interpreted as indicating that intuitive knowledge in the experiential system can be useful in solving an abstract version of the problem in the rational system. That the experiential system can prime the operation of the rational system supports the position that there are two processing systems.

There are two reasons that concrete examples increase the effectiveness of messages. One is that the experiential system encodes information primarily in the form of concrete representations. It therefore comprehends information that includes specific examples more readily than it comprehends information that is abstract. The other is that concrete representations correspond to the way events are experienced in real life, and the experiential system evolved to adapt to real-life events. Anecdotes that refer to real-life experience have been shown to increase the persuasiveness of messages (Kahneman & Tversky, 1973).

In conclusion, the observation that concrete representations are more interesting and compelling than abstract information is consistent with the assumption in CET that the experiential system primarily encodes information in the form of concrete exemplars, whereas the rational system does so in the form of verbal symbols and abstractions.

THE APPEAL AND INFLUENCE OF NARRATIVES

Despite their verbal expression, narratives are highly appealing and comprehensible to the experiential system because they are emotionally engaging, often evoke imagery, and represent the unfolding of events in the same way as they occur in real life. As in real life, narratives involve goal-oriented people engaged in events that take place in a particular location and time period, and the behavior and events that are reported mimic how they occur in real life (Bruner, 1986). The result is that narratives are intrinsically appealing in a way that the same material presented as more abstract information is not. The natural appeal and comprehensibility of narratives explains why they are so prevalent in myths and religion. It is no accident that the Bible, the most influential Western book of all time, teaches through parables and stories and not through philosophical discourse (e.g., see Vitz, 1990, for a discussion of teaching morality through stories).

IRRATIONAL FEARS

Irrational fears provide particularly compelling evidence of two ways of thinking because people with such fears recognize they are irrational but cannot eliminate them by simply regarding them from a logical perspective. Unwanted fears, such as a fear of flying, of crowds, or of giving speeches, are often maintained at great personal cost despite the recognition that they are irrational. For example, people who avoid flying in an aircraft because they fear it will crash willingly travel great distances by automobile despite knowing that travel by car is more dangerous than flying.

An interesting example of an irrational fear was reported in a newscast in the fall of 1991. A commercial airliner had to turn back because several women on the flight ran screaming away from the place where a mouse had been seen, thereby dangerously unbalancing the airliner. The degree of danger produced by their behavior, as understood by their rational systems, was apparently no match for the threat posed by the mouse as assessed by their experiential system.

SUPERSTITIOUS BELIEFS

In a Gallup poll (cited in Science News 1991), one in four people reported they believe in ghosts, one in six that they communicated with someone deceased, one in four that they have telepathically communicated with someone, one in ten that they have been in the presence of a ghost, one in seven that they have seen a UFO, one in four that they believe in astrology, and one in two that they believe in extrasensory perception. It is evident from such data that superstitious beliefs are common.

Although superstitious beliefs are irrational, they are not necessarily maladaptive. A junior business executive whom I shall call Smith was given as his first job an interview with a wealthy customer from whom he was hoping to secure a lucrative contract. Smith thought his possibility for promotion depended on his obtaining the contract, so he was very nervous on the morning of the interview. He was so nervous that he was unaware that he had put on one black and one brown shoe. Fortunately, all went well, and he obtained the contract. Many years later, when Smith was a senior manager, he continued to wear one brown and one black shoe before important meetings. Was this behavior adaptive, maladaptive, or neither? I believe it was adaptive for the following reasons. It did no harm, it automatically boosted Smith's confidence through conditioning, and it gave him an interesting conversation piece. The lesson is that it is sometimes advantageous to be irrational.

THE INFLUENCE OF EMOTIONS ON THINKING

Evidence of two kinds of information processing is provided by the difference in people's thinking when they are highly emotional compared to when they are calm. It will be recalled that, in Chapter 1, the thinking of the women in a television show who passionately expressed their anger toward two rapists compared to the logical, unemotional analysis of the psychologist directing the show resulted in a failure in communication; it was as if they had been speaking different languages. It was noted that when people are highly emotional they think in a manner that is personal, categorical, concretive, unreflective, and action-oriented, and the stronger their emotions the more they think that way.

That most people are intuitively aware that people operate with two modes of information processing according to their state of emotional arousal is indicated by the advice they typically give others who are emotionally overwrought, such as, "Get a grip on yourself. You're too emotional to think straight now. Once you calm down, you will see things differently."

THE INFLUENCE OF THINKING ON EMOTIONS

Emotions in everyday life are initiated by the preconscious thoughts and interpretations people make of events. People are angry, sad, or frightened, not as a direct response to events, but as the result of their interpretation of the events. That is, there is a critical mediating step between an event and the emotion elicited. The mediating step is the person's interpretation of the event. If a person interprets an action directed at her as an unwarranted insult, the person will most likely feel angry; however, if the same action is interpreted as a serious threat from which escape is the most desirable response, the person will likely feel frightened (e.g., Beck, 1976; Ellis, 1970; Epstein, 1984; Lazarus, 1982). (See Epstein, 1983, for the interpretations people characteristically make previous to specific emotions).

Initial construals of events are typically made so rapidly and outside of awareness as to preclude the deliberative, sequential, analytical thinking characteristic of the rational system. If the initial construal in the experiential system is subsequently identified and viewed as incorrect by the slower responding rational system, the emotion often changes. An example is a person who has a fear reaction when seeing what appears to be a snake. The fear dissipates when the person realizes it is only a rope. The difference between the initial response and the subsequent slower processing is consistent with the existence of the operation of the experiential and rational systems proposed in CET.

THE UBIQUITOUS EXISTENCE OF RELIGIOUS BELIEFS

Religion provides perhaps the most impressive evidence that there are two modes of information processing. There are few societies, if any, throughout recorded history that have not developed some form of religion. For many people, rational, scientific reasoning fails to provide as satisfactory a way of understanding the world and finding meaning and satisfaction in it as religious teaching. Why is this so? The answer, according to CET, is that religion reaches the experiential system in a way that scientific reasoning does not.

Many religious beliefs make no sense from a rational perspective. For example, some people who believe the son of God was born of a virgin regard as a myth the belief by those of another faith that their prophet was born from his mother's side. From a rational perspective, people who regard their own unrealistic beliefs as true but regard the unrealistic beliefs of others as mythical have good reason to question their own beliefs. Instead, many are certain that their unrealistic beliefs are true and that they will be rewarded with eternal happiness in heaven for realizing such truth, whereas those of other faiths who believe that their mythology is true will pay a terrible price for their folly.

That religious beliefs operate mainly within the realm of the experiential system is indicated by their attributes corresponding to those of the experiential system. Included are beliefs influenced by the hedonic principle, as indicated by beliefs in the existence of heaven and imaginary figures who live in the sky and are able to make one's wishes come true. Associative information processing is indicated by beliefs such as that all later generations of Jews are responsible for the behavior of a few Jews thousands of years ago who were responsible for the crucifixtion of Jesus. Concrete thinking is indicated by the prevalence of icons. Automatic behavior is indicated by the prevalence of rituals. Categorical thinking is indicated by judging people of one's own faith as completely good and of other faiths as completely bad and by stereotypes. The compelling quality of experiential processing is indicated by people's willingness to live and die for their faith.

CONCLUSION

It is evident from the examples given in this chapter that people exhibit two ways of thinking in everyday life that is consistent with the experiential and rational systems of CET. People think nonrationally (not necessarily irrationally) in a wide variety of ways, and such thinking is often more compelling to them than their conscious reasoning.

REFERENCES

Beck, A. T. (1976). *Cognitive therapy and the emotional disorders*. New York: International Universities Press.

Brewin, C. R. (1989). Cognitive change processes in psychotherapy. *Psychological Review*, 96, 379–394.

Bruner, J. S. (1986). *Actual minds, possible worlds*. Cambridge, MA: Harvard University Press.

Donovan, S., & Epstein, S. (1997). The difficulty of the Linda conjunction problem can be attributed to its simultaneous concrete and unnatural representation, and not to conversational implicature. *Journal of Experimental Social Psychology, 33*, 1–20.

Ellis, A. (1970). *Reason and emotion in psychotherapy*. New York: Lyle Stuart.

Epstein, S. (1983). A research paradigm for the study of personality and emotions. In M. M. Page (Ed.), *Personality: Current theory and research: 1982*. Nebraska Symposium on Motivation (pp. 91–154). Lincoln: University of Nebraska Press.

Epstein, S. (1984). Controversial issues in emotion theory. In P. Shaver (Ed.), *Annual review of research in personality and social psychology* (pp. 64–87). Beverly Hills, CA: Sage Publications.

Epstein, S., Denes-Raj, V., & Pacini, R. (1995). The Linda problem revisited from the perspective of cognitive-experiential self-theory. *Personality and Social Psychology Bulletin, 21*, 1124–1138.

Epstein, S., & Meier, P. (1989). Constructive thinking: A broad coping variable with specific components. *Journal of Personality and Social Psychology, 57*, 332–349.

Fazio, R. H., & Zanna, M. (1981). Direct experience and attitude-behavior consistency. In L. Berkowitz (Ed.), *Advances in experimental social psychology* (vol. 14, pp. 161–202). New York: Academic Press.

Kahneman, D., & Tversky, A. (1973). On the psychology of prediction. *Psychological Review, 80*, 237–251.

Lazarus, R. S. (1982). Thoughts on the relations between emotions and cognitions. *American Psychologist, 37*, 1019–1024.

Paivio, A. (2007). *Mind and its evolution: A dual-coding theoretical approach*. Mahwah, NJ: Erlbaum.

Science News. (1991). Presents statistics from Gallup poll. *Behavior*, March 9, 159.

Shiffrin, R. M., & Schneider, W. (1977). Controlled and automatic information processing: Perceptual learning, automatic attending, and general theory. *Psychological Review, 84*, 127–190.

Sternberg, R. J. (1985). *Beyond IQ: A triarchic theory of human intelligence* New York: Cambridge University Press.

Vitz, P. C. (1990). The use of stories in moral development: New psychological reasons for an old education method. *American Psychologist, 45*, 709–720.

Wagner, R. K., & Sternberg, R. J. (1986). Tacit knowledge and intelligence in the everyday world. In R. J. Sternberg & R. K. Wagner (Eds.), *Practical intelligence* (pp. 51–83). New York: Cambridge University Press.

CHAPTER 3

The Content and Organization of the Experiential System

With an Emphasis on Basic Needs and Beliefs

In this chapter, I discuss implicit basic needs and the implicit beliefs derived from them. I also consider the relation between emotions and implicit beliefs, the encoding of implicit beliefs, and their organization into an overall adaptive system.

THE NATURE AND INFLUENCE OF THE IMPLICIT BELIEFS IN THE EXPERIENTIAL SYSTEM

Let us begin by comparing two women with very different implicit beliefs to demonstrate how the content of such beliefs affects their lives. Imagine one of them views the world as a dangerous place. She is distrustful of others, believes she will fail in all her important ventures, and she is convinced she will never find someone to love her. She lacks the motivation to work hard because she believes she will fail anyway. She also does not try to make herself look attractive because she believes it will be of no use. The other person has an opposite outlook on herself, others, and life in general. She regards the world as a wonderful and exciting place, is trusting of people (within reason), is highly confident of her abilities, and is enthusiastic about the future. She puts her heart into her work because she enjoys doing it and because she believes it will be appreciated. Assume the two are of equal intelligence, are physically equally attractive, come from the same socioeconomic background, and have equal opportunities available to them. Given the content of their beliefs, it can reasonably be expected that the second woman will function at a much more satisfactory level than the first one. She will interpret and experience events in a manner that contributes to personal fulfillment, happiness, and well-being. Implicit beliefs obviously matter, and they matter perhaps more than anything else, with the possible exception of health, which they also influence (Epstein, 1992).

A caveat is in order with respect to the interpretation of the example just given. It is an easy matter to forget that the beliefs under consideration are implicit beliefs and therefore encoded in a nonverbal form of representation and not in the form of conscious, verbal representations. This raises the question of how such implicit beliefs differ from people's conscious beliefs. The answer is that they usually do not differ, but, when they do, it can be a source of conflict and stress. Evolution can be assumed to have caused the two processing systems in humans normally to operate harmoniously. If the beliefs in the two processing systems differed greatly, people would be in a continuous state of conflict and stress. When, in the course of evolution, grammatical language and a resultant rational system were added to the information processing repertoire of the predecessors of early *Homo sapiens,* it can be assumed to have occurred in a manner that coordinated the rational system with the extant experiential system. This raises an interesting question: if the content of the two systems usually coincides, then why are implicit beliefs regarded as so important in cognitive-experiential theory (CET)? If one wants to know people's implicit beliefs about something, why not simply ask them? This is certainly true in many situations and is one of the reasons why self-report inventories are often useful.

Despite the frequent correspondence between implicit and explicit beliefs, the differences between them can be an important source of maladjustment. For example, a person may be explicitly motivated to make as much money as possible because he believes it will bring him happiness. He does so in a highly competitive manner that takes advantage of others, who therefore dislike him. Because this makes him unhappy, he devotes all the more effort to making more money. At the implicit level, based on his reinforcement history, he believes that being liked by others will bring him happiness. Thus, what he does to bring him happiness makes him unhappy because it violates an experiential belief that is intimately related to affect.

It is important to recognize that although it is emphasized in CET that people acquire their implicit beliefs by automatically learning from direct or observed real-life experience, this does not mean that it is a simple matter to predict the beliefs people acquire from having certain experiences. Unfortunately, the relation is neither simple nor direct. For example, although it is easy to understand why many abused children develop a distrust of authority figures, it is not so easy to understand why some identify with their aggressors and become abusers of their own children, whereas others become empathic and protective of their own and others' children.

There are at least three reasons why the same situation produces different implicit beliefs in people. One reason is that temperament, a biologically determined variable, influences how people interpret events. What is threatening to a vulnerable, shy child can be an exciting challenge to a more self-reliant child. A second reason is that how an event is interpreted depends on a person's extant belief system. A woman who is distrustful of men because she was sexually abused as a child may interpret a hug by an acquaintance as a sexual advance, whereas another interprets it as merely a warm greeting.

A third reason why people interpret the same event differently is that people's psychodynamics (i.e., the interaction of their motives with each other and with their defenses) influence their interpretations of events. For example, because all people are motivated to feel good because of the universal operation of the hedonic principle, it will tend to bias their interpretation of events in a favorable way. Although this tendency is restrained by reality considerations, people differ in the degree of such restraint. Thus, students who, when they fail a test, are likely to attribute it to the poor selection of items by an incompetent instructor will tend to retain their self-esteem in the short run but at a significant long-term cost. A habitual way of feeling better by self-serving interpretations will increasingly reinforce a person's belief that other people are at fault when things go wrong. This way of thinking can prevent people from learning from their mistakes and will alienate and antagonize others. In contrast, other students tend to react to their failures by attributing them to insufficient studying. This motivates them to study harder, which produces more favorable results and contributes to a long-term gain in self-esteem. For the reasons just indicated, it is impossible to predict how specific events will influence an individual's implicit beliefs, with the exception of very extreme events, such as traumas, that have highly common effects.

Fortunately, post hoc understanding is much more viable than prediction and can produce useful information. For example, it can help individuals and therapists understand maladaptive implicit beliefs by exploring where they may have come from, given a person's history.

HOW IMPLICIT BELIEFS ARE ENCODED

According to CET, specific events are encoded in the experiential system in a nonverbal form because that is the only system in which they could be encoded in nonhuman animals, and the experiential system in humans is essentially the same system. The nonverbal form often consists of visual imagery, but it can include other sensory modalities, such as audition, odor, taste, touch, and pain responses. In addition to encoding events in the form of concrete images, human and nonhuman animals encode classes of events in the form of generalizations, including prototypes. Examples of such encoding include the broad generalizations people make about themselves, others, and the inanimate world. Thus, some people, depending on their past experiences, regard themselves favorably, are trusting of others, and consider the inanimate world as a benign place in which to live, whereas others have a low regard for themselves, distrust others, and view the inanimate world as fraught with danger. Nonhuman animals, such as dogs or cats, make similar generalizations. Depending on their past experiences, they may regard people as sources of care-giving or of punishment.

According to CET, the more intense an emotional experience, the greater the generalization and spread of activation across associated networks. For example, following discharge from the army, ex-soldiers who have experienced intense combat are highly sensitive to cues that remind them of combat. They may drop to the ground on hearing a car backfire, and, if being alert to surprise was important to survival, they seat themselves so they immediately see whoever comes into a room. Some survivors of the Holocaust report that they have anxiety reactions on seeing anyone in a uniform approaching them, including their mailman.

As affect is both a motivator and a reinforcer of behavior, it follows that, in the absence of affect, there would be no automatic learning from experience and therefore no experiential system. Affect will be discussed in greater detail in Chapter 5; for now, it is only necessary to be aware that, according to CET, almost all cognitions in the experiential system are stored with an affective component, which can vary from negligible to intense.

It has been demonstrated in research that incidental learning occurs in the absence of external reinforcement (e.g., Reber, 1993). However, it is important to consider that this is with regard only to external reinforcement and is not necessarily true for internal reinforcement because the very act of detecting a relationship is inherently reinforcing (Bechara, Damasio, Tranel, & Damasio, 1997). Such behavior would be adaptive because it would automatically contribute to people's information about their environment.

DESCRIPTIVE AND MOTIVATIONAL SCHEMAS

According to CET, there are two kinds of implicit beliefs, or schemas, in people's experiential systems: descriptive schemas and motivational schemas. The descriptive schemas correspond to implicit beliefs about what the self, others, and the impersonal world are like. Motivational schemas correspond to motives to behave in certain ways, such as to be powerful, helpful, friendly, or independent. To simplify the ensuing discussion, descriptive and motivational implicit schemas will henceforth be referred to, respectively, as implicit beliefs and implicit motives or needs.

Implicit Beliefs

Expressed in the form of verbal equivalents, some examples of implicit experiential generalizations about others include "authority figures are helpful (or harmful)," "most people are generous (or selfish), " "members of the opposite sex are warm and kindly (or cold and rejecting)." An example of an implicit generalization about the inanimate world is "the world is a bountiful, interesting, beautiful place (or a dangerous, foreboding, withholding) place." Implicit generalizations about the self include "I am a love-worthy person (or a person unworthy of love)," "I am a competent (or incompetent) person," "I am a morally good (or bad) person," and "I am a person who has much (or little) will power."

It is important to recognize that the valence of a belief depends on how an individual implicitly values the belief, as indicated by the individual's automatic affective reaction associated with the belief. Thus, a person who holds the belief, "I am a selfish person" may be implicitly pleased with behaving selfishly despite explicitly evaluating it negatively. The implicit valuation is automatically determined by the person's reinforcement history with regard to the frequency and intensity of favorable and unfavorable outcomes from having behaved selfishly, such as enjoying selfishly acquired objects or the approval bestowed on one for having behaved selfishly by significant others, whether the individual consciously approves of the selfish behavior or not.

Implicit Motives

Implicit motives or needs are nonverbal cognitive-affective beliefs about the desirability of behaving in certain ways. All implicit motives have a positive (approach) or negative (avoidance) valence and an affective component, the intensity of which determines the strength of the motive. Thus, if the thought of eating an ice cream cone on a hot summer day is associated with a positive affective reaction, a person will be motivated to eat one. In the absence of affect, cognitions in the experiential system do not move a person to action; they simply provide information about what might be done if a person wanted to do it. A robot with such information and no affective reaction would be as inert as the computer on your desk. You can type into a computer in the robot's head "I want to eat an ice cream cone," but the robot, in the absence of affect, would not act on the message because it would not feel like eating an ice cream cone.

Not all affectively driven motivation is a result of a person's reinforcement history. It has been demonstrated that imagined experience can influence the experiential system in a manner similar to a real experience (Crisp & Turner, 2009; Dadds, Bovbjerg, Redd, & Cutmore, 1997; Epstein & Pacini, 2001; Kosslyn, Ganis, & Thompson, 2001). It is therefore possible to develop an affectively driven motive by imagining the satisfaction one would obtain from behaving a certain way.

If motivation in the experiential system normally requires an affective component, the question may be raised as to whether the affect-free rational system is capable of any motivation at all. One way it can be motivated is by infused affect from the experiential system. It will be recalled that, according to CET, all behavior is influenced by both systems, with their relative contribution varying along a dimension from negligible to almost complete influence. Thus, a person can be passionately engaged in an intellectual activity because of the person's past reinforcement history or imagination. Although the source of the motivation is in the experiential system, it can motivate behavior in the rational system.

Consistent with the view in CET that an affective component is present in motivation, it has been demonstrated that people with injuries to the emotional centers in their brains, despite having normal intelligence, make poor judgments in laboratory tasks and disastrous decisions in real life (Damasio, 1994). Of particular interest, they have great difficulty in making any decisions at all and often spend inordinate amounts of time mulling over the advantages and disadvantages of inconsequential alternatives. Without affect to guide their decisions, they find it difficult to make them.

THE ORGANIZATION OF IMPLICIT THEORIES OF REALITY

It is assumed in CET that an implicit theory of reality consists of cognitive-affective networks hierarchically organized into a predominantly coherent, adaptive, unified system. Although there are exceptions to people's conceptual systems being unified, as when the systems include dissociated complexes (isolated cognitive-affective systems), there is a natural tendency to assimilate such complexes into a unified system. This is illustrated in repetitive, unbidden intrusions of dissociated content following traumatic events that continue to occur until the material is assimilated (e.g., Epstein, 1991; Figley, 1985; Horowitz, 1976, 1979; Janoff-Bulman, 1992; McCann & Perlman, 1990).

The Assumption of a Hierarchical Organization of an Implicit Theory of Reality

Support for the assumption that implicit theories of reality are hierarchically organized according to levels of generality is provided by both logical and empirical considerations. Logically, more general beliefs by definition must encompass less general beliefs. It follows that the highest levels of belief in an implicit theory of reality must be the most general beliefs, and the lowest level must consist of narrow beliefs about specific events. For example, at a highly general level in a woman's implicit theory of reality, she regards herself as a worthy person. At a mid-level of implicit beliefs, she views herself as a competent, love-worthy, and moral person. At a more specific level, she regards herself as academically and artistically gifted, as getting along well with some people but not with others, as being good in some sports but poor in others, and so on. At the lowest level in the hierarchy, she has representations of specific experiences, such as receiving an award in an art contest.

It is self-evident that people hold implicit beliefs in their everyday lives about themselves, others, and the world that range from broad generalizations to highly specific beliefs concerning single events and attributes. There is a high degree of connectivity among associative networks across all levels of generality, making it possible for them to be components of a unified, adaptive system (e.g., Baars, 1989; Gazzaniga, 2008, Posner, 1994; Posner & Dehaene, S., 1994; Shallice, 1988; Tonini & Edelman, 1998).

An advantage to a hierarchical organization is that it provides stability at the upper levels of the hierarchy and flexibility at the lower levels. This is because the more general implicit beliefs are supported by a far greater number of associative connections than are the more specific implicit beliefs. Thus, any one event is likely to make only a relatively small contribution to a highly general belief. A second reason is that highly general beliefs are conceptually removed from highly specific beliefs.

Although higher order implicit beliefs are difficult to invalidate, should they be invalidated, it would have a major effect on a person's overall conceptual system. Even the effect of very favorable, unexpected events could be destabilizing because it could conflict with people's need to maintain a stable and coherent conceptual system. For example, a person who believed no one could ever love him could have a transforming experience by someone falling deeply in love with him, an effect that many a novelist has mined to good advantage. In the process of transformation, the person at first is likely to resist acceptance of being loved. For example, the person might react with suspicion to acts of kindness. In support of the view that highly favorable experiences can be threatening, Morling and Epstein (1997) found that, in an experiment in which levels of favorable feedback were manipulated over a wide range, the most preferred level was only slightly more favorable than a person's self-assessment, which was interpreted as indicating a compromise between a motive for self-enhancement and a motive to maintain the stability of one's conceptual system.

Dramatic negative changes in personality are most likely to be observed following traumatic experiences that invalidate fundamental beliefs in people's implicit theories of reality. For example, uncontrolled aggression and self-destructive behavior may be exhibited in previously normal people following traumatic combat experiences (Epstein, 1991; Figley, 1985).

Of particular interest, sometimes people react to traumatic events by embracing the trauma. They exhibit a dramatic change in personality that is consistent with the traumatic experience, which protects them from being overwhelmed by a repetition of the experience, but at a terrible cost. Scheppele and Bart (1983), in a study of 94 women who were victims of rape, reported that all but two of them took great pains to avoid exposing themselves to further danger. The two notable exceptions behaved in an opposite way. One was a woman who had been raped twice in a single day who exhibited a dramatic change in personality. She began to take drugs and became a prostitute. The other was a student from an advantaged background who had been attending a prestigious university when she was raped. She dropped out of school, took to frequenting all-night bars, carried a knife, and became highly promiscuous. Such examples provide dramatic evidence of how a single intense event that invalidates basic beliefs about the safety of the world and the trustworthiness of people can produce major changes in personality.

Disorganization as Support for Organization

Having provided support for the assumption that implicit theories of reality are hierarchically organized, it remains to be demonstrated that the organization is normally unified. Although the interrelatedness among associative networks at different levels of generality, as previously noted, suggests the possibility of the existence of an overall unified organization, more definitive support is required to conclude that this possibility is a reality. Such evidence is provided by the capacity of implicit theories of reality to disorganize. This is demonstrated in nonhuman animals as well as in episodes of acute schizophrenic disorganization (e.g., Bleuler, 1978; Epstein, 1979; Kaplan, 1964; Laing, 1965; Perry, 1976).

I have selected two cases to illustrate the occurrence of disorganization. One case is that of a dog in Pavlov's laboratory and the other is that of a schizophrenic girl. I selected the dog to demonstrate that the need to maintain a stable, coherent conceptual system is so fundamental that it can be observed in nonhuman animals. The disorganization in Pavlov's dog was precipitated by the animal's inability to maintain a learned discrimination (Pavlov, 1928). The dog had been trained to produce a conditioned response (CR) of salivation when a circle but not an ellipse was the conditioned stimulus (CS) that signaled the delivery of food, which was the unconditioned stimulus (UCS). After the discrimination was well established, the ellipse was increasingly made to resemble a circle. When the dog could no longer distinguish between the two forms, a strange thing happened; it became frightened and disorganized to the point of being a dysfunctional animal. It lost all its previously established conditioned responses and exhibited a profound change in its personality.

Although previously it had been a calm, mild-mannered, well-behaved dog, it trembled, whined, and tore at its leash. When removed to a farm to recover, it remained in a disturbed state for an extended period. After recovering, it continued to exhibit signs of anxiety when exposed to cues associated with its previous traumatic experience.

Several aspects of the dog's reaction to the experimental situation warrant further consideration. First, there was no noxious physical stimulation. The disorganization was produced solely by the animal's inability to maintain a significant discrimination. Second, the animal not only lost its ability to maintain the discrimination it had recently acquired, but it lost all its other conditioned responses, including simple ones that did not require discrimination. It also exhibited a profound change in its personality. Third, it took a long time for the animal to recover in a protective environment, but it continued to be sensitive to cues associated with the disorganizing event, which can be considered an adaptive assimilation because it alerts the animal to a realistic source of danger. These reactions are consistent with the assumption in CET that higher order organisms have a basic need to maintain a stable, coherent conceptual system and that the conceptual system is subject to disorganization when it is unable to assimilate emotionally significant experiences. Over sufficient time in a protective environment, a new assimilation may take place in which the organism assimilates previously inassimilable information, including the incorporation of adaptive responses that protect it against a reoccurrence of the trauma.

We turn next to an example of disorganization in a schizophrenic girl. The following event describes, in the girl's own words, her reaction to a meeting with her therapist.

> I experienced a figure of ice which smiled at me. And this smile, showing her white teeth, frightened me. For I saw the individual features of her face, separated from each other. Perhaps it was this independence of each part that inspired such fear and prevented my recognizing her even though I knew who she was.... Then I heard this marvelous voice, which, like a talisman, could give me again a moment of reality, a contact with life.... Warmed again, encouraged,... I went home. Once in the street, however, I saw again the pasteboard scenery of unreality. (Sechehaye, 1970, pp. 37–38)

This account provides a particularly interesting example of disorganization because, although the individual features of the therapist's face were perceived, they were not meaningfully organized into the appearance of a human face. It is noteworthy that there was also a dissociation between intellectually knowing who the therapist is, which is in the domain of the rational system, and perceptually experiencing who she is in an emotionally meaningful way, which is in the domain of the experiential system. Of further interest, the passage not only describes an experience of disorganization, but also indicates a condition in which it was temporarily restored; namely, in perceiving the warmth in the therapist's voice. This is consistent with the view in CET that the primary reason for the disorganization of a conceptual system is its failure to fulfill a basic need and that the condition for reestablishing a coherent reorganization is to fulfill the need, if only, in this case, momentarily. Here, the basic need was for relatedness and, more specifically, probably for feeling loved. In the case of Pavlov's dog, it was the need to maintain a stable, coherent conceptual system. These basic needs will shortly be discussed in greater detail.

THE DESIGNATION OF IMPLICIT BASIC NEEDS AND BELIEFS

I divided implicit needs into three levels: basic, mid-level, and low-level. The most important levels to determine are the basic and mid-level needs because the low-level implicit needs are innumerable. In this chapter, I discuss the basic needs; in the next, I discuss the mid-level needs.

Selection of Basic Needs and Beliefs

The following six basic needs have been proposed by various authors, with most proposing what they regarded as a single most basic need: (1) the need to react according to the hedonic principle, (2) the need to control arousal, (3) the need to maintain the stability and coherence of the conceptual system, (4) the need for security, (5) the need for relatedness, and (6) the need for self-esteem. In the discussion that follows, we will examine the reasons that these needs were considered basic by their authors and evaluate whether they warrant such a designation.

The Hedonic Principle

Freud at first proposed a single basic need that he referred to as the *pleasure principle*, which is the motivation to seek pleasure and to avoid pain (Freud, 1900/1953). Later, he introduced a second principle that could override the pleasure principle, the *repetition compulsion*. The repetition compulsion principle refers to a tendency to repeat traumatic experiences. He assumed the purpose of the repetition compulsion was to gain mastery of a traumatic experience, and he explained it by a "death instinct," which he considered so important that it caused him to reevaluate the pleasure principle as the most important motive and, accordingly, to revise his theory of personality.

Freud's esoteric speculation about a death instinct is unwarranted because the repetition compulsion can more reasonably be explained by a need to construct and maintain a unified conceptual system According to this view, intrusive, dissociated material continues to appear in people's imagery and thoughts until the material is assimilated into a unified conceptual system (Epstein, 1981, 1991; Horowitz, 1986), which is consistent with the existence of a basic need to construct and maintain a stable and coherent conceptual system Although this explanation of the repetition compulsion is similar to Freud's view about belated mastery, it makes no assumption about a death instinct and the considerable conceptual baggage such an assumption carries with it.

Many learning theorists make an assumption similar to Freud's pleasure principle that is incorporated in their views on reinforcement. Thus, Thorndike (1911) proposed a "law of effect," according to which responses that are followed by positive affect are reinforced and therefore tend to be reproduced, whereas responses that are followed by negative affect are avoided. A great amount of research with both nonhuman animals and humans has supported Thorndike's law. For example, the importance of positive affect as a motivator of behavior has been demonstrated in a classic series of experiments by Olds and his associates using electrical brain stimulation (Olds, 1958; Olds & Milner, 1954). Laboratory rats taught to perform a variety of tasks, such as pressing levers and running through mazes to obtain electrical stimulation to the pleasure center of their brains, became so highly motivated to receive this stimulation that they pressed the levers that delivered the stimulation at a rate of hundreds of times a minute. As a result, many blissfully died of thirst because they would not relinquish pressing the bar long enough to drink water. Similar results have been obtained with other species. Humans when receiving similar stimulation to their brains report feelings of euphoria. In a great amount of research, various species of animals, including humans, have learned a wide variety of tasks to obtain pleasurable outcomes and to avoid unpleasant ones.

The Need to Control Arousal

Clark Hull (1943, 1952) introduced a highly influential view of reinforcement that differed from Thorndike's. According to Hull, reinforcement occurs when a response is followed by a decrease in a previously elevated state of arousal or "drive state," as he preferred to call it. Hull considered the level of such a drive state as the sum of all aversive and appetitive biological states, such as hunger, thirst, sex, and pain, active at a moment in time.

A somewhat similar view of arousal had earlier been proposed by Pavlov (1928), with one important difference. Pavlov emphasized the importance of controlling cortical excitation rather than the arousal produced by appetitive and aversive states. According to Pavlov, a variable even more fundamental than conditioning is the need of higher order organisms to protect their brains from excessive excitation. He reported that when cortical excitation mounts, it triggers an inhibitory reaction that produces anomalies in conditioning that he referred to as *paradoxical responses*, such as responding more strongly to weak than to strong stimuli. When a sufficient state of inhibition is reached, a stage that he referred to as *transmarginal inhibition* occurs in which previously conditioned responses are no longer present. In a later development, Pavlov classified animals and subsequently humans as belonging to inhibitory, normal, or excitatory types, depending on their normal level of cortical excitation. He later employed this typology to explain psychopathology in humans.

In sum, a basic need for controlling two kinds of arousal was introduced from different sources of research on learning and conditioning; namely, arousal produced by appetitive and aversive reactions and cerebral excitation.

There is a problem in measuring "arousal" because different indexes of arousal are not highly correlated. This may be because of the different functions of the different kinds of arousal and the different systems that control different kinds of arousal. For example, heart rate decreases during periods when people pay close attention to a real or anticipated stimulus; this occurs during a period of increased arousal, as indicated by increases in other physiological indexes, such as blood pressure and skin conductance. Moreover, the time frame for inhibitory reactions that modulate increases in arousal differs among the different indexes of arousal. Nevertheless, there is a general state of arousal that varies along a dimension from deep sleep to intense emotional excitement. I will use the word "arousal" to refer to this general state, which encompasses all forms of arousal, including autonomic arousal, striped muscle tension, and cortical excitation. It is assumed that there is a biological necessity to control such arousal, as well as each of its components, within homeostatic limits.

The Need for a Stable, Coherent Conceptual System

According to Carl Rogers (1951), the organism has one basic tendency "to actualize, maintain, and enhance, the experiencing organism," which is associated with a growth principle in which people's conceptual systems become increasing differentiated and integrated. This is assumed to be facilitated by a condition of unconditional positive regard. Rogers considered the preservation of the stability and coherence of a person's conceptual system to be the most important motive of all. Others with similar views were Lecky (1945), Raimy (1948), and Snygg and Combs (1949), all of whom emphasized the importance of maintaining the stability and coherence of people's conceptual systems. In the course of conducting psychotherapy, they were impressed with the importance of an overriding motivation in their clients to discover their authentic beliefs, which they considered to be beliefs based on direct experiences rather than on what had been introjected from others. These researchers believed that the need people have for a coherent, stabile, and authentic belief system that is consistent with their experience is more important in understanding people and in conducting psychotherapy and counseling than any other need, including the pursuit of pleasure and the avoidance of pain. Interestingly, the beliefs acquired from direct experience correspond to the implicit beliefs in the experiential system of CET.

The Need for Security

Maslow (1970) proposed a hierarchy of needs that vary from most basic needs essential to survival, such as physical needs for food and water, to higher level needs that are only motivating after lower level needs have been satisfied. Immediately below the physiological needs in Maslow's hierarchy is the psychological need for safety or security. The importance of this need is self-evident because a failure to fulfill it is a major source of anxiety and psychopathology. Examples of conditions that are sources of such failure are traumas, fear of abandonment, rejection, inconsistent child-rearing, abusive child-rearing, and overprotection. People obviously need to feel secure in the world as a condition for their normal development and well-being.

The Need for Relatedness

For object-relations theorists such as Bowlby (1988) and Fairbairn (1954), the most important need is the need for relatedness. They believe that children establish core beliefs about relationships that provide the foundation for their later relationships in adulthood. These beliefs determine how people relate to others and also determine, based on others' views about them, how they feel about themselves. Accordingly, Bowlby and Fairbairn consider the need for relatedness to be of unique importance in determining how people think, feel, and behave.

The Need for Self-Esteem

For Allport (1961), the most basic need is the need for self-esteem. For Kohut (1971), the need for self-esteem and the need to maintain a coherent, stable conceptual system are the two most fundamental needs. That the need for self-esteem is a very prominent motive in everyday life is supported by research in which college students kept records of their daily emotional experiences over several weeks (Epstein & Pacini, 1999). Assaults on their self-esteem were the most common source of the distressing emotions they reported. Sheldon et al. (2001), in a cross-cultural study that included participants from South Korea as well as the United States, found that self-esteem was the most important source of satisfaction in everyday life.

Which of the Implicit Basic Needs Warrants the Designation of Basic According to Designated Criteria?

On what basis can one decide whether a proposed basic need should qualify as basic? To answer this question, I required a basic need to meet the following four criteria: the need has to be universal; it cannot be derived from other needs; it has to be capable of dominating all the other basic needs, as well as mid-level needs; and it has to be of such significance that its failure to be fulfilled can destabilize a person's conceptual system. Let us examine how well the proposed basic needs meet these criteria.

Is the hedonic principle basic? The hedonic principle readily meets the criterion of universality because it is a fundamental source of reinforcement in nonhuman animals, as well as in humans. Moreover, there are reward (e.g., Olds, 1958; Olds & Milner, 1954) and punishment (e.g., Delgado, Roberts, & Miller, 1954) centers in the brain. There is a vast amount of research supporting the hedonic principle as a source of motivation and reinforcement. As previously noted, without affect, people would be unable to learn automatically from experience and would have great difficulty in making decisions (e.g., Damasio, 1994; Lehrer, 2009). It may be concluded that the hedonic principle is a universal aspect of human behavior. It is also readily demonstrated that the hedonic principle can dominate all the other basic needs except the biological need to control arousal. That it can dominate the need to maintain a stable and coherent conceptual system is demonstrated by the occurrence of acute psychotic reactions in response to torture. That it can dominate the need for relatedness is demonstrated by people under torture betraying their loved ones and their identity groups. That the hedonic principle can dominate the need for self-esteem is demonstrated by people being deeply disappointed with themselves for having provided secret information under torture.

Is the control of arousal basic? Turning to the proposed basic need to control arousal, it is biologically necessary to maintain arousal within homeostatic limits. Its effects are so insistent that at sufficiently intense levels it can dominate all other basic needs and disrupt cognitive functioning (e.g., Cannon, 1932; Cozolino, 2006; Duffy, 1962; Epstein, 1967; Pavlov, 1928; Sargant, 1957). Not only can very high levels of arousal destabilize people's belief systems, very low levels can do the same. In research on sensory deprivation, participants after 48 hours of sensory deprivation exhibited an intense desire for stimulation (e.g., Heron, 1967). They tried to provide themselves with stimulation by reciting poetry, whistling, recalling movies, singing, and attempting to engage the experimenters in conversation. Following a sufficient period of sensory deprivation, they developed hallucinations, paranoid delusions, spatial disorientation, an inability to think clearly, an inability to control their thoughts, and instability of their feelings and perceptions.

Is the need for maintaining the stability and coherence of the conceptual system basic? Turning next to the need to maintain the stability and coherence of people's conceptual systems, it can reasonably be assumed to be universal because people could not function without a conceptual system for interpreting events and directing behavior. That this need can dominate all other basic needs under appropriate circumstances except the need to control arousal is indicated by the following considerations: that it can dominate the need to avoid pain is demonstrated by people, such as the early Christian martyrs, preferring to accept death and torture rather than renounce their faith; that it can dominate the need for relatedness is demonstrated by people rejecting relationships with loved ones who demand they accept their world view. This is also demonstrated by the parting of partners when one remains in a commune that endorses beliefs unacceptable to the other or by the rejection by parents of their children who marry outside their faith.

That the need for maintaining a stable, coherent belief system can dominate the need for self-esteem is demonstrated by people enduring deep humiliation rather than give up certain of their beliefs, as demonstrated by some prisoners at Abu Ghraib who, despite great humiliation, maintained their beliefs. Experimental support for the dominance of maintaining the stability and coherence of one's beliefs over an increase in self-esteem is provided by the study noted earlier, in which levels of favorable feedback were experimentally manipulated (Epstein & Morling, 1995; Morling & Epstein, 1997). It was found that participants preferred feedback that was only slightly more favorable than their self-assessments, indicating that although an increase in self-esteem is desirable, it is constrained by the need to maintain the stability of people's self-concepts.

Is the need for security basic? People in all cultures have a need for security. Conditions invariably arise that are anxiety-producing either because they are directly aversive or are a source of uncertainty. Anxiety is a fundamental adaptive reaction for anticipating adversity and uncertainty, although it obviously can be maladaptive if excessive. According to CET, people's implicit beliefs reflect their life experiences. Accordingly, everyone has feelings that vary along a continuum from highly secure to highly insecure, depending on how their experiences are registered in people's implicit belief systems.

The need for security is a very general need that is influenced by a variety of sources and therefore cannot be derived from any other need. Very high levels of insecurity can override the influence of all other needs. That it can destabilize the personality is demonstrated by the symptoms of post-traumatic stress disorder, which include the shattering of assumptions in people's conceptual systems.

Is the need for relatedness basic? Turning to the basic need for relatedness, it is clearly universal as human infants and young children could not survive without caretakers. In the absence of adequate caring, infants, despite receiving adequate nutrition, not only do not thrive, they often fail to survive (Blum, 2002; Lehrer, 2009, Malinosky-Rummell, & Hansen, 1993; Rutter, 1979). Fulfilling the need for relatedness is even of critical importance for nonhuman animals. For example, baby monkeys reared in isolation grow up into dysfunctional adults (Blum, 2002; Harlow & Harlow, 1971). The basic need for relatedness is not only also exhibited in the attachment to caretakers, but also in the strong relationships people establish with their identity groups. One of the most distressing experiences people can have is being rejected by an identity group (Cozolino, 2006).

That the need for relatedness can dominate all basic needs other than the need to control arousal is demonstrated in the following situations. It can dominate the hedonic principle, as indicated by physically abused spouses remaining in their abusive relationships. That the need for relatedness can dominate the need for maintaining a stable, coherent belief system is indicated by the occurrence of acute psychotic reactions following rejection by a loved one (Bowers, 1974; Grinker & Holzman, 1973). That it can dominate the need for self-esteem is indicated by people maintaining relationships with psychologically abusive partners who humiliate them and make them feel inadequate. That deep frustration of the need for relatedness can destabilize people's overall belief system is demonstrated by rejection from a loved one producing acute schizophrenic reactions (Bowers, 1974; Grinker & Holzman, 1973).

Is the need for self-esteem basic? The need for self-esteem may appear to be the least likely of the proposed needs to meet the criteria for a basic need. However, a strong defense can be made for including it. As support for the universality of self-esteem, according to CET, self-esteem is a further development of the need for relatedness in which young children internalize the values of significant others. As a result, people's self-evaluations become as important as evaluations by significant others (Epstein & Pacini, 1999). Sheldon et al. (2001), in a cross-cultural study that included participants from South Korea as well as the United States, found that self-esteem was the most important source of satisfaction in everyday life.

Research with the implicit association test has demonstrated that people have implicit self-evaluations that differ from their explicit self-evaluations (see review in Greenwald & Benaji, 1995). In my own research, people judged their unidentified productions more favorably than they judged the productions of others and their own identified productions (Epstein, 1955). That is, they judged the personality of a presumably unknown person whom they thought produced the participant's own disguised productions more favorably than they judged other people's productions as well as their own identified productions.

The need for self-esteem can readily meet the criterion of dominating all the other basic needs except the biological need to control arousal. That it can dominate the influence of the hedonic principle is indicated by people committing suicide when their self-esteem was seriously compromised by having behaved in a manner that deeply shamed them. Hara-kiri is an institutionalized manifestation of such behavior. That the need for self-esteem can dominate the need to maintain a stable, coherent conceptual system is illustrated by people developing delusions of grandeur that frustrate their need to maintain realistic, coherent beliefs about themselves. That the need for self-esteem can dominate the need for relatedness is demonstrated by people renouncing relationships with those who denigrate them. Examples include spouses who leave their disparaging partners and children who run away from families in which they are constantly ridiculed and otherwise demeaned. That an inability to maintain self-esteem can destabilize a person's conceptual system is indicated by assaults on self-esteem being among the most frequent causes of acute schizophrenic reactions (Bowers, 1974; Grinker & Holzman, 1973).

Why All the Proposed Basic Needs Qualify as Basic

It may be concluded that all six proposed basic needs meet the criteria for a basic need: namely, the need is universal, it cannot be derived from other needs, and it can dominate all the other basic needs except for the biological need to control arousal. Although all proposed implicit basic needs meet the criteria for being basic, that does not mean they are equally fundamental. There are two implicit needs that are present in all other needs: the hedonic principle and the need to control arousal within homeostatic limits. Accordingly, these two needs are henceforth referred to as *superordinate basic needs,* and the other basic needs as *subordinate basic needs.* In elevating the hedonic principle to a superordinate need, a subdivision of it, the need to pursue sensory pleasure and to avoid sensory displeasure, is relegated to a subordinate basic need.

Summarizing the basic needs, there are two superordinate basic needs: the need to behave according to the hedonic principle and the need to control arousal, and there are five subordinate basic needs: the need for sensory pleasure and the avoidance of sensory discomfort, the need to maintain a stable and coherent conceptual system, the need for security, the need for relatedness, and the need for self-esteem.

THE DERIVATION OF BASIC BELIEFS FROM BASIC NEEDS

Implicit basic needs are an important source for the formation of implicit basic beliefs. People automatically attend to the outcomes of their attempts to fulfill their implicit basic needs. As a result, they acquire implicit beliefs about themselves, their environment, and other people. For example, people who have been highly successful in fulfilling their implicit basic need for relatedness will likely have implicit beliefs that they are love-worthy and that other people are mainly kindly and helpful. A person's implicit beliefs can be represented on bipolar belief dimensions anchored at their ends by opposite extremes, such as that one is a highly worthy person versus an extremely unworthy person and that others are kindly and helpful versus unhelpful and hostile.

The two most general and influential implicit beliefs are those acquired from the fulfillment and frustration of the two superordinate implicit basic needs. The endpoints of the implicit belief dimension regarding the hedonic principle are that the self, others, and the environment are sources of joy and fulfillment versus sources of distress and frustration. Taking into account the influence of the hedonic principle on people's thinking and behavior, most people can be expected to fall toward the favorable end of the dimension, with the number of people decreasing along the dimension as a function of increasing proximity to the endpoints.

For the implicit belief dimension derived from the superordinate need to control arousal, one end of the implicit belief dimension is represented by the belief that others and the environment are lacking in stimulation and interest, and the self is bored and lethargic. The opposite end of the dimension is represented by the belief that others and the environment are extremely overstimulating, and the self is overstimulated to the point of being overwhelmed.

The anchoring points of the five subordinate basic implicit belief dimensions are as follows: the endpoints of the implicit belief dimension associated with the subordinate implicit need for sensory pleasure and avoidance of sensory pain and discomfort are the implicit belief that the self, others, and the impersonal world are sources of great sensory pleasure versus sources of pain and physical discomfort. For the implicit belief dimension associated with the implicit need for a stable, coherent conceptual system, the endpoints of the dimension are represented by the implicit belief that one's life is stable, orderly, and meaningful versus the implicit belief that one's life is meaningless, chaotic, and disorganized. The endpoints of the implicit belief dimension associated with the implicit need for security are that the self is frightened and threatened by others and the impersonal world at one end of the dimension and that one is secure and others and the impersonal world are sources of safety. The implicit belief dimension associated with the implicit need for relatedness is represented at one end of the dimension by the belief that one is a loving, helpful person and that most people are good of heart, trustworthy, and helpful and at the other end by the implicit belief that most people are aggressive, untrustworthy, and dangerous. The implicit belief dimension associated with the implicit need for self-esteem is represented at one end by the implicit belief that one is a worthy person, including competent, moral, and love-worthy and at the other end by the implicit belief that one is unworthy, including incompetent, immoral, and unlovable. It can be concluded that people's positions on their basic implicit belief dimensions will greatly affect their personality, including how they interpret events, feel, and behave. Their conscious thinking will also be biased by the influence of their basic implicit beliefs.

It is important to recognize that the interaction between implicit beliefs and implicit needs is bidirectional, with implicit beliefs influencing the fulfillment and frustration of implicit needs, and the fulfillment and frustration of implicit needs influencing the acquisition and maintenance of implicit beliefs. It follows that changes in implicit beliefs can produce corresponding changes in implicit needs and vice versa.

REFERENCES

Allport, G. W. (1961). *Patterns of growth in personality.* New York: Holt, Rinehart, & Winston.

Baars, B. J. (1989). *A cognitive theory of consciousness.* Cambridge: Cambridge University Press.

Bechara, A., Damasio, H., Tranel, D., & Damasio, A. R. (1997). Deciding advantageously before knowing the advantageous strategy. *Science, 275,* 1293–1296.

Bleuler, M. (1978). *The schizophrenic disorders: Long-term patient and family studies.* Translated by S. M. Clemens. New Haven, CT: Yale University Press.

Bowlby, J. (1988). *A secure base: Parent-child attachment and healthy human development.* New York: Basic Books.

Blum, D. (2002). *Love at Goon Park: Harry Harlow and the science of affection.* Cambridge, MA: Perseus Publishing.

Bowers. M. B., Jr. (1974). *Retreat from sanity.* New York: Human Sciences Press.

Cannon, W. B. (1932). *The wisdom of the body.* New York: W. W. Norton.

Cozolino, L. (2006). *The neuroscience of human relationships: Attachment and the developing social brain.* New York: W. W. Norton & Co.

Crisp, R. J., & Turner, R. N. (2009). Can imagined interactions produce positive perceptions? *American Psychologist, 64,* 231–240.

Dadds, M. R., Bovbjerg, D. H., Redd, W. H., & Cutmore, T. R. (1997). Imagery in human classical conditioning. *Psychological Bulletin,122,* 89–103.

Damasio, A. R. (1994). *Descartes error: Emotion, reason, and the human brain.* New York: Avon.

Delgado, J. M. R., Roberts, W. W., & Miler, N. E. (1954). Learning motivated by electrical stimulation of the brain. *American Journal of Physiology, 179,* 587–593.

Duffy, E. (1962). *Activation and behavior.* New York: John Wiley & Sons.

Epstein, S. (1955). Unconscious self-evaluation in a normal and a schizophrenic group. *Journal of Abnormal and Social Psychology, 50,* 55–70.

Epstein, S. (1967). Toward a unified theory of anxiety. In B. Maher (Ed.). *Progress in experimental personality research* (vol. 4, pp. 1–89). New York: Academic Press.

Epstein, S. (1979). Natural healing processes of the mind: I. Acute schizophrenic disorganization. *Schizophrenia Bulletin, National Institute of Mental Health, 5*, 313–321.
Epstein, S. (1981). The unity principles versus the reality and pleasure principles, or the tale of the scorpion and the frog. In M. D. Lynch, A. A. Norem-Hebeisen, & K. J. Gergen (Eds.), *Self-concept: Advances in theory and research* (pp. 17–37). Cambridge, MA: Ballinger Publishing.
Epstein, S. (1991). The self-concept, the traumatic neurosis, and the structure of personality. In D. Ozer, J. M. Healy, & J. A. Stewart (Eds.). *Perspectives in personality* (vol. 3A, pp. 63–98). London: Jessica Kingsley.
Epstein, S. (1992). Constructive thinking and mental and physical wellbeing. In L. Montada, S. H. Filipp, & M. J. Lerner (Eds.), *Life crises and experiences of loss in adulthood* (pp. 385–409). Hillsdale, NJ: Erlbaum
Epstein, S., & Morling, B. (1995). Is the self motivated to do more than enhance and verify itself? In M. H. Kernis (Ed.)., *Efficacy, agency, and self-esteem* (pp. 9–29). New York: Plenum Press.
Epstein, S., & Pacini, R. (1999). *Constructive thinking and coping with distress in the daily lives of college students.* (Unpublished, analyzed data).
Epstein, S., & Pacini, R. (2001). The influence of visualization on intuitive and analytical information processing. *Imagination, Cognition, and Personality: Consciousness in Theory, Research, and Clinical Practice, 20*, 195–217.
Fairbairn, W. (1954). *An object-relations theory of personality*. New York: Basic Books.
Figley, C. R. (1985). *Trauma and its wake*. New York: Brunner/Mazel.
Gazzaniga, M. S. (2008). *Human: The science behind what makes us unique*. New York: HarperCollins.
Greenwald, A. G., & Banaji, M. R. (1995). Implicit social cognition: Attitudes, self-esteem, and stereotypes. *Psychological Review, 102*, 4–27.
Grinker, R. R., Sr., & Holzman, P. S. (1973). Schizophrenic pathology in young adults. *Archives of General Psychiatry, 28*, 168–175.
Harlow, H., & Harlow, M. K. (1971). Psychopathology in monkeys. In Kimmel, H. D. (Ed.), *Experimental psychopathology: Recent research & theory* (pp. 203–229). San Diego, CA: Academic Press.
Horowitz, M. J. (1976). *Stress response syndrome*. New York: Jason Aronson.
Horowitz, M. J. (1979). Psychological stress to serious life events. In V. Hamilton & D. M. Warburton (Eds.), *Human stress and cognition*. New York: Wiley.
Horowitz, M. J. (1986). *Stress Response Syndromes*. Northvale, London: Aronson.
Hull, C. L. (1943). *Principles of behavior*. New York: Appleton-Century-Crofts.
Hull, C. L. (1952). *A behavior system*. New Haven, CT: Yale University Press.
Janoff-Bulman, R. (1992). *Shattered assumptions*. New York: Free Press.
Kaplan, B. (1964). *The inner world of mental illness*. New York: Harper & Row.
Kohut, H. (1971). *The analysis of the self: A systematic approach to the treatment of narcissistic personality disorders*. New York: International Universities Press.
Kosslyn, S. M., Ganis, G., & Thompson, W. L. (2001). Neural foundations of imagery. *Nature Reviews Neuroscience. 2*, 635–642.
Laing, R. (1965). *The divided self.* Baltimore: Penguin Books.
Lecky, P. (1945). *Self-consistency: A theory of personality*. New York: Island Press.
Lehrer, J. (2009). *How we decide*. Boston: Houghton Mifflin Harcourt.
Malinosky-Rummell, R., & Hansen, D. J. (1993). Long-term consequences of childhood physical abuse. *Psychological Bulletin, 114*, 68–79.
Maslow, A. H. (1970). *Motivation and personality* (2nd ed.). New York: Harper & Row.

McCann, I. L., & Perlman, L. A. (1990). *Psychological trauma and the adult survivor*. New York: Brunner/Mazel.

Morling, B., & Epstein, S. (1997). Compromises produced by the dialectic between self-verification and self-enhancement. *Journal of Personality and Social Psychology, 73*, 1268–1283.

Olds, J. (1958). Self-stimulation of the brain. *Science, 127*, 315–324.

Olds, J., & Milner, P. (1954). Positive reinforcement produced by electrical stimulation of the septal area and other regions of the rat brain *Journal of Comparative and Physiological Psychology, 47*, 419–427.

Pavlov, I. P. (1928). *Lectures on conditioned reflexes*. New York: Liveright Publishing Corporation.

Perry, J. W. (1976). *Roots of renewal in myth and madness*. San Francisco: Jossey-Bass.

Posner, M. I. (1994). Attention: The mechanisms of consciousness. *Proceedings of the National Academy of Sciences, 91*, 7398–7403

Posner, M. I., & Dehaene, S. (1994). Attentional networks. *Trends in Neuroscience, 17*, 75–79.

Raimy, V. C. (1948). Self-reference in counseling interviews. *Journal of Consulting Psychology. 12*, 153–163.

Reber, Arthur, S. (1993). *Implicit learning and tacit knowledge: An essay on the cognitive unconscious*. New York: Oxford University Press.

Rogers, C. R. (1951). *Client-centered therapy*. Boston: Houghton Mifflin.

Rutter, M. (1979). Maternal deprivation, 1972–1978: New findings, new concepts, new approaches. *Child Development, 50*, 283–305.

Sargant, W. (1957). *Battle for the mind*. Baltimore: Penguin.

Sechehaye, M. A. (1970). *Symbolic Realization: A new method of psychotherapy applied to a case of psychotherapy*. New York: International Universities Press.

Shallice, T. (1988). *From neuropsychology to mental structure*. Cambridge: Cambridge University Press.

Scheppelle, K. L., & Bart, P. B. (1983). Through women's eyes: Defining danger in the wake of sexual assault. *Journal of Social Issues, 39*, 63–81.

Sheldon, K. M., Elliot, A. J., Youngmee, K., & Kasser, T. (2001). What is satisfying about satisfying events? Testing 10 candidate psychological needs. *Journal of Personality and Social Psychology, 80*, 325–339.

Snygg, D., & Combs, A. W. (1949). *Individual behavior*. New York: Harper & Row.

Thorndike, E. L. (1911). *Animal intelligence: Experimental studies*. New York: Macmillan.

Tonini, G., & Edelman, G. M. (1998). Consciousness and complexity. *Science, 282*, 1846–1851.

CHAPTER 4
Motivation Further Considered and Emotions

In this chapter, I discuss mid-level implicit needs and beliefs, lower level implicit needs and beliefs, emotions, and other feeling states.

MID-LEVEL NEEDS AND BELIEFS

If one is to understand motivation in everyday life, it is insufficient to consider only implicit basic needs. It is also necessary to employ a more fine-grained analysis that considers people's implicit mid-level needs, such as their desire for power, acquisitions, achievement, affiliation, aggression, and nurturance.

Proposal of a List of Mid-Level Implicit Needs

As I knew of no theoretical basis for identifying mid-level needs, I adapted the list of needs proposed by Murray (1938). I dropped and added a few needs, modified the labels of some, and condensed and simplified the descriptions of several. Because Murray does not distinguish between mid-level and basic needs, I omitted two Murray needs because of their similarity to ones I included as basic needs. Table 4.1 presents the modified list of Murray needs and their descriptions.

Derivation of Mid-Level Beliefs from Mid-Level Needs

In a corresponding manner to the derivation of basic beliefs from basic needs, mid-level beliefs can be derived from mid-level needs based on the assumption that people acquire implicit beliefs about themselves from how they have fared in fulfilling their needs. For example, people tend to acquire implicit

Table 4.1. A LIST OF MID-LEVEL NEEDS, ADAPTED FROM MURRAY (1938)

Abasement: To passively accept blame, criticism, punishment, and accusations without defending oneself; to readily acknowledge inferiority, error, wrongdoing, and defeat

Achievement: To accomplish something difficult, overcome obstacles, attain a high standard, excel and surpass others

Acquisition: To acquire possessions, to become wealthy, to delight in one's possessions, to admire people who are wealthy

Aggression: To fight, seek revenge, punish, attack

Autonomy: To be independent, resist influence from others, defy authority

Counteraction: To undo a failure, not accept defeat or humiliation, persist in rectifying situations, turn defeat into victory, overcome obstacles, difficulties, weakness, and fear

Defendance: To defend the self against criticism, blame, or assault; to defend one's reputation or honor; to rationalize the reasons for failure, misdeeds, or questionable behavior

Deference: To admire, praise, honor, or support superiors, give in to others, be a follower, emulate others, conform, consider others' needs before one's own

Dependency: To be dependent on someone or others; to be taken care of, helped, nursed, supported, protected, comforted, advised, consoled

Aesthetic appreciation: To appreciate beauty and to reject ugliness, to make things and people attractive; to sing, dance, appreciate or create art, music, poetry, architecture; to delight in a sunset or in the sounds of a babbling brook

Exhibition: To be noticed, to draw attention to oneself, to be seen or heard, to entertain others

Harm-avoidance: To avoid pain, injury, illness; to take protective measures against possible dangers

Nurturance: To feed, console, comfort, nurse, heal; to provide help, support, protection, sympathy, or understanding to those who are weak, disadvantaged, helpless, in a weakened condition, or in a vulnerable situation

Power: To influence the behavior of others; to control the outcome of events and the behavior of people; to use persuasion or force to get what one wants and to keep people from behaving in ways of which one disapproves

Psychological harm-avoidance: To avoid humiliation, disapproval, risk-taking, failure, embarrassment

Order: To put things in order, make things neat, orderly, precise, accurate

Play: To behave for fun, to laugh, make jokes, engage in games, sports, dancing, attend parties

Rejection: To reject someone or something; to have nothing to do with a person, object, or idea that once attracted you; to dismiss a person, object, or idea from further consideration

Security: To feel secure, safe, protected

Sex: To engage in and enjoy sexually related activity; to seek sexually stimulating objects, pictures, or people

Understanding: To understand oneself, others, events, or nature; to generalize, analyze, explain, develop theories; to find solutions to problems; to make sense of complex issues, situations, behavior

beliefs about their general level of competence from their degree of perceived success and failure in fulfilling their need for achievement. Such self-views are not only influenced by actual achievement; they are also influenced by the reactions of significant others and by psychodynamic considerations, such as feeling guilty about defeating an older sibling.

Mid-level beliefs, like basic beliefs, can be represented on bipolar dimensions anchored by opposite beliefs at the poles. For example, a woman's belief in her competence can be represented by her position on a bipolar dimension anchored at one end by the belief that she is extremely competent and at the other end that she is extremely incompetent.

Low-Level Implicit Needs and Beliefs

The lowest levels of implicit needs and beliefs are of very limited generality and consequence. Included are memories of specific, transient desires and of the occurrence of specific events. An example of a low-level implicit need concerning a specific event is the motivation to win in a game of tennis with a friend. An example of a lower level belief is a person's evaluation of herself as a tennis player.

Although the vast majority of beliefs concerning single events are low-level beliefs, some are sufficiently important to qualify as mid-level and even subordinate basic beliefs. An example of a single event that could influence a person's basic belief about his self-esteem is of an aging tennis star playing in the finals of a national tournament. He previously decided that the outcome of the match would determine whether he would continue to play competitively or retire. The outcome of this single tennis match therefore can have a profound effect on his overall level of self-esteem, depending on the extent to which his tennis playing is a significant aspect of his overall evaluation of himself as a worthy human being. Thus, individual events do matter if they are sufficiently important to a person.

How Limiting Is the Derivation of Implicit Beliefs from Implicit Needs?

I have inferred basic and mid-level beliefs from the fulfillment and frustration of basic and mid-level needs. How justified is this procedure? Within limits, this is a defensible procedure because people who are motivated by their needs automatically attend to the outcome of their relevant behavior. As a result, they acquire implicit beliefs about themselves, others, and the impersonal world based on their life history of fulfillment and frustration of their needs. Yet this does not mean that there are not other sources for acquiring mid-level and basic beliefs. Although most important events in people's lives are usually determined by their motivated behavior, this is clearly not always the case. There are at least three conditions in which people acquire beliefs for reasons that are unrelated to their own behavior. One such condition is the occurrence of accidental events, both good and bad, such as natural disasters and winning a lottery. Another is the occurrence of assaults by others, as in muggings, rapes, and warfare. A third is by observing what happens to other people.

At first consideration, it may seem that such situations reveal a significant limitation in deriving beliefs from needs. However, this argument turns out to be specious because in all the presumably nonmotivated situations, needs are necessarily involved and determine the influence of unmotivated events on beliefs. For example, the occurrence of a devastating hurricane from which people unintentionally suffer great harm will likely influence their basic implicit belief about their security and their mid-level implicit belief of harm avoidance. Thus, no matter what the source of an event, its influence on an implicit belief will be determined by the interaction of the situation with a person's relevant implicit needs. In other words, if there are no implicit needs regarding the occurrence of certain events, the events will have no effect on a person's beliefs. Therefore, the only limitation there can be in deriving beliefs from needs is when there is an insufficient selection of needs. The obvious solution is to add mid-level needs as required.

Emotions

Emotions are of such central importance in cognitive-experiential theory (CET) that without emotions there would be no CET. This is because in the absence of emotions there would be no automatic learning, because affect is necessary both as a source of motivation in the experiential system and as a source of reinforcement. Without automatic learning from experience, there would be no experiential system, and without an experiential system, there would be no CET.

If one is to understand emotions, it is necessary to distinguish between primary and secondary emotions. A failure to do so can be the source of confusion, for, despite superficial similarities, the two kinds of emotion involve basically different processes. The former are true emotions, whereas the latter are culturally simulated emotions that are treated as if they were true emotions because of their cultural consequences.

Primary emotions can be defined as reaction patterns in which an action tendency is the central component. Ancillary components include physiological reactions, a positive or negative affective state, cognitive processes, and expressive reactions (Epstein, 1984).

The view of an action tendency as the central aspect of an emotion from which several adjunct reactions follow is consistent with Darwin's position, as indicated in the following passage: "Unless an animal thus does act, or has the intention, or at least the desire, to attack its enemy, it cannot properly be said to be enraged. An inherited habit of muscular exertion will directly or indirectly affect various organs in nearly the same manner as does great bodily suffering" (Darwin, 1872/1955, pp. 74–75).

Primary emotions evolved in a manner that provided them with critically important adaptive features. They can be viewed as a bridge between instincts and learned behavior, being more flexible than the former and less so than the latter. Primary emotions, according to CET, include fear, anger, sadness, joy, and affection. Perhaps a few other emotions, such as disgust, surprise, and contempt can be added, but I am less certain about these; although they probably meet all the other criteria of a primary emotion, disgust and contempt are not present in nonhuman animals. Depending on the importance one wishes to attribute to representation in nonhuman species, they therefore may or may not be regarded as primary human emotions. Research that could help to settle this issue would have to determine whether disgust and contempt are exhibited in all societies. Surprise is questionable as a primary emotion because of its lack of an action tendency. The reaction it produces is an orienting response, which is a reflex and not a controllable behavioral tendency that may or may not be overtly expressed. In any event, for present purposes, it will suffice to consider the five emotions I have listed as primary, with the consideration that there may be a few more.

Primary emotions can be distinguished from secondary emotions by their attributes. A primary emotion can be identified independently from the situations that instigate it. Thus, a person can be judged to be angry, fearful, sad, happy, or affectionate by that person's behavior and expressions without requiring information about the eliciting condition. That is, primary emotions can be observed in nonhuman higher order animals as well as in humans so long as they behave in certain ways and exhibit appropriate expressions for a specific emotion. For example, a dog cavorts when happy; seeks proximity and often licks the object of its affection when affectionate; is unresponsive, droops, and is sluggish when sad; yelps and flees or freezes when frightened; and growls, bares its teeth, and attacks when angry. People also exhibit their emotions in ways that can be identified. They are energized, cavort, laugh, and sing with joy when happy; are unresponsive, withdrawn, tired, droopy, and seek isolation when sad; seek proximity, hug, kiss, or rub noses when affectionate; are wide-eyed, feel cold, shudder, may cry or flee when frightened; and clench their jaws and fists and shout when angry.

Primary emotions are universal. The evidence is fairly strong that the emotions I listed as primary can be observed in all cultures (Ekman, 1989). Primary emotions include physiological patterns that are supportive of the action tendencies of an emotion (e.g., Ekman, Levenson, & Friesen, 1983; Epstein, 1984). Primary emotions have distinctive expressive reactions that can reliably be observed (e.g., Darwin, 1872/1965; Ekman & Oster, 1979). An integrative position that ties all this together is that emotions evolved because of their adaptive significance, which is to provide animals with automatic behavioral tendencies that are adaptive for critical life events (e.g., Darwin, 1872/1965; Ekman, 1992; Epstein, 1984; Frijda, 1986; Izard, 1977; Lazarus, 1991; Panksepp, 1994; Plutchik, 1980; Tooby & Cosmides, 1990).

The Action Tendencies of the Primary Emotions

The essence of a primary emotion is an action tendency that evolved because it prepares the organism for adaptive action to critical life events. It follows that every primary emotion must have one or more adaptive action tendencies.

The Action Tendencies for Fear

Fear has two major action tendencies: flight (either away from a threatening source or toward a protective one) and freezing. Both reactions provide a way of escaping from a source of threat. Freezing is adaptive under circumstances in which flight is either impossible or unlikely to be successful. It is adaptive under such circumstances because it reduces the likelihood of detection and it avoids stimulating the chase response in predators. Humans often find themselves in fearful situations in which they have chosen to confront a threat rather than flee from it, such as being interviewed for a position they wish to obtain or giving a speech to a large audience. In such situations, they show all the physiological symptoms of fear and feel like escaping, which they control.

The Action Tendency for Anger

For anger, the action tendency is to attack. Attack is adaptive for taking resources from others and for defending oneself against others. The action tendency in humans can be expressed in the form of a physical or verbal attack or a verbal threat. It can be expressed immediately, delayed, or suppressed. It can consist of social aggression, which refers to indirectly attacking by harming a person's reputation or turning others against the person.

The Action Tendency for Sadness

The action tendency for sadness is withdrawal and disengagement. When a nonhuman or human animal is defeated in a physical struggle, it is adaptive to remove the self from further confrontation, which can reduce injury, conserve energy, and provide an opportunity for recovery to occur. When the motive consists of coping with a loss, such as the death of a loved one, withdrawal and disengagement serve to conserve energy and to provide a period for assimilating the event in the absence of distracting stimulation.

The Action Tendency for Happiness and Joy

The action tendency for happiness and joy is the opposite of that for sadness, namely, engagement. When happy, people and nonhuman animals tend to be expansive and to be increasingly engaged in their environment. A dog frolics, romps, and barks with joy. Humans sing, jump with joy, do a jig, and extend their bodies and raise their arms when victorious. Humans and other animals when they are joyous are more willing to take risks and explore their environments than at other times. Such reactions are adaptive because they facilitate obtaining information about the environment under conditions that are perceived to be safe.

The Action Tendencies for Love and Affection

Love and affection have two main action tendencies: seeking proximity and expressing affection. Examples include cats rubbing against the legs of their owners and dogs greeting their owners by running up to them, jumping on them, and licking them. Humans hold hands, hug each other, and kiss on the lips or rub noses. Such reactions facilitate bonding, cooperation, and procreation.

Ancillary Components of Primary Emotions

The physiological component of an emotion prepares an organism for expressing the action tendency elicited by an emotion, such as fight or flight. The affective component of an emotion is a positive or negative feeling state that motivates, respectively, approach or avoidance behavior toward the source of the emotion. It is also a source of reinforcement. Behavior that is followed by positive affect or a reduction in negative affect tends to be repeated, and behavior that is followed by negative affect tends to be avoided, both of which are normally adaptive.

The cognitive component of an emotion consists of the appraisal, perception, or interpretation of an event, which is the proximal instigation of the emotion (as distinguished from the objective event, which is the distal instigation). That is, the immediate cause of an emotion is not the occurrence of an event but the interpretation of the event. For example, if a person believes a curved stick is a poisonous snake, the person will be frightened; whereas, if the person believes a poisonous snake is a stick, the person will not be frightened. As another example, if a person interprets a remark as an inexcusable insult, the person will feel angry; if the same remark is interpreted as an indication of poor social skills by someone who is under great stress, it may evoke an emotion of sympathy and an attempt to put the person at ease. It is important to recognize that it is the interpretation of events, not the events themselves, that determine people's emotions. This indicates that if one can change one's interpretations, one can change one's emotions, a topic that will be discussed in Part 3.

The expressive component of an emotion, such as smiling, frowning, or clenching one's fists and jaw, serves a communicative function. By communicating an action tendency, it signals to others what to expect, which can set the stage for a more adaptive interaction between individuals. For example, if anger is communicated by a frown or clenched fists, it can alert the other party to be prepared to defend herself or to make peaceful overtures. When a dog growls and bares its teeth at another dog, it signals its readiness to attack, which can then be avoided by the other dog leaving the field or adopting a submissive posture. In contrast, when a dog reacts to another dog by wagging its tail, it signals friendly intentions that invite reciprocal behavior. This is obviously adaptive because it promotes bonding and cooperative behavior and avoids hostile interactions. Observation of expressive reactions, such as smiling, frowning, and head shaking affirmatively or negatively is useful for the cues they provide about people's action tendencies, which may or may not be consistent with their verbal statements.

Primary Emotions as Nature's Compromise Between Instinctive and Learned Behavior

Emotions are less biologically determined than instincts and more biologically determined than learned behavior. Instincts are reflexive, biologically determined ways of responding to the environment. An example of an instinct is salmon swimming thousands of miles in oceans and rivers to spawn in the same stream in which they were hatched. The salmon do not have to learn to behave in this manner. They are biologically wired to respond adaptively to certain environmental cues. Emotions also have a biological component that influences the behavior of human and nonhuman animals, but they do so in a much more flexible way than instincts because emotions involve only a disposition to behave in a certain manner. A person or nonhuman animal experiencing an emotion may or may not express the behavioral tendency activated by the emotion, and if the person or animal does express it, it may do so in a variety of ways. A frightened cat may freeze, attack, or flee from a source of threat. What triggers an instinct is wired in or reflexive, whereas what triggers an emotion is influenced by learning. Thus, what angers one person does not anger another, and when a person is angered he or she may physically attack, verbally attack, plan on future retribution, obsess over the emotion, or just let it pass.

Secondary Emotions

Secondary emotions are usually considered to be learned emotions that are combinations of primary emotions. In contrast, secondary emotions are regarded in CET as culturally established syndromes modeled after primary emotions and treated as if they are primary emotions. Although they share some common features with primary emotions, such as a state of heightened arousal and a positive or negative affective state, secondary emotions do not share the other attributes of primary emotions. They are not universal, they do not exist in nonhuman animals, and they do not have specific action tendencies, specific physiological states, or specific expressive behaviors. Rather than being defined as a syndrome with a central action tendency, they are defined primarily by the situations that elicit them. Examples of secondary emotions are envy, jealousy, pride, relief, guilt, shame, and pity. To illustrate how secondary emotions differ from primary ones, let us consider envy as an example. All that is required for an interpretation that a person is envious is information that the person is distressed because someone has something the first person desires. There is no specific inner state or action tendency for envy. An envious person can be sad, angry, or just distressed and have any of several action tendencies or none at all. Thus, envy cannot be defined by any particular state of the organism, including an action tendency that is the central component of a primary emotion. It is interesting, in this respect, to compare the secondary emotions of envy and jealousy. The only way they differ is that the former involves some kind of distress because someone possesses something that the distressed person would like to have, whereas the latter involves someone being distressed because someone possesses a relationship with a person with whom the distressed person would like to preserve or have a relationship with.

Unresolved Feeling States

Considerable attention has been devoted to emotions, moods, and general arousal. Little attention has been paid to another class of feelings that involve unresolved arousal states that are more specific than diffuse states of arousal but less specific than emotions. Such unresolved states include anxiety, agitation, tension, disquietude, distress, and excitement. They are subjective feeling states that vary in positive or negative affect and therefore are sources of motivation and reinforcement, and they have physiological components that influence people's psychological and physical well-being. They evolved because they are adaptive: they provide an additional level of flexibility beyond that provided by emotions. In a comparable manner in which shifting the gears of an automobile provides the driver with greater flexibility than if only a single gear were involved, unresolved arousal states provide people with an additional degree of flexibility. I refer to such states as *unresolved feeling states* because they are unstable states that arise in preparation for a more specific emotion that has an adaptive action tendency, such as fight or flight. Thus, they can be viewed as precursors of emotions, in the same way that emotions can be regarded as precursors of certain kinds of behavior.

As an example of the difference between an unresolved feeling state and an emotion, let us compare the unresolved feeling state of anxiety with the emotion of fear. The essence of fear is that it is an aversive feeling state that produces an action tendency to flee. In contrast, the essence of anxiety is that it is an aversive feeling state without a specific action tendency. Often, anxiety is defined as fear from an unknown source. A more useful definition is that anxiety is fear without an action tendency, which subsumes the previous definition because, without the identification of a source, there can be no action tendency for coping with it. Moreover, even when people know the source of a threat, they feel anxious rather than frightened when they have no way of reacting to it. For example, soldiers in combat find long-delayed anticipated assaults from the enemy more distressing than the assault when it finally arrives. Waiting is particularly nerve racking. As another example, wartime pilots have on occasion crash-dived their aircraft to their certain deaths because they could not tolerate the constant anxiety produced by an impending but uncertain likely death (Bond, 1952).

It is obviously adaptive for unresolved feeling states to be experienced as more aversive than specific emotions because it would motivate a resolution in the form of converting a less differentiated state into a more differentiated one for which more specific action is appropriate. That is, similar to a known evil, a known fear is likely to be less disturbing than an unknown one because at least one may be able to cope with it.

Agitation is another unresolved feeling state that can be highly distressing and has no action tendency. The person knows that something is wrong and that it is important to take action, but does not know what action to take. If the person resolves the uncertainty by deciding that there is a person whose behavior is the source of the agitation and therefore can be attacked, the agitation is converted to anger.

Vibes

There is a particularly important kind of feelings that I refer to as "vibes." Vibes are subtle feelings that are often unnoticed but exert an important influence on behavior. They are important for practical as well as theoretical reasons because awareness of them provides useful information for making decisions and for putting people in touch with their intuitive knowledge. To appreciate the importance of vibes, it is instructive to consider the behavior of nonhuman animals. Much animal behavior is controlled by subtle feelings because it is more efficient than being controlled by stronger feelings. As an animal repeatedly responds to situations that were initially highly emotionally charged, its behavior becomes increasingly routine and less emotional. For example, if one observes a monkey in an avoidance conditioning experiment in which it receives an electric shock following a tone, at first it become frantic when it hears the tone. Through trial and error it learns that by pressing a lever after the tone it can avoid receiving the shock. Over increasing trials in which it avoids the shock, it becomes increasingly less distressed. Eventually, when it hears the tone, it nonchalantly presses the lever with hardly missing a beat in the activity with which it was engaged. However, if one were to prevent it from pressing the lever after the tone, it would again exhibit its previous frantic behavior. What is true of the monkey is true of humans, who have a similar experiential system. Vibes control more of people's behavior than they are aware of.

Although much is the same between the experiential systems of monkeys and people, there is one extremely important difference. Whereas the behavior controlled by vibes in monkeys is motor behavior, in humans, it is also conscious thought. This is particularly important because it means that if people want to be able to think objectively, they have to take into account the biasing influence of their vibes, which means they have to be able to identify them. Another complication is the result of the bidirectional interaction between vibes and conscious thought. Not only do vibes influence thought, but thought also influences vibes. Namely, analytical thought interferes with the ability to attend to vibes (e.g., Epstein & Yanko, 1999; Wilson & Schooler, 1991). It follows that if one wishes to access the information provided by vibes, it is necessary to suspend reasoning and attend to one's feelings.

A dramatic example of the adaptive use of vibes is provided in a book on decision making by Jonah Lehrer (2009), in which he recounts a situation in which a naval commander, by attending to his feelings, made a critical decision that saved an aircraft carrier and many lives. The commander had to make a rapid decision about a radar blip that indicated an object was rapidly approaching an American aircraft carrier. He had to decide whether the object was a returning aircraft or an enemy missile. He ordered it shot down with a surface-to-air missile. The decision was a correct one, and everyone marveled on how he made it. He explained that there was something about the enemy missile that he could not identify but that gave him twinges of anxiety, and he decided to act on his feelings. A later investigation identified the cue that made the discrimination possible. The flight patterns of returning aircraft and missiles were slightly different. The commander was apparently able to react to the cue because of his considerable experience with the flight patterns of returning aircraft. As a result of such experience, his experiential system could identify cues that he was consciously unaware of. This analysis is consistent with research that has demonstrated that people can detect complex patterns unconsciously, as indicated by physiological measures, long before they can identify them consciously (Becchara, Damasio, Tranel, & Damasio, 1997).

THE IMPORTANCE OF FEELINGS IN COGNITIVE-EXPERIENTIAL THEORY

Emotions are of special importance in CET for several reasons. First, affect is the source of reinforcement for the automatic learning of the experiential system. Thus, as previously noted, without emotions, there would be no automatic learning and no experiential system. Second, affect is the source of motivation in the experiential system because behavior is directed in the experiential system by the anticipation of positive or negative affect based on past experience, which motivates approach or avoidance behaviors. Without affect, there would therefore be no action directed by the experiential system. This would not only keep the experiential system from influencing behavior, it would keep it from influencing conscious thought, which is simply another kind of behavior. Third, emotions provide ready-made cognitive-affective modules that serve as nuclei around which more extensive networks are constructed in the course of development. These extended networks are important components of people's implicit theories of reality and therefore of their personalities. Thus, there are people whose personalities can be described by their characteristic emotions, such as angry or disgruntled people, sad or depressed people, frightened or insecure people, affectionate or loving people, and happy or joyous people.

A fourth reason why emotions are important is that they indicate the strength of people's implicit beliefs. The stronger the emotional accompaniment of the expression of a belief, the more it can be assumed that the belief occupies an influential position in the hierarchy of a person's implicit theory of reality. From this relation, a fifth reason for the importance of emotions can be deduced: emotions are the royal road to the beliefs in people's implicit theories of reality. By attending to people's emotions, the implicit beliefs that guide their everyday behavior can be inferred (Epstein, 1973), which may or may not be congruent with their conscious beliefs.

REFERENCES

Bechara, A., Damasio, H., Tranel, D., & Damasio, A. R. (1997). Deciding advantageously before knowing the advantageous strategy. *Science*, *275*, 1293–1296.

Bond, D. D. (1952). *The love and fear of flying*. New York: International Universities Press.
Darwin, C. (1872/1965). *The expression of the emotions in man and animals*. New York: Appleton (1965 Chicago: University of Chicago Press.)
Ekman, P. (1989). The argument and evidence about universals in facial expressions of emotion. In H. Wagner & A. Manstead (Eds.), *Handbook of social psychophysiology* (pp. 143–163). New York: Wiley.
Ekman, P. (1992*a*). An argument for basic emotions. *Cognition and Emotion, 6*, 169–200.
Ekman, P. (1992*b*). Facial expressions of emotions. New findings, new questions. *Psychological Science, 3*(1), 34–38.
Ekman, P., Levenson, R. W., & Friesen, W. (1983). Autonomic nervous system activity distinguishes between emotions. *Science, 221*, 1208–1210.
Ekman, P., & Oster, H. (1979). Facial expressions of emotion. *Annual Review of Psychology, 30*, 527–554.
Epstein, S. (1984). Controversial issues in emotions theory. In Shaver (Ed.), *Annual review of research in personality and social psychology* (pp. 64–87). Beverly Hills, California: Sage Publications.
Epstein, S., & Yanko, J. (1999). *Providing reasons can interfere with children's intuitive understanding*. (Unpublished analyzed data).
Lazarus, R. S. (1991). *Emotion and adaptation*. New York: Oxford University Press.
Lehrer, J. (2009). *How we decide*. New York: Houghton Mifflin Harcourt.
Murray, H., A. (1938). *Explorations in personality*. New York: Oxford University Press.
Panksepp, J. (1994). The basics of basic emotions. In P. Ekman & R. J. Davidson (Eds.), *The nature of emotion* (pp. 20–24). New York: Oxford University Press.
Plutchik, R. (1980). *Emotion: A psychoevolutionary synthesis*. New York: Harper & Rowe.
Tooby, J., & Cosmides, L. (1990). The past explains the present: Emotional adaptation and the structure of ancestral environment. *Ethology and Socio-biology, 11*, 375–424.
Wilson, T., & Schooler, J. W. (1991). Thinking too much: Introspection can reduce the quality of preferences and decisions. *Journal of Personality and Social Psychology, 60*, 181–192.

CHAPTER 5

Interactions Between and Within the Two Systems

Conflict, Compromises, Synergy, Repression, and Dissociation

In this chapter, I discuss two major kinds of interaction: that between the experiential and the rational systems and that within the experiential system. The former shares some common ground with psychoanalytic theory, whereas the latter has no comparable representation in psychoanalysis.

INTERACTIONS BETWEEN THE EXPERIENTIAL AND RATIONAL SYSTEMS

There are several ways in which the experiential and rational systems interact with each other, including conflicting with each other, establishing compromises, reacting synergistically, and exhibiting a bidirectional dance between them.

Conflicts Between the Two Systems

Conflicts Between the Hedonic and Reality Principles

Most often, the hedonic principle and the reality principle interact with each other in seamless harmony. At other times, the two motives conflict with each other, as exhibited in everyday conflicts between the heart and the head. Although such conflicts are often of minor significance, they are sometimes the source of considerable distress, including difficulty in deciding between alternatives and experiencing serious post-decisional regret. Examples of everyday minor conflicts are deciding on whether to eat a tempting desert or to forego it and deciding whether to buy the car that looks more attractive or the one that has a better service record. An example of a more serious conflict is when a woman must decide whether to marry the suitor who makes her laugh or the one who is more responsible; many a novel has been written about a young woman paying a terrible price for following her heart, as in *Anna Karenina* by Tolstoy.

A particularly important way in which the two systems conflict is by the biasing influence of the experiential system on the rational system. It is important because it can explain why humans, despite their remarkable intelligence, often behave irrationally, at great cost to themselves and others. A finding of considerable interest in this respect is that interpersonal relationships are more likely to evoke responses according to the hedonic principle and less likely to elicit responses according to the reality principle than are impersonal situations (Epstein, Pacini, Denes-Raj, & Heier, 1996; Norris & Epstein, 2001; Pacini & Epstein, 1999a).

According to Einstein, if humans are not to destroy each other in the future, they will have to learn to think differently (Calaprice, 1996). But how are people to learn to think differently? The first step is to understand why people do think irrationally. In interpersonal situations, people apparently tend to think in ways that make them feel good or less bad, rather than in ways that are logical and realistic, and, when they try to be logical, their reasoning is often biased by the motivation to feel good. As a result, they rationalize by believing their biased reasoning is rational. This chain of reasoning readily results in people believing that those who think differently from them are unrealistic and illogical, whereas their own thinking is realistic and logical. Such reasoning can explain why a species that exhibits outstanding intelligence with regard to solving problems of an impersonal nature has a history of solving problems at the group level by armed conflict and at the individual level by a high rate of divorce, crime, and dysfunctional parenting.

The biasing influence of the hedonic principle on the operation of the reality principle can explain why brilliant people like Einstein, who solved the most conceptually difficult impersonal problems, were unable to solve conceptually much simpler problems involving their own family relationships. For example, Einstein said he could not understand what women want. He apparently did not understand why his first wife was miserably unhappy in their marriage when all he expected of her was that she should behave as a normal housewife, taking care of his every need and delighting in his success (Isaacson, 2007). He ignored the consideration that, at the time, she was one of the few women in the world to be enrolled in a doctoral program in physics at a prestigious university. He helped to ruin her career by having unprotected sex with her and making her pregnant, which made it very difficult for her to continue her studies. After he married and later divorced her, he rationalized his treatment of her by concluding that women lacked the ability of men and should not aspire to be physicists. After his second marriage, he stated, "Very few women are creative. I would not send a daughter of mine to study physics. I'm glad my wife doesn't know any science; my first wife did" (Calaprice, 1996, pp. 218–219). He also stated, "I am referring to certain obstacles in a woman's system which we must regard as given by Nature and which forbid us from applying the same standard of expectation to women as to men" (Calaprice, 1996, p. 219). This is an excellent example of how people can rationalize almost anything, and their intelligence simply contributes to their ability to rationalize. In other words, it demonstrates the power of the hedonic principle to dominate the influence of the reality principle in certain situations.

Freud acknowledged a similar problem in understanding what women want. The answer to the question that neither of these brilliant men could answer is simple: what women want is no different from what men want; namely, to be treated with respect and fairness and to be equally appreciated and rewarded for their accomplishments.

Having provided an explanation from the perspective of cognitive-experiential theory (CET) of why people think irrationally despite their ability for outstanding reasoning, the obvious question is "What can be done about it?" Because answering this question would take us into the realm of remediation, which will be considered later, only a general answer will be provided now; namely, that people can be taught to understand the operation of the experiential system in general and, even more importantly, to observe its operation in themselves and control its influence. They can also learn to train their experiential system to make it better socialized so that there is less need to control it.

Approach-Avoidance and Avoidance-Approach Conflicts

Approach-avoidance conflict was introduced by Lewin (1935) and further developed by Miller (1944). It is of special interest in CET because people experiencing such conflicts are trapped by conflicting approach and avoidance motives and are neither able to attain a goal nor give it up. As can be seen in Figure 5.1, this occurs when a steeper gradient of avoidance intersects a less steep gradient of approach. At a distance from the goal, approach is greater than avoidance, so the person moves toward the goal. When closer to the goal, avoidance becomes greater than approach, so the person retreats from the goal. Approach-avoidance conflicts of this kind can occur between the experiential and rational systems or entirely within the experiential system, which will be discussed later.

The critical condition for an approach-avoidance conflict is that the avoidance gradient is steeper than the approach gradient, and the strengths of the

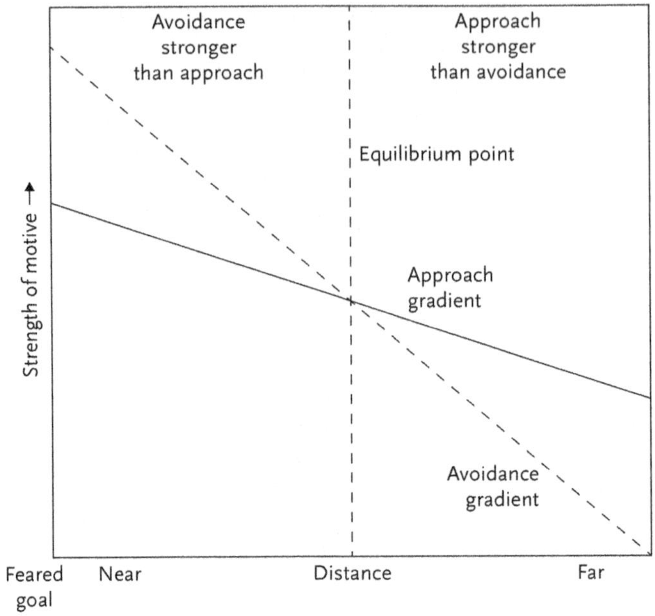

Figure 5.1
Approach-avoidance conflict. The individual approaches the goal when at a distance, vacillates at the intersection of the gradients, and avoids the goal when closer to it. The result is that the individual becomes trapped by his or her own motives, neither being able to fulfill nor abandon the approach motive.

This figure is reproduced with slight modification and with permission by The McGraw-Hill Book Companies from the figure in a book, *Personality and Psychotherapy*, authored by John Dollard and Neal E. Miller and published and copyrighted in 1950 by the McGraw-hill Book Company, Inc.

gradients, as represented by their heights, must be such that the gradients intersect. Such conditions readily occur in conflicts between the experiential and rational systems because the former has a shorter time perspective and therefore a steeper gradient as a function of time or distance. A common example of a conflict between the two systems occurs when people are enthusiastic about engaging in a challenging event some time before the event, but their enthusiasm wanes and their fear increases as the event approaches. For example, a person may enthusiastically accept an invitation to give a speech to a large professional audience thinking it is a good opportunity for advancing her career. As the time for giving the speech approaches, she begins to wish she had never accepted the invitation because her fear is now greater than her approach motivation.

To study approach-avoidance conflict, one of my research assistants, who was a sport parachutist, and I conducted a series of studies on the mastery of anxiety in sport parachuting (e.g., Epstein, 1962; Epstein & Fenz, 1965; Fenz & Epstein, 1962, 1967). In one of the studies (Epstein & Fenz, 1965), we had aspiring parachutists rate their enthusiasm for making their first jump and their fear of making the jump along a time dimension from the time when they signed up to make their first jump to shortly after landing. At a remote time from the jump, they rated their enthusiasm for making the jump very high and their fear of jumping very low. As the time to jump approached, their enthusiasm ratings decreased and their fear ratings increased, until the fear ratings for most exceeded their enthusiasm ratings. Shortly before the scheduled jump, several parachutists reported wondering what had possessed them to sign up to jump in the first place. A few decided at the last minute to abort the jump and forfeit the fee they had paid for their training and equipment. Most who jumped despite their fear ratings being greater than their enthusiasm ratings said they did so because they did not want to be regarded as cowards by their friends in the group.

Avoidance-approach conflict, in which a steeper approach gradient intersects a less steep avoidance gradient, was originally dismissed as unimportant because a person with such a conflict would normally stay away from the conflicted goal. However, the conflict can be important under certain circumstances (Epstein, 1978). If a person were brought up in a way that fear of a particular goal was strongly internalized and therefore relatively constant, it would have a relatively flat fear gradient. If, in contrast, approach tendencies to the same goal varied as a function of cues indicative of their availability, the approach gradient, as a function of time or distance, would be relatively steep. A person with such avoidance and approach gradients would have the gradients intersect if they were at appropriate levels and would therefore have an avoidance-approach conflict. Such a person would normally avoid the conflicted goal, but if circumstances or coercion placed the person on the goal side of the intersection of the gradients, the person would rapidly approach the goal that was otherwise avoided. Such conflicts can explain dramatic ego-alien behavior, as when an apparently well-behaved young man sexually assaults a woman whom he unintentionally saw through a window getting undressed.

Repression

Repression provides an example of one of the ways in which the two systems conflict with each other. Freud defined repression as a conflict between the expression of unconscious mental content in the id and a counter force in the ego that prevents the repressed material from becoming conscious (Freud, 1933/1964). According to Freud, mental energy is consumed by the effort exerted by the two opposing forces, which makes repression costly. Freud considered repression to be the most fundamental of the defense mechanisms and, as noted in Chapter 3, to lie at the heart of psychopathology. He also believed repression was important because it produced resistance to awareness of unacceptable thoughts and impulses, and it was therefore necessary to remove the resistance if treatment were to progress. It is for such reasons that Freud regarded repression as "the foundation stone on which the whole structure of psycho-analysis rests" Freud. 1924/49 (p. 297).

Although Freud's position on repression and the position of CET differ in several important ways, they are similar in other ways. Thus, the Freudian view of repression as a conflict between conscious and unconscious mental processes is accepted in CET, as is the view that repression is emotionally costly. However, according to CET, the reason that it is costly is because it involves a conflict between the experiential and rational systems, which is a source of stress, and not because repressed mental content has a force of its own that strives for expression, like steam in a steam boiler. The impression that repression has a force of its own is explained in CET by a basic implicit need to assimilate mental content into a unified system. The intrusions into consciousness are viewed as abortive attempts at such assimilation.

Repression is regarded in CET as a learned avoidance response that operates as follows. When a person's conscious thoughts approach an area of repressed mental content, the person experiences a twinge of anxiety. The anxiety motivates the person to think in ways that veer away from pursuing the line of thought that, if continued, would lead to awareness of the repressed material. The repeated avoidance of anxiety by this procedure increasingly reinforces the avoidance response, or, in Freud's terms, strengthens the repression. Thus, although some have doubted its existence, there is nothing esoteric or even remarkable about repression. In fact, when one considers the important automatic influence of the pleasure principle on conscious thinking and the readiness with which avoidance responses are learned in animals, it would be surprising if repression, conceived of as a learned avoidance response in the experiential system, did not occur in humans. This view is in essential agreement with Freud on how repression operates, although he expresses it in different terms, such as by referring to signal anxiety as a cue for avoiding awareness of repressed content.

Cognitive-experiential theory does not include other assumptions that Freud makes about repression, such as that there are two kinds of repression, *repression proper* and *primal repression*, with repression proper depending on associations with primal repressions acquired in childhood. According to CET, avoidance responses can be learned at any age and are not dependent on associations with childhood repressions. This is well demonstrated by learned avoidance responses in adult animals. It follows, according to CET, that what is true of the experiential system of nonhuman animals is likely true for the experiential system of humans.

Sensitivities and Compulsions

When people are exposed to a highly threatening event, they become sensitized to cues that are reminders of the event, and they tend to acquire a compulsion to respond in a way that reduces the anxiety evoked by these cues. Sensitivities are automatic, experiential responses that alert organisms to repetitions of a danger. Compulsions are automatic responses that may remove the organism from repetitions of the danger. Such inherently adaptive behavior is understandably highly resistant to control by the rational system.

The problem with sensitivities and compulsions is that they are so focused on a particular source of danger that they can be seriously maladaptive in situations that differ from the initial threatening experience, including fixating a person's attention, thought, and behavior on the past threat to the neglect of awareness of other sources of danger. A fighter pilot in the Eighth Air Force, which suffered extremely high casualties in the Battle of Britain in the Second World War, became fixated on attacks from the left after he was nearly shot down in such an attack. As a result of continuously searching the sky for attacks from the left, he became highly vulnerable to attacks from the right. In addition to becoming sensitized to being attacked from the left, he developed a compulsion to fire at any flying objects that approached from the left, including flights of ducks (Bond, 1952). It is noteworthy that no repression was involved in this behavior because the pilot was well aware of the source of his sensitivity and compulsion. Nevertheless, he experienced an intense conflict between an experientially determined behavior and an awareness that could cost him his life.

COMPROMISES BETWEEN THE TWO SYSTEMS

Compromises between the two systems commonly occur between the hedonic principle of the experiential system and the reality principle of the rational system and also between the attributes of the two systems.

Compromises Between the Hedonic and Reality Principles

Compromises between the principle motives of the two processing systems most often are accomplished in a manner that is harmonious, effortless, and adaptive. Under the influence of the hedonic principle, people's judgments and interpretations tend to be favorable, and, under the influence of the reality principle, the biases produced by the experiential system are constrained within adaptive limits. Because people are very good at rationalizing, under the influence of the hedonic principle, the experiential system co-opts the rational system into believing that self-serving biases and optimistic judgments are rational.

In a book aptly named *Intuition, Its Powers and Perils*, David G. Myers (2002) includes a review of research on the unrealistic favorable judgments that people frequently make, often in a way that makes them feel good and does no harm. Under certain circumstances, however, he notes that favorable biases can have seriously unfortunate consequences. In other words, most of the time, people function as strategic optimists in a way that makes them feel good at little or no risk of harm, but, in certain other situations, people's thinking is too positive for their own good, as well as for the good of others who rely on their judgment. Among some of the research findings reported by Myers on people's unrealistic positive beliefs, college students believe they are more likely to have good and not bad things happen to them than to their classmates. They believe they are more likely to get a good job, remain in better physical shape, and live ten years longer than their classmates, and that they are less likely to have a drinking problem, have a heart attack at an early age, be fired from a job, or get divorced. Most business executives, politicians, and fund managers are overly optimistic in their financial predictions. In several studies concerning betting on horse races, people overestimated the likelihood that long shots, which have high pay-offs, will win. In summary, most people make unrealistically favorable judgments about future events.

Most people accept greater responsibility for their good deeds and successful performance than for their transgressions and failures, for which they rationalize. In games of chance, people attribute their winnings to their skill and their losses to accidents or near misses that could easily have been hits. When people evaluate their performance in the stock market, they report that they have done better than they actually have. Most people regard themselves as more intelligent and better looking than most others. Most managers believe they are better managers than most managers, and most workers believe they are better workers than most workers. In national surveys, most business people regarded themselves as more ethical than other business people Thus, people tend to evaluate themselves in an unrealistically favorable way.

The phenomenon of people having favorable biases is not restricted to psychologically naïve people. When psychotherapists from various theoretical schools searched for early childhood experiences in their clients' lives, they usually found that their own theories but not the theories of others were supported. Most social psychologists, despite being aware of the research findings on self-serving biases, consider themselves to be more ethical than most social psychologists.

What is one to make of the widespread prevalence of such unrealistically favorable assessments? How maladaptive is it to be unrealistic? Before proceeding to answer this question, it is important to consider that most people are unrealistic only to a very modest degree, exactly what one would expect from a compromise between the two information-processing systems, one motivated to make people feel good and the other motivated to make them realistic. Moreover, as noted previously, people are unrealistic mostly in situations where it can do them no harm and do them some good in terms of positive feelings. Such situations include those that are ambiguous and those in which overly favorable judgments are not costly. That this is adaptive is indicated by research in which it was found that people who are strategic optimists are generally better adjusted than others. They make decisions more easily than others do, and they live happier lives than others (Baumeister, 1989; Taylor & Brown, 1988).

Some psychologists have concluded from the considerable research that has demonstrated that most people are unrealistically favorable in their judgments that this indicates that reality awareness is not an appropriate criterion of mental health. The findings can more reasonably be interpreted as indicating that reality awareness should not be treated as the *only* criterion of mental health. Because feeling good and having high self-esteem are also important criteria of mental health, when putting these criteria together with being realistic, it is not surprising that people behave as strategic optimists who form self-serving compromises that make them feel good within realistically acceptable limits. People who behaved only according to the pleasure principle would be unrealistic to the point of being psychotic, and people who behaved only according to the reality principle would be depressed. The challenge for everyone is to accomplish an appropriate compromise between the two principles that takes into account cost effectiveness in terms of feelings and reality considerations. Although most people operate as strategic optimists and self-serving self-evaluators, this is not true of everyone and, as previously noted, varies according to the person and the situation. Some people are more unrealistic than others, and some situations elicit more unrealistic behavior than others. Gamblers, stockbrokers, and those who risk their health by taking unreasonable risks, such as by smoking and engaging in unprotected sex, are being unwisely optimistic. Surgeons, soldiers in combat, fire fighters, and people who engage in potentially dangerous sports, such as sky diving and mountain climbing, are better off if they consider worst-case scenarios than if they assume that all will be well. Positive thinking may feel good, but there are circumstances in which it can cost people and those who depend on them their well-being and even lives.

Modest self-serving biases and slightly unrealistic optimism are not the only compromises produced by interaction between the pleasure principle and the reality principle. Another frequent compromise is between the desire for immediate gratification and the consideration of long-term consequences. Mary is concerned about her weight. She compromises by requesting only a sliver of a birthday cake instead of a full slice. Jack receives a tip from a highly successful stock broker on how he can make a great deal of money. He decides to compromise by putting only some of his discretionary funds into the recommended investment and the rest into more conservative investments. Such behavior is common in everyday life, and we make such decisions without realizing they are compromises between two different ways of processing information, one that operates primarily by the hedonic principle and the other by the reality principle.

Compromises Between the Attributes of the Two Systems

As an example of a compromise between the attributes of the two systems, the concrete, holistic processing of the experiential system can produce a compromise with the abstract, analytical processing of the rational system. The ratio bias (RB) phenomenon provides a demonstration of such a compromise. It also demonstrates alternative paths that the interaction between the attributes of two systems can take, including a conflict between the systems and complete dominance by the rational system.

The RB phenomenon refers to the judgment of the occurrence of a low-probability event as greater when the same probability is expressed in larger (e.g., 10 in 100) than in smaller (e.g., 1 in 10) numbers. The phenomenon has been investigated in a variety of ways, some involving a game of chance (e.g., Kirkpatrick & Epstein, 1992) and others involving responses to vignettes that compare events with different probabilities (e.g., Denes-Raj, Epstein, & Cole, 1995). In a study involving a game of chance (Denes-Raj & Epstein, 1994), participants were presented with two trays of red and white jellybeans. They were informed that on every trial in which they blindly drew a red jellybean, they would receive a dollar. It was up to them to decide on each trial from which tray they wished to draw. The smaller of the two trays always contained 10 jellybeans, one of which was red, and this tray was labeled, "10 percent red jellybeans." A larger tray contained 100 jellybeans and, depending on the trial, the number of red jellybeans varied between 5 and 10, and the trays were labeled with the probabilities they offered. Not surprisingly, a considerable number of participants consistently chose the tray that offered the greater probability of winning, which in all cases except the one in which both trays offered a 10 percent probability of winning. Of particular interest in this and in all similar experiments, the majority of participants chose to draw from the large tray that contained more red jellybeans despite it offering a lower probability of winning.

Participants were well aware of what they were doing. Some made statements such as, "I know I should pick from the tray that offers a better probability, but I feel I have a better chance of getting a red bean when there are more of them." Others defended their nonoptimal choices in a variety of ways to show why they believed their choice was rational. For example, a student who said he had taken several courses in statistics stated authoritatively that statistics do not apply to just a few trials (as in the experiment) and that, in the present situation, it was preferable to draw from the tray that had more red jellybeans. Another student said that, in a statistics test, she would indicate that it was better to select from the tray with the better probability but that, in real life, it was better to select from the tray that offered more winners. Such comments provide striking evidence of the ability of the experiential system to co-opt the rational system into rationalizing irrational decisions promoted by the experiential system. It is apparently highly compelling for people to think that if something feels right, it is right.

The RB experimental paradigm is of particular interest in CET because of the conflict it presents between experiential and rational ways of responding. The source of the conflict is that the experiential system comprehends concrete information, such as frequencies, better than ratios, which are more abstract, whereas the rational system, at least in adults, understands both kinds of information equally well.

It is noteworthy that most of the responses to the RB experimental paradigm consisted of compromises between the two systems. Compromises were indicated by the limited number of nonoptimal choices people made. Although most favored a 9 percent probability in the large tray over a 10 percent probability in the small tray, as the probabilities became more discrepant fewer participants chose the large tray. For example, few preferred a 5 percent frequency advantaged and probability disadvantaged choice (e.g., 5:100) over a 10 percent probability advantaged and frequency disadvantaged choice (e.g., 1:10) choice. Thus, the results demonstrated compromises between the experiential system favoring frequencies and the rational system favoring probabilities. In summary, most people compromised between the two systems, behaving according to their experiential processing but only within constraints imposed by their rational processing.

The RB experiment is instructive not only for producing compromises, but also for providing almost the full range of reactions to the interaction of the two processing systems. Although most participants exhibited modest compromises, a substantial number behaved consistently rationally and a few behaved in an extremely nonoptimal manner. Among those who made nonoptimal responses, some were comfortable following their feelings so long as their behavior only slightly departed from their rational thinking. Others acknowledged they were troubled by a conflict between their feelings and their reasoning. Among them, some decided to compromise between the promptings of their experiential and rational systems, whereas others decided to respond completely in terms of their rational system. Some participants were concerned about appearing irrational in the eyes of the examiner and felt compelled to explain why their behavior was actually rational because "it felt right."

The RB phenomenon is highly robust and has been replicated in many experiments (e.g., Denes-Raj & Epstein, 1994; Epstein & Pacini, 2001; Kirkpatrick & Epstein, 1992). When the experiment was conducted with children (Yanko, Epstein, Pacini, & Barrows, 1998), the only difference from the results with adults was that the children's compromises were more nonoptimal than the compromises of adults. Apparently, with maturation, people give increasing priority to their rational over their experiential processing and shift their compromises accordingly, with some shifting all the way to complete rationality.

The question may be raised as to whether those who made completely optimal responses in the jellybean experiments are better adjusted than those who made compromises. We found that those who made more nonoptimal responses than others did not differ in level of adjustment from others but reported more superstitious and Pollyannaish thinking (Pacini, Muir, & Epstein, 1998). Of particular interest in that study, those who received high scores on a measure of depression exhibited a surprisingly strong correlation ($r = 46$, $p < .01$) between nonoptimal responses in the RB task and an experiential thinking style, whereas a normal control group did not exhibit even a tendency for such a relation. There was also a significant positive relation ($r = .38$, $p < .02$) between nonoptimal responses and a measure of effective behavioral coping in the depressed group but not in the control group. The overall results suggest that, in normal individuals, making slight compromises between the two systems is not maladaptive and that, in depressed people, it may even be adaptive because it facilitates increasing engagement with the environment.

In another study of the RB effect (Pacini, Muir, & Epstein, 1998), those who made more nonoptimal responses than others did not differ in their degree of an experiential thinking style from others but had a lower rational thinking style than others. This was interpreted as indicating that everyone has a similar tendency initially to react experientially, but that its expression is controlled by individual differences in the rational system that influence the expression of the experiential system.

It is noteworthy that the results for compromises between the different processing attributes of the two systems in the RB paradigm parallel those for compromises between the primary motives of the two systems. In both cases, most adults prefer slight compromises over completely optimal responses.

THE INFLUENCE OF THE EXPERIENTIAL SYSTEM ON THE PERFORMANCE OF THE RATIONAL SYSTEM

Depending on the situation, the experiential system can facilitate or interfere with the performance of the rational system. In the research on positive biases, it was found that the experiential system influenced people to make unrealistic, favorable judgments that were usually harmless but, in some circumstances, could have dire consequences. It will be recalled that in the research on the RB phenomenon the experiential system influenced most people to prefer slightly nonoptimal responses.

Extreme Domination by the Experiential System

In the most extreme circumstances, the experiential system can overwhelm the constraints imposed by the rational system. Phobias and superstitions provide examples of such behavior. A woman who is terrified of mice knows in her rational mind that she is bigger and stronger than a mouse and that it has more reason to fear her than she has to fear it. Yet such reasoning is powerless to control her dread of mice. She becomes panic stricken when she sees a mouse, which may cause her to behave irrationally. Such a situation was reported in the newspapers some years ago, in which the flight of a commercial airliner was endangered by a mouse. A woman who saw the mouse in her aisle ran shrieking to the opposite aisle. Other women followed suit, which unbalanced the plane and required the pilot to make an emergency landing.

Another example of extreme dominance by the experiential system is provided by repetitive self-destructive behavior, such as when a woman repeatedly subjects herself to abusive relationships. Such behavior appears at first to make no sense either from the reality principle of the rational system or from the pleasure principle of the experiential system. Why should any sane woman who has been abused by an alcoholic husband and who vows never to make the same mistake again nevertheless does so, and even does it more than once? Why should a man who has been abused as a child put himself into abusive situations with authority figures as an adult? Since it might seem that no one would behave that way by their own volition, it is understandable why the behavior was once attributed to possession by evil spirits. A more reasonable explanation is that it is a natural phenomenon that can be explained by the need to maintain a stable, coherent conceptual system. To depart significantly from familiar ways of thinking, feeling, and behaving is anxiety provoking because it destabilize people's belief systems. Accordingly, people are motivated by their experiential processing to retain their major implicit beliefs. The motivation to behave more rationally is dominated by their experiential processing. Most of what the rational system contributes in such circumstances are rationalizations for experientially determined irrational behavior.

It may be concluded that the experiential system readily promotes maladaptive behavior even when people know better in their rational system. Emotional problems, neurotic and psychotic disorders, and maladaptive habits are all conditions in which people are often powerless to overcome unwanted behavioral tendencies promoted by the experiential system. Even understanding why a situation occurs may make no difference. There are simply situations in which the reasoning of the rational system is no match for the experiential system.

Dominance of the Experiential System in Heuristic Responses

Granted, there are extreme situations in which the experiential system can dominate the rational system and this can be a source of serious maladaptive behavior; however, there are more often less extreme situations in which the experiential system can interfere with the performance of the rational system. Such effects are well illustrated in a series of research studies my associates and I conducted on conjunction problems. Conjunction problems require the application of the conjunction rule, one of the simplest and most fundamental rules in probability theory. According to the conjunction rule, the occurrence of two events is less likely than the occurrence of either one of them. Although this rule seems self-evident, it is routinely violated when presented in the context of the "Linda problem." Normally, people can solve concrete versions of problems more easily than they can solve abstract ones, yet the opposite is true for the Linda problem. It will be seen that the research on this problem illustrates the conditions in which the experiential system can interfere with the performance of the rational system.

Linda is described as a 31-year-old, single woman who majored in philosophy in college and was concerned about social justice. Participants were asked to rank order the probability of a number of events, including the following: Linda is a feminist, Linda is a bank teller, and Linda is a feminist and a bank teller. The majority of respondents, including many trained in probability theory and statistics, judged the probability that Linda is both a feminist and a bank teller as greater than the probability that she is just a bank teller. A vast amount of research has been conducted to understand why people make this conjunction error.

When Tversky and Kahneman (1982) first presented their results on the Linda vignette, it stirred up a great deal of interest because the findings are so counterintuitive. As a result, the Linda vignette is probably the most researched vignette in the history of psychology. What is one to make of the strange findings from the Linda vignette? Does it mean that people simply do not understand the conjunction rule? Or do they perhaps understand the conjunction rule, but not in the context of the Linda problem, which somehow diverts them from applying the knowledge they have? The answer is that people do understand the conjunction rule when it is presented in a normal context, as will be seen in the following summary of the findings from our research about the conditions in which the experiential system can facilitate as well as interfere with the performance of the rational system (Donovan & Epstein, 1997; Epstein, Denes-Raj, & Pacini, 1995; Epstein, Donovan, & Denes-Raj, 1999).

- The experiential system performs best when problems are presented in a concrete, natural form, with natural defined as the similarity of the presentation of the problem to how it normally occurs in everyday life. Examples of concrete, natural conjunction problems are judging the likelihood of winning two lotteries or two bets on horse races compared to winning only one of them. Almost no one makes conjunction errors with such concrete, natural problems. They make more errors with abstract natural problems, such as when the problem is presented in the form of abstract symbols, and they make by far the most errors when the problem is presented in the form of concrete unnatural problems, as in the Linda problem.

- People perform best when the two systems operate in harmony with each other and poorest when they operate in opposition to each other. Thus, whereas presenting the Linda problem in a concrete unnatural version that engages the experiential system interferes with the performance of the rational system, presenting the problem in a concrete natural version, such as the likelihood that a person will win two lotteries or bets on two horse races or just one of them, allows almost everyone to solve it correctly.
- The experiential system under certain circumstances can outperform the rational system on intellectual problems. This was demonstrated when those who were unable to solve an abstract version of a conjunction problem had no difficulty in solving a natural concrete representation of the problem.
- Priming intuitive knowledge in the experiential system can facilitate performance in the rational system. This was demonstrated when we presented a lottery conjunction problem first, after which more people solved a subsequent abstract version of the problem than when the abstract version was presented first.
- People often incorrectly generalize from the specific to the general rather than correctly from the general to the specific. This was demonstrated by most participants selecting an incorrect conjunction rule that supported a conjunction error in preference to selecting the correct rule that would have prevented a conjunction error. This same conclusion has been supported by other research using different experimental paradigms.
- The overall picture that has emerged from our research is that the experiential system can interact with the performance of the rational system in three ways, most often compromising with it in a manner that results in self-serving, noncostly slight err ors; sometimes interfering with it by operating in an incompatible way; and sometimes facilitating its performance by operating harmoniously with it.

THE RATIONAL SYSTEM CAN TRAIN AND LEARN FROM THE EXPERIENTIAL SYSTEM

The rational system can influence the operation of the experiential system in two ways: by suppressing or modifying unacceptable response tendencies in the experiential system and by training the experiential system to respond in a more acceptable manner that requires little or no control. In addition, it can use its understanding of the experiential system to learn from it.

As the slower reacting system, the rational system is in a position to respond to the automatic thoughts, interpretations, and impulses initiated by the experiential system. To do so, the person must be aware of the reactions in the experiential system. In the absence of such awareness, experiential reaction tendencies will have an unobstructed path to directing behavior, including biasing conscious thinking Thus, a person can either be aware of and consequently exert conscious control over the experiential system or be automatically controlled by it.

Not everyone's experiential reactions require equal control. Some people have more appropriate experiential reactions to begin with and therefore require less control than others. People with a fortunate reinforcement history can give freer rein to their experiential reaction tendencies and still act appropriately than can those who have been less fortunate. This raises the question of what most people can do whose initial reactions are not what they would like them to be. The answer, according to CET, is that they can use their rational system to understand, train, and learn from their experiential systems in a manner that improves the operation of their experiential systems. It can also explain why many people behave more adaptively over time. The rational system may become aware of the long-term effects of failures and successes and develop strategies to minimize the former and maximize the latter. This is a life-long process of learning from experience.

An important advantage that the experiential system has in influencing the rational system is that, as an automatic, preconscious, rapidly reacting system, it can bias the operation of the rational system without the latter having any awareness that it is being influenced. In addition to an initial advantage over the rational system, the experiential system has an additional subsequent advantage in its influence on rationalization, in which it co-opts the rational system into regarding the person's experientially determined behavior as rational. To the extent that the operation of the experiential system is not countered by awareness of its operation, people will be automatically controlled by the influence of the experiential system.

By understanding the operating rules and attributes of the experiential system and, even more importantly, attending to its operation in oneself, the rational system can consciously decide whether the promptings of the experiential system are constructive and deserve to be implemented or whether they are counterproductive and should be rejected or altered. Important as such corrections are, they are at best damage control. Two more effective, albeit more difficult, procedures are training the experiential system to react initially more adaptively and learning from the automatic learning experience of the experiential system. How this can be accomplished will be discussed in Part 3, which explores therapy based on CET.

The rational system can also learn from the experiential system. Because the experiential system has a repertoire of implicit information that it empirically learned from experience, much of it outside of a person's awareness, by attending to experiential processing a person can acquire important information commonly referred to as *intuitive wisdom*. Apart from learning from such tacit information, the rational system can learn from the processing mode of the experiential system in responding to entirely new situations. Of course, people have to use their judgment in deciding when to obey the promptings of their experiential system and when to override it based on the scrutiny of their rational system.

BIDIRECTIONAL INTERACTION BETWEEN THE TWO SYSTEMS

Interactions between the two systems often involve a bidirectional, reciprocal chain of reactions corresponding to a dance between them. John is taking a mathematics test and working on a problem that requires determining which of two drivers will arrive at the same destination first. One has a faster car, but the other has a shorter distance to travel. Although it might seem at first that John's behavior in this situation will be completely determined by his rational system, remember that, according to CET, both systems contribute to all behavior and that, outside the occurrence of reflexes, no behavior can occur outside the context of past experience. John approaches the problem with confidence because he knows that he is good in mathematics and is familiar with this kind of problem. While he is immersed in his calculations, the thought occurs to him that the faster car is traveling at a dangerously high speed. This automatically triggers a memory about a serious accident he had when driving too fast. He becomes momentarily anxious and is unable to think well. He finally pulls himself together, takes a few deep breaths, relaxes, returns to concentrating on the mathematics problem, and correctly solves it. He goes through the appropriate operations and arrives at a correct solution.

Note that John's initial confidence stems from his experiential system, as it is based on his past successful performance in mathematics. Note further that his self-confidence, which corresponds to an automatic appraisal in his experiential system of his ability to solve such problems, is associated with a positive affective state that facilitates the performance of his rational system. John then has an association in his experiential system that produces an acute anxiety reaction that interferes with the performance of his rational system. He consciously (in his rational system) employs techniques for gaining control over his experiential system. Using both the abstract reasoning of his rational system and overlearned responses that were once in the rational system but, through practice, have become relegated to the experiential system, he is able to solve the problem.

Many reactions in real life consist of such bidirectional reciprocal chains of interactions. They occur so automatically that people are normally aware only of their conscious thoughts and an occasional intrusion of a salient emotion. They therefore regard their thoughts as a single process with the occasional intrusion of an emotion.

Psychodynamics

Psychodynamics refers to the interaction of unconscious wishes, fears, beliefs, and defense mechanisms in conjunction with conscious processes that can account for a particular kind of behavior. Unlike the explanations of relatively simple interactions that we have considered up to now, psychodynamic explanations are often more complicated because they involve an interaction of many variables, both simultaneously and sequentially. Moreover, the attempt to understand overt behavior by covert reactions further complicates explanation and invites speculation, making the task of providing useful psychodynamic explanations more of an art than a science.

Let us consider an example of how knowledge about individual variables considered in isolation can be misleading and how interactions of conscious and unconscious, experientially generated motives and beliefs can provide more meaningful explanations. When Mary reported for treatment of her depression, a social worker took down her case history, and a psychologist administered a battery of diagnostic tests that included the Thematic Apperception Test (TAT). Based on the stories she told to the TAT, the psychologist hypothesized that Mary had a great deal of unconscious hostile feelings toward her mother. In the absence of a psychodynamic approach, you might expect that if Mary had feelings of hostility to her mother she would move far away from her and have little to do with her. Yet, Mary behaved in the opposite manner. When she got married, it was important to her to live close enough to her mother so she could visit her on most weekends. Why is Mary behaving opposite from what would be expected based on her presumed hostility? Are the tests wrong? Not necessarily; when one understands the psychodynamic interactions behind Mary's behavior, all the information, including case history material and information obtained during her therapy sessions, falls into place. As a child Mary felt guilty about her anger toward her mother for favoring a sibling. When she accused her mother of loving her less than her sibling, she was reprimanded for her lack of appreciation of all her mother did for her that showed how much her mother loved her. But even more important than Mary's guilt were the practical consequences of what she understood would happen if she expressed her hostile feelings toward her mother or her sister; these consequences would be counterproductive to obtaining what she desperately wanted—her mother's love.

Mary decided to try to win her mother's affection by being an exceptionally good daughter. But trying to be good while having hostile feelings was difficult to do and felt terrible, so Mary avoided hostile feelings toward her mother by changing her thinking. She decided that her mother loved her less than her sister not because her mother was a bad mother but because she, Mary, had not been a good daughter who sufficiently appreciated all her mother did for her. She resolved that she would from then on become an exceptionally good daughter. By thinking she was bad and her mother was good, she was able to maintain the hope that if she became good enough her mother would appreciate her. Thinking that she was good and her mother was bad would have been counterproductive because it would have removed the only hope she had that if she changed her behavior and became exceptionally good her mother would love her.

What evidence is there that this interpretation is correct? It can best be regarded as a series of hypotheses that can be judged by their explanatory power. What, then, can the hypotheses explain? They can explain why Mary, an attractive, competent woman, has a very low opinion of herself and an unrealistic, stereotyped, favorable view of her mother. They can explain why Mary's solicitous behavior to her mother has a compulsive, driven quality to it that includes an excessive concern about her mother's welfare. On inquiry, it is learned that Mary fears that something terrible will happen to her mother. This can be explained by a hidden wish for it to occur, which is denied by consciously wishing to protect her mother from harm. Also, it is noteworthy that her extremely solicitous behavior toward her mother makes her mother uncomfortable. Is Mary perhaps killing her mother with kindness while consciously meaning to be helpful to her?

Most importantly, Mary occasionally has ego-alien outbursts in which she angrily complains about her mother's lack of appreciation for all that Mary does for her. When Mary is reminded later of what she said, she denies it and says she was misunderstood. The hypothesis provides a tentative explanation for Mary's depression, which is that the depression stems from Mary's negative views about herself, which in turn are based on her need to see herself as bad so she can view her mother as good. This hypothesis can provide a focus for further investigation during her psychotherapy sessions, which may provide additional support for it or require that it be modified or discarded.

Although it is easy to go astray with such psychodynamic explanations, they are a powerful way of addressing the complexity of human behavior. In short, if you want to understand people, you have to understand the interactive patterns of their conscious and unconscious wishes, fears, beliefs, and defenses, or, in other words, you have to understand their psychodynamics.

The following are two cases of normal individuals who provide examples of the operation of more simple psychodynamics in everyday life. Some years ago, I had a graduate student, whom I shall call Judith, who had a very high IQ and an outstanding academic record as an undergraduate. However, she was very poor at conducting research. Nothing she did seemed to work. She was very good at accumulating academic information and demonstrating her knowledge on paper-and-pencil tests, but she could not effectively apply her knowledge in the real world. Judith was very sensitive to criticism. It was more important for her to defend her ego than to improve her performance by learning from her failures. When I corrected her research designs, she would be deeply hurt and defend herself. She apparently interpreted my attempt to help her as attacks on her as a person. She complained that I made too many corrections on her papers and that I should be more accepting of what she did. The difficulty with what she asked for was that if she were to obtain a position at a prestigious university, which is what she wanted, she would have to learn what I was trying to teach her. Instead, she spent her energy defending herself. I was able to help many of my other students to obtain impressive publication records and desirable positions, but I was unable to do the same for Judith because she resisted all my efforts to help her. Judith had somehow managed to turn a benevolent situation into one that she viewed as threatening and that should be resisted at all costs.

This example indicates how an underlying implicit need to protect her ego resulted in Judith's self-destructive behavior in everyday life. Her behavior can be explained by her unconscious need, under the influence of the hedonic principle, to view herself as a competent person and to view me as someone who threatened the fulfillment of this need. This provided a momentarily satisfactory solution at the experiential level but at a terrible cost in terms of future consequences. Using the perspective of CET, one can speculate that this destructive behavior came from past experiences in which she had learned not to trust authority figures because she had been terribly hurt when she did.

As illustrated in the following example of a young child's response to threat, not all behavior is as it seems, and sometimes a little self-deception, as we have seen before, can be adaptive. My grandson, Casey, who was three years old at the time, often complained at bedtime that he wanted to stay up and play. One evening, I observed Casey shortly before his bedtime playing with his teddy bear. He was telling Teddy in no uncertain terms that it was time to go to bed. He was not at all sympathetic to Teddy's protests but seemed to be thoroughly enjoying the role of being a stern parent. He told Teddy in his firmest voice that crying and pleading would make no difference, and Teddy had better go to sleep without protesting or Casey would be very angry with him. At that point, I decided to enter the play. I assumed Casey would find my behavior amusing and that we would both get a good laugh out of it. I pretended I was Teddy, and, speaking in a falsetto voice I said, "I don't want to go to bed. I want to stay up and play. I'm not sleepy, so I shouldn't have to go to bed. I don't like you when you won't let me play and have fun." The joke turned out to be not so funny. Casey became visibly distressed. He ran around aimlessly in circles for a few moments, muttering gibberish. Then he threw himself on the floor and looked in the direction of his mother. When he saw that she was looking in his direction, he let out a wail and continued to sob. She ran over to him, picked him up, and asked what happened. He told her that he fell down and hurt himself. She kissed the imaginary wound, comforted him, and, when he was sufficiently soothed, put him down. All was well once more with Casey, and he happily resumed his playing, but not with Teddy.

This scenario well illustrates sequential interactions between the reality and pleasure principles. Casey had been enjoying the play in which he identified with the aggressor instead of being the helpless victim that he was in reality. According to the hedonic principle, it feels better to be an aggressor than a victim. I spoiled Casey's enjoyment of being a powerful aggressor in fantasy when I made the situation too real for him to continue behaving in the realm of fantasy. By mimicking his behavior as a victimized child with whom he could readily identify, it was too much for a three-year-old to cope with because it changed the good feelings of being a powerful aggressor into confusing and uncomfortable ones that were difficult to sort out. Being confused, he was motivated to find an acceptable explanation for his discomfort, one that would remedy the confusion and make him feel better (the equivalent of rationalization). He did this by creating a situation in which he could attribute his distress to a situation that made sense to him and would replace a bad feeling of being victimized with a good feeling of being comforted. Casey had illustrated, in the coping manner of a three-year-old, the same sequential interactions between the hedonic and reality principles that adults illustrate in other ways when they rationalize by providing favorable conscious explanations for behavior instigated outside of their awareness by their experiential systems.

INTERACTIONS WITHIN THE EXPERIENTIAL SYSTEM

Among the reaction tendencies and conflicts within the experiential system that can be sources of serious problems in daily life are the positive reinforcement of maladaptive behavior, approach-avoidance conflict, avoidance-approach conflict, dissociation, and the lack of fulfillment of basic needs as a result of their interactive influences on each other.

Positive Reinforcement as a Source of Maladjustment

People may be positively reinforced either intentionally or inadvertently for their maladaptive behavior. For example, children can be rewarded by explicit or implicit approval from their parents or by unintended events for certain kinds of maladaptive behavior such as being excessively aggressive, self-sacrificing, selfish, blaming others for their failures, being extremely timid, taking unreasonable risks, and behaving in a myriad of other ways that can produce problems in living. The point is that maladaptive behavior is not only produced by negative affect but also by positive affect. An element of repression may be involved in some positively reinforced behavior because learning in the experiential system occurs automatically, without requiring conscious intent, and therefore can create a conflict with conscious beliefs and values. Nevertheless, the essential problem in such circumstances is not the repression when it is present but the maladaptive behavior. Thus, even if there is resistance to awareness of such processing, insight is not necessarily the solution to the problem but may only be the beginning of a solution. That is, gaining insight into a repression may simply identify a problem that remains to be resolved; namely, how an underlying maladaptive behavioral tendency can be extinguished.

One example is a client for whom a major problem in living arose from the accidental positive reinforcement of a highly emotionally charged favorable experience. Jonathan was the younger of two siblings. When he was a very young boy, he greatly admired his brother who was two years older and therefore could do everything better than he could. Everyone admired the brother's athletic prowess and intelligence. When Jonathan entered the first grade, his teachers were disappointed with him because, although his performance was satisfactory, it was not equal to his brother's performance. Neither he nor anyone else regarded him as exceptional in any way. He wished he could be as accomplished as his brother, but he had to settle for being average. When he entered high school, everything changed. His brother fell in with a group of students who were more interested in having a good time than in studying, and he was thrown off the baseball team for misbehaving and poor grades. In the meantime, Jonathan blossomed. He became a star student and was elected captain of the debating team. His newfound superiority over his brother was a heady experience. He never dreamed anything like that could happen, and now it had happened beyond his wildest dreams. The result was a tremendous boost to his self-esteem. One might think Jonathan had undergone a wonderful growth experience. Instead, it turned out to be a disaster because it reinforced an intense desire to defeat others and to recapitulate the exciting emotional experience he had in surpassing his brother. This, of course, occurred automatically in his experiential system and was not the way he viewed himself consciously. Consciously, he considered himself a normally competitive person. From then on, Jonathan had problems in his relations with others. He alienated people by acting superior to them and by embarrassing them when an opportunity arose for doing so. He was not reelected to be captain of the debating team. Rather than maintaining a high level of self-esteem, his self-esteem plummeted because he did not get along with others and did not understand why. He later was married twice, and both marriages ended in divorce. In therapy, Jonathan at first resisted becoming aware of the role that his behavior had in alienating others. Instead, he found fault with others, including his previous wives.

Although some degree of repression may be based in Jonathan's resistance to awareness of his aggressive behavior, making the unconscious conscious was a very minor part of his therapy. The problem that remained was controlling and then extinguishing his automatic impulse to defeat others. In summary, this example indicates how people can be seduced by seemingly good experiences into developing maladaptive behavioral tendencies that can be every bit as destructive as problems produced by rejection or failure.

Approach-Avoidance and Avoidance-Approach Conflicts Within the Experiential System

Approach-avoidance and avoidance-approach conflicts were previously discussed as conflicts between the two systems. What was said for such conflicts between the two systems applies equally well to conflicts within the experiential system.

Approach-avoidance conflict was introduced by Lewin (1931) as one of three conflicts. Miller (1944, 1948, 1951, 1959) later reformulated Lewin's model in stimulus-response terms and extended its application. He and other researchers supported it mainly through research with animals (e.g., Brown, 1948; Miller, 1951; Miller & Kraeling, 1950; Rigby, 1954), and others later added research with humans (Whiting & Sears, 1949). Miller extended the model by including a time dimension for reaching a goal, in addition to a distance dimension. He also indicated how the model could elucidate a wide variety of behavior including in psychotherapy, in drug addiction, and in displacement along a dimension of goal dissimilarity. As a result, it is Miller's conflict model that has attracted the most attention.

It is noteworthy that approach-avoidance conflict occurs in nonhuman animals that have no rational system. This strongly suggested, and was verified in research, that both arms of the conflict can occur completely within the experiential system of humans (e.g., Whiting & Sears, 1949). As an example of an approach-avoidance conflict in humans in which both arms of the conflict are in the experiential system, consider the following conflict between a person's sex and fear motives. A man is sexually attracted to a woman other than his wife. He is obsessed with the person and cannot get her out of his mind, but he fears the consequences of an illicit affair. He can neither give up the attraction nor fulfill the sex drive, and he keeps ruminating about a sexual encounter but makes no attempt to have one. Instead, he makes subtle overtures but goes no further.

Turning to the feasibility of avoidance-approach conflict in which a steeper gradient of approach intersects a less steep gradient of avoidance, it has been found that either gradient can be steeper than the other depending on certain variables: the amount of training in stimulus discrimination, number of reinforced trials, and the degree to which the gradients are based on external relative to internal stimuli (Epstein, 1978). Thus, manipulation of any of these variables can make avoidance gradients less steep or steeper than approach gradients. For example, fear reactions can be internalized to the extent that they depend mainly on internal rather than on external cues, which would produce a relatively flat avoidance gradient, and approach gradients can be based primarily on external cues and therefore have a steep gradient. An avoidance-approach conflict within the experiential system could arise in the following manner. Assume a person was brought up to have very strong inhibitions against sexual or hostile behavior. Such a person would have a relatively flat avoidance gradient for the expression of sexual or hostile impulses. Now consider that this person's sexual or hostile approach tendencies are mediated more by stimulation from external cues than by an internal state. The person's approach gradient would then be steeper than the avoidance gradient. This analysis suggests that overcontrolled people are more apt to exhibit ego-alien behavior than are undercontrolled people, a conclusion supported by studies of criminal violence. It was found in such studies that the most extreme crimes tend to be committed by individuals whose hostility is characteristically overcontrolled (e.g., Blackburn, 1968, 1971; Megargee, 1966).

Avoidance-approach conflict is also significant because of its implications for diagnosis and psychotherapy. For example, if an avoidance-approach conflict with an antisocial approach tendency is diagnosed, it can be controlled by reducing the height of the approach gradient, by increasing the height of the avoidance gradient, or by increasing the steepness of the avoidance gradient through discrimination training. This latter procedure could be implemented, for example, by training a person to make discriminating judgments about degrees of assertiveness and aggression.

Complexes

The concept of a "complex" as used in CET is a modification of the concept introduced by Jung (1928). It refers in CET to a highly influential, emotionally charged network of thoughts, feelings, and behavioral tendencies that are organized around a central theme, or nucleus. This concept is incorporated into CET without the more esoteric aspects of Jung's views, such as his belief in a collective unconscious that contains archetypes, which are dispositions to react in ways determined by heredity from one's racial background. According to CET, complexes are simply highly influential cognitive-affective networks learned through intense or repetitive reinforcement. The strength of a complex is considered to be a direct function of a low threshold for its activation, a wide range of cues to which it is responsive, the strength of the emotion associated with its activation, and a compulsive need for its expression. There are two kinds of complexes, integrated and dissociated.

Integrated Complexes

Complexes that are integrated into the conceptual system are cognitive-affective networks that provide the overall system with a particular emphasis. For example, a man with a mother complex is unusually reactive to anything associated with his mother. He may go out of his way to get her unusual gifts for Mother's Day, be attracted to women who resemble her, establish a dependent relationship with his wife, and emphasize to their children the importance of demonstrating their appreciation of their mother. Because integrated complexes have strong and widespread associative connections with other networks, they exert an important influence on a person's personality.

Dissociated Complexes

Dissociated complexes are isolated from the main conceptual system. They remain dissociated because their assimilation would evoke anxiety because of their incompatibility with the overall system. Because there is an implicit basic need to assimilate mental representations into a unified experiential system, there is an inherent conflict between the implicit need to assimilate dissociated material and the implicit need to protect the overall system from a threat to its coherence that would occur from incorporating the complex. An important symptom of a dissociated complex is an increase in stress and anxiety when external events or associations activate the dissociated complex. Symptoms of dissociated complexes include sensitivities and compulsions (discussed shortly); fleeting intrusions of the content of the complex into the main conceptual system, which temporarily destabilizes it; ego-alien breakthroughs into overt behavior of material related to the complex; and a tendency for the dissociated complex to grow by assimilating new information. This latter reaction has been observed in post-traumatic stress disorder, in which some soldiers following discharge from the military resolve the conflict produced by dissociated traumatic memories by identifying with a combat personality (Epstein, 1991; Fletcher, 1988).

Sensitivities and Compulsions Produced by Interactions Within the Two Systems

Sensitivities and compulsions within the experiential system are similar to repression but, rather than protecting a person from awareness in the rational system of distressing mental content, they protect the person from the destabilization that would occur if the dissociated material were incorporated into a person's implicit theory of reality. The sensitivity is thus a protective response to the anxiety that would occur from destabilization. As in the case of repression, there is an automatic compulsion to avoid the distress that could be activated in the dissociated complex. The person therefore engages in whatever thoughts or behavior have been helpful in the past in reducing such anxiety. The problem produced by sensitivities and compulsions is that they are the source of a variety of symptoms, including fixated responses for reducing the anxiety and a narrowing of attention to avoid activating the dissociated complex and, relatedly, a reduction in the ability to cope with other issues. Moreover, the defenses activated by sensitivities and compulsions are never completely successful in avoiding automatic attempts to assimilate the dissociation, which results in distressing and destabilizing intrusions of the dissociated material that produce acute states of anxiety followed by compensatory states of broad inhibition and reduced reactivity.

INTERACTIONS AMONG BASIC NEEDS WITHIN THE EXPERIENTIAL SYSTEM

An important result of the interactions among he five implicit subordinate basic needs is that they serve as checks and balances against each other. When a need is fulfilled at the expense of fulfilling other needs, the motivation to fulfill the other needs is increased. This contributes to keeping all the needs operating within adaptive levels. However, under extreme circumstances, the motivation to fulfill a particular need may be so great that the fulfillment of other needs is sacrificed, which creates an imbalance and serious consequences. For example, a person can be so driven to compensate for a loss in self-esteem that he or she develops exaggerated views of self-importance at a significant cost to the fulfillment of other basic needs. To take the sacrifice of the need for relatedness as an example, people are likely to become alienated from someone who greatly exaggerates his own importance and degrades others in the process. Thus, in fulfilling the implicit need for self-esteem, the person sacrifices fulfillment of the implicit need for relationships. In Chapter 9 on psychopathology, I will discuss the further implications of sacrificing some of the subordinate implicit basic needs in the fulfillment of others.

There are three ways in which the five implicit subordinate basic needs can interact with each other. They can conflict with each other, react synergistically with each other, and establish compromises with each other. Interactions that produce conflict occur when the fulfillment of one implicit need interferes with the fulfillment of other implicit needs. Synergistic interactions occur when the fulfillment of some implicit need is accomplished in a manner that also fulfills other implicit needs. Compromises occur when the fulfillment of an implicit need is accomplished at a less than optimum level in order to fulfill other implicit needs.

Well-adjusted people characteristically fulfill their implicit basic needs in a synergistic manner, whereas poorly adjusted people do so in a conflicted manner. Mary is an emotionally stable and happy person. She has a high level of self-esteem, is adept at establishing mutually rewarding relationships with others, and derives great pleasure from being helpful to them. This not only contributes to her happiness, favorable relationships, and therefore to her security, but it also contributes to her self-esteem because she is proud of her behavior and because others admire her for her thoughtfulness. It also contributes to the stability of her views about herself and others because her behavior is consistent, and most people respond to her in a consistently favorable manner. Thus, Mary satisfies all five subordinate implicit basic needs in a harmonious, synergistic manner.

Michael characteristically fulfills his implicit basic needs in a conflicted manner. He is so intensely compelled to elevate his low self-esteem that he does so in counterproductive ways, as by acting superior to others, which alienates them and sacrifices his implicit need for relatedness. Because his experiential system is failing to fulfill all of his implicit subordinate basic needs, it is under the stress of potential disorganization, which he experiences as anxiety and insecurity.

People often satisfy their implicit basic needs in a manner that produces compromises. For example, as noted in Chapter 3, people's need for self-enhancement often interacts with their need to maintain a stable implicit conceptual system in a manner that causes them to establish a compromise as strategic self-enhancers who favor modest increases in self-esteem over greater increases.

Interactions Involving Mid-Level Needs

Everything that has been said about interactions among basic needs in the experiential system can be applied to mid-level needs as well. In general, however, the effects will be less extreme because the fulfillment of mid-level needs is normally less consequential for maintaining the stability of a person's conceptual system than are the basic needs. However, there are exceptions: certain conflicts between mid-level needs or between mid-level and basic needs can be of such significance in the organization of people's conceptual systems that they play as important a role as conflicts between basic needs.

It is not feasible to discuss the interactions between mid-level implicit needs with each other and with the basic needs because there are too many mid-level needs. However, one interaction between an implicit mid-level need and an implicit basic needs warrants special consideration because of its significance and prevalence. It is a conflict between the implicit mid-level need for autonomy and the implicit basic need for relatedness. Part of the human condition is for children to be dependent on their parents for a far longer period than that for any other animal. Without care from adults, children could not survive, let alone learn all they need to know to successfully adapt to society. Because of their dependence on parenting adults, children normally develop strong attachments to their parents or parent surrogates and, relatedly, a strong need to please them. As part of the task of growing up and functioning as competent adults, they must also learn to function independently, and they must do this in a manner that establishes mutual and reciprocal dependence and independence.

Depending on the circumstances in which children are raised, many fail to develop an adaptive balance between dependency and autonomy. An extreme group among these includes some who experience a strong conflict between a desire for independence and a deep need to please others. Interestingly, such conflicts can arise from two opposite childhood environments, rejection and overprotection. These are not people who derive satisfaction from pleasing others. Rather, they are people who please others because of their fear of disapproval or rejection. They feel trapped by their need to please others, and they resent both those whom they feel obligated to please and themselves for being fearful of disapproval and rejection, all while maintaining a pleasant, happy façade.

This is a serious conflict because it produces enduring feelings of despair and suppressed hostility. Moreover, it is not evident to others that these people are suffering because of the façade they successfully maintain. Some psychologists, such as LeShan (1977) and Temoshock and Dreher (1992) believe that people with this syndrome are particularly likely to develop cancer. Although there is some support for this position (e.g., Cunningham & Watson, 2004; Katz & Epstein, 2005; LeShan, 1977; Temoshok & Dreher, 1992), it remains a highly controversial issue. However, apart from whether the cancer connection with personality is valid or not, the conflict is a serious one because of the distress it produces.

REFERENCES

Baumeister, R. F. (1989). The optimal margin of illusion. *Journal of Social and Clinical Psychology, 8*, 176–189.

Blackburn, R. (1968). Personality in relation to extreme aggression in psychiatric offenders. *British Journal of Psychiatry, 114*, 821–828.

Blackburn, R. (1971). Personality types among abnormal homicides. *British Journal of Criminology, 11*, 14–31.

Bond, D. D. (1952). *The love and fear of flying*. New York: International Universities Press.

Brown, J. S. (1948). Gradients of approach and avoidance responses and their relation to level of motivation. *Journal of Comparative Physiological Psychology, 41*, 450–465.

Calaprice, A. (1996). *The quotable Einstein*. Princeton, NJ: Princeton University Press.

Cunningham, A. J., & Watson, K. (2004). How psychological therapy may prolong survival in cancer patients: New evidence and a simple theory. *Integrated Cancer Therapy, 3*, 214–229.

Denese-Raj, V., & Epstein. S. (1994). Conflict between experiential and rational processing: When people behave against their better judgment. *Journal of Personality and Social Psychology, 66*, 819–829.

Donovan, S., & Epstein, S. (1997). The difficulty of the Linda conjunction problem can be attributed to its simultaneous concrete and unnatural representation, and not to conversational implicature, *Journal of Experimental Social Psychology, 33*, 1–20.

Epstein, S. (1962). Theory and experiment on the measurement of drive and conflict. In *Nebraska symposium on motivation*, M. R. Jones (Ed.), Lincoln: University of Nebraska Press, 127–209.

Epstein, S. (1978). Approach-avoidance, the fifth basic conflict. *Journal of Consulting and Clinical Psychology, 46*, 1016–1022.

Epstein, S. (1991). The self-concept, the traumatic neurosis, and the structure of personality. In D. Ozer, J. M. Healy, Jr., & A. J. Stewart (Eds.), *Perspectives in personality, Vol 3A*, pp. 63–98.

Epstein, S., & Fenz, W. D. (1965). Steepness of approach and avoidance gradients in humans as a function of experience: Theory and experiment. *Journal of Experimental Psychology, 20*, 1–12.

Epstein, S., Denes-Raj, V., & Pacini, R. (1995). The Linda problem revisited from the perspective of cognitive-experiential self-theory. *Personality and Social Psychology Bulletin, 21*, 1124–1138.

Epstein, S., Donovan, S., & Denes-Raj, V. (1999). The missing link in the paradox of the Linda problem: Beyond knowing and thinking of the conjunction rule, the intrinsic appeal of heuristic processing. *Personality and Social Psychology Bulletin, 25*, 204–214.

Epstein, S., Pacini, R., Denes-Raj, V., & Heier, H. (1996). Individual differences in intuitive-experiential and analytical-rational thinking styles. *Journal of Personality and Social Psychology, 71*, 390–405.

Fenz, W. D., & Epstein, S. (1962). Theory and experiment on the measurement of approach-avoidance conflict. *Journal of Abnormal and Social Psychology, 64*, 97–112.

Fletcher, K. E. (1988). *Belief systems, exposure to stress, and posttraumatic stress disorder in Vietnam veterans*. Unpublished doctoral dissertation, University of Massachusetts at Amherst.

Freud, S. (1924/1949). *Collected Papers, Vol. 1. Translated by Joan Riviere*, London, The Hogarth press.

Freud, S. (1933/1964). *New introductory lectures on psychoanalysis* (Translated by J. Strachey). New York: W. W. Norton.

Isaacson, W. (2007). *Einstein*. New York: Simon & Schuster.

Jung, C. G. (1928). *Contributions to analytical psychology*. New York: Harcourt.

Katz, L., & Epstein, S. (2005). The relation of cancer-prone personality to exceptional recovery from cancer. *Advances, 21*, 1–15.

Kirkpatrick, L. A., & Epstein, S. (1992). Cognitive-experiential self-theory and subjective probability: Further evidence of two conceptual systems. *Journal of Personality and Social Psychology, 63*, 534–544.

LeShan, I. (1977). *You can fight for your life*. New York: Evans & Co.

Lewin, K. (1931). Environmental forces in child behavior and development. In Murchison, C. (Ed.), *A handbook of child psychology* (pp. 94–127). Worcester, MA: Clark University Press.

Lewin, K. (1935). *A dynamic theory of personality: Selected papers* (translated by D. K. Adams & K. E. Zener) New York: McGraw-Hill.

Megargee, E. I. (1966). Undercontrolled and overcontrolled personality types in extreme antisocial aggression. *Psychological Monographs, 80* (3, Whole No. 611), 1–29.

Miller, N. E. (1944). Experimental studies of conflict. In Hunt, J. McV (Ed.), *Personality and the behavior disorders*. (431–465). New York: Ronald Press.

Miller, N. E. (1948). Theory and experiment relating psychoanalytic displacement to stimulus-response generalization. *Journal of Abnormal and Social Psychology, 43*, 155–178.

Miller, N. E. (1951). Comments on theoretical models illustrated by the development of a theory of conflict behavior. *Journal of Personality, 20*, 82–100.

Miller, N. E. (1959). Liberalization of basic S-R concepts: Extensions to conflict behavior, motivation, and social learning. In S. Koch (Ed.), *Psychology: A study of a science* (vol. II, pp. 196–292). New York: McGraw-Hill.

Miller, N. E., & Kraeling, D. (1950). Displacement: Evidence for more generalization of approach than avoidance in an approach-avoidance conflict generalized to a new stimulus situation (unpublished manuscript).

Myers, D. G. (2002). *Intuition: Its Powers and Perile*. New Haven: Yale University Press.

Norris, P., & Epstein, S. (2001). An experiential thinking style: Its facets and relations with objective and subjective measures criterion measures. *Journal of Personality, 79*, 1043–1079.

Pacini, R., & Epstein, S. (1999). The relation of rational and experiential processing styles to personality, basic beliefs, and the ratio-bias phenomenon. *Journal of Personality and Social Psychology, 76*, 972–987.

Pacini, R., Muir, F., & Epstein, S. (1998). Depressive realism from the perspective of cognitive-experiential self-theory. *Journal of Personality and Social Psychology, 74*, 1056–1068.

Rigby, W. K. (1954). Approach and avoidance gradients and conflict behavior in a predominantly temporal situation. *Journal of Comparative Physiological Psychology, 47*, 83–89.

Taylor, S. E., & Brown, J. D. (1988). Illusions and wellbeing: A social-psychological perspective on mental health. Psychological Bulletin, 103, 193–210.

Temoshok, L., & Dreher, H. (1992). *The type-C connection*. New York: Random House.

Tversky, A., & Kahneman, D. (1982). Judgments of and by representativeness. In D. Kahneman, P. Slovic, & A. Tversky (Eds.), *Judgment under uncertainty: Heuristics and biases*. New York: University of Cambridge Press, pp. 84–98.

Whiting, J. W. M., & Sears, R. R. (1949). *Projection and displacement in doll play*. Cambridge, MA: Harvard University Laboratory of Human Development (mimeographed).

Yanko, J., Epstein, S., Pacini, R., & Barrows, P. (1998). Comparisons between intuitive and rational processing as a function of age. *Unpublished raw data*.

PART TWO

Development and Adjustment

CHAPTER 6
Development

First, some general principles of early development from the perspective of cognitive-experiential theory (CET) are discussed in this chapter. This is followed by a discussion of issues more specifically related to CET, including the development of emotions, basic needs and beliefs, and the self-concept, including self-esteem. Next, development across the lifecycle of the experiential and rational systems and their interaction are considered. This is followed by a discussion of stages in the lifecycle according to CET. In the last section, the views of a variety of other developmental theories are presented and evaluated from the perspective of CET.

DEVELOPMENT FROM THE PERSPECTIVE OF COGNITIVE-EXPERIENTIAL THEORY

The challenge in describing the course of human development is to determine how the newborn infant who initially reacts predominantly by biological reflexes develops into an adult whose behavior is primarily determined by psychological and social influences. From the perspective of CET, this requires consideration of representations of the self, of other people, of the inanimate world, and of the interactions of these representations with each other and with the environment. In other words, it involves developmental issues concerning the construction of an implicit theory of reality through the operation of the experiential and rational systems and their interactions.

Infancy: Origins of an Implicit Theory of Reality

The infant does not emerge into the world as a blank tablet on which experience freely leaves its imprint. Its behavior is primarily determined by biological influences, including reflexes, temperament, and feelings, and by some very limited intrauterine learning. Far from being a helpless creature, the infant is able to exert a powerful influence on its environment with the use of biologically provided adaptive behaviors. It can suck, cry, see, hear, feel, grasp, and make associative cognitive connections. A touch on its lips evokes a sucking reflex, and a feeling of distress reflexively evokes a crying response, both of which are highly adaptive. Sucking in response to touch facilitates the acquisition of nutrition by helping the infant to locate and respond to a nipple. Crying gains attention from adults who hasten to shut off the harsh alarm by attending to the infant's needs. At about one month of age, babies exhibit reflex smiling. Although this behavior is a reflex response, parents usually regard it as an endearing social response, which serves the purpose of strengthening the bond between infant and caretaker. At about two-and-a-half months, a true social smile appears that allows the mother to determine what pleases the baby. By behaving accordingly, she is rewarded with cooing and more smiles, which further strengthen the bond between mother and infant. Thus, nature has provided the infant with a "carrot and stick" that provide it with an important degree of control over the behavior of its caretakers.

The newborn is also well equipped for experiential learning. It has the basic ingredients for reacting to the energetic and cue components of stimulation, for reacting to affect with approach and avoidance responses, and for forming connections among stimuli, responses, and outcomes.

Infants react to the energetic component of stimuli by alerting reactions to stimuli of mild to moderate intensity and by startle responses to sudden, intense stimulation. Alerting reactions play an important role in the representation of stimuli. Habituation is a form of learning that occurs in response to repeated presentations of the same stimulus. At first, an infant responds to a stimulus mainly because of its intensity, reinforcement history, or novelty. With repetition, the stimulus becomes less arousing, until the infant no longer responds to its repetition. However, an interesting set of processes occur during this course of events from an original alerting reaction to a state of boredom. Not only has the infant developed an internal representation of the stimulus over a wide range of arousal levels, but it now responds to other stimuli because of their similarity to the habituated stimulus. Thus, habituation sets in motion a systematic process of expanding representations. In a sense, it involves a transfer of reactivity from the energetic to the cue component of stimulation. In sum, habituation is one of the processes by which the infant acquires an expanding repertoire of inner representations of the environment.

Whereas habituation occurs from the repeated presentation of a single stimulus, associative learning occurs from relations between stimuli with each other and with responses and outcomes. There are three fundamental kinds of associative learning: classical conditioning, operant conditioning, and observational learning. In classical conditioning, the organism connects stimuli with each other and with outcomes that produce desirable or undesirable feelings. In a study, the sucking response of infants who were two hours old was conditioned to strokes on the forehead. After a number of pairings of such stroking and the ingestion of a sweet solution, the newborns began to suck when just stroked (Rosenstein & Oster, 1988). Through such conditioning, an expansion of experiential learning occurs as infants acquire a repertoire of internal representations, including their predictive value for the occurrence of other stimuli and outcomes.

In instrumental conditioning, an organism forms an association between a response and its consequences, such as pressing a bar and obtaining food or jumping off a shelf that has an electrified grid to avoid receiving an electric shock. Newborns learn to suck faster to receive a reward, such as the presentation of an interesting visual stimulus, music, or a human voice (Sansavini, Bertonicini, & Giovanelli, 1997). Such behavior provides information on the effect of behavior on outcomes, including good and bad feelings.

Learning by observation provides a vicarious way of learning from other people's behavior. Many animals train their young by example. Young chimpanzees learn to gather termites, a favorite food, by watching older chimpanzees insert a stick into a termite mound and extract it with termites clinging to it. Young bears learn to fish for salmon by watching adult bears. Humans learn a variety of activities by watching other humans perform them. Even newborn humans are capable of imitation. Meltzoff and Moore (1977) showed that infants less than three weeks old will stick out their tongues and open their mouths in imitation of adults.

Through all these ways of learning about themselves, their caretakers, and the environment, infants construct an expanding model of the world or an implicit theory of reality. Depending on how its needs are fulfilled, the infant develops cognitive-affective representations and beliefs concerning stimuli, responses, events, and relationships. Because the satisfaction of implicit basic needs and the verification of associated implicit beliefs provide the foundation for further cognitive development, they establish at a very fundamental level a cognitive structure that will vary according to a dimension of stability versus vulnerability to disorganization. Alerting and startle reactions, habituation, associative learning, and imitation are not the only ways in which infants acquire representations of their environment. In addition, they are preprogrammed by emotions to make adaptive responses to critical life events, a topic to which we turn next.

The Development of Emotions as a Function of Experience

Basic emotions are either present at birth or develop very shortly thereafter. In the former case, they are initially biologically determined response tendencies that are modifiable by experience. In the latter case, they are initially based on the interaction of biological dispositions and automatic learning from experience. In both cases, they soon consist of cognitive-affective networks that provide infants with adaptive responses to critically important life events, such as anger that supports aggressive action, fear that supports avoidance behavior and flight, sadness that supports withdrawal and disengagement, happiness that supports engagement and exploration, and affection that supports attachment and seeking proximity.

The difficulty with determining whether the newborn has specific emotions and, if so, establishing what they are, is that the infant cannot speak and its emotion-like responses and expressions cannot unambiguously be identified as emotions. For example, when an infant reacts to restraint with agitation and vigorously pushes away a restraining object, there is no way of determining whether such behavior is a display of anger or of a more diffuse state of agitation that has yet to develop into anger. It is tentatively assumed that the newborn has only precursors of emotions, such as agitation, withdrawal, distress, and pleasurable excitement, which correspond to the arousal states discussed in Chapter 4 and are precursors to the primary emotions of fear, anger, sadness, joy, and affection.

The Development of Superordinate Basic Needs and Beliefs

The superordinate basic needs of the hedonic principle and the need to control arousal are biologically determined and therefore present at birth. Both of these needs, which are present in all other needs, have an important influence on behavior throughout the lifespan.

The Superordinate Need of the Hedonic Principle and Its Associated Beliefs

The hedonic principle, as the source of reinforcement in all automatic learning from experience, influences the development of all descriptive and motivational implicit beliefs in people's implicit theories of reality, including all the implicit subordinate basic needs and beliefs. For the newborn infant, the hedonic principle operates exclusively through sensory pleasure, but very soon it expands to the need to maintain the stability and coherence of an emerging conceptual system and the need for relatedness. Only after the child develops a self-concept will the hedonic principle be involved in the fulfillment and frustration of the need to maintain self-esteem. If the infant is provided with appropriate nutrition, a comfortable temperature, an absence of physical pain or discomfort, and a caretaker who holds it, comforts it, and provides it with appropriate stimulation, it will be a happy infant. Deprive it of any of these, and it will be unhappy.

As the infant matures, the sources of hedonic stimulation that the child receives become increasingly determined by subordinate basic needs and beliefs other than the sensory pleasure principle and its associated beliefs. Sources of hedonic stimulation from the need and beliefs associated with the maintenance of self-esteem are the last among the subordinate basic needs and beliefs to develop because they are contingent on the development of a self-concept.

Depending on the degree of fulfillment of the hedonic principle, the infant will develop an implicit belief that is located on a bipolar dimension, with poles that indicate a highly optimistic attitude and an implicit belief that life is good or the opposite attitude and implicit belief. Fulfillment of the hedonic principle and a favorable implicit belief about the world contribute to the construction of a strong foundation for the development of an implicit theory of reality. Serious frustration of the hedonic principle and resultant unfavorable beliefs about what life has to offer produce the foundation of a cognitive-affective system that is vulnerable to disorganization.

The Superordinate Need to Control Arousal and Its Associated Beliefs

The need to control arousal, like the hedonic principle, is a biologically determined superordinate need that is present at birth and is a component of all other needs throughout the lifecycle. Fulfillment and frustration of the need to control arousal has similar effects on the infant as the fulfillment and frustration of the hedonic principle. Limited increments in arousal are sources of positive affect, whereas insufficient or excessive increments in arousal are sources of negative affect. At first, arousal is controlled through reflexive alerting and inhibitory reactions. With maturation, the infant learns to control arousal through its own behavior. For example, it controls excessive arousal by communicating with its caretaker that it is in distress by crying. With further maturation, the child learns to reduce excessive arousal with self-soothing behavior and with more deliberately enlisting the aid of adults. Exposure to appropriate, manageable levels of arousal produces a favorable position on a bipolar belief dimension that varies from an implicit belief that the world is a source of pleasant and exciting stimulation to the belief that the world is a source of stress and distressing levels of stimulation. As with the fulfillment of the hedonic principle, the robustness versus the vulnerability of the cognitive-affective system is influenced by the fulfillment of the need to control arousal. Appropriate levels of stimulation result in a stable foundation for the cognitive affective system, whereas excessive or insufficient stimulation results in an unstable foundation that is vulnerable to disorganization and other sources of maladjustment.

Development of the Subordinate Basic Needs and Beliefs

The Subordinate Basic Need to Fulfill the Sensory Pleasure Principle and Its Associated Beliefs

As physical sensations of pleasure and pain or discomfort are by far the major sources of fulfillment or frustration of the superordinate hedonic principle in infancy, what was said about the importance of the hedonic principle in general can be reinterpreted in infants almost completely in terms of physical gratification and discomfort. Depending on the fulfillment of the need for sensory pleasure and the relief from sensory pain, the infant will develop a belief that life is a source of positive sensations and relief from unpleasant sensations. This early belief about the world as a source of positive or negative sensations is particularly important because it contributes to a conceptual foundation that influences the interpretation of all later experiences. However, it can be greatly modified by emotionally significant experiences later in life. Thus, an enduring painful illness at a later period than in infancy will likely change a person's anticipations about future sensory comfort in a negative direction, whereas experiences that involve significant gratification of sensory pleasure can have an opposite effect. A particularly influential source of sensory gratification and frustration occurs during adolescence, when the intensity of the sex drive is greatly increased.

The Subordinate Basic Need to Maintain a Coherent, Stable Conceptual System and Its Associated Beliefs

The need to maintain a coherent, stable conceptual system becomes increasingly important as the newborn constructs an increasingly complex conceptual system. Depending on how well the need to maintain the stability of the conceptual system is fulfilled, infants will develop a belief about whether the world and other people behave in ways that are predictable, orderly, and controllable or chaotic, disorderly, and uncontrollable. Inconsistent behavior by caretakers will result in a frustration of this need and a corresponding weakness in the foundation of a person's conceptual system. However, this is not the only source of such a vulnerability to disorganization. As previously noted, the development of an implicit theory of reality does not occur for its own sake. It occurs because of the advantages it provides in adapting to the environment. Thus, if an implicit theory fails to accomplish the fulfillment of any basic need, it will be vulnerable to disorganization and other sources of maladjustment.

Although infancy is the stage that exerts the most fundamental influence on the implicit belief in a stable, predictable, and controllable world, later developments can importantly influence this belief. Thus, disconfirming experiences of central beliefs in the experiential system at any time in life can frustrate the need for maintaining a stable and coherent conceptual system and disconfirm a person's belief about the predictability and controllability of the world. Positive experiences can have an opposite effect. As an example, a significant love relationship could produce a favorable reorganization of a maladaptive conceptual system. On the negative side, an extremely distressing experience, such as rejection by a loved one, could precipitate a psychotic reaction.

The Subordinate Basic Need for Security and Its Associated Beliefs

The need for security exists since birth. To develop properly, the infant must feel secure. It develops such a feeling based on the interaction of temperament and the fulfillment of basic needs. Some infants are more robust than others, and others are more vulnerable (e.g., Kagan, Kearsley, & Zelazo, 1978). Depending of the fulfillment of the need for security, the infant will have an implicit belief that the world is a safe or dangerous place, which will influence its later adjustment to the world, including the susceptibility to disorganization of the conceptual system.

The Subordinate Basic Need for Relatedness and Its Associated Beliefs

The need for relatedness occurs very shortly after birth, following the experience of the caretaker as a source of good feelings and relief from bad feelings. As a consequence, infants become attached to their caretakers, which then generalizes to relationships with others. Depending on how the need for relatedness is fulfilled or frustrated, the infant develops an implicit belief about people as trustworthy and desirable to relate to or as untrustworthy and dangerous (Ainsworth, 1993; Ainsworth, Blehar, Waters, & Wall, 1978). This view is consistent with Bowlby's (1979) belief that the manner in which the need for relatedness is fulfilled by a caretaker is a particularly important component of the infant's representation of what people are like. In contrast to infants who had a secure attachment to their caretaker, those who had an insecure attachment as children tend to have avoidant (Klohnen & Bera, 1998) or ambivalent (Rothbard & Shaver, 1994) relationship styles as adults.

The Development of the Subordinate Basic Need for Self-Esteem and Its Relation to the Development of a Self-Concept

The development of the need for self-esteem is the last subordinate basic need to develop because it is contingent on the development of a self-concept.

I therefore discuss the development of a self-concept followed by a discussion of the development of self-esteem.

The Development of a Self-Concept

To understand the development of a self-concept, it is necessary to consider two of its aspects: the self-concept as an object of belief and the self-concept as an agent of behavior with growth properties. Children develop views about themselves through direct observation and logical inference. They observe that they have a body that has features in common with the bodies of other people and that differs from that of other creatures, such as the family's pet dog or cat. They also observe that, just as others differ from each other, they have features that are uniquely theirs.

It was demonstrated in research with chimpanzees that after a few exposures to a mirror, a chimpanzee will point to a spot the researcher marked on its forehead, thereby indicating it has an objective self-concept (Gallup,1968). Unlike chimpanzees and children older than 10 months, lower order animals, infants less than 10 months old, and older mental defectives fail to exhibit such self-recognition. When these individuals look into a mirror, they think it is someone else. Thus, a certain amount of cognitive development has to take place for a child to have an objective self-concept. Although there are parts of the older children's bodies that they cannot see, such as their eyes, nose, ears, and foreheads, they can infer that if they are like people in other ways, their eyes, nose, ears, and foreheads probably also look like those of other people. Moreover, they can readily confirm this inference by touching these parts or looking into a mirror.

In addition to observing that one has a body similar to that of other people, there is also evidence that one's body is uniquely one's own. Included in such evidence are (a) saliency—it hurts more when one's own arm is pinched than when someone else's is; (b) continuity—no one's body is with one as much as one's own; (c) control—one can make one's own limbs respond to one's wishes more easily and dependably than anyone else's; and (d) double sensation—when one touches one's nose, the finger doing the touching and the nose both feel touched, whereas when one touches someone else's nose, only the part doing the touching receives sensation. Not only are there a multitude of cues that support the inference that one has a unique body self, there is also strong social reinforcement for formulating this concept. A child who thought he was a dog or a cat would be ridiculed and corrected. Second, the distinction between self and non-self allows one to behave in the world more effectively than one not having such a distinction because it is one of the most fundamental divisions in an implicit theory of reality on which a great deal of understanding and adaptive behavior depends.

Once the concept of having a unique body self has been established, it facilitates the subsequent development of awareness of having an inner self. Here, the implicit reasoning in the child is as follows: "If I am a human being similar to other human beings in all outward manifestations, then I probably am similar to them in other ways as well. If I have wishes, fears, and thoughts that influence my behavior, they must also have them. Just as they are different from each other in this respect, I must also be different from them. Accordingly, I must have a unique inner self as well as a unique outer self."

Other sources for inferring an inner self include ego involvement (i.e., some things matter to oneself, whereas other things are unimportant); the ability to introspect, a feeling of continuity of experience; awareness of the need to defend some inner aspect of one's being, such as self-esteem; awareness of having feelings and desires that are not outwardly expressed; awareness of a tendency to evaluate oneself and others automatically; and awareness that one can pretend and dissimulate. All of these observations make it evident that one has an inner self that operates privately and is different from an outwardly manifested physical self.

Having developed a body self and an inferred inner self, an important further development is that of a moral self. This will be discussed later in this chapter in which the views of CET on moral development are compared to those in Kohlberg's (1969) theory of moral development.

The development of an inner self as an agent of behavior that has growth properties is more complicated than the development of an objective self. It cannot be directly observed because it refers to an abstract concept and not to a corporal self. Unlike an objective self, people are not normally aware that they have an agentic self. However, they intuitively recognize something like it in the concept of a soul. Like other aspects of experiential processing, an agentic self operates normally outside of awareness. A theory of a self that directs behavior and grows is an important component of a person's implicit theory of reality that develops across the lifespan and, under appropriate circumstances, becomes increasingly differentiated and integrated.

The Development of Self-Esteem and Its Associated Beliefs

As one of five subordinate basic needs, the need to maintain and enhance self-esteem is one of the most powerful of human motives. In a study in which participants kept daily records of their emotions and the degree to which fulfillment and frustration of each of the subordinate basic needs was the source of an emotion, situations that influenced self-esteem were by far the most common source of people's emotions (Epstein, 1999). When people were unable to sleep at night, it was blows to self-esteem more than assaults on the fulfillment of any other subordinate basic belief that kept them awake. Why is maintaining and fulfilling the need for self-esteem such a prevalent and strong motive? The importance of self-esteem both as a need and a belief can be attributed to its developmental origin. In agreement with Mead (1934) and Sullivan (1953), I believe that the most fundamental source of self-esteem is the internalization by a child of the evaluation of the child by the child's caretakers. A young child is dependent on a caretaker not only for its survival but because the caretaker is the most important source of the child's experiences of pleasure and relief from distress. Thus, the worst fear a child can have is of being abandoned. As a result, a child is strongly motivated to please its caretakers. A particularly effective way of accomplishing this is by adopting the caretakers' values and beliefs, including the caretaker's evaluation of the child. Once the child has internalized such an evaluation, it can then behave spontaneously in ways that are most likely to please its caretakers. From then on, whenever the child behaves according to its self-evaluation it feels comfortable, and when it behaves otherwise it feels distressed. The most important value of the caretaker that the child internalizes is the caretaker's evaluation of the child as love-worthy. This internalization by the child is its most fundamental source of self-esteem. Additional sources of self-esteem are the child's evaluation of its competence and morality, but neither is as fundamental as the implicit belief in one's love-worthiness. However, with maturation, particularly for boys, competence may eventually become more important than love-worthiness.

Self-esteem operates as the nucleus of a cognitive-affective network that has a widespread influence on a child's feelings, behavior, and interpretation of the events that influence the child's development. As favorable self-evaluations produce good feelings (analogous to receiving love from a parent) and unfavorable self-evaluations produce bad feelings (analogous to rejection, disapproval, or hostility from a parent), the child acquires an affect-driven implicit motive to behave in ways that are anticipated to increase self-esteem and avoid a decrease in self-esteem.

Self-esteem influences thought, behavior, and feelings both as a basic implicit belief about the self and as a motive to maintain and enhance self-esteem. As a basic, subordinate implicit belief, a high level of self-esteem is associated with feelings of security, happiness, confidence, and general well-being (Coopersmith, 1967; Epstein, 1979, 2006; O'Brien & Epstein, 1988; Rogers, 1951). Viewing oneself in a highly favorable way facilitates effective performance and is a buffer against the negative consequences of adversity. As a basic subordinate implicit motive, the anticipation of positive affect from increases in self-esteem and of negative affect from decreases in self-esteem are powerful motives for superior levels of accomplishment and for overcoming adversity.

In a study by O'Brien and Epstein (1974), college students recorded the daily events that produced changes in their self-esteem during a six-week period. They noted whether the sources of influence were related to competence-incompetence, acceptance-rejection, power-powerlessness, and moral self-approval-guilt.

As hypothesized, the most frequent sources of self-esteem involved competence-incompetence and acceptance-rejection. Women reported more changes in self-esteem related to acceptance-rejection, and men reported more changes in self-esteem related to competence-incompetence. Increases in self-esteem were reported to produce strong and enduring positive feelings to a greater extent than were decreases in self-esteem reported to produce strong and enduring negative feelings. These results may have been influenced by a self-serving reporting bias observed in many other situations (Myers, 2002), or they may be the result of adaptive operations in which people tend to experience events in a way that maximizes good feelings and minimizes bad feelings.

In a study of people's constructive thinking across the lifespan (reported in Epstein, 1998), it was observed that, for males, self-esteem was moderately high at age 10 increased gradually to age 35, then increased more sharply until it reached its highest level at age 50, after which it remained constant to age 60. The trajectory for females was similar except for one dramatic difference. There was a sharp decrease in girls' self-esteem from age 10, when it was at the same moderately high level as for boys, to age 20, when it reached its nadir. From age 20 to age 40, there was a steady increase in the self-esteem of the women until they almost caught up to the relatively high level of the men. The women then remained at this level up to age 60.

How is one to account for the dramatic extended decrease in the self-esteem of girls beginning at age 10? The answer is suggested by research that found that girls, unlike boys, aged 10–20 become increasingly displeased with their appearance (Harter, 1999). This fits into a broader picture in which girls receive a mixed message as they are about to enter puberty about what it means to succeed in life as a woman. Unlike boys, who are admired for being intelligent, competent, and assertive, girls receive the message that although it is desirable to be accomplished, it is also important to be physically attractive and to behave in ways that please others, including parents, teachers, and boyfriends. The result is that adolescent girls experience a conflict between being competent and pleasing others. Consistent with this interpretation, it has been found that a major factor in determining which children are successful in solving problems is the extent to which they are mastery-oriented rather than approval-oriented (Dweck, 1986). For the most part, boys are socialized to be mastery-oriented, whereas girls are socialized to be approval-oriented. This can explain why girls do better than boys in the lower grades by behaving well but not in the higher grades where problem-solving ability is more important.

Development of the Two Systems Across the Lifespan

The rational system first enters into developmental considerations when children begin to represent events in verbal symbols; that is, when they begin to use language. As previously noted, preverbal infants operate exclusively in the mode of the experiential system. With the development of language, the rational system plays an increasingly important role, until its primacy is achieved in young adulthood. That is, with continuing maturation of the brain and increasing socialization and formal and informal training in reasoning, the balance of influence between the two systems gradually shifts from dominance of the experiential system to dominance of the rational system. Thus, the reality principle becomes increasingly more influential, and people's behavior and reasoning become increasingly determined by deliberative reasoning and less influenced by their emotions and impulses. It will be recalled that in the ratio bias experiment with children, the children established compromises between the two processing systems that were more in the direction of experiential dominance than was observed for adults.

The development of a rational system provides children with an ability to reason abstractly with the aid of verbal symbols and, accordingly, to delay gratification, control emotions and impulses, and plan for the future. Figure 6.1 compares the trajectories during the period from age 10 to age 60 of rational intelligence, as represented by mental age, and experiential intelligence, as represented by scores on the Constructive Thinking Inventory (CTI). It can be seen that intellectual ability sharply increases from childhood to late adolescence and reaches its apex at age 20, after which it gradually declines until age 60. Experiential intelligence exhibits an almost opposite course. It decreases sharply up to late adolescence, then increases sharply up to early adulthood, after which it exhibits a steady increase up to age 51, and then gradually decreases to age 60. Apparently, as people age, they become less cognitively acute but are able to compensate for it by their greater experience. The discrepancy between the two kinds of intelligence is particularly interesting in adolescence because it is a period in which intellectual intelligence is at its apex and experiential intelligence is close to its nadir. As a result, adolescents are able to argue very well in defending their inappropriate behavior. A caveat is in order about interpreting the trajectories in Figure 6.1. It should be kept in mind that these trajectories represent average figures and that there are marked individual differences. Not all individuals exhibit a sharp decrease in constructive thinking in adolescence. In fact, as previously noted, the sharp decrease in adolescence is produced mainly by females. Nor do all older people decline in constructive thinking after age 50. Some continue to increase in their experiential intelligence and to gain in wisdom to an extent that more than compensates for whatever reduction in intellectual acuity they experience.

The rational system develops by formal and informal training in reasoning, imitation, and directly experiencing the consequences of making correct and incorrect inferences. Children are trained to reason during their many years

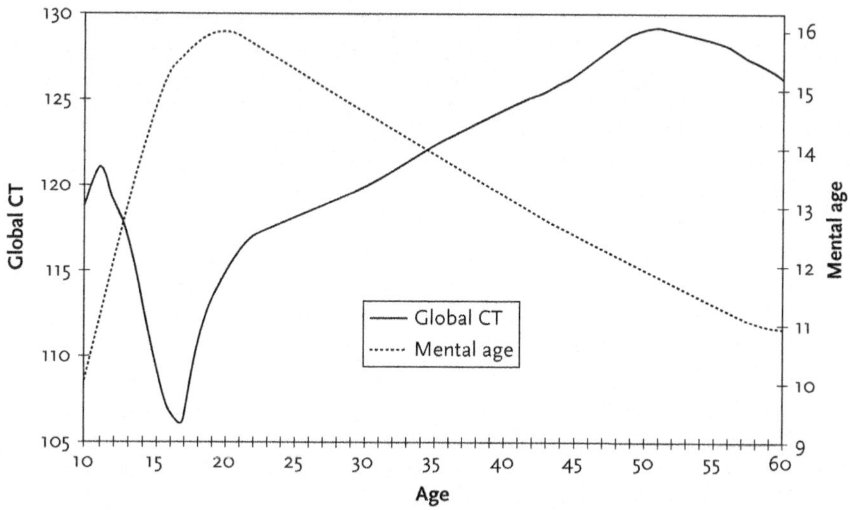

Figure 6.1
Comparison of mental age and global constructive thinking as a function of age.
Mental age was measured by the Wechsler-Bellevue Intelligence Test. Constructive thinking was measured by the Constructive Thinking Inventory (CTI). The curve for mental age was adapted from D. Wechsler, *The measurement of adult intelligence* (Baltimore: Williams & Wilkins, 1939).

of formal education. They are also trained to reason informally by their parents, other adults, and peers who dispute their reasoning in arguments and discussions. In addition, they learn from direct experience that they can solve problems by reasoning correctly and that, when they reason incorrectly, they fail to solve problems.

Cognitive-experiential theory (CET) has little that is new to say about the development of the rational system. For the most part, the views of developmental psychologists, such as Piaget, are accepted. Children obviously learn to reason more logically as they mature until late adolescence, after which their mental acuity gradual declines, as indicated by the course of mental age over the life course as shown in Figure 6.1.

The rational system has been found to be more homogeneous than the experiential system. When subjected to a factor analysis, the Experiential Scale of the CTI divided into several facets, whereas the Rational Scale retained its homogeneity (Norris & Epstein, 2011). In an experiment on heuristic processing, participants responded from two perspectives, rational and experiential. When they responded from a rational perspective, they made more consistent responses across situations than when they responded from an experiential perspective (Denes-Raj & Epstein, 1994), in support of the view that experiential processing is situation-specific whereas rational processing operates by cross-situational principles.

So far, only the course of the global aspect of constructive thinking across the lifecycle has been discussed, but it is also informative to examine the developmental trajectory of the facets of constructive thinking. Figure 6.2 presents the developmental trajectory for males and females of the two most important facets of constructive thinking, emotional and behavioral coping.

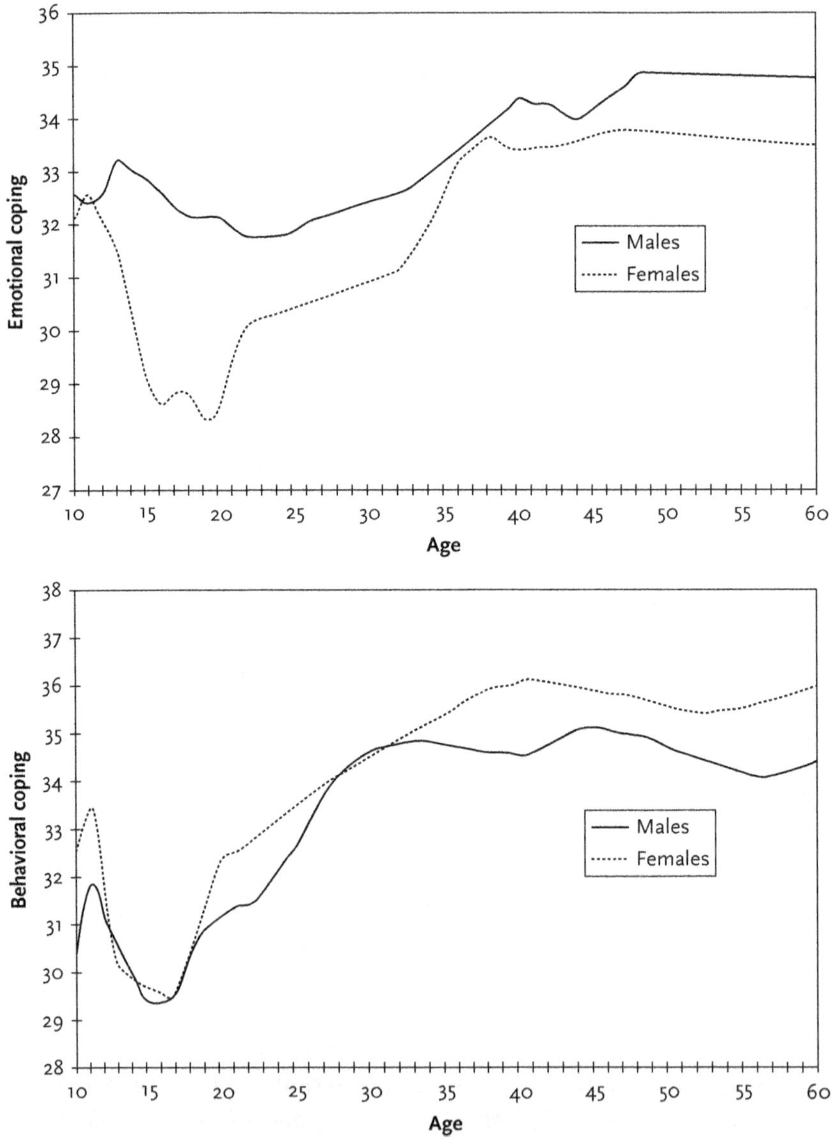

Figure 6.2
Average scores on the Constructive Thinking Inventory (CTI) scales of emotional coping and behavioral coping at different age levels.

It can be seen in Figure 6.2 that there is a sharp decrease in emotional coping for girls from age 11 until its nadir at age 20. Boys exhibit a decrease in emotional coping between ages 14 and 18, but it is not nearly as great as that for girls. Both groups thereafter experience a continuous increase in emotional coping up to about age 47, after which their emotional coping levels off at a relatively high level and continues until age 60, with women lagging slightly behind men.

Turning to behavioral coping, the main difference compared to emotional coping is that both groups show the same sharp decrease in behavioral coping in adolescence that only the girls showed for emotional coping. As can be seen in Figure 6.2, both groups reach the nadir of their behavioral coping at about age 16, with the males exhibiting a sustained increase up to about age 46 and the females up to about age 41. The apex reached by women is slightly higher than the apex for men. Following their apexes, both groups exhibit a slight decrease in behavioral coping from ages 45 to 55, followed by a recovery at age 60 to the level of their earlier apex in their 40s. The women maintain their advantage in behavioral coping after both groups reach their initial apexes in their 40s.

Most notable in Figure 6.2 is the equally sharp decline in emotional and behavioral coping during adolescence for girls compared to the much smaller decline for adolescent boys in emotional than in behavioral coping. Also of interest, the highest levels of both emotional and behavioral coping are reached and maintained in later adulthood, from about 40 to 60 years of age and perhaps beyond.

Global Constructive Thinking, Emotional Coping, and Behavioral Coping are CTI scales that measure adaptive automatic thinking (which invariably includes a component of rational thinking). The CTI also includes two scales of poor constructive thinking, Categorical Thinking and Esoteric Thinking, and one scale of mixed constructive thinking, namely Naïve Optimism, in which the positive feature tends to cancel out the unrealistic one. Figure 6.3 presents the scores on these three scales across the lifespan for the period age 10, which is the youngest period in which the children's form of the CTI can be administered, to age 60. It can be seen in Figure 6.3 that categorical thinking increases sharply in boys from age 10 to its apex at age 18, after which it rapidly decreases until age 21, when it reaches a level that is slightly below where it was at age 10. From age 21, it gradually decreases over a prolonged period until it reaches a nadir in the mid-40s, after which, during another prolonged period, it slightly increases to age 60. For females, the curve for categorical thinking is similar to that for males except that the increase in categorical thinking from age 10 to late adolescence in girls is much smaller than it is for boys, and females exhibit lower levels of categorical thinking than males across almost the entire lifespan.

The striking increase in categorical thinking at adolescence for boys and a similar but less dramatic increase for girls warrants some discussion of why

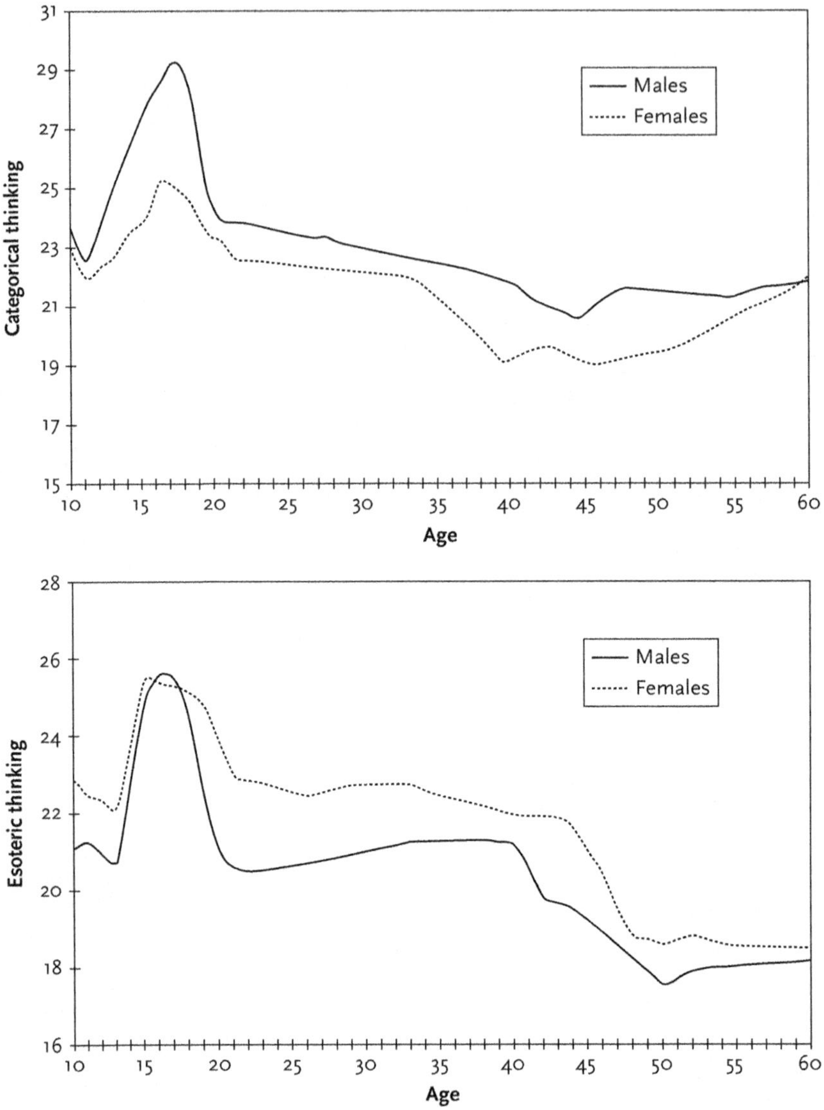

Figure 6.3
Average scores on the Constructive Thinking Inventory (CTI) scales of categories thinking, esoteric thinking, and native optimism at different age levels.

it occurs and its implications. Categorical thinking has three main components: polarized thinking, distrust of others, and intolerance. Adolescence is a period often accompanied by identity confusion (e.g., Erikson, 1963) as a result of adolescents having to change their identity from that of a child to an emerging adult. Categorical thinking provides a decisiveness that is lacking in more mature, nuanced thinking. The adolescent, by thinking categorically,

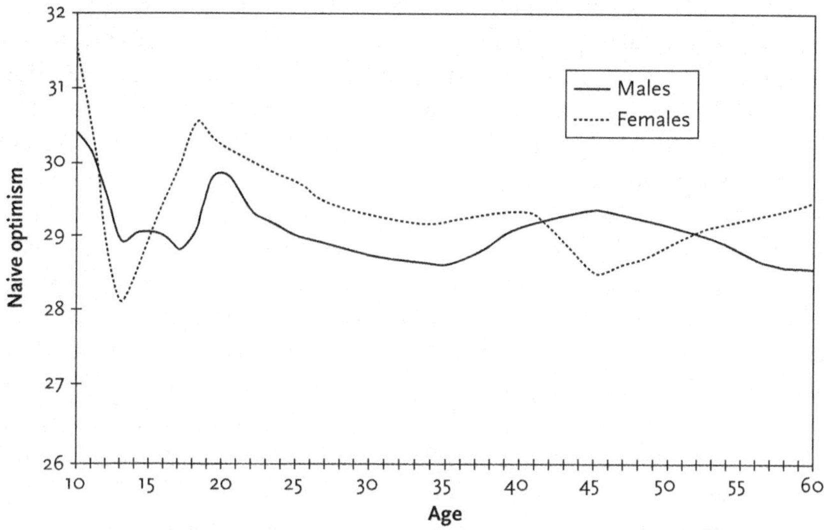

Figure 6.3 (Continued)

is able to compensate for feelings of uncertainty with feelings of excessive certainty. Black is black and white is white, and that is all there is to it; no wishy-washy shades of gray. In seeking a new identity that is different from that of a child who is dependent on adults, adolescents often bond with others of their own age and are antagonistic to adults as a way of distancing them from their dependency on them.

Turning to the information from the scale of the Esoteric Thinking figure in Figure 6.2, it can be seen that esoteric thinking in boys and girls slightly diminishes from ages 10 to 13, then rapidly increases until it reaches its apex at age 17, after which it drops off sharply until it returns at age 21to the same level as before the rise at age 13. Thereafter, it levels off to about age 42, after which it sharply decreases to age 50, and then levels off to age 60. The sexes produce similar curves, except that females exhibit slightly greater esoteric thinking across most of the lifecycle. The most dramatic result is the sharp increase in this form of maladaptive thinking in adolescence. Since esoteric thinking includes beliefs about questionable phenomena such as ghosts, astrology, and good and bad omens, the results suggest that adolescents are suggestible and undisciplined in their thinking and that they are readily influenced by their experiential systems. It may further indicate that they accept unusual beliefs as a way of demonstrating their independence from authoritatively recommended ways of thinking.

Naïve optimism refers to thinking that is unrealistically optimistic, simplistic, and often stereotyped. It can be seen in Figure 6.1 that such thinking is at its apex for both sexes at age 10. It then decreases sharply to a nadir at age 17 for boys and to an even lower nadir at age 13 for girls. Following their nadirs, the boys exhibit a sharp increase to its apex at age 18, and the girls to a considerably higher apex at age 20. This is followed by a gradual decline in both groups to about age 30, after which both groups exhibit variations around otherwise generally flat gradients at a relatively low level of esoteric thinking. Over the course of the lifecycle, females exhibit slightly higher levels of esoteric thinking than males. The most notable results are the high level of naïve optimism in 10-year-olds followed by a sharp decrease for a few years, after which there is a sharp increase in naïve optimism up to a relatively high level in late adolescence. The high level of naïve optimism in late adolescence reminds me of the estimates my college seniors made of their expected salaries after graduating. I was astonished by how unrealistically high their estimates were. According to Figure 6.1, young people gradually come down to earth as they experience the real world after school. It is of further interest that, at a period when adolescents are at the peak of their intellectual intelligence, they exhibit simplistic thinking at the experiential level in addition to poor emotional and behavioral coping, categorical thinking, and esoteric thinking. Thus, parents of adolescents must contend with their children having a high level of intellectual ability combined with unrealistic, maladaptive ways of thinking.

The Interaction of the Two Systems

As noted throughout this book, the interaction of the experiential and rational systems is considered to be a particularly important determinant of human thought, feelings, and behavior. It is thus necessary if one wishes to understand mental development to consider not only the separate course of development of each of these information-processing systems but also to consider their interactions over the lifespan.

An important developmental principle is that, with maturation, the balance of influence between the two systems shifts in favor of increasing dominance by the rational system. However, rational processing never completely displaces experiential processing. A further principle is that the development of each system influences the development of the other. Thus, a child who has serious emotional problems is unable to use her intelligence to full advantage to the extent that she is preoccupied with her emotional problems. Moreover, distressing experiences encoded in a child's implicit theory of reality can interfere with the development of the rational system. A child who has experienced a highly stressful experience or series of experiences, particularly within the family, may avoid consciously thinking in certain directions because of the anxiety it causes. The child may then generalize such a reaction tendency to avoid thinking deeply about anything. Alternatively, a child can develop a specific way of conscious thinking that reduces anxiety in the short run but that is counterproductive in the long run, thereby influencing the rational system to continue to develop in a maladaptive way. These are some examples of how the interaction between the two systems can motivate ways of thinking and behaving that interfere with the development of the ability to think rationally about everyday problems.

Developmental Stages

It is accepted in CET that certain stages in the lifespan have a particularly important influence on the development of the two information-processing systems. However, the influence of such stages in CET is accorded much less importance than in theories such as Erikson's (1963) stage theory. This issue will be further discussed when the views of Erikson on developmental stages are evaluated from the perspective of CET later in this chapter. For now, it will suffice to note a few stages of particular importance, according to CET.

The Preverbal Stage

As previously noted, this stage is considered particularly important because it lays the foundation for further cognitive and emotional development. It is the only stage in which the child operates completely in the mode of the experiential system because the operation of the rational system requires the use of language. The major implicit basic beliefs acquired at this stage are beliefs that fall along dimensions anchored by implicit beliefs about the general goodness versus badness of the world; the orderliness, predictability, and controllability of the world versus the degree to which it is considered disorderly, chaotic, and unpredictable; the degree to which the child feels secure versus insecure; and the trustworthiness and helpfulness of people versus the view of them as untrustworthy and threatening. Depending on the preverbal child's position on these implicit belief dimensions, the child will be provided with a foundation that will determine the degree to which the person's conceptual system will later be resilient or vulnerable to disorganization and other maladaptive conditions.

The Post-Language Stage

With the onset of the use of language at about the age of two, most children begin to acquire a rational system that ultimately will provide them with a level of abstract reasoning that distinguishes the human species from all other species and is the source of humankind's remarkable intellectual accomplishments.

But what if a child failed to develop the normal use of language, as occurs in some cases of brain damage and autism? Such a child would obviously be seriously impaired. It is well established that most cases of autism have a biological source. However, there may be some cases of autism that have a psychological cause, and this follows directly from some basic assumptions in CET about the establishment of a self-concept and an implicit theory of reality.

When Kanner (1943) introduced the disorder identified as autism, he and others believed it was the result of inadequate mothering, or so-called "refrigerator mothers" who lacked normal warm feelings toward their child. This view was later abandoned because of evidence of brain anomalies in cases of autism. However, basic assumptions in CET make me suspect it was premature to dismiss a psychological source of autism in all cases.

According to CET, children construct a conceptual system because it is rewarding to do so. If this is true, there should be cases in which children fail to develop a self-concept because it would be punishing to do so. This could happen if a caregiver were sufficiently hostile to a child so that adopting the parent's view of the child by the child itself would be punishing rather than rewarding. As a result, the child, according to CET, could avoid developing a self-concept. This view receives some support from the following observations. First, some autistic children begin to use language but abandon it after learning self-referent words like "I" and "me"; they regress and abandon what language they had learned up to then. Second, I have participated in the treatment of a mother who had an autistic child she hated. The child behaved exactly as would be expected of a child who had reason to avoid developing a self-concept. He exhibited all the classic symptoms of autism, with one exception. Most autistic children prefer to sit next to their mother rather than next to a stranger. This child avoided being in the proximity of his mother. When she entered the room in which he was completing his session with his therapist, he would scream in terror. The case is described in greater detail in Chapter 9 on psychopathology.

The Grade-School Stage

This stage is referred to by psychoanalysts as the latency period. It is a stage in which children are in school learning, in addition to academic material, social skills by interacting with other children and their teachers. According to CET, such experiences can influence implicit beliefs about relatedness. For example, depending on their experiences with other children, children in grade school will develop the implicit belief that peers are a source of positive feelings and therefore desirable to relate to or a source of distress to be avoided when possible. Their experiences with their teachers will influence their implicit beliefs about authority figures, such as whether they are viewed as kindly and helpful or threatening. Depending on how successfully they compete with other children and how their teachers regard them, this period may also influence their self-esteem as by now they have developed a self-concept that can be esteemed.

Adolescence

Cognitive-experiential theory is in agreement with Erikson about the special importance of adolescence. As the result of physical maturation, including changes in appearance and an intensified sexual drive, as well as new social and sexual demands, adolescents have to begin to replace their familiar identity as a child with a new identity that prepares them for adulthood. Such a significant change in identity can be highly stressful. As Erikson notes, some adolescents experience identity confusion, and others establish an identity in which they adopt the beliefs and values of a cult. Implicit beliefs about identities are not only acquired from direct experience but are also influenced by observations of other people's behavior, particularly by the behavior of significant adults such as caretakers and teachers who may provide attractive or unattractive role models of what it means to be an adult. Thus, adolescence is a double-edged sword. It is a common source of stress and confusion, but it also provides an opportunity for establishing a new and more adaptive identity than before.

As previously noted, an interesting problem for many adolescents and therefore for their parents is that they are at the peak of their intellectual ability but, because of the immature development of their brain centers that control inhibition and restraint, as well as because of their lack of experience, they lack good judgment. As previously noted, they are thus in the ironic position of being able to argue logically in defense of their unreasonable behavior.

The Early Adult Stage

In the early adult stage, young adults are faced with new responsibilities related to work and establishing a family. An adjustment that was adequate up to this stage may not be equal to meeting these new challenges. This may be why schizophrenic reactions are often first exhibited at this stage. How a person negotiates this stage may influence one or more of that person's basic implicit needs and beliefs, particularly the need to maintain and enhance self-esteem, including a person's implicit beliefs about the self as competent and love-worthy.

How successfully the person negotiates the work situation is most likely to influence implicit beliefs about the competence component of self-esteem, whereas how a person meets the challenge of establishing a family is likely to influence implicit beliefs about relatedness and self-esteem, such as whether marital relationships are viewed as a source of happiness and fulfillment or frustration and distress, and whether one's relationship with one's partner makes one feel love-worthy or not. Establishing a successful marriage can repair previous unfavorable beliefs about the self as lovable and others as helpful and desirable to relate to, whereas the failure to establish a successful marriage can have an opposite effect.

Midlife Issues

At this period in people's lives, they are likely to realize that they do not have forever to reach their goals, and they take stock of how well they have done so. Included are considerations of how satisfactory their work and their marriages are. If work is unsatisfactory, there may be an interest in changing careers. If marriage is problematic, it may result in divorce. In both cases, there may be an increase in drug and alcohol abuse. The implicit beliefs likely to be affected concern self-esteem and competence for work issues and self-esteem and relatedness for marriage issues.

Old Age and Attitudes Toward Death

There comes a time when people become aware that the end of their life is approaching. This is a period when individuals are not as alert, energetic, and intellectually acute as they once were, but this is largely balanced by their greater reservoir of experience. Depending on what they have learned in their earlier years, they may become rigid, dogmatic, and opinionated in their thinking or flexible and wise, or they may simply continue to be just as they were when younger. Wisdom, according to CET, requires a symbiotic combination of experiential and rational intelligence, which requires an understanding of how the experiential system operates in general and, more importantly, how it operates in oneself. The essence of knowing oneself, according to CET, means being in touch with the operation of one's experiential system and therefore being aware of one's implicit needs and beliefs and being able to compensate for their biasing influence on one's judgment. A wise person, according to CET, views the two processing systems as partners, each with its advantages and disadvantages, and is able to use them in a manner in which they correct and supplement each other.

A successful resolution at this stage consists of making peace with the awareness that one's life is nearing its end. This is accomplished by different people in different ways. Some gain satisfaction from the belief that they have been good people and will be leaving the world a better place for having lived in it. What is important to others is that they have contributed to the welfare and happiness of their loved ones. Yet others are satisfied because, on looking back on their lives, they believe they have lived life to the fullest and made the most of what life had to offer. Others simply enjoy their daily activities and give little thought to weighty issues such as how well they have lived their lives. Yet others derive strength from their religion, believing that they are going to a better place where they will be together with departed loved ones.

An important question that I have thought about considerably but found no compelling answer for is how important it is in facing one's ultimate death to find a larger meaning in one's life. For Viktor Frankel (1939/1963), having such a sense of meaning determined his own and others' ability to survive the horrors of being incarcerated in a Nazi concentration camp. I do not doubt that having a significant reason for living can be very helpful and even life-saving under conditions of terrible adversity. However, I doubt how necessary such a belief is for facing death with equanimity under more benign circumstances. In the behavior of people I have observed, and in my own experience, it is evident to me that the degree to which one is absorbed in some kind of activity serves to reduce stress from other sources. When I studied sport parachutists, some told me that so long as they jumped, they felt stable and calm, and they slept well at night. However, when there was an extended period of bad weather when they could not jump, old anxieties and conflicts returned that kept them awake at night. The same kind of effect has been reported in the return of post-traumatic stress disorder (PTSD) in war veterans after they retired from work. Many had achieved a satisfactory level of adjustment during their working years, but when they lost their main source of activity and direction in their lives, their PTSD returned. In sum, such evidence, as well as logic, suggests that personally important issues, such as devotion to loved ones, involvement in a career, and an intense interest in solving an important problem, can provide a source of meaning and absorption that reduces the influence of distressing beliefs or unfavorable living conditions in one's existence. What I am less sure of is whether an abiding serious interest or activity is necessary for confronting the end of one's life with equanimity. I suspect that many people who spend their last days on earth playing golf or bridge with friends or engaging in otherwise enjoyable mundane activities may die peacefully without regret.

Some Caveats About Stages

Although it is helpful to recognize the challenges and the adaptive and maladaptive resolutions of different life stages, it is important to consider that the same basic needs affect behavior at all stages and that the different stages simply indicate likely issues that affect many but not all people in certain ways. It is also important to recognize the influence of the occurrence of potent individual events, such as traumas and love relationships, which at any stage can dominate the effect of a presumably stage-specific influence.

THE DEVELOPMENTAL VIEWS OF CET COMPARED TO THOSE OF COGNITIVE, RELATIONAL, NEO-PSYCHOANALYTIC, AND MORAL DEVELOPMENTAL THEORIES

In this section, summaries of the developmental theories of Piaget, Erikson, Bowlby, and Kohlberg are presented with two aims. One aim is to increase an understanding of the views of CET on development by contrasting it with other views on development. The other aim is to indicate how CET can provide a useful perspective for evaluating other developmental theories.

Piaget's Theory of Cognitive Development

The Theory

Piaget (1929/1975) constructed his developmental theory of cognition by observing the behavior of children in situations designed to examine their thought processes. His observations at various stages of development led him to conclude that children of all ages actively seek to understand and control their world. From his studies of cognition throughout childhood, he concluded that cognitive development can be described according to the following stages. During a *sensorimotor stage*, from birth to about two years, infants learn about the world through their sensory and motor reactions. They are unable to use mental images and symbols to represent objects and events. By nine months, they learn "object permanence"—the existence of an object even when it is out of sight. They also acquire a rudimentary understanding of cause-and-effect relations. At a *preoperational stage* between the ages of approximately two and seven, children begin to use symbols and acquire language. Piaget considered this an "ego-centric" stage because children are able to view events only from their own perspective. They lack an understanding of "conservation" because they do not understand that the physical properties of an object may remain the same despite its outward appearance changing, such as when water is transferred to receptacles with different shapes. The next stage, *concrete operations*, occurs between the ages of approximately 6 and 11 years. Logical thought begins to develop at this stage but is limited to inferences about concrete objects and events and does not include abstract reasoning. The final stage is referred to as *formal operations*, which begins at the age of approximately 12. In this stage, children are able to reason abstractly with the use of symbols. However, they often come to unreasonable conclusions because of their lack of experience.

In an article based on a talk he gave to the American Psychoanalytic Association, Piaget (1973) discussed the difference between the "affective unconscious" of psychoanalysis and the cognitive unconscious that he studied.

Piaget believed that people are unaware of the operation and nature of both kinds of unconscious processing but are aware of its products, which consist of thoughts in the case of the cognitive unconscious and of feelings and motives in the case of the affective unconscious. It should be noted that this distinction is different from the distinction between the rational and experiential systems in CET because as in Piaget's theory both kinds of processing are unconscious, whereas in CET only processing in the experiential system is usually unconscious, and it includes Piaget's unconscious and some aspects of the psychoanalytic unconscious.

Piaget explains that unconscious knowledge is unavailable to consciousness because it is encoded in sensorimotor schemes and not in cognitive representational schemes. Piaget believed that sensorimotor schemes are prevented from reaching consciousness by *inhibition*, in a manner similar to repression in psychoanalysis.

Evaluation of the Theory

Piaget's theory and CET are in agreement that children from birth on are active agents who proactively seek to understand their environment. Piaget's stages are compatible with those in CET and can be mapped onto CET in terms of the trajectories of the experiential and rational systems that include an increasing shift from experiential to rational dominance. As previously noted, the jellybean and CTI research are also consistent with Piaget's stages. As Piaget's sensorimotor stage precedes language acquisition, it is a period of pure experiential processing according to CET. In the early part of the preoperational stage, the child begins to acquire language and therefore acquires a rudimentary rational system. This is consistent with Piaget's observation that although children at this stage are able to represent objects by verbal symbols, they can do so only in a very limited way and are not yet able to use language to overcome their egocentricity and to understand the principle of conservation. These limitations indicate that the rational system during the preoperational phase, despite some language acquisition, has a subordinate influence on reasoning compared to the influence of the experiential system. In the period of concrete operations, from the ages of approximately 6 to 11, the contribution of the rational system increases, as indicated by children's ability to use language to reason logically, albeit still only to a very limited degree. The considerable influence of the experiential system is indicated by the restriction of reasoning to inferences about concrete objects. Beginning at approximately age 12, the beginning of the stage of formal operations, the rational system achieves supremacy over the experiential system, as indicated by children's ability to use language to reason abstractly. Thus, Piaget's theory and CET are compatible with regard to the cognitive stages that Piaget proposes.

Despite the compatibility of the two theories with respect to cognitive development, the theories differ in several ways. First, Piaget proposes separate cognitive and affective unconscious processes, whereas CET proposes a single unconscious system in which affect is involved along a dimension that varies from negligible to a major influence. According to CET, there is always some degree of affect in all learning, including in situations in which it is not self-evident. This can be observed in the example that Piaget provides of what he regards as affect-free learning, in which children learn outside of their awareness to throw a tethered ball at right angles to a target in order to hit it. He neglects to consider that there is an initial motive to hit the target, which necessarily indicates affective involvement. Moreover, when hitting the target, the child can be assumed to experience positive affect, and, when missing it, the child can be assumed to experience negative affect, and it is through such affective reinforcement that the child learns to hit the target. This, of course, is the way in which nonhuman animals acquire proficiency, and it is therefore consistent with the operation of the experiential system in humans. Second, Piaget, in agreement with Freud, assumes that unconscious processes would be conscious if not for inhibition. In comparison, the position of CET and of modern cognitive science is that it is more parsimonious and more efficient for unconscious processing to operate outside of awareness as a natural condition rather than to require inhibition to make it unconscious.

Third, Piaget assumes that information processing advances along a single dimension from primitive to more sophisticated processing. Based on this assumption, superstitious beliefs should be replaced as a result of maturation by more realistic beliefs. In contrast, according to CET, as experiential and rational processing operate in parallel superstitious and logical thinking should occur at all ages. It will be recalled that this was found to be true for esoteric thinking, which includes a belief in superstitions, across the lifespan. Also, in a study comparing superstitious thinking in children and adults, both kinds of thinking were prevalent at all age levels from childhood throughout adulthood (reported in Epstein, 1998). It is important to consider that although adults operate more according to their rational system than do children, they also have had more opportunity to acquire superstitions through the automatic operation of their experiential systems. As a case in point, consider the following incident that was reported in a television newscast on April 15, 1993. A woman played a slot machine for 12 hours without interruption, being convinced that if she kept playing the same machine, eventually she would win. She left for a breakfast snack after an attendant promised that he would lock her machine until she returned. She ate a bagel and had a cup of coffee. When she shortly returned, she saw a crowd around her machine. A man had just won $100,000. She is suing the casino for that amount of money, claiming that she would have won it had the machine been locked as promised. She exclaimed in an interview, "I'll never eat another bagel again!"

In summary, there is much in Piaget's theory that is compatible with CET. However, there are also important differences in the two theories.

Erikson's Modified Psychoanalytic Developmental Theory

The Theory

Erikson (1963, 1987) considered his theory to be a modified version of classical psychoanalytic theory. However, many believe his modifications are so extensive as to constitute a new theory. Erikson proposes eight stages, each with a crisis based on the influences of maturation and psychosocial demands. Depending on how a stage is resolved, Erikson believes a person acquires positive or negative "ego qualities," such as trust or mistrust, which are similar to implicit beliefs in CET. Resolution of one stage paves the way for resolution of the next stage. In the event that a crisis at a particular stage is unsuccessfully resolved, it creates difficulties for resolving crises at later stages. A person remains vulnerable at the level of a poorly resolved stage. However, if a crisis at a particular stage has been poorly resolved, it can be resolved at a later stage. According to Erikson, no one emerges from a psychosexual stage with a pure positive or negative ego quality, but does so only to a degree, depending on how well the person has resolved the crisis at that stage.

Erikson's eight stages of life:

1. *The oral-sensory stage: trust versus mistrust*. Depending on how well and how consistently a parenting figure meets the needs of an infant, the infant develops a basic trust or mistrust of people and a belief in the orderly and predictable occurrence of events.
2. *The muscular-anal stage: autonomy vs. shame and doubt*. Toilet training is of special importance at this stage because it provides a situation in which a child can refuse to do what its parents wish. If the parents shame or discourage the child, the child feels doubt or shame whenever it attempts to exert its will. A successful resolution of this stage results in "willpower," the ability to exercise willpower and self-restraint.
3. *The locomotor-genital stage: initiative vs. guilt*. This is a period when preschoolers gain a sense of mastery as the result of acquiring new abilities, such as standing up and running. This is also a period in which children experience the Oedipus complex and develop a super ego as an outcome of the Oedipus complex. A successful resolution results in the acquisition of impulse control and a sense of purpose, which Erikson regards as pursuing valued goals without fear of punishment.
4. *The latency stage: industry vs. inferiority* (ages 6–11). Erikson, like Freud, views the latency period as a lull before the storm. It is characterized by sublimation

of sexual and aggressive impulses into curiosity and a desire to learn. Children develop self-esteem at this stage, depending on their success in competition with their peers. They become socialized in school into establishing work habits for contributing to society, and, if they succeed in this, it contributes to a sense of industry. A successful resolution of this stage produces high self-esteem, whereas an unsuccessful resolution produces low self-esteem.

5. *The adolescence stage: identity versus role confusion*. Children at this stage experience significant biological development and become interested in sex. They experience a conflict between a childhood and a more adult identity. Adolescents may emerge from this stage in three ways. They may feel secure about having achieved the beginning of an adult identity that includes the ability to work and to love; they may experience "identity confusion" and a prolongation of adolescence; or they may develop a destructive identity, as by identifying with a cult.
6. *The young-adulthood stage: intimacy versus isolation*. The challenge for the young adult is to establish close relations with others. Those with insecure identities have difficulty accepting and caring for others, whereas those with secure identities establish mutually rewarding relationships with others.
7. *Adulthood stage: generativity versus stagnation*. Generativity refers to raising children, guiding the next generation, and exhibiting creativity in art and productivity in work. In the absence of generativity, people suffer from "stagnation" and a sense of emptiness. Successful negotiation of this stage results in caring, responsible people who are accepting of their obligations.
8. *Maturity: ego integrity versus despair*. This stage occurs in old age, when a person realizes that death is not far off. Depending on how the previous seven stages were resolved, a person will experience either ego integrity or despair. Ego integrity refers to a feeling that one has lived one's life well. Despair refers to a feeling that one has not led a meaningful life. A successful balance in favor of ego integrity over despair results in "wisdom," defined as "a detached concern with life itself, in the face of death itself" (Erikson, 1963, p. 269).

Evaluation of the Theory

Erikson's stage theory makes a significant contribution by drawing attention to the special challenges that occur at certain periods in the lifespan and to the adaptive and maladaptive ways in which people respond to these challenges. However, it does have important limitations.

Erikson's theory and CET are similar in that both emphasize the relation between emotionally significant events and the implicit beliefs derived from them, which influence people's feelings and behavior and therefore the quality of people's lives.

Despite the reasonableness of many of Erikson's views about particular stages, there are serious problems with his theory. Perhaps the most important problem is that there is little research evidence to support the stages he proposes. A second problem is that the stages and their resolutions are not always logically coherent. For example, a crisis in the locomotor-genital stage concerns a conflict between initiative and guilt. Initiative and guilt hardly seem like incompatible opposites. In fact, people can exhibit initiative because of guilt without experiencing a conflict between them.

A third problem with Erikson's theory is that he assumes a one-to-one relation between a particular stage, a particular crisis, and a particular resolution. Yet similar crises can arise at different stages, and the theory fails systematically to consider how the crisis at one stage relates to the crises at other stages. It would be instructive to follow the resolution of a crisis through all stages in which it is relevant. There is also a failure to consider the occurrence of highly influential events that can occur at any stage, such as traumas and transforming love relationships. Moreover, there can be multiple common influences at a particular stage rather than the one major influence assumed by Erikson. For example, the crisis in the latency stage is said to involve a conflict between industry and inferiority, and the manner in which it is resolved is considered to depend on how children fare in competition with their peers. However, the influence of teachers can be as important as the influence of peers in this stage, and relationships with teachers can influence not only beliefs about industry versus inferiority (which, parenthetically, does not identify the endpoints of a coherent bipolar dimension) but also about relationships with and attitudes toward authority figures, which are no less important than beliefs about industry versus inferiority.

Bowlby's Relational Theory

The Theory

Although Bowlby's theory emphasizes interpersonal relationships, he regarded interpersonal relationships as so influential in all aspects of life that his theory comes close to being a general theory of personality. He stated his position on this issue as follows: "Intimate attachments to other human beings are the hub around which a person's life revolves, not only when he is an infant or a toddler, but throughout his adolescence and his years of maturity as well, and on into old age" (Bowlby, 1980, p. 442).

Bowlby (1969) assumes the existence of a biological adaptive attachment system in infants that is manifested in several ways that contribute to survival. Included are its promotion of proximity seeking, of fear reactions that motivate avoidance of danger, of engagement in social and interpersonal behavior, and of novelty seeking, including exploratory behavior. The attachment system draws parents and children together, which protects children from harm. The positive emotions derived from attachments make attachment inherently rewarding, which promotes parents caring for their children and children bonding with their parents. The need of children to be close to their parents in times of distress and for parents to respond to their children's distress are inherent adaptive reactions that promote survival of the species.

Bowlby emphasized the importance of "working models," which refers to inner representations. Inner representations are similar to the implicit beliefs or schemas in CET because they influence the interpretation of events, guide behavior, and influence emotions. The working models derived from early relationships with parents are particularly important in this respect. Children learn from imitation, as well as from their own experience. From observing their parents' behavior toward them and others, children learn about nurturing behavior. From their own experience, children learn about people's need to be cared for and protected. The working models derived from such observations and experience influence expectancies, behavior, and feelings toward others, including peers, younger children, older children, and adults in various roles. The children's behavior, in turn, influences how others react to them. Although working models tend to be stable, Bowlby believed they can be modified by emotionally significant new experiences. Support for such modification is provided in a study by Shaver and Brennan (1992), who found that people who were distrustful of others early in life changed this attitude when they had rewarding relationships later in life.

As in CET, Bowlby (1969) attributes special significance to the adaptive function of emotions. He notes that an adaptive bond with caretakers develops because of its reinforcement by positive feelings and by relief from negative feelings. Under such circumstances, children form a working model in which people are viewed as a reliable source of positive affect and relief from distress.

Bowlby's ideas on the secure relationships of infants with their caretakers have inspired considerable research. Based on his view that the security of the attachment bond determines infants' motivation to explore their environments, Ainsworth developed "the strange situations test" (Ainsworth et al., 1978), which is a controlled sequence of timed events among a baby, the baby's mother, and a stranger. It was found with this test that there are four basic types of attachment: a secure attachment and three types of insecure attachment. In a secure attachment, babies take comfort and explore their environment in the presence of their mother. Babies with an avoidant attachment do not cry when their mother leaves and ignore or avoid her when she returns, as if they have learned to avoid being hurt by not caring. Babies with a resistant attachment have an ambivalent or approach-avoidance conflict regarding attachment to their mothers. They cry when she leaves but push her away when she returns. Babies with a disorganized attachment exhibit disorganized, strange attachment behaviors. They look away when the mother holds them, and they exhibit stiff or otherwise strange postures when she tries to comfort them.

In support of Bowlby's views on the importance of early attachment, children who were observed to be securely attached to their caretakers as infants were found to be better adjusted as older children and even as adults than children who exhibited a disorganized attachment as infants (Dozier, Stovall, & Albus, 1999; Greenberg, 1999; Lyons-Ruth & Jacobvitz, 1999; Sroufe, 1997). There is also support for Bowlby's view that very early attachment styles are related to the kinds of relationships people establish as adults (Hazan & Shaver, 1990; Shaver & Hazan, 1994).

Evaluation of the Theory

Bowlby's theory is highly compatible with CET. His constructs of internal mental representations and working models that determine how people interpret events, feel, and behave are very similar to the views in CET about implicit beliefs and their activation by relevant situations. In fact, Bowlby's theory could well be regarded as a more developed subset of CET, one that is more specifically focused on attachment.

Although they share much in common, there are important differences between the two theories. A major difference is that Bowlby's theory is a theory of attachment, whereas CET is a more global theory of personality, in which the need for attachment, although considered extremely important, is one of five basic subordinate implicit needs. Another important difference is that CET assumes the existence of two parallel, interacting information-processing systems, whereas Bowlby does not address this issue, but emphasizes what CET considers processing in the domain of the experiential system. Although Bowlby's concept of world models is similar to CET's personal theories of reality, there is an important distinction between the two constructs. A personal theory of reality refers to a hierarchically organized system of interactive cognitive-affective networks. In contrast, a model of the world says nothing about its organization. There is no discussion in attachment theory about the integration of schematic networks into a unified system that is susceptible to disorganization.

Although both theories emphasize the importance of early childhood relationships for later adjustment, CET places greater emphasis on the significance of the occurrence of emotionally significant arbitrary events that have nothing to do with attachment and on later experiences than does attachment theory. An example of such arbitrary events is the experience of trauma and of the unintentional reinforcement of maladaptive behavioral tendencies. In agreement with attachment theory, it is assumed in CET that children are more readily influenced by emotionally significant events related to attachment figures than are adults and that attachment schemas acquired early in life are more influential than those acquired later in life. However, as important as such events are, personality is importantly influenced by other factors, and there is a danger of misinterpretation if one seeks to understand behavior only in terms of the influence of relationships.

Kohlberg's Theory of Moral Development

The Theory

Kohlberg proposes three major stages of moral development, each with two substages. To determine a person's moral developmental stage, he designed a test consisting of vignettes that describe moral dilemmas. Respondents indicate what they consider to be the preferable way of responding to the dilemmas. Their responses are assigned to a moral stage on the basis of the kind of moral reasoning they exhibit.

Kohlberg's major stages are a "preconventional level," a "conventional level," and a "postconventional level." Young children usually respond at the preconventional level, in which they judge morality in terms of whether the outcome of the behavior is good or bad without considering the motivation for the behavior. Actions that are rewarded are considered to be good and ones that are punished are judged as bad. In other words, children respond according to the hedonic principle of CET. An example of a response at the preconventional level is "The man should not steal the drug because he will be punished."

As their cognitive abilities increase, children advance to the conventional level by considering social responsibilities and the importance of the law. As an example of a response at the conventional level, a vignette is presented about a man considering whether he should steal a drug he cannot afford to buy to save his sick wife. "It is wrong to steal the drug because it is against the law, and it is important for everyone to follow the law." This response, according to CET, can be viewed as a compromise between the two conceptual systems. It is an advance in the direction of the rational system because it goes beyond the application of just the hedonic principle of the experiential system because it considers a general principle and not simply a consideration of punishment, as in the previous example. However, it is not a completely abstract response based on a moral principle in the mode of the rational system, as is required at the next level.

Many, but not all, people advance to the postconventional level of moral reasoning. Reasoning at this level requires the consideration of fundamental values or principles that transcend the rules of society. An example of a response at the postconventional level is found in the vignette about the man who has to decide whether he should steal a drug to save his wife: "We have here a conflict between two principles, following the law and saving a human life. I regard saving a human life as more important than someone making a profit, so I think the man, under the circumstances, would be doing the right thing to steal the drug." Here, we have highly abstract thinking consistent with dominance by the rational system.

Evaluation of the Theory

Research has provided mixed support for Kohlberg's theory. On the positive side, people progress in their moral reasoning according to the stages in Kohlberg's theory (e.g., Walker, 1988). On the negative side, people do not consistently respond at the same level to different moral dilemmas. Most importantly, people's moral behavior frequently does not correspond to their moral reasoning (Wark & Krebs, 1996). A further consideration is that the highest level of moral reasoning requires abstract thinking and therefore may be primarily a function of intelligence.

According to CET, although Kohlberg's test is probably a reasonably good measure of moral reasoning, it is not a promising measure of moral behavior. This is because moral reasoning depends primarily on the rational system, whereas moral behavior is more likely to be controlled by the experiential system. Thus, the level of a person's moral reasoning can be expected to be influenced by general intelligence, maturation of the brain, and formal and informal training in reasoning. With the improvement of a child's conceptual reasoning during the course of development, the child's ability to reason about moral issues, as with other issues, can be expected to improve. Such improvement in reasoning, however, may have little to do with the person's behavior. This inference is supported by evidence that intellectual ability is poorly related to problem solving in everyday life (Epstein & Meier, 1989).

The stages of moral reasoning proposed by Kohlberg can be understood from the perspective of CET as a progression of the increasing dominance of the rational over the experiential system with maturation (see Figure 6.1). Thus, Kohlberg's views can readily be assimilated into CET with regard to the role of the rational system in reasoning about morality. As already noted, a major limitation in Kohlberg's theory is that it pertains to moral reasoning and not moral behavior. From the perspective of CET, moral behavior can be expected to be primarily influenced by the experiential system, but Kohlberg's theory emphasizes the information processing that occurs in the rational system.

REFERENCES

Ainsworth, M. D. S. (1993). Attachment as related to mother-infant interaction. In C. Rovee-Collier & L. P. Lipsitt (Eds.), *Advances in infancy research* (vol. 8), Norwood, NJ: Ablex.

Ainsworth, M. D. S., Blehar, M. C., Waters, E., & Wall, S. (1978). *Patterns of attachment*. Hilldale, NJ: Erlbaum.
Bowlby, J. (1969). *Attachment* (vol. 1 of *Attachment and Loss*). New York: Basic Books.
Bowlby, J. (1979). *The making and breaking of affectionate bonds*. London: Tavistock.
Bowlby, J. (1980). *Loss: Sadness and depression* (vol. 3 of *Attachment and Loss*). New York: Basic Books.
Coopersmith, S. (1967). *The antecedents of self-esteem*. San Francisco: W. H. Freeman & Co.
Denes-Raj, V., & Epstein, S. (1994). Conflict between intuitive and rational processing: When people behave against their better judgment. *Journal of Personality and Social Psychology, 66*, 819–829.
Dozier, M., Stovall, K. C., & Albus, K. E. (1999). Attachment and psychopathology in adulthood. In J. Cassidy & P. R. Shaver (Eds.), *Handbook of attachment* (pp. 497–519). New York: Guilford Press.
Dweck, C. S. (1986). Motivational processes affecting learning. *American Psychologist, 41*, 1040–1048.
Epstein, S. (1979). The ecological study of emotions in humans. In P. Pliner, K. R. Blankstein, & I. M. Spigel (Eds.), *Advances in the study of communication and affect, vol. 5: Perception of emotions in self and others* (pp. 47–83). New York: Plenum.
Epstein, S. (1998). *Constructive thinking: The key to emotional intelligence*. Westport, CT: Greenwood.
Epstein, S. (1999). *Constructive thinking and coping with stress in the everyday life of college students*. (Statistically analyzed, unpublished data.)
Epstein, S. (2006). Conscious and unconscious self-esteem from the perspective of cognitive-experiential self-theory. In M. H. Kernis (Ed.), *Self-esteem issues and answers* (pp. 69–76). New York: Psychology Press.
Epstein, S., & Meir, P. (1989). Constructive thinking: A broad coping variable with specific components. *Journal of Personality and Social Psychology, 57*, 332–349.
Erikson, E. H. (1963). *Childhood and society*. New York: Norton.
Erikson, E. H. (1987). *A way of looking at things: Selected papers from 1930 to 1980* (S. Schein, Ed.). New York: Norton.
Frankl, V. E. (1939/1963). *Man's search for meaning*. New York: Pocket Books.
Gallup, G. G. (1968). Mirror-image stimulation. *Psychological Bulletin, 70*, 782–793.
Greenberg, M. T. (1999). Attachment and psychopathology in childhood. In J. Cassidy & P. R, Shaver (Eds.), *Handbook of attachment* (pp. 469–496). New York: Guilford Press.
Harter, S. (1999). *The construction of the self*. New York: Guilford Press.
Hazan, C., & Shaver, P. R. (1990). Love and work: An attachment-theoretical perspective. *Journal of Personality and Social Psychology, 59*, 270–280.
Kagan, J., Kearsley, R. B., & Zelazo, P. R. (1978). *Infancy: Its place in human development*. Cambridge, MA: Harvard University Press.
Kanner, L. (1943). Autistic disturbance of affective contact. *Nervous Child, 2*, 217–250.
Klohnen, E. C., & Bera, S. (1998). Behavioral and experiential patterns of avoidantly and securely attached women across adulthood: A 31-year longitudinal perspective. *Journal of Personality and Social Psychology, 74*, 211–223.
Kohlberg, L. (1969). Stage and sequence: The cognitive-developmental approach to socialization. In D. A. Goslin (Ed.), *Handbook of socialization theory and research* (pp. 347–480). Chicago: Rand McNally.

Lyons-Ruth, K., & Jacobvitz, V. (1999). Attachment disorganization: Unresolved loss, relational violence, and lapses in behavioral and attentional strategies. In J. Cassidy & P. R. Shaver (Eds.), *Handbook of attachment* (pp. 520–554). New York: Guilford Press.

Meltzoff, A. N., & Moore, M. K. (1977). Imitation of facial and manual gestures by human neonates, *Science, 198*, 75–78.

Myers, D. G. (2002). *Intuition, its powers and perils.* New Haven, CT: Yale University Press.

Norris, P., & Epstein, S. (2011). An experiential thinking style: Its facets and relations with objective and subjective criterion variables. *Journal of Personality and Social Psychology, 79*, 1049–1079.

O'Brien, E. J., & Epstein, S. (1974). Naturally occurring changes in self-esteem *Personality and Social Psychology Bulletin, 1*, 384–386.

O'Brien, E. J., & Epstein, S. (1988). *The multi-dimensional self-esteem inventory.* Odesa, FL: Psychological Assessment Resources.

Piaget, J. (1929/1975). *The child's conception of the world.* Totowa, NJ: Littlefield, Adams.

Piaget, J. *(1973). The affective unconscious and the cognitive unconscious, Journal of the American Psychoanalytic Association, 21*, 249–261.

Rogers, C. R. (1951). *Client-centered therapy: Its current practice, implications, and theory.* Boston: Houghton.

Rosenstein, D., & Oster, H. (1988). Differential facial responses to four basic tastes. *Child Development, 59*, 1555–1568.

Rothbard, J. C., & Shaver, P. R. (1994). Continuity of attachment across the life span. In M. B. Sperling & W. H. Berman (Eds.), *Attachment in adults: Clinical and developmental perspectives* (pp. 31–71). New York: Guilford Press.

Sansavini, A., Bertonicini, J., & Giovanelli, F. (1997). Newborns discriminate the rhythm of multi-syllabic stressed words. *Developmental Psychology, 33*, 3–11.

Shaver, P. R., & Brennan, K. A. (1992). Attachment styles and the "big five" personality traits: Their connections with each other and with romantic relationship outcomes. *Personality and Social Psychology Bulletin, 18*, 536–545.

Shaver, P. R., & Hazan, C. (1994). Attachment. In A. L. Weber & J. H. Harvey (Eds.), *Perspectives on close relationships* (pp. 110–130). Boston: Allyn & Bacon.

Sullivan, H. S. (1953). *The interpersonal theory of psychiatry.* New York: W. W. Norton.

Walker, L. J. (1988). The development of moral reasoning. *Annals of Child Development, 55*, 677–691.

Wark, G. R., & Krebs, D. L. (1996). Gender and dilemma differences in real-life moral judgment. *Developmental Psychology, 32*, 220–230.

CHAPTER 7

Coping and Defense Mechanisms

Coping with stress has been among the most studied topics in psychology. The results, however, have been disappointing. In a special section of the *American Psychologist* devoted to stress and coping, Somerfield and McCrae (2000) summed up the accomplishments of the research as follows: "In fact, as the following articles document, the study of human adaptational processes is in crisis. Two decades of concentrated research have yielded relatively little of either clinical or theoretical value. The seemingly boundless enthusiasm for coping research seen in the 1980s has been replaced by widespread disaffection, intense scrutiny, and corresponding calls for change" (p. 620). In other articles in the same issue, more sophisticated research procedures and new areas of inquiry, such as the role of positive affect, were called for. Not surprisingly, several contributors, including Richard Lazarus (2000), who summed up the results of the research and commented on the presentations, held out the hope for a brighter future. However, I believe that unless the new research is grounded in better theory, the future results will be no more encouraging than the past research.

Coping and defense mechanisms are commonly defined as behaviors used for coming to terms with stress, with coping referring to conscious, intentional procedures and defense mechanisms referring to unconscious processes (Cramer, 2000). Although generally useful, this distinction is clouded by the influence of unconscious on conscious processes. According to cognitive-experiential theory (CET), conscious processes are often biased by unconscious processing, making the distinction between conscious and unconscious less meaningful than it appears. Moreover, the distinction does not hold up empirically if one interprets unconscious mental content from a Freudian perspective, according to which such content is considered resistant to awareness. As will be shown later, defense mechanisms clearly occur in conditions in which the mental content is readily available to awareness. The solution regarding this issue is to substitute experiential processing, which may or may not be available to awareness, for unconscious processing, which, according to Freud, is always resistant to awareness. Accordingly, I define defense mechanisms as "experientially determined automatic responses that reduce negative affect by denying or distorting reality." I define coping mechanisms as "realistic ways of responding to challenging or threatening situations." Thus, the critical distinction, according to CET, is that defense mechanisms are unrealistic whereas coping procedures are realistic. It follows that responding to an insult with a socially appropriate response is a coping response, whereas projecting one's unacceptable hostile impulses on someone else is a defense mechanism.

Having indicated how coping behavior and defense mechanisms differ according to CET, the remainder of this chapter is divided into two main sections, one on coping behavior and the other on defense mechanisms.

COPING BEHAVIOR

Limitations in Theory and in Methodology of Past Research

As an example of how limitations in theory have resulted in serious problems with research on coping and stress, let us examine a proposal about two presumably fundamental ways of coping with stress that has greatly influenced the research on coping in the past two decades. According to Lazarus, one of the most influential researchers on coping and stress, there are two fundamental kinds of coping, problem-focused and emotion-focused. To measure these two kinds of coping, Folkman and Lazarus (1988) constructed the Ways of Coping Questionnaire, which has been widely used in research on coping. In a factor analysis of the items in the questionnaire, Folkman and Lazarus found a set of factors that they believe corresponds to problem-focused and emotion-focused ways of reacting to stress. However, they failed to find primary factors of emotion- and problem-focused coping that contained subfactors. Instead, they found a group of factor that they interpreted after the fact as related to emotion-focused and problem-focused coping. Thus, their findings actually failed to support their theory that there are two basic ways of coping.

In a book that Lazarus (1991) subsequently wrote, he changed the meaning of the two kinds of coping, with problem-focused coping now referring to attempts to reduce stress by action and emotion-focused coping to attempts to reduce stress through thought or "cognitive coping strategies." Apparently, Lazarus found the first distinction wanting because some behavior could not be unequivocally labeled as one form of coping or the other and because people often used both forms of coping together. Originally, it had been expected that people would engage in problem-focused coping when possible and in emotion-focused coping when problem-focused coping was not possible or had failed. If so, people would either use one or the other form of coping in a particular situation but not both together.

The second distinction is also problematic. First, the labels are confusing because they are no longer consistent with the processes they describe. Second, the examples provided by Lazarus include some defense mechanisms, which ignore the distinction between realistic and unrealistic behavior. Third, no explanation is given as to why a few defense mechanisms, such as denial, suppression, and avoidance, are included, whereas other defense mechanisms, such as repression, projection, and displacement, are not.

The Ways of Coping Questionnaire suffers from all the conceptual problems just enumerated and is also limited by the particular items selected and the manner of test administration. Having people respond to many items with reference to a particular stressful event they report having recently experienced confounds the frequency of the kinds of stressful events people experience, along with their reactions to a particular event. Moreover, obtaining a variety of responses from a representative sample of stressful events that would justify generalizations about a person's characteristic coping style is not feasible within the limits of a single paper-and-pencil test or interview administered in a single session. Furthermore, several of the items that people rate are too vague to determine whether the behavior in question involves primarily thought or behavior. An example of such items is provided by the item "Changed or grew as a person in a good way." Did the respondent change or grow as a person as a result of behavior or thought? One cannot know without further information.

Eight scales based on factor analysis were constructed with the aim of improving the Ways of Coping Questionnaire. The scales are *Confrontive*, *Distancing*, *Self-controlling*, *Seeking social support*, *Accepting responsibility*, *Escape-avoidance*, *Planful problem-solving*, and *Positive reappraisal* (Lazarus, 1991, p. 449). Many of these scales include both emotion- and problem-focused items, so the initial presumably important distinction between problem- and emotion-focused coping that generated a great deal of research has all but disappeared. Given the conceptual difficulties with the distinction between problem- and emotion-focused coping proposed by Lazarus, it is no wonder that the vast amount of research using this distinction has produced confusing and inconsistent results.

There are at least five important limitations to much of the research on stress and coping. The major difficulty with both the past and proposed research is that it is not based on a personality theory that can guide the research and provide a framework for interpreting the results in a coherent manner. The limitations in past research as a result of inadequate theory can be summarized as follows: First, there has been insufficient attention paid to the existence of a flexible, broadly adaptive coping ability that corresponds to the concept of constructive thinking, which, according to CET, is considered to indicate primarily the intelligence of the experiential system.

Second, there has been insufficient attention paid to internal sources of threat, such as distressing thoughts and impulses. Third, there has been insufficient attention paid to the distinction between stress that may have been produced by people's own behavior and stress produced by events over which people have no control. Fourth, there has been insufficient attention to the distinction between suppressing the expression of unacceptable thoughts and having more acceptable thoughts and impulses to begin with. This distinction can be viewed as damage control versus having acceptable thoughts and impulses that can be spontaneously expressed and require no control.

What Cognitive-Experiential Theory Can Contribute to Research on Coping and Stress

Improvement in research on coping and stress requires a theory of personality that can provide an integrative framework for a coherent research program on stress and coping. In the absence of such a theory, there will continue to be isolated results that do not build on each other and that are likely to be lost in time and then rediscovered. A useful theory should facilitate the conduct and interpretation of research in three broadly general areas: the person, the situation, and their interaction. In the suggestions that follow on improving research on coping and stress from the perspective of CET, the discussion will therefore be divided into sections on the person, the situation, and their interaction. Before doing so, however, it will be helpful to provide a historical context on how this categorization has been previously regarded.

A historically important debate on the importance of the person relative to the situation took place from early in 1930 to almost 50 years later, when it was finally resolved. For a brief period, it appeared that situationists had won the day following the publication of a book by Walter Mischel in 1968, in which he claimed that the existence of traits as reliable broad behavioral dispositions was contraindicated by the finding that, with the exception of intelligence, whenever trait measures were correlated with objective data, the correlations were below 30, which he derisively referred to as "personality coefficients" (see review of the debate in Epstein & O'Brien, 1985). Since no one at first could break the presumed .30 barrier, the fields of clinical and personality psychology were thrown into disarray. A resolution that at first seemed to have some merit was that behavior is never determined by the person nor the situation alone but always by their interaction. The difficulty with this argument was that interactions fared no better in breaking the .30 barrier than main effects. The debate was finally resolved by a series of studies that demonstrated that the .30 barrier was the result of the low reliability of the objective criterion variables that had been investigated. It was shown that correlations much greater than .30 could routinely be obtained when the objective criteria were made sufficiently reliable by aggregation. It was further demonstrated that once reliability was established in the criterion variables, compelling evidence for the validity of trait variables was manifested over a wide range of measures (e.g., Epstein, 1977, 1979, 1980, 1983).

The implication of the resolution of the person-situation debate with regard to the importance of persons, situations, and their interaction is that they should not be regarded as alternative solutions to the same problem but as providing important information in their own right. Person variables provide information on broad behavioral dispositions, or traits, across situations. Situational variables provide information on situational influences across people. Interactions provide information on how different kinds of people respond to different kinds of situations. Thus, for a full understanding of behavior, it is necessary to have all three kinds of information.

Person Variables

According to CET, two kinds of person variables are particularly important in understanding how people cope with stress. One consists of individual differences in the efficacy or intelligence of the experiential system. The other consists of people's styles of thinking with regard to the degree to which they rely on experiential relative to rational processing. Cognitive-experiential theory provides reliable measures of both of these person variables.

The Constructive Thinking Inventory: A Measure of Individual Differences Primarily of the Intelligence of the Experiential System

The Constructive Thinking Inventory (CTI; Epstein, 1998, 2001) was constructed for measuring individual differences in the intelligence of the experiential system. Preliminary Items were written from hundreds of daily records made by students who recorded their emotionally significant experiences for 30 days. Additional items were obtained by observations of the thoughts and emotions of older people, by introspection related to my own thoughts preceding emotions, and by consideration of the principles and attributes of experiential processing. Reports were condensed into simple statements and made into reliable scales using standard psychometric procedures, including factor analysis and reliability procedures. According to CET, by measuring the automatic thoughts and interpretations that direct people's behavior in everyday life, the CTI should be able to determine how effectively people adapt to their environments and cope with stress (Epstein, 1998, 2001). The following is a summary of findings from the CTI that are most relevant to coping with stress.

Favorable scores on the CTI are directly associated with a wide variety of criteria of success in living, including success in the workplace, social relationships, academic achievement, emotional well-being, and physical health (e.g., Boutelle,

Epstein, & Ruddy, 1987; Epstein, 1992, 1993; Epstein & Katz, 1992; Epstein & Meier, 1989; Katz & Epstein, 1991). Scores on the CTI global scale and subscales are unrelated to intellectual intelligence but supplement it in predicting academic performance (Epstein, 1998). Apparently, good constructive thinkers are better able to reap the benefits of their intellectual ability than are poor constructive thinkers. The CTI has displaced all other measures of coping ability that have been included with it in regression equations, with the exception of predicting abilities and attributes with tests specifically designed to measure them (Epstein, 1998; Epstein & Katz, 1992; Epstein & Meier, 1989), as in the high relation between the Social Support Questionnaire (Sarason, Levine, Basham, & Sarason, 1983) and a criterion measure of social relationships. Thus, it is possible that when other general measures of coping ability are significant predictors of effective coping with stress, it may be because they are measuring aspects of constructive thinking. This can easily be determined by including such measures together with the CTI as predictor variables in regression equations.

The question may be raised as to how a single self-report instrument like the CTI can be positively associated with such a wide array of criteria for success in living. The answer is that people who automatically think and interpret events in ways that provide them with positive and adaptive views of themselves, others, and the impersonal world fare better than others in all these ways. Such people, as indicated by the subscales of the CTI, are accepting of themselves, tolerant and trusting of others, think in ways that promote effective action, live in the present, plan for the future, and do not dwell on the past. They do not overgeneralize following negative events, are not unduly sensitive to criticism, learn from their mistakes, are reasonably rather than naïvely optimistic, think in nuanced ways rather than categorically, and are realistic rather than superstitious. Given these ways of automatically thinking, feeling, and behaving, it is understandable why people who are good constructive thinkers do better on all criteria of success in living (other than abstract, intellectual problem solving) than poor constructive thinkers (Epstein, 2001).

According to CET, the CTI as a measure of individual differences in the efficacy or "intelligence" of the experiential system should be a useful measure of people's overall coping ability. So far, the research conducted with the CTI has supported its promise. The test remains to be examined with predictors of stress and coping ability other than those that have already been examined and with different populations.

The Rational-Experiential Inventory: A Measure of Individual Differences in Rational and Experiential Thinking Styles

According to CET, the extent to which people rely on their experiential and rational systems is an important measure of individual differences because it determines how people make decisions, which further determines how they experience the world and behave in it. This raises the question of how it influences the amount of stress they experience and how they cope with it.

The Rational-Experiential Inventory (REI) was constructed to investigate individual differences in experiential and rational processing. The REI is a self-report instrument with scales that indicate the degree to which people report they rely on experiential-intuitive and rational-analytical information processing (e.g., Epstein et al., 1996; Pacini & Epstein, 1999a). The items for the REI were constructed on a theoretical basis, with those for the experiential scale referring to making decisions and judgments based on feelings, immediate impressions, and intuition and those for the rational system based on making decisions and judgments based on logical, analytical, and deliberative reasoning. It might be suspected that the degree to which people engage in one of these thinking styles is inversely related to the degree to which they engage in the other thinking style. However, it has consistently been found that the two styles of thinking are independent. People can therefore be high on both thinking styles, low on both styles, or high on one thinking style and low on the other one. It has been found in several studies that a rational thinking style is inversely related to variables related to stress and coping, such as anxiety, depression, and stress in everyday life, whereas an experiential thinking style is either nonsignificantly or more weakly significantly inversely related to variables related to stress and coping (Epstein et al., 1996; Norris & Epstein, 2009; Pacini & Epstein, 1999a, 1999b).

Situation Variables

Controllable Versus Uncontrollable Stressful Events

An important distinction that has been overlooked in almost all research on stress and coping is the difference between stressful events that could have been produced by a person's own behavior and stressful events that are beyond a person's control (Epstein & Katz, 1992). Examples of the former are failing an examination, losing important items, being fired from a job, rejection by a loved one, failure of a marriage, and accidents or diseases caused by taking unreasonable risks. Examples of the latter are death of a loved one, death of a pet, serious illness unrelated to one's behavior or physical injury through no fault of one's own, and loss of income because of unavoidable circumstances. According to CET, self-produced stressful events are often the result of poor constructive thinking. People do not consciously contrive to make life stressful for themselves. Rather, they unwittingly produce stressful events because of their poor constructive thinking. This view is supported by a significant negative correlation between constructive thinking, as measured by the CTI, and the frequency of experiencing controllable stressful events. In contrast, no relation was found between constructive thinking and uncontrollable stressful events (Epstein & Katz, 1992). It was found in the same study that the number of controllable stressful events was significantly associated with total emotional symptoms, total physical symptoms, infectious diseases, psychosomatic symptoms, self-control problems, accidents, and drug problems. Uncontrollable stressful events were either unrelated to the same variables or produced much weaker relations.

The results indicate, as previously noted, that if researchers fail to distinguish between controllable and uncontrollable events, the effects they attribute solely to the unfortunate occurrence of stressors, a situation variable, may actually be determined to a considerable extent by poor constructive thinking, a person variable.

An example of work that has failed to make this distinction is the extensive research conducted with the Holmes and Rahe (1967) questionnaire on major life events. The questionnaire includes items that refer to major changes in life experiences, including such items as death of a loved one, job loss, divorce, retirement, and the empty-nest situation. The test yields a score based on the total number of such events, weighted for their self-reported stressfulness. Major life events have been found to produce significant but weak relations with a variety of health-related outcomes. It would be informative if items were written in two categories, one consisting of major life events that could have been self-produced, such as being fired from a job or a failed relationship, and the other consisting of events that are beyond an individual's control, such as being laid off from a job as a result of downsizing. If sufficient items cannot be constructed for the two categories because of ambiguities in determining personal responsibility, the test could be conducted in an interview rather than in a self-report format, with the interviewer probing for the respondent's likely contribution to the occurrence of stressful events.

A similar problem is present in a test of everyday hassles introduced by Folkman and Lazarus (1988). They conducted a series of investigations with the test in which they compared daily hassles to major life events as predictors of mental and physical well-being (DeLongis, Coyne, Dakof, Folkman, & Lazarus, 1982; Kanner, Coyne, Schaefer, & Lazarus, 1981; Lazarus & DeLongis, 1983). As a result of their findings, Lazarus concluded that "hassles are far superior to life events in predicting psychological and somatic symptoms" (Lazarus, 1984, p. 311). This finding is impossible to interpret meaningfully because the items in the daily hassles measure refer mainly to controllable stressful events, whereas the items in the major life events measure refer mainly to uncontrollable events. Thus, both tests may establish their significant relations with health-related outcomes mainly because of the inclusion of self-produced sources of stress. The reason that the questionnaire on daily hassles produces stronger relations with mental and physical well-being than the one on life events may simply be because it includes a higher proportion of stressors that may have been self-produced.

Apart from correcting the confound between self-produced and uncontrollable stressful events, studying self-produced stressful events is an important topic in its own right because it probably affects the everyday lives of most people more than do uncontrollable stressful events. People who behave in ways that contribute to a large number of stressful events in their lives are poor constructive thinkers who are likely to experience more stressful events than do those whose stressful events are not of their own making.

Inner Versus External Sources of Stress

Because the experiential system is an associative system, people routinely have thoughts and impulses that would be highly inappropriate if behaviorally enacted. A person picking up a knife may have the fleeting thought, "What if I were to stab someone with it? What if I were to stab myself?" A man seeing a sexually attractive woman might think, "What if I raped her? Could I get away with it? What would it be like for her? Would she enjoy it even as she resisted?" Most people cope adaptively with such thoughts by simply dismissing them as idle musings. However, some people experience considerable stress because they believe they are awful people for having such thoughts or that they are weak people for not being able to suppress them. Aggravating the problem, the more people attempt to suppress unacceptable thoughts or impulses, the more they tend to empower those thoughts and impulses (Wegner, 1994). The irony of the situation is that one cannot think about suppressing a thought without having the thought that one wishes to suppress. A more serious source of stress is the occurrence of antisocial thoughts or impulses accompanied by strong urges to express them. Although people often succeed in suppressing the expression of such urges, it can be at a considerable cost in stress.

The importance of recognizing the contribution of inner sources of stress is that it indicates that it is insufficient to examine only external sources of stress. It is equally important to investigate people's stress-producing thoughts and impulses, the ways people cope with them, and the most effective ways of doing so.

Stress Produced by Threats to the Fulfillment of Basic Needs or to the Validity of Basic Beliefs

How can the different sources of stress be meaningfully differentiated? I have already suggested two important ways that have been insufficiently implemented. A third way that follows directly from CET is by considering threats to the fulfillment of implicit basic needs and to the validity of implicit basic beliefs. It will be recalled that the five basic subordinate implicit needs are the need for a favorable sensory pleasure-pain balance; the need for a coherent, stable conceptual system; the need for security; the need for relatedness; and the need for self-esteem. Frustration or the threat of frustration of any of these needs and threats to or actual invalidation of any of these beliefs can be significant sources of stress. According to CET, it is insufficient to divide stressful events only according to whether they present problem-focused or emotion-focused problems or hassles versus major life events. At this point, we know little about the differences in stress associated with the different implicit needs and beliefs and how they are coped with.

Some important questions that remain to be answered include: Which implicit basic needs and beliefs are most and least often sources of stress? How serious are the consequences of stress concerning threats to the fulfillment of the different implicit needs and the invalidation of the different implicit beliefs? What kind of individuals are most and least vulnerable to stress associated with the different implicit needs and beliefs? How do people cope differently with the different kinds of stress? What kinds of coping are most and least successful in coping with threats to the different implicit needs and beliefs?

Person-Situation Interactions

There are two important kinds of information that person-situation interactions provide. First, by indicating how different kinds of people respond to different kinds of situations, person-situation interactions provide a more discriminating kind of information than broad generalizations about how people react to a particular situation or to a class of situations or how certain situations affect people in general. It thus can provide a correction for overgeneralization, which is probably all too common in research on stress and coping. Second, as will be demonstrated in an example that will shortly be presented, the more discriminating information provided by interactions can elucidate person and situation main effects.

Because there are as many person-situation interactions as there are person variables multiplied by situation variables, a very large number of interactions are possible. Thus, it is important to select for investigation those that appear particularly promising on a theoretical or empirical basis. Particularly promising candidates from the perspective of CET are the investigation of person-situation interactions in which styles of thinking, as measured by the REI, and constructive thinking, as measured by the CTI are the person variables. Promising candidates for situation variables according to CET are self-produced versus uncontrollable sources of stress, stress associated with the frustration of implicit basic needs and the invalidation of implicit basic beliefs, and inner versus external sources of stress.

To illustrate the value of studying a theoretically meaningful person-situation interaction, a study on the ratio bias (RB) phenomenon that examined the interaction of thinking styles and incentive level on nonoptimal responses in a game of chance is presented here.

As noted in Chapter 5, what makes the RB experimental paradigm particularly interesting is that it provides a conflict between experiential and rational processing to which most people respond by behaving against their better judgment. It will be recalled that most participants prefer to draw from a tray that offers a 9 percent probability of obtaining a winning red jellybean over one that offers a 10 percent probability of obtaining a winning red jellybean when the former probability is frequency advantaged for the numerator because it is a larger number (i.e., it offers more winners, e.g., 9 out of 100 in comparison to 1 out of 10 in the smaller tray). People make such a nonoptimal selection despite knowing that it is irrational, explaining that, although they know such behavior is unreasonable, they *feel* they have a better chance of drawing a winner when there are more of them. We wondered how increasing the incentive for drawing red jellybeans would affect people's behavior. Would it make them behave more or less rationally?

In a study in which we varied the level of the reward for drawing red jellybeans, most participants made fewer nonoptimal responses when the stakes were raised (Pacini, Muir, & Epstein, 1998). We concluded that although most people make nonoptimal responses when the stakes are low, they behave more rationally when the stakes are higher. This suggests that although most people give priority to their experiential processing in certain casual situations, they shift toward more rational processing in more important situations. But how general is this generalization? Does it hold for those with a predominantly experiential thinking style, as well as for those with a predominantly rational thinking style? Might those with a predominantly experiential thinking style have such confidence in their experiential processing that they become more experiential when the stakes are raised and therefore make more nonoptimal responses? To answer these questions, we conducted a study in which we examined the interaction of incentive level and thinking styles (Pacini & Epstein, 1999b).

We examined the nonoptimal responses participants made as a function of rational and experiential styles of thinking as measured by the REI, incentive level (ten cents or two dollars on each trial in which a red jellybean was drawn), and the interaction of thinking style and incentive level. We found a main effect of a rational thinking style, with highly rational thinkers making fewer nonoptimal choices than low rational thinkers. There was no main effect for an experiential thinking style. Of particular interest, there was a significant interaction between an experiential thinking style, a rational thinking style, and incentive level. On decomposing the interaction by separately analyzing groups with high and low experiential thinking styles, the rationality main effect was reproduced in both analyses. Apparently, apart from participants' experiential thinking style, if they have a highly rational thinking style, they make fewer nonoptimal responses than if they have a low rational thinking style. There was no other significant effect in the low experiential group. However, in the highly experiential group, there was a significant interaction between rationality and incentive level. Those with a low rational thinking style reacted to an increase in incentive with an increase in nonoptimal responses, whereas those with a highly rational thinking style made fewer nonoptimal responses with an increase in incentive. The interaction is interesting for two reasons. First, it qualifies the generalization from a previous study because it indicates that although most people react to an increase in incentive by making fewer nonoptimal responses, those with a highly experiential thinking style and a low rational thinking style behave in an opposite way; they make more rather than fewer nonoptimal responses with an increase in incentive. This was well illustrated by one of my undergraduate assistants who said, "Professor Epstein, I hate to tell you this, but I think you are wrong in thinking that choosing from the tray with more red jellybeans and a lower probability is a nonoptimal response. If I had to respond to the problem in a statistics class, of course I would go with the better probability, but in real life it is far better to go with the choice that offers more winners." I asked her what she would do if a million dollars were at stake, to which she replied, "Then I certainly would go with the choice that offered more winners."

The second way in which the interaction is interesting is in its elucidation of the nature of the RB phenomenon. Initially, I had suspected that the magnitude of the RB phenomenon would be inversely related to a rational thinking style and directly related to an experiential thinking style. The expectation that a rational thinking style would be inversely related to nonoptimal responding was supported in the present study, but the expectation about an experiential thinking style was not. However, the influence of an experiential thinking style was exhibited by an interaction in the highly experiential thinking style group of a rational thinking style and incentive level.

The presence of a main effect for rationality, the absence of a main effect for experientiality, and the presence of a significant interaction between incentive level and rationality only for the highly experiential group can be explained as follows. The absence of a main effect for experientiality can be attributed to a universal tendency to attend to numerosity. This follows from the consideration that attention to frequencies is one of the most fundamental of all cognitive activities, as indicated by its presence in nonhuman animals, as well as in preverbal children (Gallistel, 1989; Gallistel & Gelman, 1992; Geary, 1995; Starkey, 1992). Individual differences in nonoptimal responses must therefore be determined by the degree of rational control, which accounts for the main effect for rationality. The occurrence of the interaction between incentive level and rationality only for the highly experiential group indicates that if participants have a highly experiential thinking style and low rational thinking style, they react directly to an increase in incentive level by making more nonoptimal responses. If they have a highly experiential thinking style and a highly rational thinking style, they overcompensate for a tendency to make nonoptimal responses to an increase in incentive by making fewer nonoptimal responses to an increase in incentive. In summary, what one learns about the dynamics of the RB phenomenon from the rational-experiential-incentive interaction is that the overt responses to the jellybeans are determined not by individual differences in the initial attraction to the tray with more red jellybeans, which is probably a universal tendency, but to individual differences in the rational control of the nonoptimal tendency.

DEFENSE MECHANISMS

Anna Freud (1946) made a major contribution to psychoanalysis with her views on defensive processes. She considered the essence of defense mechanisms to be the reduction or avoidance of anxiety by unconsciously denying, distorting, or falsifying reality (AFreud, 1946). Note the similarity to my definition, which is that defense mechanisms are experientially determined automatic reactions that reduce or avoid anxiety by distorting or denying reality. However, there is one important difference: she assumes that defense mechanisms operate "unconsciously," whereas I assume that they operate "experientially" and that people can, therefore, be aware of their operation. I will shortly demonstrate how defense mechanisms can be used to reduce anxiety in situations in which repression is not involved because people are aware of the source of their distress. By lifting the restriction of requiring repression, the way is opened for recognizing an important class of defensive processes that has not received the attention it deserves.

Defense Mechanisms as Avoidance Conditioning

As noted in Chapter 5, defense mechanisms can be viewed as learned avoidance reactions. It will be recalled that in avoidance conditioning an animal receives a signal, such as a tone, which is followed by a noxious stimulus, such as an electric shock. By pressing a bar after the tone, the animal can avoid receiving the shock. After sufficient practice in pressing the bar to avoid the noxious stimulus, the animal calmly goes about its activities, nonchalantly pressing the bar whenever the tone sounds. The avoidance response at this stage cannot be considered a defense mechanism according to my definition because the response is realistic; the animal avoids receiving the shock it would receive if it did not press the bar. However, if the electric shock were to be discontinued, the avoidance response would qualify as a defense mechanism because there is no realistic threat. Such avoidance responses are highly resistant to extinction because extinction requires confronting a stimulus in the absence of reinforcement, and the animal avoids such exposure.

How similar is avoidance conditioning in nonhuman animals to the use of defense mechanisms in humans? Recall that, according to CET, the experiential system in humans is similar to the experiential system in other animals. Accordingly, humans can be expected to exhibit avoidance conditioning within their experiential systems. In other words, people can automatically respond in the absence of a real threat and of repression with avoidance reactions that reduce anxiety, thus corresponding to my definition of a defense mechanism. Such defense mechanisms obviously do not involve protection against anxiety resulting from awareness.

An example of a defense mechanism based on avoidance conditioning is exhibited by someone who learned in childhood to think in a way that avoided awareness of anxiety-producing material and who continues the avoidance reaction after it is no longer necessary. If such a person were to achieve intellectual insight, it would make no difference unless she extinguished the reaction by confronting her fear and learning that the threat no longer existed. In other words, she would simply be a neurotic with intellectual insight.

As another example of a maladaptive defense mechanism in which repression is not involved, recall the case of the fighter pilot who was aware of the source of his compulsive maladaptive defensive reaction. He was nevertheless unable to control his sensitivity to anything flying in his direction from the left and his compulsion to fire at it. The sensitivity and compulsion can both be considered as defense mechanisms according to my definition because they automatically reduce anxiety, which, in the case of the sensitivity, is the fear of being surprised and, in the case of the compulsion, is a feeling of helplessness. Moreover, both are unrealistic to the point of endangering the pilot's life. Clearly then, there are defense mechanisms that do not involve repression and that can be highly maladaptive and life-threatening even among otherwise normal people. But is this always true of defense mechanisms? Are there some defense mechanisms that are actually adaptive and, if so, what are the characteristics that distinguish them from maladaptive defenses?

Defense Mechanisms That are Adaptive

If the essence of a defense mechanism is an automatic, unrealistic avoidance response, then the question arises of whether defense mechanisms are necessarily maladaptive because they are unrealistic. The *Diagnostic and Statistical Manual of Mental Disorders* (DSM-IV-TR) Defensive Functioning Scale

(American Psychiatric Association, 2000) lists defense mechanisms hierarchically according to how maladaptive they are. At the top of the list are the most adaptive defense mechanisms, which include altruism, humor, sublimation, and suppression. At the bottom of the list are highly unrealistic defense mechanisms such as "delusional projection" and "psychotic denial." Projection and denial, which are less unrealistic, are placed in the middle of the list. From this, it appears that the distinguishing feature between adaptive and maladaptive defense mechanisms is the degree to which they are unrealistic. However, it turns out not to be so simple. Although the degree to which a defense mechanism is unrealistic is an important consideration in evaluating how pathological or maladaptive it is, it is not the only consideration, nor for that matter the most important one. To determine whether a defense mechanism is adaptive or maladaptive, it is necessary to consider its cost-benefit consequences. Does its benefit exceed its cost or is the reverse true? It is therefore necessary to consider what would likely happen if the defense were not used and what adaptive properties a defense mechanism may have in addition to reducing anxiety. Despite the problems an unrealistic defense mechanism may create, it may prevent the person from experiencing more serious problems. For example, by using the defense mechanism of projection, a paranoid person who is able to function to some extent in everyday life may avoid becoming a disorganized schizophrenic who is unable to care for himself. Thus, what appeared to be a highly maladaptive defense mechanism may, on further consideration, be considered an adaptive response. Unsatisfactory as it may be, the defense is the best bargain available to a person at a particular time for a particular situation. This is not meant to imply that all defense mechanisms are necessarily adaptive in an overall sense. Some defense mechanisms, such as the one used by the pilot who avoided attacks from the left by exposing himself to attacks from the right, are clearly a poor bargain that can cost a life. The point is that a defense mechanism cannot be properly evaluated without considering what it accomplishes at what cost.

Almost any defense mechanism can be used in an adaptive or maladaptive way. Consider denial as an example. Denial is listed in the DSM-IV scale as an immature, maladaptive defense. That it can be highly adaptive, however, is indicated by research on the mastery of anxiety in sport parachuting. Research on sport parachuting was discussed in Chapter 5 with reference to approach-avoidance conflict (e.g., Epstein & Fenz, 1962, 1965; Fenz & Epstein, 1967, 1969). It will now be reconsidered for what it can contribute to an understanding of defense mechanisms. In our research with parachutists, we found that denial plays an important role in the mastery of anxiety by novice parachutists. An important challenge for them is to avoid an incapacitating level of fear that could interfere with their performance. They attempted to control their anxiety by concentrating on what they have to do to perform well and by avoiding anxiety-producing thoughts. In a word-association test, they often misperceived anxiety-related stimulus words as other words. When we questioned them about such associations, they reported that they mistook a stimulus word for a similar word that rhymed with it. As a further indication of the avoidance of anxiety-producing thoughts, their reaction times to anxiety words were elevated compared to other words. In their responses to a Thematic Apperception Test that included pictures suggestive of parachuting, they often told stories that emphasized the attractive aspects of parachuting and that denied its threatening aspects. One example of denial of fear is the following response to a picture of a parachutist in an aircraft whose face was carefully drawn to have a neutral expression: "He is not afraid. It just looks that way because of the wind in his face." The denial of fear and the misperception of fear-related stimuli were clearly the result of a defensive process and cannot be attributed to the characteristics of the stimuli, as indicated by the absence of such responses by nonparachutists and by novice parachutists on a control day when they were not jumping. Moreover, experienced parachutists before a jump did not exhibit this defense mechanism. When we tested novice parachutists repeatedly as they gained experienced, we found their denial of fear gradually decreased as they gained mastery.

Research on parachuting has identified an important characteristic of adaptive defense mechanisms. They are flexible defenses that are used to pace the experience of anxiety by keeping it within manageable limits during the period in which mastery is being attempted, and they are gradually surrendered as they become unnecessary. In contrast to parachutists who behaved in this manner, there were two women who, instead of using defensive processes to pace their anxiety, exhibited an all-or-none defensive reaction that involved either complete denial of threat or becoming completely overwhelmed with anxiety when denial of threat was no longer possible. Unlike the other novice parachutists, who were clearly anxious and absorbed with controlling their anxiety, these women were relaxed, laughing, and chattering. This made the other parachutists feel inferior because they could not relax, but were grim, mainly silent, and anxious. Every once in a while, one of them would attempt a joke to break the tension, and the others would laugh with exaggerated hilarity. When it came time to board the aircraft for their first jump, both women were seized with panic and aborted the jump. One began to vomit and the other was ashen-faced and looked as if she were about to faint. The lesson their behavior provides is that adaptive defenses in response to threatening situations serve to keep anxiety within manageable limits and do not completely avoid the confrontation with realistic sources of threat. If the denial of the threat is too complete, the person is overwhelmed when conditions arise in which the denial cannot be maintained, as in the case of the two women when confronted with boarding the aircraft. That the process of mastering a stressful experience by pacing the awareness of anxiety-producing cues according to what a person can manage without interfering with performance is highly general is suggested by the same process having been described in combat pilots in the Eighth Air Force during the Second World War (Bond, 1952).

Studies of people's reactions to life-threatening diseases also indicate that denial used to keep anxiety within manageable limits but relinquished when no longer necessary is adaptive (Pennebaker, 1993; Suls & Fletcher, 1985), whereas complete denial is maladaptive. Patients with life-threatening diseases, including cancer, diabetes, and kidney failure, who exhibited a strong denial of threat failed to comply with medical advice (Farberow, 1980; Goldstein, 1980; Katz, Weiner, Gallagher, & Hellman, 1970; Oettingen, 1996). By denying the seriousness of their illness, they reduced their momentary anxiety but at the cost of being insufficiently motivated to take constructive action. Clearly, depending on how it is used, denial can be adaptive or maladaptive.

There are two crucial tests for determining whether denial is used in an adaptive manner. One concerns the degree of denial. It should not consist of an all-or-none response. Rather, it should be maintained at a manageable level that allows mental and behavioral coping to take place, such as following medical recommendations or learning to properly deploy a parachute and control one's descent. The other test concerns how the person behaves over time. An adaptive defense paces the experience of anxiety and is surrendered when it is no longer necessary, whereas a maladaptive defense is maintained when it is no longer required.

Some Conventional Defense Mechanisms

Given the definition of defense mechanisms as automatic reactions that reduce negative affect by denying, avoiding, or distorting reality, defense mechanisms are used more commonly than is generally recognized. This follows from the influence of the hedonic principle on conscious thinking and behavior. Since the hedonic principle operates automatically with the aim of increasing positive affect and reducing negative affect, any behavior in which it promotes unrealistically favorable thinking or behavior would qualify as a defense mechanism. Accordingly, there is no limit to the kind of thoughts and behavior that can be regarded as defense mechanisms. Thus, it is not possible to provide a complete list of defensive operations. Nevertheless, it is of interest to examine some conventional defense mechanisms that are of particular significance. According to Anna Freud (1946), the principal defense mechanisms are repression, projection, reaction formation, and fixation. They will be examined shortly from the perspective of CET, and I will include two additional defense mechanisms that are important for understanding people's behavior in their everyday lives, namely, rationalization and displacement.

It will be seen that, for defense mechanisms based on repression, the explanations provided by CET are the same as those provided by psychoanalytic theory, with the exception that, according to Freudian theory, the conflict is between the id and the ego, whereas in CET it is between the experiential and rational systems. A more important difference exists when defense mechanisms occur in the absence of repression.

Repression

As previously noted, repression, from the perspective of CET, is an automatic mental avoidance response. Under the influence of the hedonic principle, people avoid awareness of distressing mental content by letting their minds veer off from a direction that was producing twinges of anxiety. With increasing practice in making avoidance responses, the anxiety is reduced until it becomes a very weak, albeit sufficient, signal for initiating an avoidance response. Because repression involves an automatic avoidance of the negative affect that would be elicited by awareness of taboo mental content, it clearly qualifies as a defense mechanism from the positions of both Freudian theory and CET.

Projection

Projection refers to attributing one's own unacceptable thoughts and impulses to another person. It operates according to the hedonic principle by avoiding the negative affect that would occur if the person became aware that the unacceptable thoughts or impulses were his or her own. Because the experiential system is an associative system, unacceptable mental content is readily transferred to someone else's thoughts under the influence of the hedonic principle. It is hedonically supported because it feels better to oppose the unacceptable thoughts and impulses of someone else than to acknowledge them as one's own. Projection qualifies as a defense mechanism according to both CET and psychoanalysis because it automatically avoids negative affect by distorting reality.

Reaction Formation

Reaction formation consists of consciously thinking or behaving in ways that are opposite to a person's unacceptable unconscious thoughts and impulses. As an associative system, the experiential system readily associates behavior with its opposite. When a person substitutes a desirable thought for an unacceptable one, it not only reduces negative affect, it increases positive affect. The person thinks "I am not a bad. selfish person. I am a good. helpful one."

The solution is unrealistic because of the denial of the thoughts and feelings that are driving the response. It is also unrealistic because the behavior often has a compulsive quality about it and is carried out in a manner that often indirectly accomplishes the intent of the denied beliefs and feelings, such as by making the target of the reaction formation feel guilty or unworthy by excessive kindness to the person.

Fixation

Fixation is viewed somewhat differently in psychoanalysis and in learning theory. In psychoanalysis, it refers to a person's attachment to a particular developmental stage being so strong that advancement to a more mature stage is impeded or prevented. Fixation as viewed in learning theory refers to rigidly adhering to a response acquired under stress and resisting its modification or extinction. As a result, the response, such as a conditioned avoidance response, is often maintained under conditions in which the original threat is no longer present. Ironically, it is difficult to see how fixation can be regarded as a defense mechanism from a psychoanalytic perspective because neither kind of fixation requires repression. In contrast, fixation readily qualifies as a defense mechanism according to its definition by CET because it is an automatic, unrealistic way of reducing anxiety when the original threat is no longer present.

Regression

In regression, behavior under a high degree of stress returns to a previous level of development that involved a degree of fixation that had permitted only a tenuous progression. As an example, a child who gave up sucking his thumb a year ago returns to it when threatened by the birth of a sibling who is attracting most of his mother's attention. Although regression is listed as a principal defense mechanism by Anna Freud, it is difficult to see how it can qualify as a psychoanalytic defense mechanism because there is no apparent threat to awareness that motivates its adoption. It does, however, qualify as a defense mechanism according to CET because it is an automatic response that reduces negative affect by behavior that is inappropriate to the age at which it occurs.

Rationalization

Although it is not listed among Anna Freud's principal defense mechanisms, rationalization is included here because, according to CET, it is a defense mechanism that everyone routinely engages in as part of their everyday information processing. It is therefore probably the most common of all defense mechanisms. The reason it routinely occurs is because the experiential system normally operates outside of awareness. When seeking to explain their behavior, people rely on a rational interpretation of why they behaved as they did. Under the combined influence of the hedonic principle of the experiential system and the reality principle of the rational system, they usually obtain an explanation that provides the most desirable interpretation they can think of that is within acceptable reality limits. Thus, the essence of such rationalization, according to CET, is the attribution to the rational system of what was primarily determined by the experiential system. Rationalization qualifies as a defense mechanism, according to CET, because it automatically reduces negative affect by engaging in information processing that distorts reality. It probably also qualifies as a defense mechanism according to the psychoanalytic position because, in most cases, people resist awareness of the source of their rationalization.

The reason rationalization has not received much attention in psychoanalysis is very likely because it is a common reaction in everyday behavior and therefore not very useful in understanding pathology. In contrast, it is considered of great importance in CET.

Displacement

Displacement refers to the substitution of an uninhibited, related response for one that is inhibited. An example is someone expressing anger provoked by the behavior of an unacceptable or unsafe target toward a more acceptable or vulnerable target. Displacement occurs for several reasons, according to CET, and it is far more common than has been recognized. Often, it occurs as the result of repression. An example is a person with an Oedipus complex who is sexually attracted to women similar to his mother but not so similar as to evoke avoidance reactions. This form of displacement, which is the result of repression, corresponds to the Freudian model of displacement. It also fits Miller's (1948) representation of displacement by the intersection of a steeper gradient of inhibition than of expression. However, Miller's model is more general than the psychoanalytic model because it does not require the occurrence of repression.

A simple example of displacement that is not based on repression is indicated in the following case. A number of years ago, I observed children in a nursery school who were having a free-play period in which they could play with whatever toys or games they wished. Some played with other children, and some played alone. When the teacher was preoccupied with soothing a distressed child, one of the younger children, whom I shall call John, was building a fort out of blocks for his toy solders. An older child was aimlessly wandering around the room looking at what the other children were doing. He appeared disgruntled and made disparaging remarks to some of the children, telling them that what they were doing was stupid. Finally, he came to where John was playing. He kicked down John's blocks, and John began to cry. The older child then taunted him, "Cry-baby, cry-baby! I knew you are a cry-baby!" John stifled his crying, wiped away his tears, and left the scene. He aimlessly wandered around the room silently sobbing until he came upon a child who was younger and smaller than he. The child was busily building a tower of blocks. John kicked down the blocks and began to laugh. The other child began to cry, and John taunted him, "Cry-baby, cry-baby! You sure are a cry-baby!" The child cried louder. The teacher ran over, scolded John, and gave him a time-out. I observed John carefully. He had a satisfied smirk on his face and was humming.

Notice that the displacement had nothing to do with a taboo thought or impulse. John could not strike back at the older child, but he could attack a younger child, and, by doing so, it restored his self-esteem and assuaged his feelings of distress. Instead of being a helpless victim, he became a powerful aggressor, something that the experiential system, operating under the hedonic principle, appreciated. Clearly, such displacement does not conform to Freud's definition of a defense mechanism based on repression, but it does conform to the definition provided by CET because the displacement reduced negative affect and, in this case, even contributed to positive affect, and it did so automatically and unrealistically. John's behavior was unrealistic because he made a younger child cry, which was not inappropriate for the child's age, so John could unfairly call him a cry baby.

As I have pointed out elsewhere (Epstein, 1967), displacement also is an automatic adaptive process used in the control of arousal. Some years ago, I explained this process by proposing a Law of Excitatory Modulation (LEM). According to the LEM, when arousal mounts beyond a certain point, it triggers an inhibitory reaction that has a steeper gradient, which increasingly reduces and finally reverses the net increase in the mounting arousal produced by the high level of stimulation. The LEM not only explains Pavlov's (1927) observations of paradoxical reactions as a function of mounting excitation, it also explains the prevalent displacement that occurs in dreams, which I suggest occurs not only to avoid awareness of taboo mental content but also more generally to safeguard sleep by controlling arousal (Epstein, 1999).

REFERENCES

American Psychiatric Association (2000). *Diagnostic and Statistical Manual of Mental Disorders (DSM-IV-TR) Defensive Functioning Scale.*

Bond, D. D. (1952). *The love and fear of flying.* New York: International Universities Press.

Boutelle, R., Epstein, S.,& Ruddy, M. C. (1987). The relation of essential hypertension to feelings of anxiety, depression, and anger. *Psychiatry*, *50*, 206–217.
Cramer, P. (2000). Defense mechanisms in psychology today: Further processes for adaptation. *American Psychologist*, *55*, 637–646.
DeLongis, A., Coyne, J. C., Dakof, G., Folkman, S., & Lazarus, R. S. (1982). Relationship of daily hassles, uplifts, and major life events to health status. *Health Psychology*, *1*, 119–136.
Epstein, S. (1967). Toward a unified theory of anxiety. In B. Maher (Ed.), *Progress in experimental personality research* (vol. 4, pp. 1–89). New York: Academic Press.
Epstein, S. (1977). Traits are alive and well. In S. Magnusson & N. S. Endler (Eds.), Personality at the cross-roads: Current issues in interactional psychology (pp. 83–98). Hillsdal, NJ: Lawrence Erlbaum Associates.
Epstein, S. (1979). The stability of behavior: I. On predicting most of the people much of the time. *Journal of Personality and Social Psychology*, *37*, 1097–1126.
Epstein, S. (1980). The stability of behavior: II. Implications for psychological research. *American Psychologist*, *35*, 790–806.
Epstein, S. (1983). Aggregation and beyond: Some basic issues on the prediction of behavior. *Journal of Personality*, *51*, 360–392.
Epstein, S. (1992). Constructive thinking and mental and physical well-being. In L. Montada, S. H. Filipp, & M. J. Lerner (Eds.), Life crises and experiences of loss in adulthood (pp. 385–409). Hillsdale, NJ: Erlbaum.
Epstein, S. (1993). Bereavement from the perspective of cognitive-experiential self-theory. In M. S. Stroebe, W. Stroebe, & R. O. Hansson (Eds.), Handbook of bereavement: Theory, research, and intervention (pp. 112–125). New York: Cambridge University Press.
Epstein, S. (1998). Constructive thinking: The key to emotional intelligence. Westport, CT: Greenwood Publishing.
Epstein, S. (1999). The interpretation of dreams from the perspective of cognitive-experiential self-theory. In J. A. Singer, & P. Salovey (Eds.), At play in the fields of consciousness: Essays in honor of Jerome L. Singer (pp. 59–82). Mahway, NJ: Lawrence Erlbaum.
Epstein, S. (2001). Manual for the Constructive Thinking Inventory. Odessa, FL: Psychological Assessment Resources.
Epstein, S., & Fenz, W. D. (1962). Theory and experiment on the measurement of approach-avoidance conflict. *Journal of Abnormal and Social Psychology*, *64*, 97–112.
Epstein, S., & Fenz, W. D. (1965). Steepness of approach and avoidance gradients in humans as a function of experience. *Journal of Experimental Psychology*, *70*, 1–12.
Epstein, S., & Katz, L. (1992). Coping ability, stress, productive load, and symptoms. *Journal of Personality and Social Psychology*, *62*, 813–825.
Epstein, S., & Meier, P. (1989). Constructive thinking: A broad coping variable with specific components. *Journal of Personality and Social Psychology*, *57*, 332–349.
Epstein, S., & O'Brien, E. J. (1985). The person-situation debate in historical perspective. *Psychological Bulletin*, *98*, 513–537.
Epstein, S., Pacini, R., Denes-Raj, V., & Heier, H. (1996). Individual differences in intuitive-experiential and analytical-rational thinking styles. Journal of Personality and Social Psychology, *71*, 390–405.
Fenz, W. D., & Epstein, S. (1967). Gradients of physiological arousal of experienced and novice parachutists as a function of an approaching jump. *Psychosomatic Medicine*, *29*, 33–51.
Fenz, W. D., & Epstein, S. (1969). Stress: In the air. *Psychology Today*, *9/1969*, 27–29.

Farberow, N. L. (1980). Indirect self-destructive behavior in diabetics and Buerger's disease patients. In N. L. Faberow (Ed.), The many faces of suicide: Indirect self-destructive behavior (pp. 79–88). New York: McGraw Hill Goldstein.

Folkman & Lazarus. (1988). Manual for the Ways of Coping Questionnaire. Palo Alto, CA: Consulting Psychologists Press. Published later by Mind Garden.

Freud, A. (1946). The ego and the mechanisms of defense. New York: International Universities Press.

Gallistel, C. R. (1989). Animal cognition: The representation of space, time, and number. *Annual Review of Psychology, 40*, 155–189.

Gallistel, C. R., & Gelman, R. (1992). Preverbal and verbal counting and computation. Special issue: Numerical cognition. *Cognition, 44*, 43–74.

Geary, D. C. (1995). Reflections of evolution and culture in children's cognition: Implications for mathematic development and instruction. *American Psychologist, 50*, 24–37.

Goldstein, A. M. (1980). The "uncooperative" patient: Self-destructive behavior in hemodialysis patients. In N. L. Farberow (Ed.), The many faces of suicide: Indirect self-destructive behavior (pp. 89–98). New York: McGraw-Hill.

Holmes, T. H.,and Rahe, R. H. (1967). The social readjustment rating scale. *Journal of Psychosomatic Research, 11*, 213–218.

Kanner, A., Coyne, J. C., Schaefer, C., & Lazarus, R. S. (1981). Comparison of two modes of stress management: Daily hassles and uplifts versus major life events. *Journal of Behavioral Medicine, 4*, 1–39.

Katz, J. L., Weiner, H., Gallagher, T. F., & Hellman, I. (1970). Stress, distress, and ego-defenses. *Archives of General Psychology, 23*, 131–142.

Katz, L., & Epstein, S. (1991). Constructive thinking and coping with laboratory-induced stress. *Journal of Personality and Social Psychology, 61*, 789–800.

Kirkpatrick, L. A., & Epstein, S. (1992). Cognitive-experiential self-theory and subjective probability: Further evidence for two conceptual systems. *Journal of Personality and Social Psychology, 63*, 534–544.

Lazarus, R. S. (1984). Puzzles in the study of daily hassles. *Journal of Behavioral Medicine, 7*, 375–389.

Lazarus, R. S. (1991). Emotion and adaptation. New York: Oxford University Press.

Lazarus, R. S. (2000). Toward better research on stress and coping. *American Psychologist, 55*, 665–673.

Lazarus, R. S., & DeLongis, A. (1983). Psychological stress and coping in aging. *American Psychologist, 38*, 245–254.

Miller, N. E. (1948). Theory and experiment relating psychoanalytic to stimulus response generalization. *Journal of Abnormal and Social Psychology, 43*, 155–178.

Mischel, W. (1968). Personality and assessment. New York: Wiley.

Oettingen, G. (1996). Positive fantasy and motivation. In P. M. Gollwitzer & J. A. Bargh (Eds.), The psychology of action (pp. 236–259). New York: Guilford Press.

Pacini, R., & Epstein, S. (1999a). The interaction of three facets of concrete thinking in a game of chance. *Thinking and Reasoning, 5*, 303–325.

Pacini, R., & Epstein, S. (1999b). The relation of rational and experiential information processing styles to personality, basic beliefs, and the ratio-bias phenomenon. *Journal of Personality and Social Psychology, 76*, 972–987.

Pacini, R., Muir, F., & Epstein, S. (1998). Depressive realism from the perspective of cognitive-experiential self-theory. *Journal of Personality and Social Psychology, 74*, 1056–1068.

Pavlov, I. P. (1928). Lectures on conditioned reflexes.(Translated by W. Horsely Gantt). New York: Liveright Publishing Corp.
Pennebaker, J. W. (1993). Putting stress into words: Health, linguistic, and therapeutic implications. *Behavior Research and Therapy*, *6*, 539–548.
Sarason, I. G. Levine, H. M., Basham, R. B.,& Sarason, B. R. (1983). Assessing social support: The Social Support Questionnaire. *Journal of Personality and Social Psychology*, *44*, 127–130.
Somerfield, M. R., & McCrae, R. (2000). Stress and coping research. Methodological challenges, theoretical advances, and clinical applications. *American Psychologist*, *55*, 620–625.
Starkey, P. (1992). The early development of numerical reasoning. *Cognition*, *43*, 93–126.
Suls, J., & Fletcher, B. (1985). Self-attention, life-stress, and illness: A prospective study. *Psychosomatic Medicine*, *47*, 469–481.
Wegner, D. M. (1994). Ironic processes of mental control. *Psychological Review*, *101*, 34–52.

CHAPTER 8
The Maladaptive Behavior of Everyday Life

In this and the next two chapters, I discuss maladjustment from the perspective of cognitive-experiential theory (CET). I make no attempt to cover the field of abnormal psychology. Such information is readily available in many excellent textbooks, and CET has nothing new to add to most of this information. Rather, I present my views on selected topics about which I believe CET has something to contribute.

According to CET, "constructive thinking" is a concept of central importance to understanding everyday adaptive and maladaptive behavior. Constructive thinking refers to the effective operation of the experiential system in solving everyday problems in living. It therefore corresponds to the intelligence or efficacy of the experiential system. People who are good constructive thinkers automatically think and interpret events in a manner that is helpful for solving everyday problems at a minimum cost of stress to themselves and distress to others, whereas poor constructive thinkers do so in a manner that produces excessive stress for themselves and often distress for others.

Following a discussion of the implications of constructive thinking for everyday maladaptive behavior, I describe two studies that elucidate the operation of constructive thinking. This is followed by a discussion of and research on another central concept regarding everyday adjustment, namely thinking styles and, more specifically, rational and experiential styles of thinking. As will be seen, the degree to which people engage in one of these thinking styles is related to adjustment and maladjustment, whereas the degree to which they engage in the other thinking style is related to other important attributes. Next, I discuss a few other topics I consider of special significance for understanding everyday maladaptive behavior. This is followed by a consideration of what it means to be a fully functioning person according to CET.

MALADAPTIVE EVERYDAY BEHAVIOR

There is no clear dividing line between everyday maladaptive behavior and more serious problems. However, for practical reasons in the discussion of neurosis in the next chapter, I consider neurosis as beginning at a level of dysfunction in which people are almost continuously distressed or have difficulty in functioning adequately in their everyday lives. I will consider those with everyday maladaptive behavior as having less general, less continuous, and less debilitating difficulties in their everyday lives. They have problems in their lives such as not being able to get along with some of their family members or with some of the people with whom they work, in which their own behavior plays a significant role in the maladaptive relationships; they have specific fears, such as fear of flying or fear of riding on a chair lift, that keeps them from skiing; or they are excessively sensitive and take things too personally. Such problems are inconvenient and distressing, but they are far from incapacitating. Neurotic problems include a broad range of issues that overlaps with everyday problems in living but also extend beyond them, up to a point of making a person incapacitated and unable to work. Included among such states are anxiety, depression, and aggression that make it difficult for people to find a reasonable degree of happiness in living or be able to live harmoniously with others. Here, I discuss everyday problems in living and, in the next chapter, I discuss neurosis.

If we wish to understand people's everyday maladaptive behavior, we have to understand the nature of their constructive thinking. There are two fundamental aspects of constructive thinking: content and process. Content refers to the implicit beliefs in people's experiential systems about themselves, others, and the impersonal world, and process refers to the manner in which people think. A good constructive thinker has a relatively high level of self-acceptance, is reasonably but not excessively trusting of others, and has favorable views about the impersonal world, but not naïvely so. Thought process refers to the characteristic, non–content related ways in which people think, such as whether they overgeneralize, think categorically, or think in an overcontrolled or undercontrolled manner. A good constructive thinker automatically thinks and interprets events in a manner that contributes to his own and others' welfare. A poor constructive thinker thinks and interprets events in a manner that produces stress for the self and distress for others.

The Measurement of Constructive Thinking

If one is to study constructive thinking, it is useful to have an instrument for measuring it. To this end, my associates and I constructed the Constructive Thinking Inventory (CTI; Epstein, 2001; Epstein & Meier, 1989). The items in the CTI are primarily based on the reports of people who kept daily records over an extended period of their emotions and the automatic interpretations they made of the events that immediately preceded and triggered the emotions they experienced. Items constructed from these reports were supplemented with others derived from observations of the emotions that other people and I had in response to everyday events and by the views of cognitive-behavioral therapists about the automatic thoughts and interpretations of their clients that determined their maladaptive feelings and behavior (e.g., Beck, 1976; Ellis & Grieger, 1977) and influenced their conscious thinking.

Using factor analytic and reliability procedures, the items were reduced to five scales. Later, a sixth scale was added (Epstein & Meier, 1989). The CTI is a hierarchically organized test that includes scales at three levels of generality. At the most general level is a global score of constructive thinking that includes all the items in the CTI except for a few that produced low loadings on a general factor when the items were factor analyzed. At the next general level are six more specific scales: Emotional Coping, Behavioral Coping, Categorical Thinking, Naïve Optimism, Esoteric Thinking, and Personal Superstitious Thinking. All but one of these categories has several subscales that refer to particular beliefs and ways in which people think. For example, Emotional Coping includes subscales such as dwelling on unfavorable past events and overgeneralizing.

The content of the scales and subscales of the CTI and their relations with a variety of criterion measures in many studies (see review in Epstein, 2001) provide a rich source of information about the influence of people's automatic thinking and interpretation of events on their everyday feelings, behavior, and adjustment. People's performance on the CTI has been found to be related to emotional adjustment, ability to cope with stress, physical well-being, performance at work, academic performance, social facility, leadership ability, and absence of drug abuse. (For a more thorough description of the construction of the CTI and a review of the research conducted with it, see Epstein, 1998, 2001.)

The question may be raised as to how a single test can be predictive of such a wide variety of abilities and attributes. The answer is that, just as there is a general factor of intellectual intelligence that affects a wide range of intellectual abilities, there is also a general factor of experiential intelligence that affects almost all nonintellectual abilities (Epstein, 2001, 2012). Experiential intelligence has been popularized under the concept of emotional intelligence, which has been criticized because many of the tests of emotional intelligence include abilities that do not involve emotions, such as social ability, ego-strength, conscientiousness, assertiveness trustworthiness, and cooperation (e.g., Daus & Ashkanasy, 2003; Locke, 2005; Murphy & Sideman, 2006). Yet the evidence suggests that all such nonintellect abilities are related (e.g., Bar-On, 1997). This indicates that emotional intelligence is an inaccurate designation of the existence of a broadly general nonintellectual kind of ability that corresponds to what can more appropriately be labeled as experiential intelligence.

Another perspective for understanding why the CTI is predictive of a wide variety of abilities and favorable attributes is provided by an examination of the scales of the CTI. Because the scales provide information on people's implicit beliefs and manner of processing information, they indicate how people automatically think and interpret events, which determines how they experience and behave in the world, which has very widespread ramifications (e.g., Epstein, 2001; Epstein & Meier, 1989; Valach & Epstein, 1995). The following sections describe the CTI's scales.

Emotional Coping

Emotional coping refers to thinking in ways that promote adaptive emotional reactions to whatever situations arise. The scale of Emotional Coping is one of the most important scales in the CTI. The content of its subscales indicates that people who are poor in emotional coping tend to be low in self-acceptance, to overgeneralize after unfavorable outcomes, to be excessively sensitive to criticism, and to dwell excessively on negative outcomes. Some typical items are as follows: "The slightest indication of disapproval gets me upset," and "I worry a great deal about what other people think of me." Thinking in such ways has been found to be associated with emotional distress (e.g., Epstein & Meier, 1989; Epstein & Pacini, 1999; Valach & Epstein, 1995); poor work performance (Atwater, 1992; Epstein & Katz, 1992; Epstein & Meier, 1989; Green, 1988; Nadeau, 1994; Stacciarini, 1999); unsatisfactory relationships with others (Epstein & Meier, 1989); emotional symptoms, including anxiety and depression (Epstein, 1992; Epstein & Katz, 1992; Epstein & Meier, 1989; Epstein & Pacini, 1999; Pacini, Muir, & Epstein, 1998; Park, Moore, Turner, & Adler, 1997; Scheuer & Epstein, 1997; Valach & Epstein, 1995); psychosomatic symptoms; sleep problems (Epstein, 1992; Epstein & Katz, 1992; Epstein & Meier, 1989; Epstein & Pacini, 1999; Scheuer & Epstein, 1997; Valach & Epstein, 1995); control problems, as in binge eating (Kungl, Fultz, Jones, Reel, & Brookings, 1990; Valach & Epstein, 1995); and alcohol and drug abuse (Epstein & Meier, 1989, Epstein & Sherman, 1992; Gollnisch, 1991). In summary, people who automatically think in ways that promote poor emotional coping are poorly adjusted in a wide variety of ways.

Behavioral Coping

Behavioral coping, which is another major CTI scale, refers to solving problems in living by taking effective action. People who are poor at behavioral coping think in ways that promote inaction or ineffective behavior. They tend to obsess over problems or to procrastinate rather than take action, and they work less hard and give up more easily than others. In general, they tend not to think in ways that promote effective behavior. Some typical items are: "I avoid challenges because it hurts too much when I fail," and "When faced with a large amount of work to complete, I tell myself I can never get it done, and feel like giving up."

Behavioral coping is significantly associated with the same variables as emotional coping, but the strengths of the relations are not as strong. As indicated by its subscales, those who are poor at behavioral coping are pessimistic and tend to emphasize the negative aspects of events, tend not to take action in solving problems, and are not conscientious but prefer to take the easy way out. Poor behavioral coping is particularly strongly associated with ineffective performance. It is also significantly associated with emotional problems and psychosomatic symptoms, but to a lesser extent than emotional coping. It is significantly associated with alcohol and drug problems, but to a lesser extent than emotional coping, which suggests that such problems in college students are more related to controlling feelings than to controlling behavior.

Categorical Thinking

Categorical thinking includes two subscales, one that refers to the formal nature of thinking and the other to the content of thinking. The former subscales includes a tendency to judge people and events in broad, black-and-white terms and to ignore nuances, as in viewing others as good or bad people, as friends or enemies, and as being like oneself and one's "kind of people" or as a different kind of person. Items that refer to content of thinking include a tendency to regard people as threatening and untrustworthy and to be unforgiving, intolerant, and angry. It is intriguing that a formal way of thinking and the content of thinking happen to go together to form an overall scale of categorical thinking. Typical items are "There are fundamentally two kinds of people in the world, good and bad people," and "The only person I can totally trust is myself." In a battery of personality and adjustment tests, categorical thinking was associated with impulsive anger, suppressed anger, a favorable view of aggression, low friendliness, uncaring about others, poor relationships with others, high anxiety, and high physiological arousal.

Personal Superstitious Thinking

Personal superstitious thinking refers to private superstitions that prepare one for disappointment by accepting it in advance. People with high scores on the Personal Superstitious Scale are more concerned with defending themselves against threat and misfortune than with achieving happiness. Such people tend to be pessimistic, feel helpless, are prone to depression, have psychosomatic symptoms, and, to a lesser extent, have control problems (Epstein &

Pacini, 1999; Pacini et al., 1998; Valach & Epstein, 1995). Examples of items in the Personal Superstitious Thinking Scale are "If something very good happens to me I believe it will be followed by something equally bad," and "I sometimes think that if I wish for something to happen it will keep it from happening."

In a study in which students kept daily records of their average feelings of the day, personal superstitious thinking was significantly associated with sadness, feelings of unworthiness, pessimism, lack of spontaneity, and feelings of being overwhelmed (Epstein & Pacini, 1999). In the same study, personal superstitious thinking was also associated with neuroticism, suppressed anger, guilt over hostility, hopelessness, disorganization, low self-esteem, submissiveness, low positive affect, unsatisfactory relationships, and an unfavorable body image.

Esoteric Thinking

Esoteric thinking refers to believing in strange, magical, and scientifically questionable phenomena, such as ghosts, astrology, good and bad omens, and conventional superstitions. The subscales of the Esoteric Thinking scale are Unusual Beliefs and Conventional Superstitions. Typical items are "Astrology will never explain anything" (reverse scored), and "I believe in ghosts." If not excessive, esoteric thinking reveals an openness of mind and a willingness to consider a wide range of possibilities. High levels of esoteric thinking, however, are indicative of a lack of disciplined thinking and an excessive reliance on intuitive and associative impressions. Esoteric Thinking, unlike Personal Superstitious Thinking, does not include a negative bias. It therefore includes a belief in lucky charms, as well as in evil omens. Despite not including an emphasis on negative thinking, it is interesting that Esoteric Thinking is associated with a tendency to have depressive episodes, which suggests that people who are less disciplined and rational in their thinking than others are more prone than others to depression. This view is supported by high scores on esoteric thinking being associated with low scores on rational thinking (Pacini et al., 1998). However, within both a normal college group (Epstein & Pacini, 1999) and a normal middle-aged group (Valach & Epstein, 1995), within limits, esoteric thinking was neither associated with depression nor with any other indication of maladjustment. Thus, the results from these studies support the view that esoteric thinking is only maladaptive when it is also irrational.

Naïve Optimism

Naïve optimism refers to unrealistic optimism. Unlike Positive Thinking, which is a subscale of Behavioral Coping, high scores on Naïve Optimism are a mixed blessing. On the positive side, naïve optimists have high spirits, tend to be liked by others, and are popular in politics. On the negative side, high scores on Naïve Optimism are associated with a simplified view of life, a tendency to ignore unpleasant realities, and a corresponding failure to take protective action in potentially threatening situations. Scores on the Naïve Optimism Scale decrease from childhood to adulthood. In the adult years, naïve optimism is directly associated with categorical thinking, another simplified form of thinking, but one with more negative consequences. Naïve optimism is associated with self-reported conscientiousness but not with behavioral measures of conscientiousness, which indicates that naïve optimists tend to report and very likely to have unrealistically favorable views about themselves.

The subscales of Naive Optimism are Overoptimism (e.g., the belief, for example, that following a single successful performance, one will always be successful), Stereotypical Thinking (e.g., the belief that everyone should love their parents), and Pollyannaish Thinking (e.g., the belief that everyone is good at heart). In neither college students nor middle-aged adults is naïve optimism associated with any measures related to adjustment. Apparently, the positive and the unrealistic components of naïve optimism cancel each other out with respect to adjustment.

Summarizing the CTI Scales

In summary, we learn from the CTI that there are two important components of people's thinking that are related to adjustment. One component consists of the kind of thinking that people engage in, such as categorical or nuanced thinking, overgeneralized, undergeneralized, or appropriately generalized thinking, and whether they dwell on past events or move on to current concerns. The other component is the content of people's implicit beliefs, such as whether they are accepting of themselves and others or have a low opinion of themselves and others. Two particularly important kinds of thinking are thinking in ways that promote effective emotional coping and thinking in ways that promote effective action. Specific ways of adaptive and maladaptive emotional and behavioral coping are indicated by the Emotional Coping and Behavioral Coping subscales, respectively. Other ways of automatic thinking that are related to maladjustment were indicated by the CTI scales of Categorical Thinking, Personal Superstitious Thinking, and Esoteric Thinking. The scale of Naïve Optimism was unrelated to adjustment, suggesting that the optimistic component cancelled out the maladaptive naïve component.

A Study of Constructive Thinking in the Daily Lives of College Students

The most intensive study of constructive thinking was conducted with several successive classes of college students, in which they kept detailed records of their daily experiences, emotions, symptoms, and other reactions. The class was described to prospective students as providing an opportunity to learn about and improve their coping with stress based on daily self-observations. The students kept records on specially devised forms that could be computer analyzed. They did this for 30 consecutive days, during which they recorded their average mood of the day, their strongest negative emotion of the day, an objective description of the event that was the source of their negative emotion, their automatic interpretation that determined their negative emotion, the degree of stress they experienced from the event, and a variety of other variables including their secondary coping responses and any symptoms they had on the same day of the event after its occurrence. After the recording period, the data from each student's reports were summarized by a computer that provided means and correlations among relevant variables over the 30-day recording period. The results were returned to the students, who used the computerized information to write a report on what they learned from the data about their constructive thinking, followed by a program they proposed for becoming a better constructive thinker. At the beginning and end of each semester, students responded to a battery of psychological tests that included the CTI.

The Results

The findings from this study are so extensive that they will require a book-length presentation. For now, only the results on stress and the correlates of constructive thinking will be presented. Here is a summary of these results:

- The single, strongest predictor of stress over the 30-day period was the initial rating of the significance of the event that was the source of the daily negative emotion that was reported.

  In a comparison of the significance of events during the 30-day recording period and at a period shortly after the recording period, the students almost always judged the significance of a distressing event as far greater when they initially rated the event than when they reevaluated its significance later. This further supports the conclusion that a common source of maladaptive behavior in everyday life is initially overestimating the significance of distressing events. Apparently, the experiential system, as a result of its short time perspective, tends to exaggerate the immediate significance of events. The implication of this finding for improving adjustment is that it is important to recognize that distressing experiences are usually not as harmful as they initially appear to be and that one should therefore recognize the importance of compensating for a tendency initially to overreact.

- Constructive thinking as measured by the CTI was found to be inversely related to the average degree of stress reported over the 30-day recording period. Thus, people who were good constructive thinkers reported that they led less stressful lives than did those who were poor constructive thinkers. This indicates that an important way of reducing stress is to learn to make more constructive interpretations of distressing events.
- There was a relatively strong relation between stress and the interpretation of a potentially stressful event as a challenge rather than as a threat. Thus, good constructive thinkers did not experience less stress than others by avoiding potentially stressful situations. Rather, they actively confronted problems in living, but regarded them as challenges rather than as threats. This was further illustrated in a study of constructive thinking in public school administrators (Green, 1988). The better constructive thinkers voluntarily chose to become engaged in more challenging and stressful situations than did the poorer constructive thinkers and, despite doing so, reported less stress.
- An important question about constructive thinking is the relative degree to which different kinds of construals and subsequent adaptive and maladaptive secondary mental and behavioral responses contribute to the overall level of stress people experience. To answer this question, students indicated in their daily ratings the degree to which they construed each of their negative events in the following ways: how significant the event was initially perceived to be, how much the event was viewed as a challenge versus a threat, and how well the students believed they could effectively cope with the event. In addition to their initial construals, students indicated how much they engaged in each procedure in a list of adaptive and maladaptive secondary responses to the event, such as realistically rehearsing the event, asserting oneself, encouraging oneself, berating oneself, and withdrawing, among others. When the construals that were significantly related to stress were entered into a regression equation, followed by the significant secondary mental and behavioral coping responses, all the construals remained significant whereas most of the secondary responses lost their significance. Moreover, the construal of the significance of the events was a much stronger predictor of the average stress of the day than any other variable, confirming the previous observation with a different procedure. It may be concluded that the extent to which people construe potentially stressful events as significant is more important in determining their experience of stress than all their other reactions combined.
- Psychosomatic symptoms, such as headaches and stomach aches, as well as sleeping problems were significantly associated with poor constructive thinking and with higher levels of reported stress. This result was replicated in other research (Epstein, 1992).

- Control problems, such as binge eating and drug abuse, were inversely related to constructive thinking.
- A comparison of scores on the CTI at the beginning and end of the semester indicated that learning about CET and keeping records of how one interprets potentially stressful events is therapeutic. This is consistent with the view in CET that being aware of the operation of one's experiential system can contribute to improving one's adjustment. Some students reported that participating in the class changed their lives for the better and that their parents and friends spontaneously remarked about their improvement.

A Study of the Relation of Constructive Thinking and Emotional and Physical Well-Being in Middle-Aged Adults

It will be recalled that in the study with college students constructive thinking was found to be inversely related to emotional distress, psychosomatic symptoms, and control problems. Similar results were obtained in other studies with college students (Epstein & Meier, 1989; Epstein & Katz, 1992; Scheuer & Epstein, 1997). An important relation that could not be examined with college student is the relation of constructive thinking to serious diseases because the frequency of such diseases is extremely low in young adults. Accordingly, a study was conducted with a middle-aged sample in which serious diseases were much more prevalent. There were two main interests in conducting the study: to determine whether the results with college students on emotional disorders, psychosomatic symptoms, and control problems would be replicated with a middle-aged group and to determine whether a relation between constructive thinking and serious diseases would be found with a middle-aged group.

A sample of convenience of 209 middle-aged adults between the ages of 45 and 72, with a median age of 55, was administered a battery of questionnaires that included the CTI, an adjective checklist of moods and emotions, and questions on emotional disorders (e.g., depressive episodes, anxiety attacks), physical health, control problems (e.g., alcohol abuse, drug abuse, binging on food), stressful life events, and attitudes and beliefs reported in the literature to be associated with serious diseases, such as cancer and heart disease. The relations, summarized here, are based on correlations of at least .20 ($p < .01$).

Relations Between CTI Scales and Emotional and Physical Well-Being

The CTI scales of Global Constructive Thinking, Emotional Coping, and Behavioral Coping were all negatively correlated with emotional disorders, psychosomatic symptoms, and control problems. Personal Superstitious Thinking was directly associated with emotional disorders and with psychosomatic symptoms. The strongest correlations were between Emotional Coping and emotional disorders ($r = -.50$) and with psychosomatic symptoms ($r = -.29$). There were no significant relations between any CTI scale with infectious diseases or with any major disease. It is important in this regard to recognize that the participants in the study were a relatively healthy group and had not been preselected for having any diseases.

Relations of Positive and Negative Emotions and Moods with Emotional Disorders and Physical Well-Being

A relation of emotions and moods with physical disorders can be expected because emotions and moods have an important physiological component. For example, when people experience fear or anger, their breathing rate, heart rate, muscle tension, and blood pressure all increase. It was therefore hypothesized that chronic negative moods and emotions would be positively related not only to emotional disorders but also to psychosomatic disorders and that negative moods and emotions might even be related to more serious diseases. Negative emotions and moods were found to be directly associated with emotional disorders ($r = .55$), psychosomatic symptoms ($r = .37$), and control problems ($r = .31$). Positive emotions and moods were more weakly, albeit significantly, inversely associated with the same variables. Neither emotions nor moods were significantly related to major diseases, accidents, or infectious diseases. Fear, anger, and sadness were associated with emotional disorders, psychosomatic symptoms, and control problems. Fear produced the strongest relations compared to the other emotion. The strength of the relations of fear alone was comparable to the strength of the relations produced by the overall negative emotions and moods. Anger produced the weakest, albeit significant, relations.

Relations of Controllable and Uncontrollable Stressful Life Events and Emotional and Physical Disorders

Stressful life events were categorized according to whether they were controllable or uncontrollable. Examples of controllable life events are divorce and significant failures, such as being fired from a job for unsatisfactory performance or doing poorly on a job interview. Examples of uncontrollable life events are death of a loved one, separation from a loved one, and losing a job because of business downsizing. Both kinds of stressful life events were associated with psychosomatic symptoms and major diseases. Controllable, but not uncontrollable, stressful events were associated with emotional disorders. Uncontrollable, but not controllable, stressful events were associated with accidents. The relation between uncontrollable events and accidents is not easily explained but may be related to uncontrollable stressful events being more severe than controllable stressful events. If so, it is all the more impressive that only the controllable events were associated with emotional disorders, which can be explained by assuming that people who contribute to the occurrence of their stressful events are likely to be generally more poorly adjusted than others.

The Mediating Role of Negative Emotions and Moods in the Relations of Constructive Thinking and Emotional and Physical Well-Being

As emotions have both psychological and physiological components, a route by which constructive thinking could affect psychological and physical well-being is through mediation by negative emotions. Support for such mediation was obtained in the study of college students previously reported and also in another study with college students (Epstein & Katz, 1992).

In the study with middle-aged adults, the mediating role of emotions and moods in the relations of constructive thinking and psychosomatic symptoms, emotional disorders, and control problems was investigated with regression analyses. As a first step, age and gender were entered as control variables and Global Constructive Thinking scores as a predictor variable. As hypothesized, with gender and age controlled, constructive thinking was significantly inversely related to emotional disorders and psychosomatic symptoms. Constructive thinking was also significantly inversely related to control problems. In the second step of the regression analysis, negative emotions were entered into the equation. When this was done, negative emotions completely displaced Global Constructive Thinking, thereby supporting the mediation hypothesis. Thus, the results with the middle-aged group replicate the results with the college students, according to which the relations between constructive thinking and psychosomatic symptoms, emotional disorders, and control problems can be attributed to the influence of poor constructive thinking on the occurrence of negative emotions.

The failure to find relations between constructive thinking and serious diseases such as heart disease and cancer may have occurred for at least two reasons. One reason is that the incidence of such diseases was insufficiently frequent in our sample. The other reason is that the CTI scales do not measure the personality attributes that are most relevant for specific serious diseases, such as heart disease and cancer. For example, it is fairly well established that the disposition to chronic or frequent episodes of anger is associated with heart disease (e.g., Miller, Smith, Turner, Guijarro, & Hallet, 1996), which suggests a particular kind of poor constructive thinking in which a person tends to think that others behave badly and therefore warrant reactions to them of anger and aggression. This is not poor constructive thinking in general, such as poor emotional or behavioral coping; rather, it is a very specific kind of thinking that is associated with preparing the body for attack in a manner that affects the cardiovascular system.

There is also evidence from another source to support a relation between a particular maladaptive way of thinking and susceptibility to cancer. According to the concept of a cancer-prone personality, people who are characteristically helpful to others but do so at the sacrifice of fulfilling their own needs are more prone to cancer than others. One of my graduate students tested the hypothesis that remarkable spontaneous recoveries from cancer are disproportionately associated with the remediation of a cancer-prone personality. The hypothesis was tested by comparing a group of people with very unusual recoveries from late-stage cancer from which recovery was extremely unlikely with a recovered group of people with more benign forms and stages of cancer from which recovery was not unusual and also from a recovered group of people with nonexceptional recoveries from heart disease. In support of hypothesis, the exceptional cancer patients obtained significantly higher scores on a measure of a cancer-prone personality, in which they described what they were like before their diagnosis, than the other two groups reported. The group that experienced the unusual recoveries from cancer also reported a significantly greater decrease in their cancer-prone personality scores than the other two groups reported. Similar evidence of unusual recoveries by patients with cancer-prone personalities who reduced their cancer- prone way of thinking in the course of psychotherapy has also been reported by others (Cunningham & Watson, 2004). There were no significant differences in the three groups in the present study on their postrecovery Global Constructive Thinking scores.

Adjustment as Related to Individual Differences in Degree of Experiential and Rational Processing

In contrast to the CTI, which measures the quality of people's experiential thinking, the Rational-Experiential Inventory (REI) measures the degree to which people report they engage in experiential and rational processing. The REI includes two main scales, one that measures individual differences in a rational thinking style and the other that measures individual differences in an experiential thinking style. Each scale has two subscales, one that indicates the extent to which people report they engage in a thinking style and the other that indicates how effectively they believe they are able to use it. Several studies with the REI reveal that one of the styles of thinking is inversely related to maladjustment whereas the other is positively related to desirable attributes.

An important question when constructing the REI is whether the two thinking styles should be represented as opposite ends of a single dimension or by two independent dimensions. To answer this question, separate scales were constructed for each thinking style that were then correlated with each other. Because the two scales were found to be independent rather than negatively correlated, it was concluded that they represented independent dimensions. As further support for their independence, the two thinking styles were significantly correlated with different variables rather than lying in opposite directions with the same variables. Moreover, when they did correlate significantly with the same variables, it was in the same rather than in the opposite direction, indicating that, rather than being opposite ends of a single dimension, they represented two different dimensions. Because the two thinking styles are independent, it indicates that developing one thinking style does not reduce the operation of the other thinking style. Rather, it is possible to be high on both thinking styles, low on both thinking styles, or high on one and low on the other.

Table 8.1 presents a summary of the findings from all the studies in which the relations of the two thinking styles to other variables were examined by my assistants and me (Epstein, Pacini, Denes-Raj, & Heier, 1996; Pacini & Epstein, 1999a, 1999b; Pacini et al., 1998). Although some of the attributes and abilities that are significantly correlated with the REI scales are based on self-report measures, others are based on objective measures, such as performance in experimental situations, intelligence test scores, and performance on tasks that measure creativity, sense of humor, intuitive ability, and aesthetic judgment.

It can be seen in Table 8.1 that a rational thinking style is directly related to intellectual performance, self-esteem, and meaningfulness of life. It is inversely related to several measures associated with maladjustment, including measures of anxiety, depression, stress, and neuroticism. An experiential/intuitive thinking style provides a more mixed picture. On the positive side, it is associated with creativity, empathy, aesthetic judgment, intuitive ability, and establishing satisfactory interpersonal relationships. Although these variables are unrelated to an absence of maladjustment, they are related to leading a fulfilling and interesting life. On the negative side, an experiential thinking style is associated with naïve optimism, Pollyannaish beliefs, stereotyped thinking, superstitious beliefs, and unrealistic beliefs. It is important, when interpreting these findings, to recognize that a high score on an experiential thinking style can be obtained by endorsing most of the desirable attributes and abilities and few of the undesirable ones, or it can be obtained with the opposite pattern of responses.

Of particular interest regarding the relation of the two thinking styles to adjustment, the findings from the REI indicate that unless people are sufficiently engaged in rational processing, they are prone to be maladjusted, as indicated by symptoms of depression, anxiety, high levels of stress, and neuroticism. If they are sufficiently engaged in rational processing, it does not

Table 8.1. CORRELATES OF INTUITIVE/EXPERIENTIAL AND RATIONAL/ANALYTIC THINKING STYLES

Rational/Analytic Thinking Style	Experiential/Intuitive Thinking Style
Positive Attributes of Rational Thinking	*Positive Attributes of Experiential Thinking*
High level of intellectual performance	Favorable interpersonal relationships
High meaningfulness in life	High social popularity
Realistic thinking	Imaginative thinking
Low stress in living	High agreeableness
High self-esteem	High empathy
Positive world view	High spontaneity
Low neuroticism	Emotionally expressive
Low anxiety	Good aesthetic sense
Low depression	Good sense of humor
Conscientious	Creative
Open-minded	Open-minded
High personal growth	High personal growth
Negative Attributes	*Negative Attributes*
Weak tendency of a	Naïve optimism
dismissive relationship style	Polyannaish thinking
	Stereotyped thinking
	Unrealistic beliefs
	Superstitious beliefs

matter so far as their adjustment is concerned how much they engage in experiential processing so long as it is not irrational.

The Failure to Fulfill Basic Needs as a Source of Maladjustment

According to CET, one of the major reasons why people are maladjusted is that they fail to fulfill their basic needs. There are several reasons for this, including the influence of society, the influence of significant others, the existence of repression, and the presence of sensitivities and compulsions.

The Influence of Society

The values of society influence people to believe that the fulfillment of certain needs, such as acquiring fame or fortune, is a path to personal fulfillment and happiness. Thus, people may spend a lifetime to achieve such goals, only to find that when they reach them they feel depressed and disappointed rather than elated and fulfilled. Unfortunately, people often do not know what will bring them happiness because happiness is determined more by fulfilling needs in their experiential system than by fulfilling needs in their rational system, as promoted by the societies in which they live.

Marilyn Monroe was successful beyond her wildest dreams. She was beautiful, wealthy, and popular. Yet she was often miserable, addicted to drugs, and probably committed suicide (although some suspect she was murdered). Why are some people who have fulfilled their life goals not happy? This is an extremely important question that is relevant for everyone because it means that people can devote their lives to achieving a goal only to find it does not bring them the fulfillment they anticipated. Tolstoy (1887), who was given to periods of depression, asked himself this very same question. He reported that he had reached a point in life where he was famous, wealthy, respected, and had a loving and beloved wife and children. Try as he might, he could not understand why he was depressed under such favorable circumstances. The failure to understand this, he said, troubled him more than the depression itself. Although Marilyn Monroe and Tolstoy would meet the criteria for a diagnosis of neurosis or depression, the problem of false goals is relevant for everyone.

In the book *Brace for Impact* (Firman & Quirk, 2009), people who came close to death described their reactions on being informed that their airliner was about to crash into the Hudson River. Facing imminent death made many aware that their relationships with their loved ones were more important to them than anything else. Several people reported that this awareness changed their lives. Apparently, there is nothing like a near-death experience to teach people about what is important to them.

False goals can be defined as those that fail to fulfill their promise of fulfillment and happiness when achieved. Instead, achieving a false goal is often the source of disappointment, disillusionment, and even depression. According to CET, the reason people have false goals is that they pursue goals that are determined primarily by the conscious beliefs in their rational system, often derived from societal influence, rather than by their actual experiences regarding what they enjoy and are good at.

Marilyn Monroe reported that when she received applause from audiences, it passed right by her, as if the people were applauding someone else. She said that although she knew she should feel proud and happy, the applause did not reach her because she looked out onto the world with the eyes of a frightened child. This is perfectly understandable when one considers her background because she had been brought up under dreadful circumstances. She was raised in foster homes and raped and otherwise abused as a child. As a result, she had a deep craving for being loved for herself, not for being a sex goddess. Unfortunately, the personality structure that she developed, including an excessive need for assurances of love combined with defenses against rejection, made it difficult for her to obtain the love she so desperately desired or even to accept it when it was offered.

False goals are common in our society because people are taught that happiness can be obtained by achieving fame, fortune, admiration, or power. This message is often accepted in a person's rational system, whereas the source of people's real happiness lies in the fulfillment of goals in their experiential system, and these are goals of which they are often unaware. Goals that bring happiness in the experiential system are usually much simpler and more fundamental than the goals in people's rational systems. Goals in the experiential system are derived from lived experience involving the fulfillment of basic needs, such as the desire to be loved.

Influence of Significant Others

A particularly important reason why people fail to fulfill their basic needs is that they have been influenced by significant others, such as a parent, to adopt certain needs that are inconsistent with their actual experiences. As a result, they remain out of touch with the needs of their experiential system. For example, if the condition for obtaining a parent's love is perceived by a child as requiring the fulfillment of a wish by the parent that the child become an outstanding athlete, the child may strive to fulfill the parent's wish despite getting little enjoyment from the activity. The child may then unconsciously sabotage fulfilling that need. Alternatively, in the event that the person fulfills the need, he or she may feel depressed rather than happy when reaching the consciously desired goal because, although it makes the parent happy, it brings no satisfaction to the child.

Conflict Between Needs

A third reason why people fail to fulfill basic needs is because of a conflict between their needs. As previously noted, people may be so driven to fulfill a particular need that they do so in a manner that sacrifices the fulfillment of their other needs. A more adaptive way of behaving is to fulfill a basic need in a manner that is compatible with fulfilling other needs. For example, a person can be helpful to others in a way that makes her proud of herself and appreciated by others, which serves to fulfill the basic needs for relatedness and for self-esteem enhancement. Alternatively, a person can fulfill a need for self-esteem enhancement by defeating and denigrating others, which is likely to lead to their retaliation, which results in the frustration of fulfilling the need for relatedness. Another kind of conflict between the basic needs of self-esteem and relatedness is that of a highly successful person who feels alone and unloved because pursuit of career left no room for establishing and maintaining satisfactory relationships.

Repression

A fourth reason why people fail to fulfill the needs in their experiential system is because of repression. Because repression plays a more important role in neurosis than in everyday problems in living, it will be briefly discussed in this chapter and more thoroughly discussed in a section on neurosis in Chapter 9. As a result of guilt feelings about unacceptable feelings, thoughts, or impulses, people may repress awareness of thoughts or images associated with the unacceptable material. As previously noted, repression operates as follows: when a person's mind approaches an area of repression, the person experiences twinges of anxiety referred to as *signal anxiety*. The anxiety automatically triggers avoidance reactions that are reinforced by the removal of the anxiety signals. This reaction maintains the repression, but at a considerable price. One cost is that the repression remains a source of vulnerability because it can fail under certain stimulating conditions or by weakened defenses as a result of fatigue, drugs, or illness. A second cost is that, by remaining unconscious, the source of a repression cannot be identified, confronted, and then resolved. A third cost is that a repressed need tends to be fulfilled indirectly by displacement or in some other maladaptive way, such as by physical symptoms that are associatively related to the repressed need. For example, repressed hostility to a caregiver can be expressed in the form of a symptom that is demanding of the caregiver's attention.

Sensitivities and Compulsions

Sensitivities, as used in CET, refer to a low threshold for perceiving threat from the presence of certain situations. Compulsions are automatically learned rigid ways of reducing the anxiety produced by sensitivities. Sensitivities and compulsions are common sources of everyday maladaptive behavior. Because they are also prevalent in more serious pathological conditions, they will be further discussed in the section on neurosis in Chapter 9. Prevalent sensitivities and compulsions within the range of normal behavior include common phobias such fears of mice, bugs, flying in airplanes, heights, crowds, confined spaces, public speaking, and social situations. Other sources of sensitivities and compulsions are any experiences that have been highly distressing.

Sensitivities serve the adaptive function of automatically alerting people to the possible recurrence of past threatening events or to the occurrence of associatively related events. Compulsions serve the adaptive function of automatically providing people with behavioral responses that reduce the anxiety produced by sensitivities. Although sensitivities and compulsions were learned because of their adaptive functions, they are a common source of problems in everyday life. First, because they were learned under strong threat or high arousal, they are excessively intense reactions when activated by much less threatening situations. Second, there is a rigid, fixated quality about their operation that is resistant to extinction and that fails to take into account important situational distinctions. They also have a broad generalization gradient. Thus, a person who is sensitive to ridicule may misinterpret a friendly joke as an attempt to ridicule him, and a person who is afraid of mice may believe she sees them in everything remotely resembling a mouse. Third, sensitivities alert people to dangers that often no longer exist, thereby becoming a source of unrealistic anxiety. Fourth, by focusing attention on their sensitivities, people may ignore other sources of danger. Fifth, by avoiding situations that arouse sensitivities, people are often considerably inconvenienced. For example, a person with a phobia about flying in airplanes may travel great distances by automobile despite knowing that it is more dangerous as well as much more time consuming and inconvenient than air travel.

Sensitivities create problems in living not only because of the compulsive avoidance reactions they elicit but also because of the rigid behavior they instigate. For example, people who are unduly distrustful of others because of early experiences may be compulsively driven to attack people whose behavior is misperceived as violating their trust, which produces retaliatory reactions on the part of the other person, which then confirms the distrustful person's suspicion. Another example is a daughter who had a mother who interfered with her attempts to establish normal independence. As a result, the daughter becomes excessively sensitive to behavior that she perceives as interfering with her autonomy. Such a person may develop a compulsion to resist the influence of authority figures and consequently have difficulty in holding a job.

Overgeneralization as a Source of Interpersonal Problems

Undoubtedly, the most prevalent psychological problems that people have in everyday life concern interpersonal relationships. Apparently, they are unable to apply the same reasoning to solving interpersonal problems that they are able to apply so well in solving impersonal problems. This is well indicated by the history of humankind. People have made remarkable advances in science, mathematics, and technology, but they still continue to fight wars and have difficulties in their personal relations. The explanation, according to CET, is that the impersonal problems are primarily processed by the rational system, whereas the interpersonal problems are processed primarily by the experiential system. The result is that people automatically react in current relationships according to their emotions and generalizations from past relationships. Of particular importance is the acquisition of maladaptive generalizations of interpersonal relationships from childhood experiences because children have limited cognitive ability and are dependent on their parents. They may also have been involved in early relationships with family members that are unrepresentative of their relationships as adults, resulting in inappropriate generalizations in their beliefs.

Psychoanalysts, in their concept of transference, have emphasized the importance of generalizations from early experiences in influencing how people behave in future relationships, including relationships with psychotherapists. Cognitive-experiential theory extends this concept by including generalizations from relationships with all significant figures in a child's life, including parents, siblings, and teachers.

The more intense and enduring a person's early relationship is with a significant other, the stronger and broader the person's tendency to generalize from that relationship to other relationships (Bowlby, 1969; Catlin & Epstein, 1992). Thus, a person who, as a child, was constantly belittled and criticized by his parents will tend to expect such behavior from others.

Generalizations from distressing relationships with parents and other significant figures in childhood are a prevalent source of maladaptive problems regarding other relevant interpersonal relationships, including relationships between husbands and wives, between romantic partners, between parents and children, between teachers and students, between employees and employers, and between members of extended families. Such relationship problems are among the most common sources of problems in everyday life.

Self-Defeating Behavior

Robert Sternberg has done interesting research on practical intelligence (Sternberg, 1985). He has found that practical intelligence is often unrelated to intellectual intelligence. He has described people of modest intellectual ability who are highly competent in solving practical problems that are particularly important to them. He has also described people who are lacking in normal practical intelligence and seem not to obtain the important information about how to perform well on their jobs and advance in their positions that others pick up naturally. I have observed this behavior in a few of my graduate students who were academically highly competent but were poor research assistants and did not advance in their positions after they received their doctoral degrees. How is such behavior explained? Why cannot these people use their considerable intellectual intelligence to solve practical problems in living?

One route to such a pattern could develop when a parent unintentionally punishes a child's successes and rewards the child's failures. A mother could react this way by expressing displaced hostility toward her own child as the result of unconsciously generalizing from her early rivalry with a sibling of whom she was very jealous because of her sibling's superior performance. As a result, a parent with the best of intentions could fail to praise the child when she does well but be concerned and helpful when she does poorly. The child automatically learns from such behavior that she will receive highly desirable attention from her mother when she does poorly but not when she does well. As a result, when the child performs well or anticipates performing well, she automatically has bad feelings that motivate her to sabotage her own efforts. In a corresponding manner, the anticipation of failure could automatically produce good feelings, which also motivate her to sabotage her performance. Thus, as much as such a person might consciously wish to succeed, she would be unable to do so. Because she would not understand that she was sabotaging her own efforts, she would likely attribute her failures to supervisors whom she considered unreasonably critical.

Another source of self-defeating behavior is the intrusive behavior of a parent or teacher that threatens the development of autonomy in a child. In such circumstances, a child could develop an intense need to defend his autonomy. Given such a need, the child, when grown, would tend to view authority figures and mentors as threats to his autonomy and therefore resist their influence. This not only would create poor relationships with mentors and authority figures, it would interfere with the person's ability to learn from them.

THE FULLY FUNCTIONING PERSON

Because this chapter is concerned with the maladaptive behaviors of everyday life, what reasons are there for including in it a discussion of the fully functioning person? The answer is that it provides an ideal standard against which maladaptive behavior can be evaluated. Everyone will be deficient according to this standard, but some will be more so than others. Moreover, providing an ideal standard draws attention to variables that may be overlooked when attending only to maladaptive behavior.

I first present a picture of an idealized, fully functioning person according to CET, one painted with very broad strokes that present little detail. I next provide an in-depth discussion of a topic of special significance in CET, namely the challenge presented to people of having to coordinate two information-processing systems that operate by different rules and contain different schemas.

An Overview of the Fully Functioning Person

The fully functioning person utilizes the experiential and rational systems in a harmonious, mutually facilitative manner and therefore does not experience significant conflict between the two systems. This occurs because the person has trained the experiential system so that its initial responses are acceptable to the individual. Little monitoring and control is therefore required of impulses and emotional expression because initial reactions are appropriate to begin with. The person spontaneously expresses the full range of emotions and does so in a flexible manner that is appropriate for each situation. The fully functioning person has a favorable pleasure-pain balance under normal circumstances and a favorable view of himself, others, and the inanimate world. The fully functional person is therefore accepting of the self and others and is kind and warmhearted toward others. As a result, the fully functioning person is able to examine the self and others free of defensiveness. Although optimistic, the fully functioning person is not naïvely so; he entertains the possibility of worst-case scenarios in threatening situations and engages in appropriate protective actions.

The fully functioning person operates at a high level of problem solving in both the rational and experiential domains and is aware of the operation of his experiential system. Thus, the person is a logical thinker who is aware of and can compensate for the biasing influence of his experiential system. The person's experiential system is highly stable at its core and flexible at its periphery, which allows it to operate according to basic principles and yet be able to modify the implementation of those principles according to situational requirements. The fully functioning person normally operates in a growth mode but can adopt a defensive mode when threatened. When adopting a defensive mode, this is done in a manner that paces the experience of anxiety so that the person is able to acquire mastery of a challenging or threatening situation without being overwhelmed. As the threat is reduced as the result of increasing mastery of the skills and understanding required for effective performance, the person gradually relinquishes the defensive mode and behaves increasingly according to a growth mode.

The fully functioning person is not judgmental of people as good or bad but views maladaptive and antisocial behavior as problems in living to be solved. Of particular importance, the fully functioning person solves his basic needs in a harmonious rather than in a conflicted manner, so that fulfilling one need often serves also to fulfill other needs.

Finally, the fully functioning person is creative and has sufficient ego-strength to make new discoveries and to propose new ideas despite awareness that such behavior is often met with initial rejection and hostility.

The Challenge of Having Two Different Systems for Processing Information

It is no simple matter to be a human being. Unlike other animals that have only an experiential system for directing their behavior, humans have two systems that operate by different rules, have different attributes, and include different schemas. As a result of having only an experiential system, nonhuman animals have a much more limited time perspective than humans, and the most advanced among them have at most a very limited concept of self that does not include an ego, a conscience, a sense of morality, or an awareness of their eventual death. They live for the moment and are happy and secure if their current needs are fulfilled.

Humans, unlike other animals, worry about the past and the future, are distressed and angered by the transgressions of others, feel guilty about their own transgressions, and are aware of their future death. It therefore might be said that humans understand too much for their own good. However, considering that they have no choice but to operate with two conceptual systems, it might more constructively be said that they do not understand enough for their own good because only by further understanding can they resolve the problems created by having two processing systems that operate in different ways.

To make matters more complicated, the human experiential system influences the operation of the rational system, as it does all other behavior, so that, despite intending to reason logically and objectively, people are often incapable of doing so, particularly in matters concerning human relationships. This is not only a major source of problems between individuals, it is also a problem among social groups (including nations) and may determine the survival of the species. Thus, although the rational system has been the source of humankind's unique accomplishments, it has also provided humans with formidable destructive power. The challenge remains for humans to use their remarkable intelligence to understand and train their experiential systems to make it a source of personal and social well-being rather than a source of irrational thinking and behavior.

REFERENCES

Atwater, L. E. (1992). Beyond cognitive ability: Improving the prediction of performance. *Journal of Business and Psychology*, 7, 27–44.

Bar-On, R. (1997). *Bar-On Emotional Quotient Inventory: Technical manual*. Toronto, Ontario, Canada: Multiple Health Systems.

Beck, A. T. (1976). *Cognitive therapy and the emotional disorders*. New York: International Universities Press.

Bowlby, J. (1969). *Attachment* (Vol. 1 of *Attachment and Loss*). New York: Basic Books.

Catlin, G., & Epstein, S. (1992). Unforgettable experiences: The relation of life-events to basic beliefs about self and world. *Social Cognition*, *10*, 189–209.

Cunningham, A. J., & Watson, K. (2004). How psychological therapy may prolong survival in cancer patients: new evidence and a simple theory. *Integrative Cancer Therapy*, *3*, 214–229.

Daus, C. S., & Ashkanasy, N. M. (2003). Will the real emotional intelligence please stand up? On deconstructing the emotional intelligence "debate." *Industrial Organizational Psychologist*, *41*, 69–72.

Ellis, A., & Grieger, R. (1977). *Handbook of rational-emotive therapy*. New York: Springer Publishing.
Epstein, S. (1992). Constructive thinking and mental and physical well-being. In L. Montada, S. H. Filipp, & M. J. Lerner (Eds.), *Life crises and experiences of loss in adulthood* (pp. 385–409). Hillsdale, NJ: Erlbaum.
Epstein, S. (1998). *Constructive thinking: The key to emotional intelligence*. Westport, CT: Greenwood Publishing.
Epstein, S. (2001). *Manual for the Constructive Thinking Inventory*. Odessa, FL: Psychological Assessment Resources.
Epstein, S. (2012). Emotional intelligence from the perspective of cognitive-experiential self-theory. *International Journal of Transformative Emotional intelligence, 1*, 109–121.
Epstein, S., & Katz, L. (1992). Coping ability, stress, productive load, and symptoms. *Journal of Personality and Social Psychology, 62*, 813–825.
Epstein, S., & Meier, P. (1989). Constructive thinking: A broad coping variable with specific components. *Journal of Personality and Social Psychology, 57*, 332–349.
Epstein, S., & Pacini, R. (1999). Constructive thinking and coping with stress in the everyday life of college students. (Statistically analyzed unpublished data).
Epstein, S., Pacini, R., Denes-Raj, V., & Heier, H. (1996). Individual differences in intuitive-experiential and analytical-rational thinking styles. *Journal of Personality and Social Psychology, 71*, 390–405.
Epstein, S., & Sherman, D. (1992). Constructive thinking and alcoholism in college students. (Unpublished analyzed data).
Firman, D., & Quirk, K. (2009). *Brace for impact*. Deerfield Beach, FL: Health Communications.
Gollnish, G. (1991). *Drug use in methadone maintenance clients: A multi-dimensional model of motivation, coping, and personality*. Unpublished doctoral dissertation, University of Massachusetts at Amherst.
Green, M. (1988). *Occupational stress: A study of public school administrators in southeast Massachusetts*. Unpublished doctoral dissertation, University of Massachusetts at Amherst.
Kungl, C. T., Fultz, D. A., Jones, S. G., Reel, K. L., & Brookings, J. B. (1990). *Constructive thinking and bulimia*. Presented at the Midwestern Psychological Association Convention, Chicago.
Locke, E. A. (2005). Why emotional intelligence is an invalid concept. *Journal of Organizational Behavior, 26*, 425–431.
Miller, T. Q., Smith, T. W., Turner, C. W., Guijarro, M. L., & Hallet, A. J.(1996). A meta-analytic review of research on hostility and physical health, *Psychological Bulletin, 119*, 322–348.
Murphy, K. R., & Sideman, L. (2006). The falsification of emotional intelligence. In K. R. Murphy (Ed.), *A critique of emotional intelligence: What are the problems and how can they be fixed*? (pp. 283–299). Mahway, NJ: Erlbaum.
Nadeau, M. J. (1994). *Relation of constructive thinking to work performance, stress, and health*. Unpublished honors thesis, University of Massachusetts at Amherst.
Pacini, R., & Epstein, S. (1999). The relation of rational and experiential information-processing styles to personality, basic beliefs, and the ratio-bias phenomenon. *Journal of Personality and Social Psychology, 76*, 972–987.
Pacini, R., Muir, F., & Epstein, S. (1998). Depressive realism from the perspective of cognitive-experiential self-theory. *Journal of Personality and Social Psychology, 74*, 1056–1068.

Park, C. L., Moore, P. J., Turner, R. A., & Adler, N. E. (1997). The roles of constructive thinking and optimism in psychological and behavioral adjustment during pregnancy. *Journal of Personality and Social Psychology, 73*, 584–592.

Scheuer, E., & Epstein, S. (1997). Constructive thinking, reactions to a laboratory stressor, and symptoms in everyday life. *Anxiety, Stress, and Coping, 10*, 269–303.

Stacciarini, J. M. (1999). *Constructive thinking, occupational stress, job satisfaction, and well-being in Brazilian nurses*. Unpublished doctoral dissertation. University of Brazil, Rio de Janeiro.

Sternberg, R. J. (1985). *Beyond IQ: A triarchic theory of human intelligence*. New York: Cambridge University Press.

Tolstoy, L. (1887). *My confession.* New York: Crowell.

Valach, L., & Epstein, S. (1995). The relation of constructive thinking to mental and physical wellbeing in a middle-aged sample. (Statistically analyzed unpublished data).

Wagner, R. K., & Sternberg, R. J. (1985). Practical intelligence in real-world pursuits: the role of tacit knowledge. *Journal of Personality and Social Psychology, 48*, 436–458.

CHAPTER 9
Neurosis, Post-Traumatic Stress Disorder, Psychosis, and Autism

In this chapter, I discuss from the perspective of cognitive-experiential theory (CET) neurosis, post-traumatic stress disorder, psychosis, and autism.

NEUROSIS

The designation of neurosis is retained, despite its substitution in the *Diagnostic and Statistical Manual of Mental Disorders* (DSM-III) by its components, because I regard it a useful designation considering the high rate of comorbidity among its components (Brown, Campbell, Lenman, Grisham, & Mancill, 2001).

As noted in the previous chapter, neurosis and the psychopathology of everyday life differ more in degree than in kind of behavior. A person who seeks treatment from a psychotherapist is often regarded as neurotic, whereas another who is equally disturbed but does not seek treatment is usually not regarded as neurotic. To further complicate the picture, the more distressed a person is, the more likely it is that he or she will seek treatment. However, there are many people who are highly disturbed but do not seek psychotherapeutic treatment for various reasons. They may simply not believe in psychotherapy, they may regard seeking psychotherapy as a sign of weakness and take pride in not seeking treatment, or they may not regard themselves as maladjusted and attribute their problems in living to circumstances or the behavior of others. Thus, seeking therapy provides only a very approximate dividing line between everyday problems and neurosis. Because there is considerable overlap between maladaptive behavior in everyday life and neurotic behavior, almost everything I have said about everyday maladaptive behavior in the previous chapter can be applied to neurosis, and almost everything

I will say about neurosis in this chapter can be applied to everyday maladaptive behavior.

I discuss under neurosis the following topics: disorders involving the primary emotions of fear, sadness, and anger; the role of sensitivities and compulsions in neurosis; and the occurrence of dissociation, repression, and alienation from the self.

The Role of Primary Emotions in Neurosis

It will be recalled that, according to CET, primary emotions serve as the nuclei of cognitive-affective networks that influence how people automatically interpret events, feel, behave, and consciously think. They are thus critically important components of people's implicit theories of reality. Depending on the reinforcement of behaviors associated with these cognitive-affective networks, any of them can be the source of a salient personality trait. Thus, there are people who are characteristically fearful/anxious, angry, sad, happy, or affectionate. Chronically high levels of fear/anxiety, anger, and sadness produce serious problems in living. Not only do they affect mental well-being and relationships with others, they also affect physical well-being.

Fear and Anxiety

The most common symptom of neurosis is a high level of anxiety. As previously noted, anxiety is a close cousin of fear that differs from it in one important respect. Fear is a motive that has an action tendency, which is normally to flee from a source of perceived danger or toward a source of safety. Although anxiety, like fear, involves a perception of threat, it lacks an action tendency. Thus, anxiety can be defined as a state of unresolved fear, or, alternatively, as undirected arousal following the perception of danger. The danger can be psychological, as in the threat of failure, or it can be physical, as in the threat of physical injury. Anxiety is more commonly defined as fear without an identifiable threat (e.g., Lazarus,1966; May, 1950). My definition differs by emphasizing an absence of an action tendency rather than an absence of a known threat. Therefore, according to my definition, anxiety can occur in the presence of a known threat when there is no response for coping with that threat. This may occur when there is a long waiting period during which action to a threat cannot be undertaken, as in soldiers waiting for an attack by an enemy. Another example occurs when there is a desire to confront a threat rather than flee from it, as when giving a speech to a large audience. Of course, if one is unable to identify the source of a threat, then there is no way of responding to it. Thus, sometimes the two definitions coincide, and sometimes they do not.

Anxiety is assumed to have evolved as a particularly noxious arousal state. Such a reaction is adaptive because it motivates the conversion of anxiety into the less distressing state of fear by identifying a response to a threat. It follows that people who are highly anxious tend to develop specific fears, including but not restricted to phobias, to which they then can react by escaping from or avoiding the source of the threat. Fear is obviously adaptive because it promotes avoidance of or escape from a perceived threat.

That anxiety and fear evolved as adaptive reactions raises the question of why they are maladaptive in certain situations. Anxiety and fear evolved under conditions in which people were confronted with physical dangers, such as being attacked by wild animals. Under such conditions, fear and anxiety were adaptive because anxiety prepared a person for seeking an appropriate response that would convert the more noxious state of anxiety into the less noxious one of fear, which would prepare a person for flight. Thus, anxiety added a condition of increased flexibility to the fear-flight relation. In contrast, in modern society, where threats are primarily of a psychological nature that cannot or will not be escaped from, anxiety and fear are often maladaptive. For example, if a person has to give a speech to a large audience and is fearful about public speaking, but is nevertheless determined to give the speech, the anxiety that is aroused can be disruptive. Of course, even in modern society, anxiety is not always maladaptive because it can motivate people to take constructive action, such as engaging in sufficient preparation to prevent a feared outcome from occurring.

In conclusion, modern society produces a great deal of anxiety because it requires people to confront, rather than flee from, threatening events. Yet, by understanding the nature of anxiety and thinking constructively about how one can respond to it, one can convert the anxiety into the less noxious state of fear.

Why are some people more anxious than others? The answer requires a consideration of temperament, life experience, and their interaction. Like some nonhuman animals (Pavlov, 1941), some people are born with more excitable temperaments than others (e.g., Kagan, 1984). For example, bulldogs are temperamentally stable and not easily excited, whereas fox terriers are highly reactive and easily excited. Each kind of temperament has its advantages and disadvantages. Highly reactive people experience more intense positive as well as negative emotions. They are also more prone to develop conditioned responses, including conditioned anxiety and fear responses (Eysenck & Rachman, 1965; Pavlov, 1941). It follows that individual differences in temperament are one of the reasons why some people are more prone than others to become anxious and fearful.

Holding temperament constant, people who have had threatening life experiences, such as difficult family relationships, particularly in their formative years, are more prone than others to become anxious and fearful. This, of course, follows directly from the schemas people automatically acquire from emotionally significant experiences. For some situations, the interaction between temperament and experience is particularly important. For example, depending on the family in which a child is reared, highly reactive children may receive greater or less acceptance than children who are less reactive. Also, highly reactive children are likely to experience greater stress than less reactive children not only because they react more strongly to the same events, but also because they are likely to be regarded by others as more unruly and difficult to manage than less reactive children.

Returning to the assumption that the schemas in people's experiential systems are primarily generalizations from emotionally significant experiences, children who have been brought up under threatening conditions will tend to view the world and people as threatening and themselves as vulnerable. The threats they experience can consist of unavoidable life events, such as loss of loved ones, and threats produced by the behavior of the significant people in their lives, such as their parents, siblings, and teachers. The threats can consist of threats of abandonment, threats to life or limb, threats to relationships, threats to self-esteem, and threats to the fulfillment of any of the other implicit basic needs. Children who have been exposed to such threats will tend to develop schematic representations of other people and situations as dangerous and to view themselves as potential victims who have to be on guard against psychological or physical injury. People with such stable implicit beliefs will tend to be chronically tense and anxious.

Since the experiential system normally operates outside of awareness, people may feel anxiety without being able to identify its source. This inability to identify a source of anxiety is exacerbated when awareness of the source is distressing and may therefore be repressed. Because there is a tendency to convert such anxiety into fear, anxious people may attribute their feelings of being threatened to an incorrect source that makes sense to them.

Because the experiential system learns by observing the behavior of others, as well as by direct experience, people can develop anxiety reactions not only through their own experiences but also by observing the behavior of others. Anna Freud and Burlingham (1943) described the reactions of children during the bombing of London in the Second World War. The degree of anxiety experienced by the children was determined more by the fear displayed by their caretakers than by the damage caused by the bombs.

In cases in which awareness of a source of threat is repressed, as in the case of an inappropriate sexual advance by a significant other, only displaced associations with the repressed material may be identified. This is one reason why people have fears that make little sense to them. An example is demonstrated by people whose fear of mice results from the thought that mice crawl into small spaces, which, depending on what else is going on in a person's thoughts at the time the fear was acquired, may be associated with body portals. Such a person may have no idea of how or why he or she developed an intense fear of mice.

A more direct source of developing phobias, including mouse phobias, is by being startled by the phobic object when one was in a state of high arousal. Any increment in arousal for a person already highly aroused is extremely distressing because of the basic need to control arousal level. Other examples of phobias that may have occurred because of incidents involving arousal considerations are fear of bugs, bats, and snakes, which, because of their erratic movements or unexpected appearance, produce startle responses that readily become conditioned responses. Although such phobias are common in otherwise normal individuals, if they are based on associative connections with deeper problems, they can reasonably be regarded as neurotic symptoms.

Anxiety and Fear Produced by Threats to Basic Needs

Threats to the fulfillment of implicit needs or to the validity of related beliefs are another source of neurotic reactions. Examples of neurotic fears related to the need to avoid pain and discomfort include excessive fear of visiting a physician because of the anticipated pain of inoculations or an excessive fear of visiting a dentist because of the anticipated pain if one's teeth are drilled. Such fears can be considered excessive if they cause a person either to avoid such procedures or to subject themselves to the procedures at the cost of prolonged anxiety at the prospect of facing what they fear.

Threats to the stability and coherence of a person's conceptual system are less likely to be identified than threats to the other basic needs. That such a threat is very fundamental and can disrupt the conceptual system was indicated by the previously described behavior of the dog in Pavlov's laboratory. It will be recalled that when the dog could not maintain an important discrimination, it experienced a disorganization of its conceptual system and intense anxiety.

Threats to the need for security are very fundamental sources of anxiety and fear because infants and young children are extremely vulnerable. They require stable sources for fulfilling all their physical needs, such as a need for food, water, and an appropriate temperature, and all their basic psychological needs, including appropriate stimulation and caring.

Threats to fulfillment of the need for relatedness can be a potent source of fear and anxiety. Because children are dependent on their caretakers for their very existence, one of their greatest fears is that they will be abandoned. This fear can develop into an enduring sensitivity if the child has had relevant experiences, such as the death of a loved one, extended departures of a loved one because of hospitalization or divorce, and fear of abandonment because of the child's perceived unacceptable behavior or thoughts, such as having secret death wishes toward a sibling who subsequently dies. Such experiences can be the source of enduring insecurity and anxiety.

The need for self-esteem is a common source of neurotic anxiety after the development of a self-concept. The anxiety is often compounded by maladaptive coping reactions that provide further sources of anxiety. Thus, people may compensate for feelings of inferiority by acting aloof, thereby alienating others, which then produces anxiety about being rejected by others. Another self-defeating reaction occurs in people who are threatened by assaults on their self-esteem, so that they react to constructive criticism as personal attacks against which they defend themselves rather than by learning from them. Such behavior contributes to failure, which becomes an additional source of anxiety.

Repression

In the previous chapter, I discussed repression as one of the reasons that people in their everyday lives sometimes fail to fulfill their needs. In this chapter, I consider its significance for neurotic disorders. The issue has been raised of whether repression actually exists. According to CET, repression is not surprising because it is simply a learned mental avoidance response. What is avoided is awareness of content that would be disturbing if a person became aware of it. An interesting example of the powerful influence of repression on conscious thinking is demonstrated by the following incident. I was treating a young man, whom I shall call Robert, who came to his appointment one day in an acutely distressed state. After being silent for a long period, he began to say something but stopped in mid-sentence. Finally, he blurted out that a memory had come to him since his last appointment that was so awful that, if he told it to me I, would never want to see him again. I told him that I would certainly not behave in such a manner and that I do not judge my patients as good or bad people, but only regard them as having problems that I wanted to help them resolve. Amid sobs, he related the following incident. One night, when he was about four years old, he heard the bed in his parents' bedroom creaking. Out of curiosity, he got out of bed and opened the door to their bedroom a crack. He saw his father on top of his mother. He thought at first that they were wrestling and his father was winning. But then he realized his mother was moaning and groaning as if she were enjoying what was going on. It occurred to him that his father must be sticking his "thing" into her, and she liked it. He then began to sob to the point that his speech became incoherent. He finally pulled himself together and said that he must have been a depraved child because he wanted to do to his mother what his father was doing to her. He said that thereafter he would often sneak over to their bedroom and watch his mother and father having sex and want to do what his father was doing. I asked him if he had read anything about the Oedipus complex. He was shocked at the question and asked, "You mean someone else reported a similar experience?" He was greatly relieved when I told him that it is not uncommon for little boys to have such feelings and that Freud thought the experience was universal, as were the feelings of guilt and anxiety that often followed.

About a month later, Robert again came to a session very distressed. He told me a memory had occurred to him that was so awful, he was ashamed to tell it to me. He then described the same incident he had recounted before, apparently unaware that he had already told me. Apparently, he had re-repressed the memory of the event.

Having provided an example of repression as a very real phenomenon, the question remains as to its importance. Recall that Freud considered it to be the most important concept in psychoanalysis and the source of all psychopathology. According to CET, repression is important, but it is not the only reason for neurosis, let alone for all other kinds of psychopathology. Having said this, let us examine what is important about it. First, it removes an important area of information about the self from awareness and therefore from being coped with through the use of a person's intelligence. Second, it uses up cognitive resources by placing a person on guard against thinking about certain threatening mental content and having to suppress its expression if it is activated. Third, content associated with repression may intrude into consciousness and be distracting and unsettling. Fourth, it tends to be behaviorally expressed in displaced, inappropriate ways.

I believe that the view that repression is the sole source of neurosis is not only incorrect, but it can be a serious source of mistreatment. The problem is that it encourages therapists to overestimate the importance of unconscious conflict concerning early relationships with parents to the neglect of other sources of maladaptive behavior, such as the intentional or unintentional reinforcement of maladaptive ways of thinking, feeling, and behaving that are not repressed.

The Negative Consequences of Fortuitous Reinforcement of Maladaptive Behavior

Sometimes, sources of maladjustment occur in a child's life that have nothing to do with poor parenting, rejection, or the repression of unacceptable sexual or hostile thoughts or impulses. The following example is of a child being accidentally rewarded for behavior that later became a source of serious problems in living. The child learned that feigning emotions could be a useful way of getting what he wanted. By feigning sadness and sobbing when he wanted attention or to obtain something he desired, he could induce his parents and others to comfort him and give him what he desired; by feigning anger, he could intimidate younger children into doing his bidding. As he successfully practiced such behavior, the behavior became increasingly reinforced until it became automatic and no longer required conscious intent. Originally, he was in control of the behavior, but it gradually came to be in control of him, with the result that he became an unhappy and angry person. Moreover, in addition to his distressing emotions, his unconsciously manipulative behavior produced problems in his relationships with others. Having no idea of why he was sad or angry, he assumed his emotions must be produced by the behavior of other people toward him, which he was able to verify without realizing that they behaved as they did in response to his own behavior. The result was that he developed an automatic self-maintaining way of being frequently sad and angry. I cite this case to provide an example of one of the many ways in which situations can fortuitously arise that have serious negative consequences without the complication of repression.

Dissociation

Whereas repression involves a conflict between the experiential and rational systems, dissociation involves a conflict completely within the experiential system. Dissociation refers to a separation in the connections in a conceptual system or systems that interferes with coherence. The existence of dissociation as distinct from repression is demonstrated by its existence in nonhuman animals. It was previously noted in the discussion of approach-avoidance conflict that a nonhuman animal or a person can be attracted to and repelled by the same goal, with the attraction and repulsion both occurring within the experiential system. Dissociation is also observed in multiple personalities and in post-traumatic stress disorder (PTSD). Dissociations within the experiential system can occur because of experiences that cannot be coherently assimilated within a person's experiential conceptual system. Several problems are produced by such dissociation. First, the person exhibits inconsistent behavior depending on which dissociated aspect of the dissociation is dominant at a particular time in a particular situation. Second, dissociation is a source of stress because the incongruity within the experiential system violates the basic need to maintain a stable, coherent implicit conceptual system. Third, intrusions of the nondominant aspect of the dissociation into a person's consciousness are disturbing and disruptive.

Alienation from the Self

Jeffrey, despite great intellectual promise, was unsuccessful in everything he tried. Nevertheless, he was very proud of himself because of his very high ideals. His ideals were so lofty that they protected him from failure because no one could reasonably be expected to meet them. How is one to explain why he led such an unproductive and deluded life, one in which he bolstered his self-esteem by taking pride in his unrealistic ideals? Horney (1950) and Rogers (1959) both regarded people like Jeffrey as alienated from their real self, which these therspists consider to be derived from actual experience. They believed such alienation is a major source of maladjustment. Horney stated that a person's real self is the "alive, unique, personal center of ourselves; the only part that can and wants to grow" (Horney, 1950, p. 155). She believed that people who are alienated from their real self have made a pact with the devil. They have sold their soul (i.e., their real self) for the self-esteem derived from a false self that includes lofty beliefs about themselves that are out of touch with their feelings.

Rogers (1959) had a similar view regarding the real self. He believed that people like Jeffrey are out of touch with what he refers to as their *organismic experience*. As a result, they suffer from an incongruity between their experience and their self-concept, which Rogers regarded as their conscious views about themselves. Rogers, like Horney, emphasized the importance of an ideal self. Like Horney, he proposed a growth principle. According to Rogers, under conditions of unconditional positive regard, people give up their defenses and become aware of and accepting of their organismic experience, which reduces the disparity between their implicit organismic self and their explicit self-concept. He stated that, with increasing congruence between these two selves, people's behavior becomes increasingly adaptive, authentic, and fulfilling.

Thus, both Horney and Rogers had a concept of a natural self that is similar to the experiential self of CET. They also believed in a conscious self based on values introjected from others. Both authors assume the existence of a growth principle. For Horney, maladjustment occurred when fulfilling the functions of the real self was thwarted by the idealized false self. Growth spontaneously occurred when the real self was released from the control of the false self. This is accomplished by interpretation and by encouragement to give up the false self. For Rogers, growth occurred when a person received unconditional positive regard. In this condition, there is a decreased investment in maintaining an unrealistic, idealized self-concept and a resultant increase in the correspondence between the conscious self-concept and the organismic self.

Cognitive-experiential theory shares important aspects of Horney's and Rogers's views, but differs from them in some vital respects. There is a correspondence between Horney's and Rogers's false self and the representation of the self in the rational system of CET. There is also a correspondence between the real selves of Horney and Rogers and the experiential self of CET. According to CET, alienation from the real self occurs when people operate in the mode of the rational system to the extent that they ignore important information about themselves, including their implicit needs and beliefs, in their experiential system, which results in an unnatural, passionless, unfulfilling manner of existence.

Cognitive-experiential theory, in common with the theories of Horney and Rogers, endorses a growth principle. According to CET, there are two inherent sources of growth. One is the basic need to maintain and enhance the conceptual system. As previously noted, a personal theory of reality, like a scientific theory, grows through its interaction with the data of reality. In agreement with Rogers, it is assumed in CET that unconditional positive regard is an important condition for fostering growth through such an experience. In agreement with Horney, according to CET, an important source of growth in therapy is interpretation at an appropriate time about the adverse consequences of maintaining an unrealistic idealized self and encouragement for accepting a more authentic self based on one's feelings and experience. Another source of growth according to CET is due to the operation of the hedonic principle, which provides an inherent motive for reducing stress and promoting positive feelings and the reduction of negative feelings.

Cognitive-experiential theory is in disagreement with Horney's and Rogers's assumption that the real self is essentially good and therefore always a source of positive growth. According to CET, the experiential self can include both destructive and constructive schemas, both of which depend on a person's reinforcement history. Therefore, releasing the real or experiential self from cognitive control by the conscious self, as advocated by Horney, can result in serious antisocial or otherwise maladaptive behavior. Nor does CET believe that the only source of a motive for growth exists in the real or experiential self. People can consciously decide in their rational system to change their maladaptive ways of being in the world and, given an understanding of the operation of their experiential system, they can undertake constructive actions to create the conditions for producing desirable changes in their experiential system.

POST-TRAUMATIC STRESS DISORDER

According to DSM-IV, PTSD is a psychological disorder in which overwhelming anxiety is produced by a threat to life or limb experienced directly or observed in others. The major symptoms of PTSD, as listed in DSM-IV are:

1. The person has experienced or witnessed a threat to life or limb of the self or to others that produced intense fear, helplessness, or horror.
2. The event is reexperienced in one or more of the following ways: recurrent, intrusive, distressing, recollections and images of the event; recurrent distressing dreams;, reliving the experience with hallucinations, illusions, and flashbacks; intense distress; and physiological reactivity when exposed to cues associated with the traumatic event.

3. The person avoids stimuli associated with the trauma and experiences a numbing of responsiveness, as indicated by three or more of the following: efforts to avoid thoughts, feelings, conversations, activities and any other cues associated with the trauma; an inability to recall important aspects of the trauma; diminished interest or participation in significant activities; feelings of detachment or estrangement from others; restricted affect and inability to have loving feelings; limited expectancies about the future.
4. Symptoms of increased arousal are present, as indicated by two or more of the following: sleep difficulty, irritability or outbursts of anger, difficulty in concentrating, hypervigilance, or an exaggerated startle response.

Cognitive-experiential theory has a somewhat different view of PTSD. According to CET, the essence of PTSD is the experience of overwhelming anxiety in response to a highly distressing event that can neither be habituated nor assimilated. This view includes not only threats to life and limb as sources of PTSD but also other experiences of overwhelming emotional intensity, such as abandonment or rejection by a loved one. The critical consideration is that the event is so incongruous with a person's basic beliefs that it cannot be assimilated and tends therefore to disorganize the person's conceptual system, which is a source of overwhelming anxiety. Because the event cannot be assimilated, its representations are dissociated from the remainder of the conceptual system in order to protect the coherence and stability of the overall system. The result is a continuous source of tension produced by a conflict between maintaining the dissociation and attempting to assimilate it. The repetitive reexperiencing of certain aspects of the trauma is a manifestation of abortive attempts at assimilation. The numbing of affect and withdrawal, including disinterest in the future, is a manifestation of the need to maintain the dissociation and to avoid thereby the disorganization and anxiety produced by attempts at assimilation. In sum, the major conceptual difference between anxiety reactions to ordinary threats and traumatic events is the disruption of a person's conceptual system in the latter situation (e.g., Epstein, 1991; Janoff-Bulman, 1992; McCann & Pearlman, 1990).

Post-traumatic stress disorder is usually resolved in one of the following two ways: (1) the trauma is assimilated within an altered conceptual system that includes accepting the possibility of the occurrence of such traumatic events as part of an overall view of a world that nevertheless provides favorable opportunities for achieving happiness and fulfillment, or (2) the person "embraces the trauma" in a revised conceptual system in which the trauma becomes the center of an overall new conceptual organization that prepares the person for accepting similar traumas. As an example of the first kind of resolution, most Vietnam veterans with PTSD gradually improved after they returned to a safe and supporting environment (Fletcher, 1988, a summary of which is provided in Epstein, 1990). A favorable readjustment in a safe environment requires veterans to assimilate their traumatic experiences by accommodating their previous conceptual systems so that they can accept the reality that traumatic events like the one they experienced (and all it implies about the nature of people, the self, and the world) can occur. Nevertheless, the world is viewed favorably and as a reasonably secure place, although less so than previously believed. Most veterans were able to achieve this synthesis within a reasonable period of time. Having made the synthesis, they were sadder but wiser people with a more differentiated and less naïvely optimistic view of the world than previously.

Other veterans descended into what Fletcher (1988) referred to as "a negative spiral." They achieved assimilation by "embracing the trauma," meaning that their beliefs about their traumatic experience became the nucleus of a cognitive-affective network that represented a new identity. Despite their being removed to a secure and favorable environment after combat, they continued to view events from the perspective of their combat experience, which meant remaining continuously vigilant, living for the moment, and distrusting authority figures.

In a study of trauma in women who had been raped, Scheppele and Bart (1983) provided two examples of women who behaved in a manner that corresponds to embracing the trauma. One of them was raped twice in a single day. After the rapes, she began to take drugs and became a prostitute. The other, a student from an advantaged background who had been attending a prestigious university, dropped out of school, took to frequenting all-night bars, carried a knife, and became highly promiscuous. How are such remarkable changes in personality to be explained? According to CET, almost any resolution of incompatible beliefs is less distressing than no resolution. By embracing the trauma, these women are protected from being traumatized in the same way as before, and they now have a measure of control over events that they previously experienced helplessly.

Jean Jenet (1946/1994) describes a situation in which he changed an abhorrent event into one that he could endure by embracing the event. During a period when he was in prison, the other prisoners forced him to sit against a wall with his mouth open. They then had a competition to determine who could get the highest score of spitting into the target, which was his open mouth. He says he coped with the situation by welcoming it, often begging the men to play the game with him. By making the activity voluntary, it reduced the stress of being a helpless victim.

PSYCHOTIC REACTIONS

In the following discussion of psychotic disorders, I make no attempt to be inclusive. Instead, I selected a limited number of disorders about which I believe CET has something to contribute.

Schizophrenia

Schizophrenia is the most serious psychotic disorder because it involves a break with reality to the extent that a person is unable to function effectively in everyday life, and it is relatively frequent. One in a hundred people in the United States will be diagnosed with schizophrenia at some time in their lives. Its symptoms are either direct manifestations of disorganization of a person's conceptual system or defenses against disorganization.

Disorganization

Why should the debilitating disorder of schizophrenia occur with such frequency? Is it possible that it has some adaptive function that can explain why it occurs? It will be recalled that, according to CET, if a conceptual system is unable to fulfill its functions, it is subject to disorganization. Disorganizing a poorly functioning conceptual system that is unable to fulfill its functions provides an opportunity for a new, improved conceptual system to be constructed (Epstein, 1979; Jefferson, 1974; Laing, 1965; Perry, 1976; Silverman; 1970). There is, of course, no guarantee that the new organization will be any more successful than the old one, but sometimes it is, as attested to by people who describe their recoveries from psychosis (e.g., Barnes & Burke, 1971; Boisen, 1960; Jefferson, 1974; Landis & Mettler, 1964; Sechehaye, 1970).

Lara Jefferson (1974) wrote a book in which she described in great detail her experience of and subsequent recovery from schizophrenia following a state of acute distress and disorganization. Following her recovery, she offered this advice to those concerned about a loved one who is undergoing a schizophrenic reaction: "Remember, when a soul sails out on that unmarked sea called Madness they have gained release much greater than your loss—and more important.... For what the sane call 'ruin'—because they do not know—those who have experienced what I am speaking of, know the wild hysteria of Madness means salvation" (p. 199). Although she may be overstating the benefits of psychotic breakdowns, Jefferson makes a compelling case for disorganization as being adaptive in some cases, such as her own.

As an example of the therapeutic consequences of a loss of normal inhibitory control followed by assimilation of long repressed memories, Jefferson described her experience of such a reaction as follows: "And once the great Madness in me found a voice, there was no stopping it. It rolled out in such a tumult, I was amazed at it myself; wondered where it all came from. It seemed obscene and terrible that I should answer in adult language, things said to me in my childhood. Things I had forgotten until they again began to pour about me in a flood of bitter memories....As I fitted answers to all those unimportant and forgotten childish silences, they lost much of their bitterness" (p. 213).

Ultimately, disorganization is a state devoid of conceptualization and, relatedly, of feelings. Although its anticipation is dreaded, its occurrence corresponds to a state of nonbeing, a void in which there are neither pleasant nor unpleasant feelings (Jefferson, 1974). Thus, what is gained is a net improvement in the pleasure-pain balance (from a negative to a zero value). What is sacrificed is the fulfillment of all the basic needs other than the hedonic principle.

The Fulfillment and Sacrifice of Basic Needs in Schizophrenia

According to CET, an important source of schizophrenia apart from genetic and biological considerations is that the conceptual system may be prone to disorganization because it was constructed on a weak foundation during the formative period of early childhood. When such a person is placed under stress later in life by a threat to the fulfillment of a basic need, the person's conceptual system is vulnerable to disorganization, and the person may use extreme defenses to prevent the disorganization from occurring.

A failure in the fulfillment or anticipated fulfillment of the basic need to maintain a favorable pleasure-pain balance is described by several people to be a common precursor of a schizophrenic episode. Grinker and Holzman (1973), Meehl (1962), and Rado (1956) report that a salient characteristic of premorbid schizophrenics is anhedonia, an inability to derive pleasure from living. Meehl makes the following statement: "For the most part these young patients report a pervasive inability to derive much joy from life.... Further, the view of their own future described by the schizophrenic patients held little prospect of amelioration" (p. 174).

A threat to the fulfillment of the basic need to maintain a stable, coherent conceptual system is another common precipitating factor of schizophrenic reactions (e.g., Bowers, 1974; Kaplan, 1964). In an investigation of acute schizophrenic disorganization, Bowers (1974) concluded that schizophrenic reactions often occurred following an impasse at a crucial maturational step that required a new way of responding to situations. Included were problems in establishing autonomy, in forming intimate nonsexual as well as sexual relationships, in giving birth to or caring for an infant, in maintaining a marital relationship, and in coping with the emergence into consciousness of unacceptable impulses, such as homosexual attraction. In all of these situations, individuals experienced emotionally significant events beyond their capacity to assimilate them, and the result was a serious threat to the organization of their conceptual systems.

A failure to fulfill the basic need for security is also a basic cause of schizophrenic reactions. Intense states of distress produced by threats to security for any reason can promote a schizophrenic episode. As previously noted, a background in which a child is insecure because its fundamental needs were either unfulfilled or inconsistently fulfilled can be the source of the construction of a conceptual system that is vulnerable to disorganization.

A failure to fulfill the basic need for relatedness is a common precipitating factor in acute schizophrenic reactions. People who later became schizophrenic are described as withdrawn and isolated individuals who desired close relationships but were afraid to establish them because they were extremely sensitive to rejection. It is noteworthy in this respect that Bowers reported that forming intimate relationships, caring for an infant, and maintaining marital relationships are among the most important threats to assimilation in premorbid schizophrenics. That frustrations regarding the establishment or maintenance of relationships are a potent source of schizophrenic reactions is not surprising because relations with a caretaker mediate the satisfaction of all of an infant's and young child's needs. Because a parenting figure is the most important source of pleasure and alleviation from distress in infants and young children, it follows that if a conceptual system for representing reality is constructed because of its emotionally rewarding value, then relationships with significant others will be an important factor in maintaining the stability of the conceptual system, particularly if it rests on a weak foundation.

A dramatic example of the relation between attachment to a significant other and the maintenance of a coherent conceptual system is illustrated by the following account of a late adolescent schizophrenic girl when reuniting with a friend in a mental institution (Green, 1964): Deborah had just learned that Carla had been readmitted to the mental institution from which she was recently discharged. Carla failed to adjust outside of the hospital, and she returned beaten and distraught. Because both young women were extremely sensitive to rejection, they were reticent to make the first approach for fear of rejection and also because they did not wish to intrude into the space of the other person in the event that she was not ready to resume a relationship.

> No one seeing Deborah and Carla, would have known they were friends. It would have been an imposition, incomprehensible to the sane, for Deborah to greet Carla, who was in distress, and who would have been sorry later if a greeting drove her to violence or even rudeness. Deborah did not look at Carla; she only waited behind her stone mask until she would see the secret sign from Carla that meant recognition.
>
> When the sign was given, they moved toward each other appearing as elaborately unconcerned as they could. Deborah smiled very slightly, but then a strange thing happened. Into the flat, gray, blurred and two-dimensional waste of her vision, Carla came three-dimensionally and in color, as whole and real as a mouthful of hot coffee or coming-to in a pack. (p. 152)

It may be recalled that another example of a relation between reality and relatedness was presented in Chapter 2, in which in a return to reality, depth perception, and perceptual organization occurred in a schizophrenic girl during a session with her therapist, only to be lost again shortly after the session (Sechehaye, 1970). These incidents are remarkable because they demonstrate how perception of reality, including fundamental physical reactions such as depth perception, can be contingent on a relationship with a significant other.

If relatedness is implicated in the construction of reality, can self-esteem be far behind? Recall that the need for self-esteem is considered in CET to be a derivative of the need for relatedness. Where once there was the perception of acceptance or rejection by a significant other, with the advent of the development of a self-concept comes acceptance and rejection of the self. Because of its relation to the need for relatedness, the need for self-esteem similarly influences the susceptibility of the conceptual system to disorganization.

In an investigation of precursors of schizophrenic episodes, Grinker and Holzman (1973) found that a particularly important premorbid characteristic of schizophrenics is "an exquisitely vulnerable sense of self-regard" (p. 168). They noted that threats to self-esteem were the most common precursors of the schizophrenic episodes they examined.

In summary, a failure to fulfill any of the basic needs can precipitate an acute schizophrenic reaction in vulnerable individuals.

Delusions of Grandeur

The following incident, which occurred many years ago when I was an interne at a Veteran's Administration (VA) hospital for psychiatric patients, well illustrates the use of a delusion of grandeur as a compensation for feelings of inferiority. At the end of my first encounter with an ongoing psychodrama treatment group, one of the patients, whom I shall call Ken, approached me. "Welcome to our group, small fry," he said. "I have a welcoming gift for you." He then handed me a piece of paper on which was written, "Pay to the bearer $10,000,000 (ten million) dollars." It was signed with his name. Ken's diagnosis was "paranoid schizophrenia with delusions of grandeur." Aside from the occasional manifestation of his delusion of being an important and wealthy person, I observed in further sessions that his behavior was usually realistic. He told me he was very eager to get out of the hospital. Why would Ken then present himself on occasion as extremely wealthy and important when everyone knew it was not true? I believe the answer is that Ken was compensating for intense feelings of inferiority by his delusion of superiority. This was clearly demonstrated in an event that took place at a later period.

Ken had agreed to participate in a research project I was conducting for my doctoral dissertation. The purpose of the research was to compare people's conscious and unconscious self-evaluations. I hypothesized that despite people with delusions of grandeur presenting extremely favorable views about themselves, at an unconscious level, they regarded themselves unfavorably. I assessed unconscious self-evaluation by having participants rate their unrecognized self-productions, such as a mirror-image presentation of their own handwriting and a recording of their voice played backward. For comparison, they also rated the productions of others. After obtaining Ken's presumably unconscious self-assessments, I asked him to rate how favorably he consciously regarded himself. Ken gave himself the lowest possible rating. I asked why he evaluated himself so negatively when he was always telling everyone how important and superior he was. He said, "I know how important your research is to you, so I told you the truth. I am a complete failure in life, not worth anything, and never will be. I act important to make myself feel better at least for the moment." Ken happened to be a psychotic who had insight into his delusion, which is not the usual case. Most patients with delusions believe them or at least consistently act as if they believe them. Ironically, Ken set his delusion aside to be helpful to me but, in doing so, he contributed data that were contrary to my hypothesis and opposite to that of the other patients with delusions of grandeur.

It is instructive to view delusions of grandeur from the perspective of what is gained and what is lost from such a delusion. A delusion of grandeur is obviously an extreme attempt to satisfy the basic need in the experiential system to maintain and enhance self-esteem. Although it may succeed to some extent in achieving such success, it is at a considerable cost in the fulfillment of other needs, particularly the need in the rational system to behave according to the reality principle. As for the experiential subordinate basic needs other than the need for self-esteem, the fulfillment of the need for sensory pleasure is sacrificed because being incarcerated in a mental institution is not a very pleasant living arrangement. The need for maintaining a coherent, stable conceptual system for accurately representing reality is somewhat but not completely sacrificed because delusions, by definition, are unrealistic. The need for security is sacrificed because a delusion of grandeur is difficult to maintain because it is unrealistic. The need for relationship is sacrificed because people are repelled by unrealistic claims of superiority. Delusions of grandeur are maintained because, in addition to a desperate attempt to boost self-esteem, they prevent disorganization by providing a unifying theme centered on one's importance.

Delusions of Persecution

The paranoid person with delusions of persecution reacts to an internal source of threat by substituting an external source of threat. Through focusing all attention and mobilizing all resources on combating the external threat, the paranoid with delusions of persecution accomplishes two goals. First, such a stance permits the person to avoid recognition of the inner source of threat, such as an unacceptable thought or impulse. Second, it provides a high degree of coherence and stability, which protects the person from disorganization. Anger and hostility are particularly useful reactions in this regard because the underlying construal for both is that one's problems are caused by bad others against whom one must protect oneself. To the extent that a person is absorbed with protection against an imminent threat, all other problems pale in significance.

An important question is to ask what underlying threat can be so great as to threaten to destabilize a person's conceptual system. According to Freud, the underlying threat is of unacceptable homosexual attraction. As a way of denying the attraction, the paranoid is said to reason as follows: "I do not love the person, I hate him, and the reason I hate him is that he is hostile toward me."

A major problem with Freud's explanation is that there is no justification for restricting an unacceptable belief that must be defended to homosexual attraction. Any unacceptable belief or impulse that is sufficiently threatening to the maintenance of a person's belief system could have the same destabilizing effect. Another problem with Freud's explanation is that there is also no reason to restrict the sources of destabilization to unacceptable beliefs or impulses. Any physical state that temporarily or permanently weakens the strength of the organization of people's conceptual systems could also be a source of delusions of persecution. This can account for the wide variety of conditions that produce delusions of persecution, including sleep deprivation, the effect of drugs, senility, and deafness.

Turning to the basic needs that are fulfilled and sacrificed by delusions of persecution, it has already been noted that the needs that are fulfilled are maintaining the coherence and stability of the conceptual system and, to a lesser extent, enhancing self-esteem. The reality principle of the rational system is obviously sacrificed because delusions are unrealistic by definition. As for the subordinate basic needs of the experiential system, the need for sensory pleasure is sacrificed because being incarcerated is an unpleasant experience. The need for security is sacrificed because believing one is being persecuted is certain to make one feel insecure. The need for relatedness is sacrificed because others are viewed as enemies who would be dangerous to relate to and also because the paranoid person alienates people through the unreasonableness of his or her belief in being persecuted. It may be concluded that the net effect of what is lost and gained by a delusion of persecution is consistent with the operation of the superordinate hedonic principle because the delusion is probably the best bargain with respect to affect that the paranoid can make.

AUTISM

When Kanner (1943) introduced the disorder identified as autism, he believed it was the result of "refrigerator mothers" who lacked normal, warm feelings for their children. This view was later abandoned because of evidence of brain anomalies in cases of autism. However, basic assumptions in CET lead me to suspect that it was premature to dismiss the possibility of at least some cases with a psychological cause of autism. This view is supported by the following case of an autistic child who I shall call John.

John was an attractive three-year-old boy with a diagnosis of autism, He was brought to a university mental health clinic for treatment. John was accompanied by his parents and his eight-year-old brother. When he was brought into the play room, he ran around in circles shrieking. When anyone talked to him, he ignored them and continued to run around in circles, shrieking. To examine how he and the members of his family interacted, we drew a circle with chalk on the floor and had the members of the family enter the room, one at a time, with instructions to play with John in the circle. The father entered first. He offered John one toy after another without trying to fit into John's play. It was evident that he was trying very hard to please John, but did not know how to do it. John ignored him and continued to push a toy truck back and forth, sometimes shouting with glee. It was the brother's turn next. He sat on the floor next to John and made himself available without interfering with John's activity. After a while, he tried to fit into the activity. When John would push the truck in his direction, he would push it back, and John would shriek with delight. Then it was the mother's turn. When John saw her enter the room, he let out a blood-curdling shriek, jumped up and began to run around the room aimlessly, as before.

One of the graduate students in our clinical psychology program was assigned to treat John on a weekly basis, and I treated his mother at the same time. My aim was to train her to be a surrogate therapist. In my sessions with the mother, it quickly became apparent that she was extremely hostile to John. He had been adopted as an infant and behaved badly from the moment they brought him home, she said. She wanted to return him to the agency, but her husband would not hear of it. In the sessions that followed, she described how her parents had favored her younger brother over her sister and herself. Her brother could do no wrong in the parents' eyes, and they showered him with gifts even when he got into trouble, which he often did. With considerable emotion, she described incident after incident in which the daughters, despite being helpful and performing well in school, were unappreciated, whereas the son, no matter how badly he behaved, was "spoiled rotten." She emphasized that she believed that what her brother needed then and John needed now was firm discipline, including punishment for misbehavior.

In describing John's behavior, his mother said that she did not believe he was a defective child, but rather that he was a willful child who knew more than he let on and who enjoyed exasperating his parents. He did this by not learning to speak and by running around in circles, shrieking. At times he would sit on the banister at the top of the stairs and get everyone very frightened that he would fall off. They would plead with him to get off, and he would just sit there and giggle. On a few occasions, she caught him raiding the refrigerator at night to get something to eat after refusing the excellent meal she had taken the trouble to prepare for the family. He hated her, she said. On one occasion, he bit her so hard through her heavy winter coat that it left a bruise.

After several months of treatment that included discussions about whether she was taking out her anger toward her brother on John, she seemed to be more accepting of John. I gave her exercises in which she was to treat John in a way that he would enjoy. As I soon would have to depart for my sabbatical in a foreign country, I wanted to get a picture of how far the relation between John and his mother had progressed. To determine whether he would now regard her as a safe refuge when he felt threatened and to observe how she would comfort him, I had someone turn on an electric shaver, which I had been told frightened him when he had his hair cut by a barber. John could hear it through the wall of the playroom. I waited at the entrance to the waiting room where John routinely joined his mother at the end of his session. At the sound of the razor, John bolted out of the playroom. He ran past his mother in the waiting room and into the street, and then he ran down the street as fast as his legs would carry him. His therapist and I finally caught up with him. As we walked back holding his hands, we did our best to soothe him. When we arrived at the clinic, we gave him some of his favorite candy. I normally am able to maintain an appropriate therapeutic distance when hearing the problems of my clients, but this time I was deeply distressed at the thought that this poor child felt he had no one to turn to when he was upset.

Frequently, John's sessions with his therapist ended slightly after my sessions with his mother. I would then wait for him in the hall outside the playroom, greet him when he emerged, throw him in the air and catch him, and he would giggle with delight. However, he never paid any attention to my words or made eye contact with me. I felt that if a robot replaced me, it would have made no difference to him. One day, however, something very strange happened. When John came out of the playroom, I said to him, "I'm so happy to see you, John. Would you please get that truck you were playing with for me?" John wheeled around, ran into the playroom, and brought back the truck. He gave it to me and then went berserk. We were standing outside the bathroom. John ran into the bathroom, jumped into the toilet with both feet, and proceeded to stamp his feet in the water and shriek. He then jumped out of the toilet, ran into the playroom, and ran in circles, shrieking all the while. I had the feeling that he wanted to convey to me that he is a crazy child who understands nothing and that I should pay no attention to his momentary lapse into sanity. After that incident, things returned to where they had been before, and I again became no more than a child-throwing robot to him. When I spoke to him, he showed no sign that he heard me.

John had a vocabulary of four words. The words were "open," which he used when he wanted someone to open a door for him; "M&M," which he used to solicit his favorite candy; "up," which he used when he wanted to be picked up and thrown in the air; and "down," when he wanted to be put down. I decided, not long after the truck incident, to find out if I could get him to cooperate again. The next time, when I picked him up I held him and did not throw him in the air, nor did I put him down. I said, "John, when you want me to put you down, just say the word 'down,' and I will put you down right away." He paid no attention to me and stared vacuously through me. He began to squirm. I repeated, "John, just say 'down,' and I will put you down. I know you know how to say down; just say it." He began to struggle more intensely, cried, flailed at me, and finally blurted out, "up, up, up, open, open, open, M & M, M & M, M & M." I put him down and said I was sorry I had upset him. He ran back to the playroom and ran in circles, shrieking.

How is one to explain John's behavior? It will be recalled that, according to CET, people construct an implicit theory of reality, including a self-concept, not for its own sake, but because it is rewarding to do so. By representing what they, themselves, are like, what other people and the world are like, and the influence of their behavior on outcomes, people's implicit theories of reality allow them to negotiate the real world. But what if the construction of an implicit theory of reality would be more punishing than rewarding? What if it meant viewing people as hostile and more as a source of distress than of pleasure and of viewing the self as bad and unlovable? In that case, constructing a theory of reality and a self-concept would be a poor bargain. Thus, according to CET, there are at least some cases of autism that occur for psychological reasons, such as when it is unrewarding to have a concept of self. A promising area for research on this issue is the investigation of whether an autistic child prefers contact with his or her caretaker or is threatened by and avoids such contact. It is hypothesized that there is an important psychological causative component in autistic children in the latter category that is lacking in those in the former category.

REFERENCES

Barnes, M., & Burke, J. (1971). *Mary Barnes: Two accounts of a journey through madness*. New York: Ballantine Books.

Boisen, A. (1960). *Out of depths*. New York: Harper & Rowe.

Bowers, M. B. Jr. (1974). *Retreat from sanity*. New York: Human Sciences Press.

Brown, T. A., Campbell, L. A., Lenman, C. L., Grisham, J. R., & Mancill, R. B. (2001). Current and lifetime comorbidity of the DSM-!V anxiety and mood disorders in a large clinical example. *Journal of Abnormal Psychology, 110*, 585–599.

Epstein, S. (1979). Natural healing processes of the mind: 1. Acute schizophrenic disorganization. *Schizophrenia Bulletin, 5*, 313–321.

Epstein, S. (1990). Cognitive-experiential self-theory. In L. Pervin (Ed.), *Handbook of personality theory and research: Theory and research*. (pp. 165–192). New York: Guilford Press.
Epstein, S. (1991). The self-concept, the traumatic neurosis, and the structure of personality. In D. Ozer, J. M. Healy Jr., & A. J. Stewart (Eds.), *Perspectives in personality* (vol. 3A, pp. 63–98). London: Jessica Kingsley.
Eysenck, H. J., & Rachman, S. (1965). *The causes and cures of neurosis*. London: Routledge & Kegan Paul.
Fletcher, K. E. (1988). *Belief systems, exposure to stress, and post-traumatic stress-disorder in Vietnam veterans*. Unpublished doctoral dissertation, University of Massachusetts at Amherst.
Freud, A., & Burlingham, D. (1943). *War and children*. New York: Medical War Books.
Green, H. (1964). *I never promised you a rose garden*. New York: New American Library.
Grinker, R. R. Sr., & Holzman, P. S. (1973). Schizophrenic pathology in young adults. *Archives of General Psychiatry*, *28*, 168–175.
Horney, K. (1950). *Neurosis and human growth*. New York: W. W. Norton & Co.
Jenet, J. (1946/1994). *The miracle of the rose*. Published in French in 1946. (Translated into English by Bernard Frechtman.) Published in English in 1994. New York: Grove Press.
Janoff-Bulman, R. (1992). *Shattered assumptions*. New York: The Free Press.
Jefferson, L. (1974). *These are my sisters*. New York: Anchor Press/Doubleday.
Kagan, J. (1984). *The nature of the child*. New York: Basic Books.
Kanner (1943). Autistic disturbances of affective contact. *Nervous Child*, *2*, 217–250.
Kaplan, B. (1964). *The inner world of mental illness*. New York: Harper & Row.
Laing, R. (1965). *The divided self*. Baltimore, MD: Penguin Books.
Landis, C., & Mettler, F. A. (1964). *Varieties of psychopathological experience*. New York: Holt, Rinehart, & Winston.
Lazarus, R. S. (1966). *Psychological stress and the coping response*. New York: McGraw-Hill.
May, R. (1950). *The meaning of anxiety*. New York: Ronald Press.
McCann, I. L, & Pearlman, L. A. (1990). *Psychological trauma and the adult survivor*. New York: Bruner/Mazel.
Meehl, P. E. (1962). Schizotaxia, schizotypy, schizophrenia. *American Psychologist*, *17*, 827–838.
Pavlov, I. P. (1941). *Conditioned reflexes and psychiatry* (trans. W. H. Gantt). New York: International Publishers Co.
Perry, J. W. (1976). *Roots of renewal in myth and madness*. San Francisco: Jossey-Bass.
Rado, S. (1956). *Psychoanalysis of behavior: Collected papers*. New York: Grune & Stratton.
Rogers, C. R. (1959). A theory of therapy, personality, and interpersonal relationships as developed in the client-centered framework. In S. Koch (Ed.), *Psychology: A study of a science* (vol. 3, pp. 184–256). New York: McGraw-Hill.
Scheppele, K. L., & Bart, P. B. (1983). Through women's eyes: Defining danger in the wake of sexual assault. *Journal of Social Issues*, *39*, 63–81.
Sechehaye, M. (1970). *Autobiography of a schizophrenic girl*. New York: New American Library.
Silverman, J. (1970). When schizophrenia helps. *Psychology Today*, 4, 63–65.

CHAPTER 10
Depression

The most fundamental symptom of depression is a deep and enduring feeling of sadness. It follows that understanding the nature of sadness should be helpful in understanding depression. It will be recalled that, according to cognitive-experiential theory (CET), the essence of a primary emotion such as sadness is preparation for a certain kind of action. Just as anger prepares an organism for attack, fear for flight, and joy for engagement, sadness prepares an animal for disengagement. The adaptive value of sadness for a defeated or helpless animal is that it provides a period for conserving energy and assimilating the consequences of a loss or defeat. It is maladaptive only when it results in an extended state of sadness, helplessness, hopelessness, or disengagement.

To obtain further information about the relation of sadness to depression, let us consider the symptoms of depression according to the *Diagnostic and Statistical Manual of Mental Disorders* (DSM-IV; American Psychiatric Association, 2000). According to the manual, a diagnosis of depression is warranted when five or more of the following symptoms are present: (1) depressed mood; (2) diminished interest and pleasure in living; (3) significant weight loss or weight gain; (4) insomnia or hypersomnia (excessive sleep); (5) psychomotor retardation or agitation; (6) fatigue or loss of energy; (7) feelings of worthlessness or excessive guilt, which may reach delusional proportions; (8) indecisiveness and diminished ability to think or concentrate; and (9) recurrent thoughts of death or suicide. Among these symptoms, the following refer to manifestations or consequences of sadness: depressed mood, diminished interest and pleasure in living, significant weight loss (a consequence of diminished pleasure from eating), excessive or disturbed sleep, psychomotor retardation or agitation, loss of energy, and an inability to think, concentrate, and decide. Such manifestations of the sadness-disengagement reaction account for seven of the nine symptoms listed for a diagnosis of depression. All of these are experienced by depressed nonhuman animals, as well as by depressed humans. The symptoms of agitation and sleeplessness may seem incompatible with disengagement and withdrawal, but they can be explained by the inability to assimilate the distressing event that precipitated the depression. This informs us that depression is not simply a restful state of disengagement that facilitates healing, but, rather, it is a disturbed disengagement. More is going on under the surface in depression than meets the eye. For both human and nonhuman animals, the implicit cognitions underlying depression appear to be assessments of a significant loss or defeat that appears beyond correction; there is nothing that can be done about the situation, and the organism is rendered helpless with respect to regaining important rewards in living.

For humans, there is another common source of depression that is suggested by the two remaining DSM-IV symptoms, namely, feelings of worthlessness or guilt and thoughts of suicide. These are neither experienced by nonhuman animals, nor are they characteristic of normal sadness in humans. Both implicate a person's self-concept. Feelings of worthlessness involve a denigration of the self, and suicide involves its destruction. Why should turning against the self be a source of depression in humans? Why do some women following a horrifying experience, such as being raped, react with guilt and self-belittlement rather than only with fear of and anger at the perpetrator? Why do such women make statements such as, "I was treated as a piece of dirt, so I guess I am a piece of dirt, a thing that anyone can do with whatever they want, as if I don't matter at all." I will attempt to answer this question after discussing some other issues. For now, it will suffice to note that there are two kinds of depression, one that involves feelings of helplessness without a negative view of the self and the other that includes a negative view of the self. Note that although there are two kinds of depression, both involve deep and prolonged states of sadness in association with feelings of helplessness and hopelessness.

THE STRESS-DIATHESIS MODEL OF DEPRESSION

Depression of both kinds is often precipitated by the occurrence of an external event in interaction with a personal vulnerability. This is a common view about mental disorders in general, one that is referred to as the *stress-diathesis model*, which refers to the combination of an external stressor and an individual who is vulnerable to the stressor. The vulnerability can consist of either a biological or psychological predisposing factor. Although there is evidence that genetic factors may play a role in some cases of depression (Winokur, 1979), they are not considered to be the main influence in most cases (Fabry, 1980; Winokur, 1979).

Depressive episodes also occur in the absence of specific precipitating events. Brown and Harris (1989), in a review of many studies of depression, concluded that 70–95 percent of depressive episodes are preceded by an emotionally significant life event. This leaves more than a negligible number without an external precipitating event. It is quite possible that an internal precipitating event occurred, such as the cumulative influence of a disappointing lifestyle resulting in the conclusion that one has been a failure in life and always will be. Such thinking would be represented by an affectively charged cognitive network in which the self is considered unworthy, helpless, and hopeless.

SOME INFLUENTIAL THEORIES OF DEPRESSION

Freud's Psychoanalytic Theory of Depression

Freud (1917/1957) believed that depression is caused by unconscious hostility toward a lost love object, in which the hostility is turned inward. The hostility is produced by distress at the loss of an important relationship, such as the death, rejection, or departure of a loved one toward whom the depressed person had ambivalent feelings. The depressed person is assumed to maintain the relationship by incorporating aspects of the other person's personality into the person's self-concept; that is, through identification with the person for whom the relationship was lost, thereby undoing the loss to some extent. Unable to consciously accept the hostility toward the person whose relationship has been lost, the depressed person directs his or her hostility at the incorporated part of the lost person in the self. The result is that the depressed person experiences hatred of the self, which is a central aspect of the person's depression. A difficulty with Freud's explanation of depression is that it is highly speculative and complex and, as will be seen, simpler, less speculative, and more reasonable explanations are available.

Neo-Analytic Theories of Depression

Arieti and Bemporad

Arieti and Bemporad (1978) believe that a predisposing condition for depression is a sudden severe loss during childhood. The loss can be of affection or of attention as a result of the death, illness, or departure of a parent. The loss can also be a loss of freedom as the result of increasing demands for improved behavior as a child grows older or of a favored position in the family because of the birth of a sibling. The child who experiences any of these or related losses often strives to reestablish a close relationship with a parent by trying to please the parent in one of two ways. One way is by being helpful, obedient, and a very good child. The other way is by demonstrating one's worth by being very successful in one's endeavors and, relatedly, of setting very high standards for achievement. The former approach is more commonly exhibited by females and the latter by males.

The approach to regaining a lost relationship with parents by being helpful often generalizes to a desire to please parent surrogates, including authority figures and institutions. Consonant with adopting a subservient attitude for the purpose of pleasing others, the depression-prone person is likely to establish a subordinate role with a significant other, such as a spouse. The significant other then tends to be overestimated, just as a parent once was, and the importance of the self is correspondingly diminished, as if the person were still a child. The depression-prone person who wishes to gain the approval of others by being subservient tends to take responsibility for adverse outcomes even if she objectively knows she was not at fault. The result is that she develops a self-derogatory, dependent, unsatisfactory lifestyle that makes her vulnerable to depression.

As for the path to depression taken by those who hope to achieve appreciation and admiration by meeting very high achievement goals, when, as often happens, they fail to meet those goals, they consider themselves to be failures in life. This then leads, as in the other path to depression, to a negative self-concept and a corresponding state of depression.

According to Arieti and Bemporad, the two kinds of event that most often trigger severe depressive episodes are the realization that one will never realize a lifetime goal and the loss of a significant relationship by divorce, death, departure, or rejection. Both of these kinds of event have in common "the experience of a loss of what seems to the patient the most valuable or meaningful aspect of his life. Even more crucial is the feeling of being unable to retrieve or substitute what has been lost" (1978, p. 155). In summary, Arieti and Bemporad believe that the basic requirement for an event to trigger a severe depressive episode is that it consists of an irretrievable loss of an important goal or of a significant relationship that produces feelings of helplessness and hopelessness in a person who has been sensitized to such a loss by an early childhood experience of loss.

Bowlby

Bowlby's (1980) understanding of depression is based on his observations of the behavior of young children to separation from their mothers by events such as maternal death or hospitalization. He noted that young children react to such events with an initial period of acute distress and searching for the mother. This is followed by ambivalence toward her when she returns. Finally, recovery occurs after a sufficient period following the mother's return.

Bowlby also obtained his views about depression from the treatment of adults who were suffering from symptoms that followed loss of a loved one. He concluded that depression often results from incomplete mourning. He noted a variety of ways in which the normal process of mourning is aborted and the symptoms and problems in living that accompany unresolved mourning. He observed that a bereaved person may fail to go through a normal period of mourning because he or she avoids thoughts of the deceased person because such thoughts are too distressing to bear. The result is that the bereaved person feels numbed and becomes withdrawn. Another maladaptive pattern that Bowlby observed is an obsessive dwelling on the lost person and an inability to get beyond such thoughts. The person has little interest in other aspects of living and is unable to move beyond the grief reaction. A third maladaptive pattern is maintaining an unrealistic belief that the lost relationship is not really lost and that somehow it will be reinstated. This, too, keeps the person from moving ahead in life.

Bowlby believed that the reason some people are unable successfully to negotiate the process of mourning is that they were sensitized in childhood to a loss of or separation from a significant adult. He makes no claim that his theory is a general theory of depression. Rather, he views his contribution as involving an understanding of bereavement, a very important subset of depression.

As noted in Chapter 7, his theory of attachment and loss, with its emphasis on mental representations of significant early figures and relationships, is similar to that of CET but narrower in scope. In common with CET, Bowlby believes that people develop working representations of reality based on emotionally significant experiences. It is because of their vulnerability to loss of relationships with caretakers and their limited cognitive ability to understand and otherwise cope with adversity that young children develop maladaptive representations following significant loses or separations in childhood. As a result, they are sensitized to similar losses and separations in their adult years, which predisposes them to depression.

Cognitive Theories of Depression

Aaron Beck

Beck has been very influential in current thinking, research, and treatment concerning depression (Beck, 1967; Beck & Alford, 2009; Beck, Rush, Shaw, & Emery, 1979; Beck, & Young, 1985). The treatment he proposes is one of the most widely employed and successful procedures for treating depression. Similar to CET, Beck emphasizes the importance of the meanings people attribute to events and how this determines the emotions they experience. He noted, for example, that the same event, such as doing poorly on a test, can evoke sadness, anger, or fear, depending on how a person interprets it. What is a success to one person is a failure to another, and one student will attribute her failure to insufficient studying and, as a result, be motivated to study harder, whereas another will attribute it to a poor test or an unfair instructor, be angry, and not change his studying habits. Accordingly, Beck believes that depression is caused by the maladaptive ways in which depressive-prone people think.

Beck's explanation of why some people are more vulnerable to depression than others is that they have been sensitized by early experiences to think in negative ways. Predisposing experiences could be exposure to the modeling of a depression-prone significant other or by having had extremely distressing experiences, such as loss of or rejection or abuse by a parent. The result is that the child develops a maladaptive cognitive way of interpreting events with regard to both content and cognitive style of thinking. The content is biased in the direction of maximizing negative and minimizing positive interpretations of events and people, including—particularly—oneself. The cognitive style is characterized by polarized thinking (i.e., viewing events and people, including the self, in categorical ways, such as being totally good or totally bad) and by overgeneralization, such as by coming to an excessively broad conclusion based on a single experience. As a result of thinking in such ways regarding content and cognitive style, depression-prone people acquire a negative and maladaptive view of themselves, the world, and the future.

Beck's cognitive view of depression (Beck, 1967, 1976; Beck et al., 1979; Beck, & Young, 1985) is similar to the views of Bowlby and of Arieti and Bemporad regarding the kinds of event that trigger depressive episodes in adults. Beck takes issue with what he regards as an overemphasis by psychoanalysts on unconscious processes. In contrast, psychoanalysts like Arieti and Bemporad regard unconscious beliefs as the most important source of depression, and they regard conscious beliefs as superficial. It should be noted that Beck is not completely consistent in his emphasis on conscious information processing because he often refers to the importance of automatic thoughts and interpretations and the fact that people may be unaware of their significance. A second difference between Beck's explanation of depression and the view of Ariei and Bemporad is that the views of the latter are complicated by considering the interactions of unconscious thoughts, impulses, and defenses.

Beck's theory of depression is dissimilar from others in that he explains depression not only by the acquisition of negatively biased ways of thinking because of unfortunate experiences in childhood, but also by the acquisition of maladaptive cognitive styles of thinking and by the modeling by children of the depressive thoughts and behavior of significant adults in children's families.

Seligman

Martin Seligman (1975) initially proposed a cognitive theory of depression that was referred to as the *learned helplessness* (LH) theory of depression. It is similar in many respects to Beck's theory but also incorporates some other principles from learning theory. The initial LH theory was based on experiments with dogs. When dogs were placed in a situation in which they previously had received unavoidable electric shock, they did not try to escape when it later became possible to do so. They had acquired what Seligman and his associates referred to as "learned helplessness," and it was assumed that the same LH reaction could account for depression in humans. An obvious deficiency in the theory soon became apparent. It could not account for the low self-esteem that is characteristic of many depressed people. To remedy this deficiency, the theory was revised to include a concept of "explanatory style," which refers to the attributions that people make when they have unfavorable experiences. Peterson and Seligman (1984) proposed that depressed people, more than others, attribute unfortunate outcomes to internal (self-produced), stable (unchanging), and global (highly general) personal inadequacies rather than to other causes. As a result, they have low self-esteem. The predisposing conditions for acquiring such negative ways of thinking are considered to be an upbringing in which children do not have sufficient experiences that promote a sense of mastery and optimism. The implication for child rearing and psychotherapy is that it is important to provide children with experiences that cultivate self-attributions of mastery and success.

The elaboration of LH by emphasizing the importance of attributions can be viewed as a subset of Beck's theory of depression. It differs from Beck's theory in placing greater importance on the adaptive value of positive thinking, particularly with regard to attributions concerning mastery. This has obvious implications for child rearing and psychotherapy because it suggests the importance of providing people with experiences that foster a sense of mastery. This can be contrasted with the emphasis placed by others on predisposing events in childhood being primarily unfavorable experiences involving loss of significant relationships and separation. It also differs from the importance, according to Beck, of the modeling of depressive thinking and of the value of teaching and encouraging logical and realistic thinking. It is ironic that Seligman criticizes an overemphasis on negative thinking and then exhibits an equivalent opposite bias by overemphasizing the importance of positive thinking. Obviously, it is important for a complete psychology to recognize the value and limitations of both kinds of thinking.

DEPRESSION FROM THE PERSPECTIVE OF COGNITIVE-EXPERIENTIAL THEORY

Cognitive-experiential theory provides a theory of depression that draws on principles of learning theory, cognitive theory, psychoanalytic theory, and its own constructs, including sensitivities and compulsions, emotional complexes, and constructive thinking. As previously noted, there are two kinds of depression, one that does not involve negative self-assessments and one that does. The former is more likely to be associated with a reactive depression precipitated by the occurrence of unfavorable events, such as the irretrievable loss of a loved one. The latter is more likely to have a greater internal component related to the vulnerability of a person's self-concept to derogation.

Depression in the Absence of Self-Negation

That severe depression can occur in the absence of a negative self-concept is demonstrated by its occurrence in nonhuman animals, which suggests, according to CET, that it can also occur in the experiential system of humans, such as by its occurrence in a variety of distressing conditions from which escape is impossible or at least highly unlikely. Examples of such conditions include a fatal illness, intractable chronic pain, the death or departure of a loved one, and incarceration in a concentration camp. Thus, after the loss of a child, a mother may lose her interest in living. She may be depressed, not because she thinks of herself in disparaging ways, including unrealistically believing that she was responsible for her child's death, but because life has lost its joy and meaning for her, she is helpless to change the situation, and she feels hopeless regarding life ever returning to normal. Another example of severe depression in the absence of a negative self-concept is the deep depression exhibited by many prisoners in Nazi extermination camps, in which their misery was at the limit of human tolerance and there was no realistic hope of survival. Several went into a state of depression in which they lost their interest in living. They were recognized by their fellow prisoners as the living dead by their shuffling gait and their vacuous stare, and they usually died soon after they entered this state (Des Pres, 1976).

Yet not everyone reacts even to the inhumane and near-hopeless conditions of a concentration camp by entering into a deep state of depression. Some avoid doing so by finding some glimmer of meaning in life, if it is only to survive against all odds so that they can bear witness against the people or institutions that were responsible for their treatment (Des Pres, 1976; Frankl, 1939).

Based on recent research, it has become apparent that people are more resilient than has commonly been assumed. For example, it was found in several studies that only 10–15 percent of bereaved people become chronically depressed (Bonanno, 2004). Moreover, most of those without indications of acute distress were not people who were repressing or suppressing the manifestation of their grief, which was presumably the source of some form of maladjustment, such as the development of psychosomatic symptoms or a serious disease. The picture that emerged from prospective as well as retrospective studies is that most of those who did not exhibit strong signs of distress following bereavement were better adjusted both immediately after bereavement and at a later period. Such people apparently interpreted their loss in more adaptive ways than did those who were more distressed (Bonanno, 2004). In the terminology of CET, they behaved as better constructive thinkers. Another possibility, of course, is that, for some, the loss of a spouse with whom they had a poor relationship was more of a relief than a trauma.

According to CET, implicit schemas that promote interpreting events and thinking in a manner that produces feelings of helplessness and hopelessness make people vulnerable to depression when they experience the loss of a significant relationship or a significant failure from which they see no possibility of restitution. Moreover, such a way of automatically thinking and interpreting events outside of awareness makes people unable to understand why they are depressed. It is interesting, in this respect, that Tolstoy (1887/1987), who was given to periods of deep depression, reported that he was more disturbed by his inability to understand why he should feel depressed despite his favorable circumstances than by the depression itself. Apart from the influence of biological influences, such as bipolar depression, the possibility should be considered that a learned way of thinking based on very early childhood experiences may have played a role in Tolstoy's depression. Here is how he described his situation (Tolstoy, 1897/1987): "Or thinking about the fame my own writing brought me, I would say to myself, 'Well fine, so you will be more famous than Gogol, Pushkin, Shakespeare, Moliere, more famous than all the writers in the world, and so what?' And I had absolutely no answer."

"All this was happening to me at a time when I was surrounded on all sides by what is considered complete happiness. I was not yet fifty, I had a kind, loving and beloved wife, lovely children, and a large estate that was growing and expanding with no effort on my part. I was respected by relatives and friends far more than ever before. I was praised by strangers and could consider myself a celebrity without deceiving myself....

"I could not attribute any rational meaning to a single act, let alone to my whole life. I simply felt astonished that I had failed to realize this from the beginning. It had all been common knowledge for such a long time. Today or tomorrow sickness and death will come (and they had already arrived) to those dear to me, and to myself, and nothing will remain other than the stench and the worms. Sooner or later my deeds, whatever they may have been, will be forgotten and will no longer exist. What is all the fuss about then? How can a person carry on living and fail to perceive this? That is what is so astonishing! It is only possible to go on living while you are intoxicated with life; once sober it is impossible not to see that it is all a mere trick, and a stupid trick!" (pp. 29–31).

What was the vulnerability that made Tolstoy depressed despite his fame and favorable economic and family situation, and why, despite his superior intelligence, could he not understand his depression? According to CET, one possibility of why he was unable to understand it was because the answer lay in the operation of his experiential system, of which he was unaware.

Without knowing about the sensitivities and compulsions that Tolstoy acquired in his early childhood, we, too, are unable to understand his depression. However, by understanding the general operation of the experiential system and the kinds of basic needs that could have been unfulfilled in his childhood, we are in a better position to speculate than was Tolstoy. One possibility, consistent with the views of Arieti and Bemporad (1978), is that Tolstoy was driven to be successful as a way of securing the unconditional love he craved as an infant or very young child. The difficulty was that the love he craved was the unconditional love normally received only by infants. Such unconditional love cannot, by definition, be achieved by superior accomplishment, no matter how great. When Tolstoy fulfilled his conscious goal, it was therefore experienced at the experiential level as a disappointment and an indication of the futility of any achievement, rather than as a source of fulfillment and happiness.

In conclusion, one way people become depressed is by feeling helpless because of the occurrence of distressing events, often involving some form of loss that they view as irreparable. Depending on how early experiences influence people's automatic thinking and interpretation of events, some people are more predisposed than others to react to such events with the helpless form of depression. The occurrence of distressing events in childhood, such as loss or separation from a loved one that a child feels helpless to reverse and that the child does not interpret as resulting from his own bad behavior, is likely to be the source of implicit beliefs that predispose a person to such depression.

It might be argued that depression resulting from realistic conditions of helplessness and hopelessness, as in the case of a terminal illness or internment in a concentration camp, is a normal reaction that does not require sensitization by previous experiences or maladaptive styles of thinking. However, because it is realistic to be depressed in certain situations does not mean that such reactions are not influenced by previously acquired schemas, including sensitivities in a person's experiential system. Some people in the most difficult circumstances, depending in large part on how they interpret and think about events, are better able to cope with adversity than others. A case in point is exhibited by the following example.

My wife and I were recently visited by a casual acquaintance who had just lost her spouse following the sudden onset and rapid progress of a fatal cancer. I will call her Jane and him Scott. Scott was a forester who supervised the woodlot we own. We regarded him as a friend as much as a consultant. We first met Jane a year ago, when she accompanied Scott, my wife, and me on an inspection of our forest. I had not seen nor heard from Scott nor Jane for about a year, until she called to report that Scott had died from a very aggressive cancer. We were shocked at the news, as Scott was in his 40s and seemed to be in excellent health when we last saw him. She suggested we arrange for an appointment so she could deliver to us the information on our property she found in Scott's files. When Jane came to our house, after taking care of business matters, we invited her to stay for tea. Jane seemed to have a need to talk about Scott, so we reminisced with her about him, but mainly we listened. Jane told us that she and Scott had been good friends for a long time, but had not thought about each other romantically. She said that both were wary about serious relationships, but, as they got to know each other, they fell in love, and, a few months later, they became engaged. Shortly before the date of their wedding, Scott was diagnosed with a cancer that they were told he was unlikely to survive for more than a few months, which is what happened. Tears welled up in Jane's eyes. We expressed our sympathy and expected her to unburden herself about how hard the loss was on her. Instead, she talked in glowing terms about what a wonderful person Scott was and how fortunate she was for having had a wonderful, intimate relationship with him. She said it always brought a warm glow to her heart to think about Scott and that the memories it left her with will always be a source of strength and joy for her. She related all of this, not in a stereotyped, defensive way, but in a rich and expressive manner that made us feel drawn to her and to admire the way she turned what could easily have been a devastating experience into a growth experience. Someone else might have been deeply distraught and dysfunctional after having one of the most wonderful experiences in their life suddenly wrenched from them. People obviously can interpret events to a greater or lesser extent in a constructive or a destructive manner, and it is obviously constructive, not maladaptive, to appreciate what is positive in life without denying what is negative about it.

A caveat about constructive thinking is in order here, lest the view I have presented be misinterpreted. Constructive thinking is not the same as positive thinking. A good constructive thinker is positive when it is adaptive to view events in a favorable way but is not a naïve optimist, does not hesitate to entertain worst-case scenarios when appropriate, and is able to grieve at a loss, but also to recover from it and to appreciate the positive memories that remain.

Depression with Self-Negation

Why should people turn against themselves after experiencing highly distressing events for which they were not responsible, such as the loss of a loved one? Severely depressed people who have done nothing wrong of any significance sometimes say they have committed unpardonable sins that are too terrible to report. Some even confess to crimes they did not commit. A young woman I was treating described her feelings after she had been raped, as follows: "I felt like a piece of dirt, worth nothing, simply existing for others to do with as they pleased." Because the rape was not her fault, why should she direct her anger at herself rather than at the rapist?

We have already seen that Freud, Arieti and Bemporad, Bowlby, and Beck, and their associates all attribute negative evaluations of the self primarily to experiences in childhood. Although all of their views contribute to our understanding of hostility turned inward, I believe that Sullivan's (1953) views about the interaction of the "good and bad me" with the "good and bad mother" provide a particularly illuminating explanation of why some people are prone to turn against themselves. According to Sullivan, people acquire "personifications," which are similar to Bowlby's inner representations and to schemas about self and others in CET. Particularly important personifications, according to Sullivan, are of a "good me," "a bad me," "a good mother," and a "bad mother." As previously noted, it is self-defeating for children to be hostile toward a parent whom they desperately want to love and care for them. It is self-defeating not only because the feeling of hostility is distressing in itself, but because, if a child expresses the hostility, it will alienate the parent, which is the last thing the child wants to happen. A more satisfactory solution is to view the self as bad and the parent as good because that keeps alive the hope that the good parent will love and attend to the needs of the bad child if the bad child becomes a good child. Note that the hostility is not denied in such a resolution, not because of guilt but because of the strategic advantage in denying and thereby avoiding the expression of the hostility. Once such a strategic set of beliefs is adopted by the child, should she feel the slightest anger at the parent, she would experiences a twinge of anxiety that would provide a signal for suppressing or displacing the expression of the hostility. With repeated reinforcement through anxiety reduction, the compulsion to think of the self as bad and the parent as good becomes automatic and influences how the child interprets and reacts to the parent. This view of the self as bad and the parent as good automatically generalizes to other significant relationships. The suppressed hostility to the parent may also be displaced to another person, such as a spouse. The implicit beliefs underlying such reactions tend to be self-maintaining because of behavior that results in self-fulfilling prophecies.

A second route to depression that includes turning against the self involves guilt. Guilt can occur in children because of unacceptable wishes, behavioral impulses, or overt behavior. It can occur in adults because of behavior that violates their values Such behavior may occur under the influence of alcohol or other drugs, under the influence of group pressure, under the temptation to gain a desired object or behavioral outcome, under conditions of duress (such as providing information under torture that results in the capture or death of one's comrades or loved ones), and under conditions of violating one's honor or the honor of one's country, as in the institutionalized practice of hara-kiri.

More commonly, depression associated with turning against the self has its roots in unrealistic guilt reactions in childhood because of the limited cognitive ability of children. Thus, a child may be overwhelmed with guilt following the death of a sibling whose removal from the family the child had wished for. In the child's mind, the wish may be considered the cause of the death. Wishes for the removal of a new sibling who usurps a mother's attention are not uncommon and are readily forgotten if the wish is unfulfilled, as is the usual case. I witnessed an example of such an unfulfilled wish some years ago. When one of my grandchildren was three years old, I asked him how he felt about his new baby brother. He said, "I don't like him. He cries all the time, he smells, and he keeps my mother so busy she has no time for me." "What do you think should be done about it?" I asked him. He replied, "I think we should send him back where he came from." I asked him what he thought the chances were of that happening. He said, "I want to do it, but my mother likes him, so I guess we will have to keep him."

Now consider a situation in which a child, whom I shall call Jane, is very insecure about her mother's love. The mother who previously had lavished attention on Jane is preoccupied with a new baby. When Jane tries to attract her mother's attention, her mother becomes cross with her and says, "Can't you see I am busy with your brother?" The mother then talks in baby talk to the baby, sings to him, and appears to be joyous as she does so. Everyone who visits fusses about the new baby and ignores Jane. Jane is distressed and angry at the way the new baby is favored and she is neglected. She desperately wishes the new baby would disappear and life would return to normal. Suppose that the new baby dies in its sleep, diagnosed with sudden infant death (SID) syndrome. The parents are beside themselves with grief. Jane is aware that a very terrible thing has happened and that she was responsible for making it happen because that is what she wished for. Further assume that, in their grief, the parents do nothing to help Jane cope with the situation. This may convince her that she is a wicked and unlovable child. She acquires a sensitivity to the slightest sign of disapproval, which she interprets as verifying her wickedness, and she tries to compensate for it by being an exceptionally good and obedient child.

Relation of Loss of Self-Esteem to Loss of a Caretaker

If the most fundamental aspect of depression is a prolonged feeling of helplessness and hopelessness, why should depression often be accompanied by low self-esteem? In addition to the reasons I have already noted, I believe the answer can be found in the similarity of the loss or absence of a caretaker by a very young child and the loss of a love-worthy self in an adult or a child old enough to have developed a self-concept.

According to CET, the most fundamental source of self-esteem is an implicit belief that the self is love-worthy (Epstein, 2006). Although there are several other sources of self-esteem, including implicit beliefs about one's competence, morality, attractiveness, will-power, and social skills (O'Brien & Epstein, 1988), none is as fundamental as a view of the self as not love-worthy. The powerful influence of the implicit belief about the degree that one is love-worthy can be understood by considering it as a development of the basic need of a young child for the love and care of its caretaker. This basic need for relatedness provides the foundation for the development of another highly influential basic need when the child develops a self-concept, namely, the need for self-esteem in the form of regarding the self as love-worthy. Previously, all that mattered to the child was how the mother regarded the child. With the development of a self-concept, the child's feelings are determined not only by whether it feels loved and cared for by its mother but also by how much it loves itself. The two kinds of appraisal are closely related because the child regards itself as love-worthy to the extent that it feels loved by its caretaker. Because of the relation between being loved and feeling love-worthy, a loss of self-esteem in an older child or in an adult is a source of depression in a similar way as the loss or separation from a mother is a source of depression in a younger child. I believe it is for this reason that depression is often accompanied by low self-esteem.

The Relation of a Negative View of the Self in Depression to the Hedonic Principle

Why should people maintain a negative view of themselves in an apparent violation of the operation of the superordinate motive of the hedonic principle? There are several reasons why this occurs, all of which are consistent with the influence of the hedonic principle. As previously noted, turning against the self can occur for at least two reasons: the strategic advantage of regarding the self as bad and the mother as good compared to the opposite view, and the occurrence of guilt. As previously noted, it is less distressing for a child to regard itself as bad and its mother as good than to arrive at the opposite opinion, for it allows the child to avoid feeling and expressing hostility and it maintains the hope that if the child mends its ways the good mother will appreciate it. Clearly, the net emotional effect of such thinking and behaving is in accord with the hedonic principle.

The experience of guilt is also in accord with the hedonic principle. In the example previously provided, the child acquired and maintained guilt feelings following fulfillment of a death wish toward a sibling. The acquisition of the guilt reaction can be explained by the operation of the basic need to maintain a stable and coherent conceptual system. Given the child's values, the child knows it is wrong to kill someone and that a person responsible for the death of another is therefore a very bad person. To be consistent with the child's belief system, the child therefore must regards herself as a bad person for wishing for and thereby causing the sibling's death. The problem lies in the child's limited cognitive ability, according to which she believes that wishes can kill. In considering the psychoeconomics of her guilt reaction, she is caught in a conflict between two unfavorable possibilities. If she feels guilty, she suffers the consequences of regarding herself as a bad person, but she can at least try to make up for it by being very good. Not a very good bargain, but better than the alternative. The alternative is to rationalize her behavior by believing her sibling was a bad child who deserved to die, and she did a good deed by causing her sibling's death. This would create all kinds of difficulties because the child would also have to rationalize the grief the child's death caused her parents and their abhorrence if she expressed the reason for her death wish. In other words, she would have to deny reality at a considerable cost in anxiety, including the anxiety produced by the disapproval of her loved ones if she defended her belief. In sum, guilt may be the best hedonic bargain the person can make under the circumstances.

The question may be raised as to why the child maintains the guilt into adulthood when she no longer believes that wishes can kill and that a death wish by a young child toward a sibling is not wicked. The answer is that, in many cases, such understanding does resolve the problem. It does not happen in other cases because the child may have developed automatic ways of thinking, feeling, and behaving that have received a great deal of emotional reinforcement. Thus, the child could have derived satisfaction from the way others responded to her being a very helpful and good child, or the child could have found that when she was depressed and self-critical others paid increasing attention to her and tried to make her feel better. Repression is another reason that the belief does not change. Because the thought of the death wish to her sibling was highly distressing, she may have avoided thinking about it to the extent that it finally became unavailable to her conscious mind, and she therefore could not reconsider it as she matured. An important consideration is that the hedonic principle, as a motive in the experiential system, has a short time perspective. Thus, although the child's guilt feelings are irrational from an adult perspective, the short-term immediate reinforcement received for being good and for avoiding distressing thoughts in the experiential system can override the later, more logical reasoning of the rational system.

Another reason that people maintain negative views about themselves despite the apparent violation to the hedonic principle is, as previously noted, because of the basic need to maintain a stable and coherent conceptual system. Once a belief has become an important aspect of a person's conceptual system, it is anxiety-producing to change it because it would threaten the organization of the conceptual system.

Yet another reason that people maintain a negative view of themselves is because maintaining a chronically low level of self-esteem is less distressing than the distress produced by an acute reduction in self-esteem. Thus, one way of reducing the sting of disappointment is to maintain a low base level of self-esteem.

A Study of Thought Content and Thinking Style in Subclinical Depression

It is important to consider people's styles of thinking, as well as the content of their implicit beliefs, to understand why some people are more prone to depression than others. Support for the view that depression involves maladaptive ways of thinking, as well as maladaptive beliefs, is provided in a study of subclinically depressed college students (Pacini, Muir, & Epstein, 1998). Subclinical depression refers to a level of depression that, although involving great distress, is not incapacitating with regard to attending to everyday affairs, which in the case of students means attending classes, maintaining satisfying relationships, and perhaps conducting part-time work. The participants in this study were college students selected based on extreme scores on the Beck Depression Inventory (BDI; Beck, Ward, Mendelson, Mock, & Erbaugh, 1961). They endorsed items such as "I am so sad and unhappy that I can't stand it," "I hate myself," "I feel that the future is hopeless and that things cannot improve," and "I would like to kill myself." They were compared to a control group of students who obtained very low scores on the BDI. As part of a larger study, the students in both groups were administered the Constructive Thinking Inventory (CTI) and the Rational-Experiential Inventory (REI). The CTI, it may be recalled, measures a variety of adaptive and maladaptive primarily automatic thoughts and beliefs. It provides information on cognitive styles of thinking, as well as on the content of beliefs about the self and others. The REI provides scales that measure the degree to which people report they engage in rational-analytical and experiential-intuitive thinking.

The thinking of depressed students differed from that of nondepressed students in both content and styles of thinking. On the CTI, the depressed students obtained poorer scores on overall constructive thinking, on emotional coping, and on behavioral coping than did the other students. An unanticipated finding was that the depressed students obtained higher scores on intolerance and on distrust of others than did nondepressed students. This is an interesting finding, but since it was unanticipated and has not been reported in other research, it should be regarded as tentative until replicated. With respect to styles of thinking, the responses of the depressed group on the CTI, compared to those of the control group, indicated that the depressed students overgeneralized more following unfavorable outcomes, and they thought in more polarized and unrealistic ways than did those in the control group. On the REI, the depressed students reported that they engaged in and valued logical thinking less than the nondepressed students reported.

To determine which attributes of depression are predictors and which are symptoms of depression, participants were divided into three groups, a currently depressed group, a previously depressed group that was not currently depressed, and a control group that was neither previously nor currently depressed. The currently depressed group consisted of students who obtained very high depression scores on the BDI on two occasions five weeks apart. The previously depressed group obtained very high scores on the first administration but normal scores on the second administration of the BDI. The control group obtained low scores on both administrations of the BDI.

Information on precursors of depression was obtained by comparing the previously depressed students who were not currently depressed with the students in the control group. Based on this comparison, the following variables appear to be precursors of depression: low engagement in and low evaluation of logical thinking, poor constructive thinking, poor emotional coping, low action orientation, high sensitivity to rejection and disapproval, and holding many unusual beliefs.

Variables that were symptoms of depression were considered those on which the currently depressed group obtained significantly more unfavorable scores than the previously depressed group. Based on this comparison, the following variables appear to be symptoms of depression: a relatively high degree of engagement in and a favorable evaluation of an experiential thinking style, poor constructive thinking, poor emotional coping, poor behavioral coping, low action orientation, low positive thinking, high personal superstitious thinking, high categorical thinking, and high stereotypical thinking. The following variables appear to be both precursors and symptoms of depression because they were significantly more unfavorable in the previously depressed group than in the control group and significantly more unfavorable in the currently depressed group than in the previously depressed group: global constructive thinking, emotional coping, and action orientation. Of particular interest, the variables categorical thinking, personal superstitious thinking, and stereotypical thinking appeared to be only symptoms of depression and therefore would lead to errors in interpretation if they were assumed to have causal significance.

According to the present study, the only variables that can tentatively be considered to have predictive value for subclinical depression are low scores on a rational thinking style and unfavorable scores on the CTI scales of Global

Constructive Thinking, Emotional Coping, the Action orientation facet of Behavioral Coping, Sensitivity to rejection and disapproval, and Unusual Beliefs.

The results of this study support Beck's view that depression involves disorders in regard to both beliefs and style of thinking. It is therefore important in research and theorizing to consider the cognitive style of thinking, as well as the beliefs of depressed people. It is not sufficient to simply study and theorize about the schemas that people acquire from distressing experiences, such as loss of or separation from a loved one and significant failures. It is equally important to determine why people acquire and employ different styles of thinking in coping with adversity. It is also important to investigate not only depressed people's thinking about themselves but also their thinking about others. If depressed people tend to be intolerant and distrusting of others, as found in the present study, this could influence how others respond to them, which could contribute to their depression.

Some caveats are in order about the interpretation of this study's findings. Because it is a single study with a relatively small sample, it remains to be seen how well it will withstand replication. The findings about which variables are predictive and which are symptoms of depression were not hypothesized, which makes it all the more important that the results withstand replication. The participants consisted of subclinically depressed college students. The study should be repeated with more seriously depressed people.

On the positive side, the study demonstrates the importance of distinguishing between predictive and symptomatic variables, which requires examining people when they are and are not depressed. It also suggests that it is important to examine cognitive-style, as well as the content of thinking, and to investigate not only how depressed people think about themselves but also how they think about others.

CONCLUSION

In conclusion, there are two major ways in which people become depressed. One way is by feeling helpless because of an unfavorable situation that is viewed as irreparable. The other way is by feeling worthless or undeserving as a result of one's own behavior or of one's treatment by others. Depending on how early experiences influence people's automatic thinking and interpretation of events, some people are more predisposed than others to be vulnerable to either form of depression. The occurrence of events, such as loss or separation from a loved one that the child is helpless to remedy and that the child does not interpret as resulting from the child's own bad thoughts or behavior, are more likely to be the source of implicit beliefs that predispose a person to depression of the helplessness kind. The occurrence of events that lead a child to believe he or she is bad, such as a child who feels guilty about hostility to a parent who favors a sibling, who has death wishes to a sibling who dies, or who believes he or she has been abandoned by his mother because of the child's behavior are more likely to be the source of implicit beliefs that predispose a person to be vulnerable to the low self-esteem source of depression.

REFERENCES

American Psychiatric Association. (2000). *Diagnostic and statistical manual of mental disorders* DSM-IV (2nd ed.). Washington, DC.

Arieti, S., & Bemporad, J. (1978). *Severe and mild depression.* New York: Basic Books.

Beck, A. T. (1967). *Depression: Causes and treatment.* Philadelphia: University of Pennsylvania Press.

Beck, A. T., & Alford, B. A. (2009). *Depression: Causes and treatment*, 2nd edition. Philadelphia: University of Pennsylvania Press.

Beck, A. T., Rush, A. J., Shaw, B., & Emery, G. (1979). *Cognitive therapy of depression: A treatment manual.* New York: Guilford Press.

Beck, A. T., Ward, C. H., Mendelson, M., Mock, J., & Erbaugh, J. (1961). An inventory for measuring depression. *Archives of General Psychiatry, 4*, 561–571.

Beck, A. T., & Young, J. E. (1985). Depression. In D. H. Barlow (Ed.), *Clinical handbook of psychological disorders.* New York: Guilford Press.

Bonanno, G. A. (2004). Loss, trauma, and human resilience: Have we underestimated the human capacity to survive after extremely aversive events? *American Psychologist, 59*, 20–28.

Bowlby, J. (1980). *Attachment and loss, Vol. III: Loss, sadness and depression.* New York: Basic Books.

Brown, G. W., & Harris, T. O. (1989). Depression. In G. W. Harris & T. O. Harris (Eds.), *Life events and illness* (pp. 49–93). New York: Guilford Press.

Des Pres, T. (1976). *The Survivor: An anatomy of life in the death camps.* New York: Oxford University Press.

Epstein, S. (2006). Conscious and unconscious self-esteem from the perspective of cognitive-experiential self-theory. In M. H. Kernis (Ed.), *Self-esteem: Issues and answers.* New York: Psychology Press.

Fabry, J. (1980). Depression. In R. Woody (Ed.), *Encyclopedia of mental assessment.* San Francisco: Jossey-Bass.

Frankl, V. E. (1939). *Man's search for meaning.* New York: Simon & Schuster.

Freud, S. (1917/1957). Mourning and melancholia. In J. Strachey (Ed. & Trans.), *The standard edition of the complete psychological works of Sigmund Freud* (vol. 14). London: Hogarth Press.

O'Brien, E. J., & Epstein, S. (1988). *The Multidimensional Self-esteem Inventory.* Odessa, FL: Psychological Assessment Resources, Inc.

Pacini, R., Muir, F., & Epstein, S. (1998). Depressive realism from the perspective of cognitive-experiential self-theory. *Journal of Personality and Social Psychology, 74*, 1056–1068.

Peterson, C., & Seligman, M. E. P. (1984). Causal explanations as a risk factor for depression: Theory and evidence. *Psychological Review, 91*, 347–374.

Seligman, M. E. P. (1975). *Helplessness: On depression, development, and death*. San Francisco: W. H. Freeman.
Sullivan, H. S. (1953). *The interpersonal theory of psychiatry*. New York: W. W. Norton.
Tolstoy, L. (1887/1987). *A Confession and Other Religious Writings* (Translated by Jane Kentish). New York: Crowell.
Winokur, G. (1979). Unipolar depression. *Archives of General Psychiatry*, *36*, 47–52.

PART THREE

Clinical Applications

CHAPTER 11

Psychotherapy 1

Constructive Thinking, Cognitive Therapy, Behavior Therapy, Cognitive-Behavioral Therapy

As psychotherapists have become aware of the limitations of their procedures, they have become increasingly interested in what other approaches have to offer. This has resulted in proposals for thee kinds of integration: establishing a coherent, empirical eclecticism based on research and clinical observation; proposing a theoretical framework that encompasses all forms of psychotherapy; and identifying common factors in psychotherapy (Castonguay, Reid, Halperin, & Goldfried, 2003). Because cognitive-experiential theory (CET) integrates major aspects of learning theory, psychodynamic theory, cognitive science, and self-phenomenological theory, it is in a favorable position to provide an integrative framework for psychotherapy that includes all major approaches. Because of its considerable breadth, this framework can identify limitations in narrower approaches and can suggest ways in which other approaches can be extended and improved. In addition, it can provide explanations of procedures that were completely empirically derived and are lacking in adequate theory. It also can provide an integrative, therapeutic approach of its own that coherently assimilates other orientations.

According to CET, for any therapy to be successful, it must produce enduring changes in the experiential system. This is not to suggest that changes in the rational system are unimportant, but only that their importance depends on the extent to which they facilitate desirable changes in the experiential system. As noted previously, in the absence of such influence, insight may be useful to some extent by improving control of maladaptive behavioral tendencies and by reducing inappropriate generalizations. However, so far as producing changes in experiential processing, it may only serve to change a neurotic person without insight into one with insight. There are five basic ways of producing desirable changes in the experiential system, each with its own advantages and limitations. One way is by using the rational system to correct the experiential system, as occurs in educating clients about CET, providing training in constructive thinking, and conducting pure cognitive therapy (CT), which refers to the use of cognitive procedures unaccompanied by any other procedures, such as behavioral therapy. Another way is by behavioral reprogramming, as occurs in behavioral therapy. A third way is by using a combination of cognitive and behavioral procedures, as occurs in cognitive-behavioral therapy (CBT). A fourth way is by using psychodynamic therapy (PT) to identify and treat unconscious sources of behavior and interactions among needs, beliefs, and defenses. A fifth way is by humanistic-experiential approaches that communicate with the experiential system in its own medium, as occurs in providing unconditional positive regard in client-centered therapy and in the use of fantasy in Gestalt therapy and in psychosynthesis.

USING THE RATIONAL SYSTEM TO CORRECT THE EXPERIENTIAL SYSTEM

Using the rational system to correct the experiential can be an effective, relatively simple procedure for producing desirable changes in the experiential system. However, it has important limitations, among which is its unsuitability for treating certain kinds of problems and, very probably, a vulnerability to relapse. A difficulty in attempting to correct the experiential system by using only the rational system is that, as noted in the discussion of research on heuristics, processing in the experiential system can be extremely compelling and therefore resistant to changes by conscious reasoning. Moreover, because experiential processing influences all behavior, including conscious reasoning, it not only biases people's initial reasoning, but it also subsequently promotes rationalization in the sense that what was determined by the experiential system is attributed to the rational system. It is therefore useful to make clients aware that the mind operates with two systems, an experiential system that automatically learns from experience and a rational system that operates by conscious reasoning. Such information is easily comprehended, particularly when supported by examples from everyday life, such as the occurrence of conflicts between the heart and the head. Simply understanding that the experiential and rational systems process information by different rules and that people's problems are usually produced by their maladaptive schemas and ways of processing information in their experiential systems can help people understand why they have been unsuccessful in solving their problems by their reasoning and willpower alone.

It can be explained to clients that attending to emotions, bodily states, imagery, and unbidden thoughts can be useful for identifying the implicit beliefs that influence those perceptions, interpretations of events, and behavioral tendencies that are the sources of the difficulties they experience in their everyday lives. They can also be taught about the nonrational manner of information processing in the experiential system, which connects events by association rather than by logical reasoning and is prone to overgeneralize and think categorically rather than in a more nuanced manner. In the absence of awareness of their implicit beliefs and of the manner of operation of their experiential systems, clients may fail to benefit from otherwise corrective experiences by unintentionally sabotaging their efforts and then rationalizing the unfavorable outcomes to poor luck or the behavior of others.

An understanding of CET can also contribute to the development of a therapeutic alliance because when clients and therapists operate from the same orientation, they can more effectively communicate with each other. Moreover, clients appreciate sharing with their therapists the theory on which their treatment is based and by being treated as partners in a joint venture.

Understanding the nonrational, automatic operation of the experiential system can reduce resistance and defensiveness by eliminating the need of clients to defend their rationality. For example, if a client feels compelled to defend her irrational behavior, the therapist can remind her that the experiential system is not a logical system but rather operates according to the principles of associative learning, including the automatic acquisition of implicit beliefs that were emotionally reinforced by their outcomes. The therapist can then suggest that it can be useful to consider the client's feelings about the event that led her to defend her rationality.

It can be useful for clients to understand that neither the rational nor experiential system is superior to the other and that each has its advantages and disadvantages. Each system can provide useful guidance, as well as lead people astray. It follows that it is just as counterproductive to try always to be rational and to ignore one's intuition and feelings as to do the opposite. For these reasons, clients should understand the importance of being in touch with the content and manner of operation of their experiential systems, which normally operate outside of awareness but that can, with appropriate attention, be accessed.

Providing Training in Constructive Thinking

Training in constructive thinking has been demonstrated to be a useful procedure for improving feelings, thinking, and the behavior of people in their everyday lives (Epstein, 1998, 2001). Its principles are largely the same as those of CT, but it differs in regard to recognizing the significance of the experiential system. It also differs from CT in that it is mainly directed at improving overall adjustment in everyday life in normal people. Its effectiveness in treating everyday problems establishes that it is possible to use the rational system to improve the operation of the experiential system. People's constructive thinking has been found to be poor in all diagnostic conditions thus far examined (Epstein, 2001). Accordingly, it is useful for clients undergoing any form of psychotherapy to be provided with some training in constructive thinking, which can be a useful adjunct in all forms of therapy. Almost all clients, no matter what their specific problems, are poor constructive thinkers, not only because their poor constructive thinking has likely contributed to their clinical problems, but also because their clinical problems have probably influenced their constructive thinking. The reason for this is that many cases of serious maladjustment are the result of traumatic and near-traumatic experiences. Such experiences make people overly sensitive to cues that remind them of their traumas and of the possibility of something similar recurring. As a result, they are prone to worrying and to depressive thinking. In sum, no matter what their specific symptoms, almost all clients can benefit from some degree of training in constructive thinking.

The most important basic principle of constructive thinking is that people's experientially derived beliefs automatically determine their interpretation of events, feelings, and behavioral tendencies and bias their conscious reasoning. Therefore, by becoming aware of and then appropriately changing their maladaptive implicit beliefs and manner of processing information, people can improve the quality of their lives.

There are two ways in which limited training in constructive thinking can be included as a simple and effective supplement to other forms of therapy. One way is by teaching clients about the significance of experiential processing with regard to adjustment. An aphorism that well captures much of the essence of constructive thinking is the Serenity Prayer, according to which one desires to have the serenity to accept what cannot be changed, the motivation to change what can be changed, and the wisdom to know the difference. Another useful statement for controlling negative emotions is to ask oneself what thought or interpretation of an event instigated a negative emotion and then to ask oneself what would happen if one did not think that way. If it is concluded that the only effect of the thought is to make one distressed, then the thought should obviously be discontinued or at least disregarded. A third useful procedure is to seek constructive alternatives for distressing thoughts. When a destructive thought enters a person's mind, a more constructive replacement can be sought. If this is repeated sufficiently, the constructive alternative will eventually become automatic and no longer require conscious effort. Other simple exercises for improving constructive thinking can be found in my book on constructive thinking (Epstein, 1998). These procedures can be usefully implemented whenever appropriate conditions arise for doing so in therapy sessions.

My book on constructive thinking (Epstein, 1998), which is available through amazon.com, can be helpful to clients by presenting the principles of constructive thinking in a user-friendly manner, including providing many examples and exercises. Several readers who wrote reviews in amazon.com reported that the book greatly improved the quality of their lives, particularly with respect to coping with stress, correcting counterproductive thinking habits, and improving their relationships with others. Therapists have informed me that they have had very favorable results from assigning the book to their clients.

Cognitive Therapy

I use the term "cognitive therapy" to refer to cognitive procedures unaccompanied by any other therapeutic procedure. Note that, according to this definition, the inclusion of a noncognitive procedure such as behavior therapy, which is a common supplement, disqualifies the treatment as CT. Cognitive therapy is conducted by Ellis (1977) primarily by disputing irrational beliefs and by Beck (1976) by testing the rationality of beliefs in simulated and real situations. Both often combine CT with other procedures, most notably behavioral therapy, but here I am including only a purely cognitive approach. I do so for theoretical as well as practical reasons, so that treating cognition by itself can be evaluated uncomplicated by the presence of other interventions.

A fundamental assumption in CT, and one consistent with CET, is that psychopathology is primarily the result of maladaptive beliefs. However, despite this basic agreement, there is also a critically important difference between the two theoretical positions. Whereas CET emphasizes the importance of a distinction between beliefs in the rational and experiential systems, CT does not recognize the existence of an experiential system but considers only a distinction between conscious and unconscious beliefs.

The Advantages and Limitations of Cognitive Therapy

The failure to recognize the operation of an experiential system is regarded in CET as highly significant. More important than whether a belief is conscious or unconscious is whether it operates according to the principles and attributes of the experiential or the rational system. According to CET, an experientially acquired belief may not be changed at all when it is made conscious because it continues to operate according to the same rules and attributes of the experiential system as it did before. What is accomplished by making an implicit experiential belief explicit is an important first step in correcting an experiential belief because once it is identified in the rational system, it can be treated experientially. Otherwise, insight by itself has only limited advantages, which include rationally reducing inappropriate generalizations and controlling maladaptive behavioral tendencies. Note that such control is far different from extinguishing maladaptive generalizations and behavioral tendencies in the first place.

Cognitive scientists recognize that most cognition occurs outside of awareness because it is a more efficient procedure than conscious processing. Likewise, it is emphasized in CET that implicit beliefs are an important source of maladaptive behavior. Unfortunately, cognitive therapists often do not treat unconscious irrational beliefs because they cannot identify them. Moreover, they do not attribute great importance to doing so because they consider unconscious processing and beliefs a murky topic, fraught with questionable assumptions and inferences that are best avoided and that, in any case, would be very difficult to identify. The reason for this view lies in a failure to understand that most unconscious beliefs are implicit schemas in the experiential system and are not repressed beliefs in the Freudian unconscious system. They are therefore not necessarily difficult to access and often simply require learning to attend to them.

It therefore would be a useful addition to CT to identify and then treat those experientially acquired beliefs of which clients may be unaware. This can be accomplished by procedures such as making inferences from biographical information, observing repetitive patterns of behavior, attending to automatic thoughts, using projective techniques, and inferring the experiential beliefs that are the sources of particular emotions.

The effectiveness of CT can be expected to vary according to the person and the situation. With regard to the person, it can reasonably be expected that a rational thinking style is directly and an experiential thinking style is inversely related to the effectiveness of treatment by CT. This can be tested with the use of the Rational-Experiential Inventory (REI; e.g., Pacini & Epstein, 1999a). Moreover, information about thinking styles can be used therapeutically. Thus, clients with a low degree of a rational thinking style can benefit from instruction about the positive relation of a rational thinking style to adjustment, and those with a low degree of an experiential thinking style can benefit from discussions about the value of increasing their experiential processing. If it is found that it is extremely difficult to change the thinking style of a client with a very low rational thinking style, a more experiential kind of therapy than CT would be more appropriate.

As for situational variables, CT can be a relatively simple, efficient, and highly effective treatment under appropriate circumstances. As a very simple example of using the rational system to correct the experiential system, consider the following thought experiment regarding the treatment of an intense anxiety reaction. Mary is in a state of great panic because she was bitten by a snake on which she accidentally stepped. Because she believes her life is in danger, she is terrified. She goes to the nearest emergency treatment facility. When she describes the snake that bit her, she is assured that it is a harmless garter snake and that there are no poisonous snakes in the area. Mary's intense anxiety immediately dissipates. Note that despite Mary's anxiety resulting from an actual experience and being highly distressing, it was based on only a single incident of short duration, so its experiential reinforcement history is weak. Accordingly, it was easily treated by simply correcting her incorrect conscious belief.

Now let us consider common maladaptive beliefs in everyday life that have a stronger reinforcement history. It will be recalled that in the study of constructive thinking in college students reported in Chapter 8, correcting the students' irrational automatic thoughts and interpretations of events by identifying them, disputing them, testing their reality in a follow-up period, and then working on replacing them with more constructive responses was an effective treatment for improving students' adjustment. They learned that by replacing the beliefs that determined their undesirable emotions, they were able to change their emotions in ways that were more satisfactory to them. For many of them, this was a life-transforming understanding. Several said they were surprised to learn that it is possible to change emotions by such a procedure. Previously, they had believed that they could suppress the behavioral expression of maladaptive emotions but that they could not change the emotions themselves.

Similar results were obtained with adults who read my book describing the same self-help procedure that was used with the college students (Epstein, 1998). The adults reported that the procedure greatly improved their emotional well-being, their performance in their jobs, their relationships, and the quality of their lives more generally (see reviews in amazon.com by readers of the book, *Constructive Thinking: The Key to Emotional Intelligence*). Thus, the results from two nonclinical samples of people support the conclusion that using the rational system to correct the experiential system is a very simple and effective procedure for treating problems of less than clinical severity. This raises the question of how successful CT can be for treating clinically significant symptoms such as phobias, compulsions, depressive episodes, anxiety reactions, and uncontrollable aggression.

Although there are many studies that have demonstrated the effectiveness of CT combined with other procedures, such as CBT, I could not find any that evaluated CT as a stand-alone treatment. All that was available for evaluating such treatment were reports of individual cases. As an example, let us consider the following case reported by Beck (1976) of someone he successfully treated with CT. The client was a college student in a speech class who was terrified of giving speeches. When asked why he was afraid of giving speeches, the student said he was afraid of making a fool of himself. Note that Beck did not state that being afraid of giving speeches is irrational because the fear interferes with performance, produces awful feelings, and accomplishes nothing worthwhile. There would, of course, be nothing to be gained by pointing out the irrationality of the fear because the student no doubt was aware of this; it was the reason that he came for treatment. Instead, Beck explored the thoughts that were responsible for the fear.

When Beck further asked the student why giving a poor speech was threatening, the student said it was not only because he was concerned about making a fool of himself but also because of its other consequences. Beck asked the student to do a reality check on how awful giving a poor speech actually was by evaluating the likelihood of several possible unfortunate consequences. The student acknowledged that giving a poor talk would not kill him, would not ruin his future career, and would not result in his parents or his wife disowning him. He then added that although these terrible things would not happen, he would feel very bad. Beck asked him about how long the bad feeling would last. The student said for a day or two. Following this discussion, the student acknowledged that his assessment of the consequences of giving a poor speech had been exaggerated. Beck then stated that the obvious resolution of the student's intense fear was to be more realistic and not exaggerate.

After his next speech, the student reported that he performed poorly and felt bad about it for a few days, but he recognized it was certainly not a terrible tragedy. After giving more speeches, the student reported that he was less distressed about his performance than before.

What do we learn from this example? One thing we learn is that a clinically significant symptom can be simply and effectively treated with CT without the use of supplementary procedures. We also learn that the essence of the treatment was not in disputing the rationality of the symptom, but in disputing the beliefs that were the source of the symptom. The irrational fear corresponded to an abstract belief that was disembodied from its empirical underpinnings. When the fear was disassembled into its more specific and testable components, their validity was found wanting. Remember that the experiential system encodes events primarily in the form of specific, concrete representations and is more responsive to such representations than to broad abstractions. We may also learn something about the likelihood of relapse in cases similar to this. I suspect that there is little likelihood of relapse in this case for a very important reason, which is that giving speeches with reduced fear was continuously reinforced by an improvement in performance.

There is one more important lesson to be learned from this example, which is that an *unidentified* source of support was provided by the therapeutic relationship. This interpretation is supported by the client later reporting a problem that was beyond simply giving speeches, which was also effectively treated by CT. The problem was that the client had an unrealistic need for approval, which can explain his extreme anxiety about giving speeches. A likely reason for the exaggerated need for approval is that he had failed to receive reasonable approval from his family. In contrast, Beck provided an experience with a significant-other who approved of him and was trying to help him reach his goal. It will be recalled that, according to CET, a fundamental source of self-esteem is the introjection of evaluations by significant others. It is noteworthy that the therapeutic relationship is considered to be one of the few important variables common to all forms of psychotherapy (Castonguay et al., 2003; Martin, Garske, & Davis, 2000). In conclusion, the case provides an example of how a purely rational approach can change beliefs in the experiential system and remove a clinically significant symptom when administered by a caring therapist.

Despite many case histories that illustrate the successful treatment of clinically significant disorders by CT, the question remains as to the boundary conditions of its effectiveness. Because of the lack of research on CT, it will be necessary to propose the conditions in which it is most and least likely to be effective based on logical and theoretical considerations.

Cognitive therapy is a highly efficient and effective procedure under certain conditions. This was illustrated in the thought experiment about the girl bitten by a snake, by the improvement in the lives of college students who received training in constructive thinking (which is a form of CT), and by the case treated by Beck. The following are suggestions concerning the conditions in which CT is likely to be most and least effective. Although all of the conditions are stated in terms of poor outcomes, the obverse is equally true for favorable outcomes. For example, the statement that the intensity of the emotional charge of an irrational belief is directly related to its resistance to correction by CT can be restated as the likelihood of a favorable outcome by CT is inversely related to the emotional charge of an irrational belief. From the framework provided by CET, it is suggested that the conditions in which CT is least likely to be successful are as follows:

1. The symptoms are based on irrational beliefs that are unconscious and therefore presumably cannot be identified and treated by CT. How serious a limitation this is for CT depends, of course, on how often unconscious irrational beliefs are the sources of clinical symptoms and whether unconscious beliefs can be identified.
2. The treatment does not receive sufficient reinforcement at the time of the treatment as well as subsequently.
3. The more intense the emotional charge of an irrational belief, the more resistant it is to treatment by CT. Thus, treatment of post-traumatic stress disorder (PTSD) by CT is considered unlikely to succeed.
4. The longer the reinforcement history of an irrational belief, such as those having their roots in childhood experiences, the more resistant it is to treatment by CT.
5. Irrational beliefs that are embedded in a network of other beliefs are more resistant to treatment by CT than isolated irrational beliefs.
6. The treatment of secondary sources of symptoms that have primary sources is unlikely to be successfully treated by CT and is particularly subject to relapse.
7. Cognitive therapy will not produce enduring favorable symptom reduction if an unfulfilled need that is the source of a symptom remains unfulfilled.

Some Further Considerations Regarding the Limitations of Cognitive Therapy

Of particular importance regarding the limitations of CT are the lack of an adequate theory for understanding the operation of CT, a failure to distinguish between two different divisions of cognitive processing (conscious vs. unconscious and rational vs. experiential processing), a presumed inability to identify and treat unconscious experiential beliefs, and limitations in the range of effective treatment by CT.

The lack of an adequate theory for understanding the operation and limits of CT. An interesting example of the confusion about the operation of CT is provided by Ellis (1987) in an article in which he courageously acknowledged his failure to understand why his patients often relapsed following what he thought had been successful treatment. What most puzzled him, he said, was why intelligent people continue to think irrationally after their incorrect beliefs have been corrected. He concluded that there must be something inherently maladaptive in the architecture of the human mind, but what that something is eluded him. He then added: "We find that literally hundreds of major irrationalities exist in all societies.... These irrationalities persist despite people's conscious determination to change;... they persist among highly intelligent, educated, and relatively little disturbed individuals;... people who strongly oppose them in principle nonetheless perpetuate them in practice;... they often seem to flow from deep-seated and almost ineradicable human tendencies toward fallibility, overgeneralization, wishful thinking, gullibility and short range hedonism; and they appear at least in part tied up with physiological, hereditary, and constitutional processes" (Ellis, 1987, p. 364).

In seeking an explanation for the resistance of people to think rationally, Ellis unknowingly cites attributes of experiential processing. According to CET, people have a strong propensity to think in nonrational ways because experiential processing is the dominant processing mode in everyday life. It is therefore highly compelling, it biases conscious thinking, and it makes associative rather than logical connections. The inherently compelling nature of experiential processing can explain why people's conscious desire to change in their rational systems is often unable to produce permanent changes in the operation of their experiential system. The influence of experiential on rational processing can account for why intelligent people are often unable to use their intelligence to solve their problems, why they often behave in ways that are inconsistent with their conscious beliefs, and why they have an inherent propensity to overgeneralize, engage in wishful thinking, and be motivated by short-term hedonism, all of which are attributes of experiential processing.

Ellis (1987) later makes the following statement: "I am again hypothesizing, most overly anxious, depressed, and hostile people, because of their feelings about the ease of becoming disturbed and the hopelessness of undisturbing themselves, after awhile only try moderately, if at all, to become really undisturbed" (p. 368). According to CET, behaving in irrational ways is easier and more natural than deliberative reasoning because the experiential system operates in a manner that is automatic, effortless, associative, and minimally demanding of cognitive resources in comparison to the more effortful, deliberative processing of the rational system. Thus, it is difficult permanently to correct seriously maladaptive beliefs in the experiential system by purely cognitive procedures. However, it can more readily be done in less extreme conditions, and it can be done in more extreme conditions under appropriate circumstances.

Failure to distinguish between two different processing divisions (conscious vs. unconscious and rational vs. experiential processing). As previously noted, a serious limitation in CT, according to CET, is treating the distinction between conscious and unconscious processing as similar to the distinction between rational and experiential processing. This error has important implications with respect to understanding the limitations and extensions of CT. According to CET, experiential beliefs can be conscious or unconscious, and, in either case, they operate by the same rules and have the same attributes. Thus, making unconscious experiential beliefs conscious does not change their manner of operation. It simply makes them accessible to treatment and somewhat increases conscious control, as by reducing inappropriate generalization. However, this often is no more than a first step because the beliefs still operate by the same rules and attributes as before. Unconscious experiential irrational beliefs are far more common than has been recognized by cognitive therapists. Fortunately, they are also more easily accessed and treated than are Freudian repressed beliefs.

Although cognitive therapists note that they cannot treat unconscious beliefs, they recognize and treat what they refer to as *automatic thoughts*, which are manifestations of experiential processing. Knowing the rules and attributes of such processing can provide an understanding of their operation and therefore a pathway for correcting maladaptive experiential beliefs, whether they are unconscious or conscious.

Failure to use procedures for identifying unconscious beliefs. According to CET, maladaptive experiential beliefs are the most common source of symptoms. Many of these beliefs are unconscious because the experiential system normally operates outside of awareness; thus, it is highly limiting to be unable to identify and treat them. It would therefore greatly increase the range of effective treatment by CT if unconscious beliefs were identified, a topic shortly to be discussed. Identifying unconscious experiential beliefs can reduce the possibility of unsuccessfully treating secondary sources of symptoms because their primary sources are unconscious and therefore unidentified.

Limitations in the effective range of CT. As previously noted, CT can be a very efficient procedure for the treatment of maladaptive behavior in the psychopathology of everyday life. According to CET, the more extreme the pathology, the less likely it can be successfully treatable by purely cognitive procedures.

In more serious pathology, as in PTSD, as previously noted, treatment by CT alone is likely to result in failure. This is because symptoms such as flashbacks, sensitivity to cues associated with a trauma, intrusive thoughts, and the persistence of automatic attempts to assimilate dissociated representations into a unified conceptual system are so fundamental and insistent that they are beyond the capacity of effective treatment by conscious reasoning. Thus, attempting to do so by discussing their irrationality can only empower them by drawing attention to the futility of consciously controlling them by reasoning alone. It is preferable to understand and accept passively the automatic operation of the experiential system in such circumstances (Segal, Williams, & Teasdale, 2002). This is not meant to deny the usefulness of CT for treating less fundamental symptoms of PTSD, such as overgeneralization of the consequences of traumatic beliefs to life in general.

The futility of treating fundamental PTSD symptoms with purely cognitive procedures can be extended to conditions that are less extreme, but where the limits are still determined by the relative potency of the experiential beliefs compared to that of the beliefs in the rational system.

Extensions of CT. Considering the highly compelling nature of strong, experientially acquired beliefs, the ability to produce lasting changes in such beliefs solely by rational thinking can be expected to be insufficient in most circumstances. It is therefore important to consider the conditions in which a purely cognitive approach is likely to be sufficient and when it is necessary to supplement or replace it with other procedures.

It should be noted that despite the considerable attention given to the frequency and treatment of relapse, the research on relapse does not include any studies on CT alone, but only studies that employ CT combined with behavioral procedures, such as CBT. Although the results vary among studies, the overall results for CBT are favorable and suggest the importance of supplementing CT with behavioral procedures. This, of course, is a well-recognized important extension of CT that is commonly practiced.

Other extensions recommended by CET have not been recognized, let alone implemented. One is recognition of the importance of the role of experiential processing in irrational beliefs, and another is the use of procedures for identifying implicit irrational beliefs so that they can be treated by CT. The latter can be accomplished by observing patterns of repetitive behavior, by the automatic occurrence of intrusive beliefs and automatic thoughts, and by inferring implicit thoughts from the emotions they elicit.

BEHAVIOR THERAPY

In the previous section, I discussed pure CT while acknowledging that even those who refer to themselves as cognitive therapists almost always combine it with behavioral procedures. The theoretical reason I treated it separately is that cognitive and behavioral procedures operate according to different principles, with CT being based on correcting maladaptive beliefs and therefore related most closely to cognitive psychology and behavioral therapies being based on correcting maladaptive behavior and therefore based on learning theory. As a result, it is confusing to try to evaluate and understand the advantages and limitations of a combined procedure when each procedure operates in different ways and uses different procedures. Thus, although CT is an efficient procedure for treating some kinds of maladjustment, it is limited in treating other, often more severe conditions. Adding experiential to cognitive procedures greatly increases their range of effectiveness. Using only behavioral procedures for correcting problems is more feasible than CT for treating serious disorders, but it is best suited for treating specific behavioral problems. Because of these considerations, I first discuss behavioral therapy by itself, after which I discuss the combination of CT and behavioral therapy in CBT.

As emphasized throughout this book, it is assumed in CET that schemas in the experiential system automatically determine people's interpretation of events, their feelings, and how they tend to behave. They are therefore major determinants of people's adjustment. Because these schemas are acquired by automatically learning from experience, the most direct way of changing them is by providing new learning experiences that counteract the old learning. This can be accomplished by a variety of corrective learning procedures.

Although correcting maladaptive behavior by learning from experience is highly compatible with CET, there is a major theoretical difference between CET and the theory underlying behavior therapy. In behavioral therapy, the emphasis is on correcting maladaptive behavioral responses, whereas in CET it is on correcting maladaptive beliefs. It is interesting that the very same behavior is interpreted differently in these two approaches, with one approach viewing the maladaptive behavior itself as the essential problem and the other approach considering the maladaptive beliefs that underlie the behavior as the basic problem.

Basic Principles of Behavior Therapy

Behavior therapy is consistent with the associative learning component of the framework provided by CET. Although there are a wide variety of behavioral procedures, all of them operate according to one or more of the following kinds of associative learning: classical conditioning, operant or instrumental conditioning, and observational learning. The influence of learning in all of them is determined by the variables of reinforcement, punishment, extinction, and amount of exposure, such as number of trials. There are two kinds of reinforcement, both of which strengthen responses. *Positive reinforcement* strengthens a response by providing a desirable outcome following the response, and *negative reinforcement* does so by removing or reducing an aversive stimulus following a response. *Punishment* reduces the strength of a response by the presentation of an aversive stimulus following a response or by the removal of a desirable outcome. Increasing the amount of reinforcement or punishment, respectively, increases or decreases the strength of a response. *Extinction* refers to the decrease or elimination of a response that occurs following repeated trials in the absence of reinforcement or punishment. Following extinction, spontaneous recovery normally occurs after a period of time without reinforcement or punishment. As demonstrated by innumerable studies, these are extremely powerful variables for controlling behavior of all kinds and are the basic variables that determine the operation and learned content of the experiential system. Behavior therapy uses various combinations of them to correct a wide variety of maladaptive behaviors.

Behavioral therapists typically target overt symptoms and are unconcerned about beliefs or inferred sources regarding unconscious processes and interactive patterns. In contrast to classical psychoanalysts and psychodynamic therapists, they are therefore minimally, if at all, interested in early childhood relationships. Accordingly, treatment in behavioral therapy is symptom-oriented, less inferential than in psychodynamic therapy, and therefore usually of much shorter duration.

Basic Procedures in Behavior Therapy

Any or all of the variables governing associative learning are used in behavioral therapy to promote adaptive changes in behavior or to reduce or eliminate maladaptive behavior. Not only is this done with real and imagined exercises in therapy sessions, it is also accomplished with real-life assignments, homework assignments, record keeping of adaptive and maladaptive behavior and of their relation to symptoms, and obtaining practice in behaving in adaptive ways. The variety of conditions that behavioral therapists have successfully treated is very great and beyond the scope of this chapter. For present purposes, it will suffice to present a few examples of the use of behavior therapy in the three kinds of associative learning procedures.

Classical Conditioning Procedures

Classical conditioning has been used effectively to treat phobias, such as fear of heights, fear of flying, claustrophobia, agoraphobia, fear of traversing bridges, and social anxiety. Treatment consists of extinction of fear either in imagination or in real life by fully facing the feared object or event in the absence of reinforcement. Therapeutic procedures include systematic desensitization, implosion therapy, flooding, and a variety of other procedures.

In systematic desensitization in imagination, a client uses a relaxation procedure, such as deep muscle relaxation, while responding to increasing levels of an anxiety-producing stimulus. For example, a client afraid of heights may be asked vividly to imagine looking down from the first floor of an apartment house. When the client is able to do so while remaining relaxed, the client progresses to a more challenging level, such as looking down from a second story window and so on, until the client can vividly imagine looking down from the uppermost level in a state of relaxation. A similar procedure is used with real-life experiences in which a client maintains a state of relaxation in the company of a therapist while looking down from increasingly higher levels of a building. In both procedures, the anxiety response is extinguished as the result of experiencing the anxiety-producing stimulus in the absence of the feared outcome.

In implosion therapy and in flooding, the client is encouraged to react to an aversive stimulus with full emotional intensity. In implosion therapy, the event is imagined (Stampfl, 1975), whereas in flooding the client is placed in a real-life threatening situation (e.g., Morganstern, 1973). In both cases, the client is encouraged to keep reacting emotionally until the anxiety reaction dissipates. Real exposure has been found to be more effective than imaginary exposure. On its surface, experiencing a threatening stimulus in its full emotional intensity might seem to operate in an opposite way from systematic desensitization, in which the stimulus is experienced in a state of relaxation. However, the same basic principle is involved, namely, the extinction of a feared stimulus by fully facing it in the absence of the feared outcome. As a thought experiment, consider a child who believes that a ghost resides at night in his bedroom closet. One night during a thunderstorm, the door to the closet blows open. In terror, the child expects to see the ghost. When nothing happens, after a sufficient period of time, the fear extinguishes. Note that it would not matter if the child had been in a relaxed state or in a state of terror. All that mattered is that the threat was fully faced in the absence of an aversive outcome.

Operant Conditioning Procedures

Unlike in classical conditioning, in which extinction only requires exposure to an unreinforced stimulus, in operant conditioning, what matters is the consequences of a person's behavioral response to a stimulus. The response is strengthened by rewards and weakened by punishment or the removal of rewards. Operant conditioning is illustrated by the use of *token economies*, in which rewards and punishments are administered in the form of desirable tokens or fines. Desirable tokens can be converted into desirable items, such as attractive food and privileges, whereas fines operate in the opposite way, by reducing rewards and privileges. Token economies have been used to influence the behavior of people in mental institutions (e.g., Ayllon & Azrin, 1968) and in institutions for the intellectually deficient by rewarding adaptive behavior and punishing maladaptive behavior (reviews are available in Hurley & Sovner, 1985; Kazdin & Bootzin, 1972; Rimmerman, Finn, Schnee, & Klein, 1992).

Token economies have also been effectively used to improve the behavior of difficult children. Usually, this is a joint procedure that involves training parents and their children. With the use of token economies and other operant techniques, children can be taught to behave more acceptably, and parents can learn to control their children's behavior.

Parents may unintentionally reinforce maladaptive behavior in their children. For example, a mother could reinforce her child for failing in school by rewarding him with attention whenever he fails. She believes that admonishing the child for failing will motivate him to succeed. With the help of a therapist, she learns that the attention he desperately craves is obtained only when he does poorly, which motivates him to fail. She is told to ignore his failures, attend to any improvements in his behavior, and attend to him in other ways as well. When she behaves in this manner, his performance improves.

Lovaas (1987) conducted an intensive study in which three-year-old autistic children were treated by their parents for 40 hours a week for two years. The parents were trained to use positive reinforcement of desirable behavior and punishment or ignoring for maladaptive behaviors, such as self-punishment and aggression to others. By the first grade, 9 of the 19 children who were treated in this manner were functioning normally in school.

Homework assignments are often used in behavioral therapy. For example, a shy person may be encouraged to meet others by introducing herself to a few strangers before the next therapy session. The therapist may also train the client and have her rehearse the skills required to engage in successful encounters. The likelihood is that she will learn that most people are friendly and cooperative and that the event is not as threatening as she had anticipated it would be.

Modeling Procedures

It will be recalled that the experiential system learns not only from personal experience but also from observing the behavior of others. Thus, nonhuman animals learn vital lessons in living from observing the behavior of more experienced members of their species. Young bears learn to fish by fishing with their mothers, and young chimpanzees learn to capture termites by observing adults extracting them from mounds with specially fashioned sticks. If the experiential system of nonhuman animals can learn in this way, it can be assumed that the experiential system of humans can do the same.

Modeling has been used therapeutically in a wide variety of situations, including the control of anger and aggression (e.g., Bandura, 1986; Schneider & Byrne, 1987), and overcoming phobias (e.g., Bandura, 1986). Typically, clients are exposed to someone who demonstrates how a problematic situation can be dealt with in an effective way.

Evaluation of Behavior Therapy from the Perspective of Cognitive-Experiential Theory

As noted previously, behavior therapy is consistent with CET in its emphasis on the use of direct or observed experience for producing changes in the experiential system. This can account for why it is a particularly effective form of psychotherapy for treating specific behavioral problems. Conversely, the emphasis in the theoretical orientation underlying behavior therapy is inconsistent with the emphasis in CET on beliefs as the source of most maladaptive behavior. Of course, from the perspective of CET, changes in behavior are associated with changes in implicit beliefs in the experiential system. The emphasis on learning theory is both an advantage and a disadvantage in behavioral therapy. It is an advantage in that it can use well-established principles of associative learning for changing behavior without having to treat the underlying beliefs assumed in CET to be the source of the maladaptive behavior. The disadvantage is in the limited range of problems that can be treated because many maladaptive conditions not only involve maladaptive behavior but a thought disturbance as well. It would therefore extend the range of behavior therapy to combine it with CT, as in CBT.

COGNITIVE-BEHAVIORAL THERAPY

Ellis and Beck were psychoanalysts who became disenchanted with psychoanalytic theory and practice. In contrast to psychoanalysis and psychodynamic therapy, they preferred a form of treatment that is less inferential, less concerned about the past, less complicated, better supported by research, and of shorter duration. The major thesis underlying CBT is that maladaptive feelings and behavior are determined by the content of maladaptive beliefs and by ways of thinking.

Cognitive-behavioral therapy can more accurately be considered CT supplemented with behavioral procedures than behavior therapy supplemented with cognitive procedures. The theoretical emphasis in CBT is on cognitions. Thus, when a practitioner of CBT uses behavioral procedures, it is either to provide a test of the validity of a client's beliefs or to change behavior as a way of changing a belief related to the behavior. For example, if a painfully shy person says she cannot possibly meet new people because she is terrified that she will not know what to say and will make a fool of herself, she may be given an assignment to initiate a conversation with five strangers before the next therapy session. Note that although a behavior therapist and a cognitive-behavioral therapist may both use the same procedure, the behavior therapist does so from a learning theory perspective and an interest in changing the person's behavior per se, whereas the CBT therapist operates from a cognitive perspective with an interest in changing the underlying beliefs and, thereby, the behavior.

Among those who refer to themselves as cognitive therapists, almost all also employ behavioral procedures. It is noteworthy in this respect that Ellis, who had previously referred to his therapy as *rational emotive therapy* (RET) later changed its name to *rational emotive behavior therapy* (REBT; Ellis, 1993). Cognitive-behavioral therapy is a widely applicable form that has produced favorable results in the treatment of depression, anxiety disorders including phobias, PTSD, eating disorders, and other forms of maladjustment.

Theory and Principles of Cognitive-Behavioral Therapy

According to both Ellis and Beck, people are maladjusted because they process information inappropriately with regard to both content and form of thinking. According to Ellis, examples of maladaptive content are holding negative views about oneself, believing that one "must" have something one wants to be happy, and engaging in catastrophic thinking. Examples of maladaptive forms of thinking are overgeneralization and all-or-none or categorical thinking. Ellis's explanation of why people think in self-defeating, irrational ways is that they have automatic reactions stemming from strong desires for love, safety, comfort, and success.

According to Beck (1976), people are maladjusted because they engage in self-defeating and self-fulfilling hypotheses in which they selectively perceive the world as harmful and ignore contradictory evidence, overgeneralize from limited information, exaggerate the significance of undesirable events, and engage in absolutistic, all-or-none thinking. They also exaggerate the importance of negative outcomes and tend to see the world as a dangerous place.

Procedure

Operating out of the same theoretical position and using similar procedures that include disputing clients' irrational thinking and a variety of behavioral procedures, the therapeutic approaches of Ellis and Beck differ mainly in style. Ellis relies more on direct confrontation in which he vigorously challenges the logic of his clients' irrational beliefs. Beck's approach is a gentler one. Although he, too, challenges his clients' logic, he engages in more hypothesis testing. He and his clients typically map out the latter's questionable beliefs and subject them to empirical testing. Beck often has his clients keep a log of their automatic thoughts and their emotional and behavioral consequences. He also encourages his clients to engage in activities that counter the effects of their pathology. For example, depressed clients are assigned activities that involve action to counter their state of withdrawal and lassitude. They may also be asked to recall times when they were happy and to attend to any current fleeting states of well-being. Ellis, like Beck, in addition to behavioral hypothesis testing, gives behavioral homework assignments that may involve hypothesis testing. Although there are some procedural differences between them, in general, Beck and Ellis use whatever behavioral procedures they believe will usefully supplement their cognitive approach.

Evaluation

Cognitive-behavioral therapy is particularly effective because it adds an important component to CT, the inclusion of behavioral procedures that directly influence the experiential system, and it has been shown to be effective in treating a wide range of disorders, including depression, anxiety, phobias, eating disorders, and PTSD. Nevertheless, it shares some of the same limitations as CT, including a failure to recognize the existence of an experiential system and a failure to identify and treat unconscious beliefs. Because these limitations have already been discussed regarding CT, they need not be repeated here.

Why Intelligent People Think Irrationally

It is noteworthy that the reasons that both Beck and Ellis give for maladjustment correspond to the attributes of experiential processing, such as all-or-none thinking and overgeneralization. In the normal course of development, it was previously shown that there occurs a gradual shift from the dominance of experiential processing to an increasing dominance of rational processing. Because the experiential system is a more fundamental system than the rational system, it can reasonably be assumed that, under stress, people will tend to regress and revert to thinking more experientially.

Given the potency of experiential processing, the influence of early distressing experiences is apt to result in the acquisition of strongly held experientially derived beliefs. Such beliefs are likely to have an enduring influence on people's interpretation of events and on their behavior and to bias people's rational processing. As noted previously, Ellis stated that the reason he believes people have irrational beliefs and reason improperly is because they have automatic reactions stemming from very strong needs for love, safety, comfort, and success. It is noteworthy that these needs correspond to four of the five subordinate basic needs proposed in CET, with love corresponding to the basic need for relationship, safety to the basic need for security, comfort to the basic need to behave according to the pleasure principle, and success to the basic need for self-esteem. It is also consistent with the view in CET that irrational beliefs often have their origin in early childhood experiences (Blatt, 1995). In sum, one reason why otherwise intelligent people think irrationally is that they acquired maladaptive basic needs that lacked fulfillment in early childhood.

Note the implications of these views for the importance of obtaining diagnostic information concerning early childhood experiences. As previously noted, such information can be helpful by indicating the therapeutic value of identifying and treating unconscious needs and beliefs. From the framework provided by CET, this would be an important extension of CBT.

REFERENCES

Ayllon, T., & Azrin, N. H. (1968). *The token economy: A motivation system for therapy and rehabilitation.* New York: Appleton-Century-Crofts.

Bandura, A. (1986). *Social foundations of thought and action: A social-cognitive theory.* Englewood Cliffs, NJ: Prentice-Hall.

Beck, A. T. (1976). *Cognitive therapy and the emotional disorders.* New York: International Universities Press.

Blatt, S. J. (1995). The destructiveness of perfectionism: Implications for the treatment of depression. *American Psychologist, 50,* 1003–1020.

Castonguay, L. G., Reid Jr., J. J., Halperin, G. S., & Goldfried, M R. (2003). *Handbook of psychology: Clinical psychology* (vol. 8., pp. 327–366). Hoboken, NJ: John Wiley & Sons.

Ellis, A. (1977). The basic clinical theory of rational-emotive therapy. In A. Ellis & R. Grieger (Eds.), *Handbook of rational-emotive therapy.* New York: Springer.

Ellis, A. (1987). The impossibility of achieving consistently good mental health. (1987). *American Psychologist, 42,* 364–375.

Ellis, A. (1993). Changing rational-emotive therapy (RET) to rational-emotive behavior therapy (REBT). *Behavior Therapist, 16,* 257–258.

Epstein, S. (1998). *Constructive thinking: The key to emotional intelligence.* Westport, Conneticut: Greenwood Publishing.

Epstein, S. (2001). *Manual for the Constructive Thinking Inventory.* Odessa, Florida Psychological Assessment Resources.

Hurley, A. D., & Sovner, R. (1985). Behavior modification: III. The token economy. *Psychiatric Aspects of Mental Retardation Reviews, 4,* 1–4.

Kazdin, A. E., & Bootzin, R. R. (1972). The token economy: An evaluative review. *Journal of Applied Behavior Analysis, 5,* 343–372

Lovaas, O. I. (1987). Behavioral treatment and normal educational and intellectual functioning in young autistic children. *Journal of Consulting and Clinical Psychology, 55,* 3–9.

Martin, D. J., Garske, J. P., & Davis, M. K. (2000). Relation of the therapeutic alliance with outcome and other variables: A meta-analytic review. *Journal of Consulting and Clinical Psychology*, *68*, 438–450.

Morganstern, K. P. (1973). Implosive therapy and flooding procedures: A critical review. *Psychological Bulletin*, *79*, 318–334.

Pacini, R., & Epstein, S. (1999). The relation of rational and experiential information processing information styles to personality, basic beliefs, and the ratio-bias phenomenon. *Journal of Personality and Social Psychology*, *76*, 972–987.

Rimmerman, A., Finn, H., Schnee, J., & Klein, I (1992). The rehabilitation of persons with severe mental illness in adult homes: The NYPCC study. *Psychosocial Rehabilitation Journal*, *15*, 55–66.

Schneider, B. H., & Bryne, B. M. (1987). Individualizing social skills training for behavior-disordered children. *Journal of Consulting & Clinical Psychology*, *55*, 444–445.

Segal, Z. V., Williams, J. M. G., & Teasdale, J. D. (2002). *Mindfulness based cognitive therapy for depression. A new approach for preventing relapse.* New York: Guilford Press.

Stampfl, T. G. (1975). Implosion therapy: Staring down your nightmares. *Psychology Today*, *8*, 66–68, 72–73.

CHAPTER 12
Psychotherapy 2
Psychodynamic Therapy, Client-Centered Therapy, Gestalt Therapy, Psychosynthesis, Cognitive-Experiential Therapy, Relapse

It is beyond the scope of this chapter to discuss from the perspective of cognitive-experiential theory (CET) the many kinds of psychotherapy that exist. In the previous chapter, as well as here, examples are provided of four approaches for influencing the experiential system: (1) using the rational system to correct the experiential system, (2) using behavioral approaches to correct the experiential system, (3) using a psychodynamic/eclectic approach, and (4) communicating with the experiential system in its own medium. In the previous chapter, examples were provided of influencing the experiential system by using the rational system to correct the experiential system, as demonstrated in cognitive therapy (CT) and cognitive-behavioral therapy (CBT). As examples of using behavioral procedures to correct the experiential system, I discussed behavioral therapy (BT) and CBT. In this chapter, as an example of a kind of therapy that can use all three basic approaches, I discuss a psychodynamic/eclectic approach, and, as examples of communicating with the experiential system in its own medium, I discuss client-centered therapy, Gestalt therapy, and psychosynthesis. I next consider therapy conducted according to the framework of CET. I close the chapter with a discussion of relapse and offer suggestions for reducing or preventing it.

PSYCHODYNAMIC PSYCHOTHERAPY

Psychodynamic therapy (PT), including its various eclectic approaches, is the most widely practiced form of psychotherapy (Norcross, Hedges, & Castle, 2002; Svartberg & Stiles, 1991).

Procedure

Psychodynamic therapy is a greatly modified, less intensive version of psychoanalysis, using 50 to 60-minute sessions usually held once or sometimes twice a week. Unlike standard psychoanalysis, the client and therapist sit facing one another and converse in a normal manner rather than having the client lie on a couch with the therapist seated unseen behind the couch, listening and interpreting. In other ways, as well, there is less conformity in PT with classical psychoanalytic theory and practice. Psychodynamic therapy also often includes procedures from other forms of therapy, such as cognitive, behavioral, and experiential approaches.

Blagys and Hilsenroth (2000) conducted a study in which they compared manualized PT with manualized CBT. As revealed by transcripts and recordings of sessions, a greater emphasis was placed in PT compared to CBT on affect and expression of emotions, exploration of resistance to discussing distressing thoughts and feelings, identification of recurring themes and patterns, developmental issues concerning past experiences, interpersonal relationships, the therapeutic relationship (e.g., transference), and on exploration of fantasy life. This study was only concerned with specific techniques and processes. At a more general level, one would have to include the emphasis in PT on unconscious processes. Thus, psychodynamic therapists believe that it is misguided to treat only manifest symptoms. They believe that it is particularly important to determine and treat the unconscious roots of symptoms.

Evaluation of Psychodynamic Psychotherapy

In common with CET, PT uses an eclectic approach and emphasizes the significance of unconscious beliefs and needs and their influence on behavior and conscious thinking. It also considers the interactions of needs, beliefs, and defenses. On this basis, it might seem that, from the perspective of CET, PT would be among the most effective forms of psychotherapy. However, its evaluation has been highly controversial. The evaluation of PT is considered here from two perspectives: empirically based on outcomes and conceptually based on theoretical and logical considerations.

The Empirical Evaluation of Psychodynamic Therapy

How effective is PT? Among several meta-analyses that have compared the outcome of PT with other forms of therapy, the general conclusion is that the differences are generally small and inconsistent, with one notable exception. Psychodynamic therapy has generally been found to be inferior to CBT in the treatment of depression, although this conclusion is not accepted by everyone. For readers who wish more information on this controversy, see Shedler (2010) on PT; for responses to his article, see McKay (2011), Thombs, Jewett, and Bassel (2011), Anestis, Anestis, and Lilienfeld (2011), and Tryon and Tryon (2011). For Shedler's defense of the efficacy of PT, in which he cites a variety of meta-analyses in which PT is compared to control groups or to other procedures, see Shedler (2011). Shedler concludes that PT produces results that are at least as favorable as those from the most successful other procedures, such as CBT. He notes, for example, that the meta-analyses referred to by his critics do not include some measures of particular significance to PT, such as general psychological health, fulfillment, and well-being He cites several meta-analyses in which it was found that those treated with PT exhibited further improvement at follow-up, whereas in other approaches a decline is generally observed at follow-up.

The heterogeneity of psychodynamic therapy. A serious difficulty in evaluating psychodynamic therapy is that the therapy is extremely heterogeneous. Thus, some psychodynamic therapists adhere more closely than others to classical psychoanalytic theory, dogma, and practice; some incorporate more procedures from nonanalytical forms of therapy than others; and some emphasize transference reactions much more than others. Accordingly, in research comparing the effectiveness of PT with other forms of therapy, much depends on the particular sample of psychodynamic therapists examined. In a meta-analysis conducted by Svartberg and Stiles (1991), this problem was dealt with to some extent by classifying therapists in various ways, such as by their experience in using a particular procedure, their consideration of demographic variables, their consideration of whether an approach was event- or personality-centered, their consideration of whether the duration of therapy was fixed or flexible, and whether emphasis in interpretations was on transference relations or on other kinds of behavior. Although such an approach is commendable, other theoretically important variables were not considered, such as an emphasis on unconscious versus conscious beliefs and the inclusion of outcome measures of fulfillment and overall well-being, along with more specific measures of symptoms.

The self-selection by clients of their therapies. The results on the effectiveness of different therapies can be influenced by the self-selection by clients of the therapies they receive. If patients who are more disturbed than others select treatments that differ from those chosen by clients who are less disturbed, they may have less favorable outcomes not because their therapy was poorer but because they were more disturbed to begin with.

As an example of the complications that arise because of a confound between outcomes and the self-selection of therapies, let us consider a study in which it was found that behavior therapists were more likely to choose PT for themselves than behavior therapy (Gochman, Allgood, & Geer, 1982). How is this finding to be interpreted? At first consideration, it may seem that behavior therapists value PT more favorably than the therapy they practice. However, the following interpretation is just as plausible and perhaps even more so: behavior therapists seek treatment for conditions such as relationship problems or unconscious conflicts that they regard as more appropriate for their treatment by PT than by behavioral procedures. Moreover, because they are experts in behavior therapy, they may be able to treat their own behavioral problems but require help with other kinds of problems. If this is true, it would indicate that they regard PT as superior to behavior therapy only for certain kinds of problems but not for others.

Ideally, clients would be randomly assigned to different treatments for the same disorders. This, of course, has not yet been done for practical reasons—many clients have preferences for particular treatments. The result is that the studies so far conducted have an important confound between selection of treatment and outcome, which allows for alternate interpretations. Moreover, even with the degree of psychopathology controlled, differences among clients in personality and in beliefs about therapies could influence outcomes, which again would make it impossible, in the absence of random assignment to therapies, to assume that differences in outcomes can be attributed to the general effectiveness of the treatments.

The importance of comparing therapies on theoretically relevant variables. A particularly important consideration when comparing different therapies is the kind of variables on which they are compared. This issue has been dealt with in many studies by examining outcomes for therapies as a function of diagnosis, such as depression, anxiety reactions, and relationship problems. This is obviously a desirable procedure, but it does have an important limitation. Namely, more theoretically important than dividing therapies by standard diagnostic categories is dividing them according to relevant distinctions for different kinds of therapies.

If PT is superior in any way to other forms of therapy, as previously noted, it would have to be judged so with regard to such variables as the identification and treatment of unconscious needs and beliefs and the consideration of transference relationships. Also important are the significance of early childhood experiences and the identification and treatment of interactions among needs, beliefs, and defenses, It is therefore important to include the influence of these variables in comparisons of PT with other forms of therapy.

The Evaluation of Psychodynamic Therapy Based on Logical and Theoretical Considerations

Psychodynamic therapy as a complex, inferential therapy that has its dangers as well as its virtues. According to CET, there is much in favor of the concepts of unconscious processes and psychodynamics. Although these concepts add a level of complexity and inference in interpretation that increases the likelihood of error, they also are powerful constructs that recognize how people operate in real life. Nevertheless, psychodynamic therapists may tend to emphasize these concepts more than is warranted in certain cases. They may assume the operation of unconscious motives and defenses where none exist, and they may also be unduly influenced by a strong hypothesis that almost all maladjustment is the results of dysfunctional parenting during the early formative years of development. To some degree, an overemphasis on unconscious processes and interactions by psychodynamic therapists may be related to a failure to recognize the limitations inherent in the Freudian view of how the unconscious mind operates and to recognize instead that many problems in living are produced by the influence of experiential processing in the absence of repression. The extent of this problem will vary according to the degree to which psychodynamic therapists adhere to psychoanalytic dogma.

The advantages and disadvantages of the interpretations of transference. Transference relationships are particularly important according to CET because relationship variables fall strongly into the domain of the experiential system. However, many, but not all, psychodynamic therapists regard the interpretation of transference relations as a central aspect of their therapy. In a meta-analysis in which psychodynamic therapists were divided according to the extent of their interpretations of transference reactions, those who emphasized such interpretations outperformed those who emphasized other kinds of behavior (Svartberg & Stiles, 1991). Moreover, the former, unlike the latter group of therapists, did not perform more poorly than cognitive-behavioral therapists.

Let us consider in greater detail the advantages to interpreting clients' transference reactions toward their therapists. In interpreting such reactions, therapists consider their clients' reactions to them as an indication of how they probably react to others. Such transference interpretations have an advantage over the interpretations of self-reported information because they are based on the observation of behavior of which the client may be unaware. However, there is still a problem concerning the subjective judgment of the therapist, although many therapists are probably aware of this possibility and try to avoid it.

Another kind of transference interpretation is more likely to be a serious problem. It is an interpretation that is made with regard to the verbal report of a client about a significant other. Given a strong hypothesis by some psychodynamic therapists that current problems in living are almost always the result of dysfunctional parenting, there is the danger of accepting a biased report of what actually occurred. This is illustrated in the following example based on an observation of a specific case. The therapist made the following interpretation: "It seems from what you have repeatedly told me about your father that it can help us to understand your problem with male authority figures. You describe your father as behaving in an authoritarian, know-it-all manner that made you feel very inadequate until you got older and began to rebel against it. I suspect that his behavior sensitized you to such behavior in others. No doubt some others are, in fact, authoritarian like your father, but most are probably not that way. That is, you may be ultra-sensitive to seeing bossy, know-it-all behavior in others at times when it is not there. Moreover, people with a sensitivity like yours may tend unintentionally to elicit behavior in others that confirms their expectations. Let's discuss what you think about this explanation of your problem with authority figures."

Note that if this latter interpretation is correct, it can be helpful in improving the client's relationships with authority figures. It can do so partly by identifying and controlling self-verifying behavior and thereby teaching that not all authority figures behave as anticipated. This raises the critical question of whether the interpretation is correct and, if incorrect, its cost. It can easily be incorrect for the following reasons. The client may be providing a distorted representation of his father as part of a general tendency toward blaming others and denying his own responsibility for unfavorable outcomes. Moreover, the therapist may be particularly susceptible to accepting such information as accurate because of a strong hypothesis that maladjustment almost always has its roots in dysfunctional parenting. Unfortunately, such an incorrect interpretation is reinforcing for both the therapist and the client in the short run, but at a significant long-term cost. The therapist is reinforced by the verification of the hypothesis, and the client is reinforced by the boost in self-esteem from support of his maladaptive defense mechanism. The costs of the incorrect interpretation are that it can be disruptive of family relationships, and it reinforces the continuation of a maladaptive defensive response.

An important danger in transference relationships is that they can occur in therapists as well as in clients. When transference occurs in a therapist, it is referred to as *countertransference*, which is recognized as a serious impediment to therapy because it distorts the therapist's judgment and leads to incorrect interpretations. Fortunately, there is a useful procedure that can help to control countertransference reactions: according to CET, therapists must attend carefully to their own emotional reactions elicited by their clients' narratives, which can help to prevent therapists from being influenced outside of their awareness.

In addition to its usefulness in controlling countertransference reactions, such awareness can make another important contribution. It can provide an additional source of information that is not based on self-report. Thus, the therapist's own emotional reactions elicited by a client can provide useful information about how the client, intentionally or unintentionally, influences and may attempt to control others. For example, a therapist makes the following comment: "In attending to my own feelings while listening to your recounting of your many unfortunate experiences, I note that it tends to elicit a feeling of pity in me. This makes me wonder how much you elicit the same feeling in others. If so, I wonder if you do it intentionally or unintentionally, and in either case what it does for you. If you agree that you may do this, I think it would be useful for us to discuss what you gain from it and at what cost."

Psychodynamic therapy may be more resistant to relapse than other therapies. According to CET, PT may be more resistant to relapse than other forms of therapy. As noted previously, in several meta-analyses reported by Shedler (2010), outcomes of PT improved in a post-therapy period, which is the opposite of what usually occurs. Thus, PT may be more resistant to relapse than other forms of therapy. One reason for this may be because PT is more likely to treat the unconscious sources of symptoms rather than just the symptoms themselves. A simple analogy may help to explain why finding and treating an underlying cause may prevent relapse. The example involves the treatment of a car's transmission, and the usefulness of the analogy rests on the assumption that the operation of the human brain is at least as complicated as the operation of an automobile transmission.

I obtained two estimates for repairing the transmission of my car. The first was from a large automobile dealership that specializes in the sales and repair of the kind of car I own. The second was from a nationally syndicated firm that specializes in repairing transmissions. The diagnosis by the first garage was that the car required a new transmission and that the cost would be considerable. The diagnosis from the second establishment was that there was a flaw in an electronic unit that influences the operation of the transmission, which would again break down after a period of satisfactory operation if the transmission were replaced. The breakdown of the transmission following a period of recovery can be considered analogous to a relapse following a period of recovery in psychotherapy. Thus, if only the surface manifestation of a problem is treated, and it has an underlying, untreated cause, relapse is likely. Conversely, if the underlying cause is successfully treated, then relapse is more unlikely.

In a case I treated as a co-therapist (fully described in the next chapter), the client remained symptom free and without relapse for more than 20 years after previously enduring unremitting depression. The client says she now is unable even to imagine how she felt when depressed, and she attributes her recovery to a major reorganization of her implicit cognitions that allowed her to fulfill unsatisfied needs.

I do not believe that failure to treat an underlying source of a symptom is the only reason for relapse, but I do believe it is at least one important reason for relapse. To the extent this is true, it follows that PT should have an advantage with regard to relapse prevention in comparison to other forms of therapy that treat only symptoms.

In conclusion, although PT has not exhibited an advantage in empirical research, this may be due to limitations in the research and that it is simply too early to make a definitive judgment based on purely empirical grounds regarding the relative effectiveness of PT. The best one can do at this stage of research is to make reasonable decisions based on logical and theoretical considerations as to which kinds of therapy are likely to be most effective for which kinds of problems and clients. From the perspective of CET, PT has an important contribution to make with respect to identifying and treating unconscious sources of symptoms and interactive patterns involving needs, beliefs, and defenses. Also, according to the framework provided by CET, it should have an advantage over other forms of therapy that are less eclectic because it can include all other therapeutic approaches. These two reasons are both strengths and weaknesses of PT. They are strengths according to CET because of the importance of unconscious processing and the assimilation of other forms of therapy. They are weaknesses because of the complexity they introduce into understanding and treating maladaptive behavior. Of particular significance, the added degree of inference in interpreting unconscious processes introduces an important source of error. Thus, if a therapist can adequately deal with the complexity, he or she would be among the very best of therapists, and if the therapist cannot do so, he or she would be among the very worst of therapists. Put the two together and one obtains a medium level of performance, which is another reason why PT may not have fared better in empirical comparisons with other therapies.

INFLUENCING THE EXPERIENTIAL SYSTEM BY COMMUNICATING WITH IT IN ITS OWN MEDIUM

Three humanistic-experiential therapies are discussed in this section: the client-centered therapy of Carl Rogers (1951, 1961), the Gestalt therapy of Fritz Perls (1967, 1969), and the psychosynthesis therapy of Roberto Assagioli (1965) and his disciple Piero Ferrucci (1982).

In client-centered therapy, a single fundamental procedure is used to communicate with the experiential system in its own medium, which is achieved by the attitude and behavior of the therapist toward the client. In Gestalt therapy and psychosynthesis, communication with the experiential system is achieved by a variety of procedures including the use of imagery, fantasy, metaphors, narratives, role playing, associations, free drawing, dream analysis, and attending to bodily states and feelings.

Client-Centered Therapy

In the introductory chapter of this book, it was noted that the foundation of CET was suggested by two properties of the self that were proposed by

Rogers and rejected by others as scientifically indefensible. One property was that the self is an agent of behavior, and the other is that it operates according to a growth principle. In response to this criticism, I suggested that these two properties could be reasonably explained if the self-concept is identified as a self-theory because all scientific theories have these properties. They are agentic because they direct the behavior of the scientists who hold them, and they operate by a growth principle by becoming increasingly differentiated and integrated through their interaction with the data of reality. And so CET was born out of two disputed views of Rogers, indicating that there is a fundamental affinity between Rogers's theory and CET.

An important area of agreement between Rogers's theory and CET is that both assume that people's beliefs are the most important determinants of their feelings and behavior. The two theories are also in agreement that discrepancies between beliefs directly acquired from experience and those introjected from significant others are an important source of maladjustment. According to CET, the beliefs acquired from experience often exist outside of awareness in the experiential system, whereas the introjected beliefs in client-centered therapy reside primarily consciously in the rational system. Only CET recognizes the existence of an experiential system. Although Rogers refers to organismic beliefs acquired from experience, they are a far cry from an experiential system, which is an organized adaptive system that operates by rules and attributes that differ from those that govern the operation of a rational system.

Rogers's theory and CET share the belief that people have a fundamental need to maintain and enhance their conceptual systems. However, for Rogers, this is the only basic need whereas for CET it is one among five subordinate basic needs and two superordinate needs. Thus, from the viewpoint of CET, Rogers's theory has important theoretical limitations that are the source of applied limitations. For example, according to Rogers, all maladjustment is the result of incoherence within or between belief systems. Such a theory would have difficulty in explaining all depression, low self-esteem, poor relationships, or antisocial behavior; surely, some maladjustment could obviously occur from coherent maladaptive beliefs. This does not deny that incoherence is a source of any of these symptoms; it simply indicates that symptoms can occur for reasons other than incoherence.

Another problem with Rogers's theory is that it is almost completely phenomenological, assuming as it does that all needs and beliefs, with one exception, vary along dimensions that differ among individuals. The exception is that everyone is assumed to have a need to maintain and enhance a coherent self-concept. The assumption that people's needs and beliefs differ among individuals considerably complicates research on Rogers's theory. In contrast, according to CET, people vary mainly in the degree to which they hold the same needs and beliefs.

The two theories also differ in whether people's self-concepts are conscious, unconscious, or both. According to Rogers, the self-concept is always conscious. According to CET, people have two self-concepts, one in their rational system and another in their experiential system, which is largely unconscious.

Client-centered therapy relies primarily on the use of one basic procedure, which is to "reflect" what clients report in a manner that conveys empathy and unconditional positive regard. It is impressive when conducting such therapy or reading case histories about it that clients often solve their own problems when provided with appropriate conditions. In the absence of interpretations or guidance from their therapists, clients exhibit the kind of psychological growth predicted by Rogers's theory. That is, they construct a more coherent belief system that is consistent with their emotionally significant experiences and, as a result, become more self-accepting, accepting of others, and better adjusted.

The technique of client-centered therapy is a simple one that is relatively easy to learn using the many examples and training exercises provided (e.g., Rogers, 1951, 1961). One obvious pitfall that the beginning therapist must learn to avoid involves mechanically reflecting what a client says in a manner that is closer to mimicry than to attentive listening, empathy, and positive regard. Thus, a key element in this therapy is for the client to experience feedback from the therapist as authentic acceptance.

Client-centered therapy can be expected to be most effective for clients with problems concerning autonomy, self-acceptance, relationships, and alienation from experientially acquired beliefs. Thus, there is a large group of clients for whom client-centered therapy is appropriate.

A problem with client-centered therapy that will require research to resolve concerns the possible adverse effect of unconditional positive regard in people with antisocial tendencies. According to CET, and in contrast to Rogers's theory, people are neither inherently socially good nor bad but may have predominantly pro- or antisocial tendencies, depending on their reinforcement history. Thus, if those with experientially based antisocial beliefs, needs, beliefs, and behavioral tendencies were to become more accepting of such responses by receiving unconditional positive regard, they could become dangerously antisocial. It would, of course, have far-reaching implications, both theoretically and practically, if Rogers's view on this issue were found either to be correct or incorrect.

An important extension of client-centered therapy from the perspective of CET is to shift, at an appropriate time in therapy, from a purely reflective procedure in the initial phase of treatment (i.e., phase 1) to an interactive relationship in a subsequent phase (i.e., phase 2). So long as the same positive attitude toward the client is retained in phase 2, it should enhance the communication of unconditional positive regard by demonstrating the therapist's confidence in the client's ability to behave in a cooperative, equal, and mature interaction. Phase 2 could therefore be regarded as a step beyond phase 1 in the communication of unconditional positive regard.

In my own experience, I have found client-centered therapy during phase 1 to be a very effective way of establishing trust and a therapeutic alliance with almost all clients. After I have established a satisfactory level of trust and a therapeutic alliance, I advance to phase 2, but so gently so that I can readily retreat if I miscalculated. My aim in phase 2 is to establish a partnership in which the client and I work together to solve the client's problems. I freely express my views but always in a tentative manner, as material for discussion. In sum, I attempt to change our relationship in phase 2 to one that is more equal and in which we both feel free to express our views. I believe this is not only a more authentic way of conveying unconditional positive regard but that it provides the client with practice in communicating with others in a mutually advantageous and mature manner. I therefore believe it would be a desirable extension of the more traditional practice of one-sided reflection of a client's meaning and that Rogers (1980) was moving in this direction.

GESTALT THERAPY AND PSYCHOSYNTHESIS

The primary aim of Gestalt therapy and psychosynthesis is to establish a state of wholeness and harmony in place of one of conflict, isolated beliefs, and a lack of coherence and integration. To accomplish this, both employ a variety of exercises for communicating with the experiential system in its own medium. Among the procedures are the use of imagery, fantasy, free drawing, associations, dream interpretation, metaphors, narrative processing, concrete representations, and attention to bodily states and feelings. This, of course, is consistent with CET because the exercises involve many of the attributes of experiential processing listed in Chapter 1. The most important attributes of experiential processing used in both Gestalt therapy and psychosynthesis are imagination and visualization. Also, like CET, Gestalt therapy and psychosynthesis recognize the significance of beliefs that are unconscious for reasons other than repression. Unlike CET, Gestalt therapy and psychosynthesis focus on the present, on what clients feel and think currently, and not on why or where it came from. A limitation with regard to evaluating both of these therapies is that little outcome research has been done with them.

Gestalt Therapy

Gestalt therapy was developed by Frederick Perls (1969) as a way to teach clients to become aware of their bodily and emotional states, with the aim of identifying and integrating blocked and isolated aspects of their personalities. An example of an exercise is the "the two chair technique" in which a client sits in one chair while acting out one side of a conflict and in another chair while acting out the other side of the conflict. Another example is the "empty chair technique," in which a client imagines and talks to an imaginary person, such as a deceased parent. The client is likely to bring up issues with the imagined person that Perl refers to as "unfinished business," which consists of problems that require resolution before integration and harmony can be achieved. While imagining their interaction, clients are asked to report their emotions and the feelings they have in different parts of their bodies.

Dream analysis is used in Gestalt therapy, in which the content of the dream is interpreted together with the client's free drawings and associations to aspects of the dream. Clients are often asked to role play items of particular interest in their dreams. Fritz Perls (1969, pp. 81–82) recounts the following role playing by one of his clients of the image of an old license plate lying on the bottom of a drying out lake.

L: "I am an old license plate, thrown in the bottom of a lake. I have no use because I'm no value—although I'm not rusted—I'm outdated, so I can't be used as a license plate . . . and I'm just thrown on the rubbish heap."

Fritz Perls (F): "Well, how do you feel about this?"

L: "I don't like it . . . useless."

F: "Could you talk about this?"

L: (sighs). " Useless. Outdated. . . . The use of a license plate is to allow—give a car permission—to go . . . Now I can't give anyone permission to do anything because I'm outdated."

F: "Okay, now play the lake."

L: "I'm a lake . . . I'm drying up, and disappearing, soaking into the earth . . . dying. But when I soak into the earth, I become part of the earth—so maybe I water the surrounding area . . . so, even in the lake . . . flowers can grow. . . . New life can grow . . . from me (cries)."

F: "You get the existential message?"

L: "Yes, I can paint—I can create—I can create beauty. . . . I can play a part in something."

F: "You see the contrast: On the surface you find something—some artifact—the license plate, the artificial you—but when you go deeper, you find the apparent death of the lake is actual fertility. . . . "

L: "And I don't need a license plate, or a permission, a license in order to. . . . "

F: "Nature doesn't need a license plate to grow. You don't have to be useless, if you are organismically creative, which means if you are involved."

L: "And I don't need permission to be creative. . . . Thank you."

It is interesting to consider the different interpretation that would be made according to CET. It will be recalled that, according to CET, the major motive of the experiential system is to operate according to the hedonic principle (i.e., to feel good and avoid feeling bad). Viewing the drying out lake as a source of regeneration and beauty can be explained by the motivation to find a favorable way of reinterpreting a distressing experience that is consistent with the operation of the hedonic principle.

Psychosynthesis

Among the procedures used in psychosynthesis for communicating with the experiential system in its own medium are a lighthouse exercise, a butterfly exercise, free drawing, and, most importantly, the identification and transformation of subpersonalities. In the lighthouse exercise, a client imagines being on a small ship at sea during a fiercely raging storm. The wind is howling, and the ship is pitching and rolling. The client is wrestling with the wheel, trying to keep the ship on course. With great relief, a light is seen from a distant lighthouse that will lead the client to safety. The client is told that after a period of time the image should be dropped while retaining the sense of support and security.

In the butterfly exercise, the client imagines being a caterpillar that surrounds itself with a cocoon made of soft, silken threads. With the passage of time, a ray of light penetrates the cocoon as it begins to open. A surge of energy is felt as the caterpillar emerges from the cocoon. It leaves the cocoon, and, in imagining a higher form of existence, the client is told to leave his defenses and concerns about the past behind because they will no longer be necessary. The caterpillar has now been transformed into a beautiful butterfly that can fly, which gives it a feeling of exhilaration and freedom beyond what was thought possible. The butterfly descends to a meadow full of beautiful flowers and gently settles on one after another. The client is told to take his time in experiencing, as a butterfly, the freedom, lightness, and beauty with which it is surrounded. The vivid use of metaphors in these exercises is consistent with their communication with the experiential system according to CET.

In the free drawing exercise, clients are asked to let their hand draw whatever it wishes without conscious direction. When finished, they are asked to examine their drawings and report whatever associations and images come to mind and what they may be revealing. They are then asked to turn the drawing over, write whatever occurs to them, and note any new information that may be revealed. The drawing and writing may be repeated several times while seeking a common thread of meaning and attending to the significance of any differences that occur.

Working with subpersonalities is considered to be an extremely effective procedure for addressing the most important aspects of humanistic theory. Subpersonalities represent isolated belief systems that prevent wholeness from being achieved. To establish wholeness, each subpersonality must be elevated to a higher, more adaptive level in which it is capable of accepting and cooperating with the other subpersonalities. Subpersonalities are considered to be components of an overall observing self. Each subpersonality has a personality of its own, complete with feelings, beliefs, attitudes, needs, motives, and behavioral tendencies.

Subpersonalities represent personal attributes that clients wish to understand. They include both admired and unacceptable attributes and ways of being in the world. Thus, they include favorable attributes such as being courageous, competent, creative, kind, assertive, intuitive, empathic, and hopeful, and unacceptable attributes and ways of being in the world, such as being cowardly, incompetent, cruel, self-sacrificing, selfish, deceitful, controlling, and pessimistic. The existence of such subpersonalities is consistent with the concept of complexes in CET, which are isolated cognitive-affective networks.

Subpersonalities are vividly imagined and assigned a name. The construction of subpersonalities, although only the first step, is itself considered therapeutic because it promotes "disidentification," which refers to the recognition that the self is more than the sum of separate subpersonalities. The self is regarded as the stable, unifying core of the personality that exists in the form of "pure consciousness," which is considered to be present at a higher conceptual level than all other beliefs. As the result of a very high level of generality and stability, the self is said to "disidentify," meaning it can view specific beliefs and feelings from a position of objective, therapeutic distance (Ferrucci, 1982). It therefore makes it possible for a person to gain therapeutic distance from each subpersonality by regarding it objectively and recognizing that it is less than the observing self.

A second major step is to elevate a subpersonality to its highest level by "taking it up the mountain." The journey begins in a meadow in which there are beautiful wildflowers and singing birds. There is a trail that becomes steeper as it wends its way up the mountain. The subpersonality takes this trail and, near or at the top of the mountain, becomes transformed. If the transformation is unsatisfactory, the subpersonality is taken up the mountain again, as many times as necessary for an acceptable transformation to occur. What is remarkable about this process is that it appears to have a life of its own, much like a dream in which the client does not know what to expect and is often surprised.

The final major step is to achieve a synthesis of the subpersonalities by teaching the subpersonalities in their transformed state to accept each other and behave cooperatively, with the aim of establishing a unified conceptual system.

THERAPY CONDUCTED ACCORDING TO THE THERAPEUTIC FRAMEWORK PROVIDED BY COGNITIVE-EXPERIENTIAL THEORY

The main contribution of CET for psychotherapy is to provide an integrative framework for all therapeutic procedures. In addition, it provides an approach to therapy in which theory is intimately related to practice. Cognitive-experiential therapy is readily shared with clients and can serve as a source of guidance throughout the course of therapy. In other words, CET can be regarded as a "give-away" theory, working to the advantage of both client and therapist.

Understanding how the mind operates according to CET narrows the selection of procedures and, equally important, it allows for the organization of new and old information into a cohesive system that can guide the choice of a therapeutic procedure. Cognitive-experiential theory is not only a compelling theory of how the mind operates, it is also well supported by research and real-life phenomena. In addition, it is easily comprehended by ordinary people because it corresponds to their own experience, and it explains in a comprehensible manner why they think and behave irrationally despite their capacity for logical reasoning. They are well aware that they have conflicts between the heart and the head and that they have unbidden thoughts that they are unable to control. When the principles of CET are explained to them, for the first time they are able to comprehend what before seemed inexplicable.

It is a relatively simple matter to explain, using examples from people's everyday lives, that there are two ways in which humans adapt to their environment. One way is based on the automatic operation of an experiential associative learning system that often operates outside of awareness and that humans share with other animals. The other way is based on a conscious, deliberative, verbal, rational system that is unique to humans. Clients learn that each of the systems processes information according to its own rules and attributes. They further learn how the two systems interact. Most importantly, they learn that their problems most likely lie in the content and operation of their experiential systems and that it is this system that needs to be corrected. Cognitive-experiential therapy indicates the various ways in which malfunctioning can be fixed, which may or may not involve the use of the rational system. Such an understanding of how the mind operates prepares clients to behave in a theory-guided manner to solve their problems in living.

As previously noted, sharing CET with clients has an advantage beyond providing information about how the mind operates. It facilitates the development of a therapeutic alliance, which provides an important corrective emotional experience regarding trust and working cooperatively with others. Moreover, the unconditional positive regard provided by a therapist in CET-based therapies contributes to elevating self-esteem. Both of these developments provide a secure base from which clients can explore their problems.

One of the advantages in recognizing two distinct systems is that it can reduce defensiveness. Once it is understood that the experiential system operates according to associations based on past experience, it becomes meaningless for clients to defend their experientially determined behavior by intellectual argument. The only meaningful response is to investigate the operation and content of the experiential system, which frequently means relating present events to emotionally significant past events in order to uncover maladaptive schemas.

Although CET offers no new specific procedures of its own, it does offer several emphases that can be implemented in a family of CET-related therapies. One such emphasis is on the use of a coherent eclectic approach. Unlike other eclectic approaches that are derived empirically, primarily through clinical experience and whatever limited information is available, the selection of procedures can be conducted in CET-related therapies in a theoretically directed manner. For example, procedures can be classified according to whether they involve using the rational system to correct the experiential system, using a psychodynamic/eclectic approach, providing corrective emotional experiences in or outside of therapy, and communicating with the experiential system in its own medium. The therapist and client together can consider which of these procedures would be best used at the beginning of therapy or later. In the event that they choose communicating with the experiential system in its own medium, they can consider whether it would be best to use it to learn about the experiential system, to learn from it, or to influence it. Of course, all this depends on the nature of a particular problem at a particular time. Note that this approach provides a way of organizing therapeutic procedures from all orientations within a single, coherent framework.

I do not mean to imply that, at this stage of knowledge, therapists have much objective data to rely on in making the kinds of decisions that are required to operate according to the CET framework. However, providing the framework is at least a beginning for the development of a theoretically based, coherent eclecticism. Moreover, the framework I have proposed can not only organize old research; it can guide new research by indicating where the most important gaps are. Until sufficient research is conducted, therapists will, of course, have to rely on their clinical experience as well as on the limited research available. But, even here, the framework can be useful because it can provide an impetus for clinicians to familiarize themselves with what is available from various orientations and to make comparisons and selections among them in a theoretically coherent manner.

Another emphasis in CET is on the importance of need fulfillment for producing enduring changes in the experiential system. In the absence of need fulfillment, treatment of symptoms may be prone to relapse, which will be discussed in greater detail later.

Cognitive-experiential therapy-emphasizes the interaction of the experiential and rational systems. It will be recalled that the typical sequence of reactions following an emotionally significant event is first to process the information experientially, which then may bias conscious thinking as well as influence behavior. Being unaware of such influence, people consciously try to explain their behavior and think in a rational way; that is, they rationalize behavior by attributing to their rational system what was determined by their experiential system. This process is important to consider because it prevents people from learning from experience. People can all too easily find acceptable ways of attributing unfavorable outcomes to the behavior of other people or to circumstances beyond their control. By defending their own maladaptive behavior, they have no incentive to change how they think and behave.

Another hallmark of CET-related therapies is to employ fantasy, viewed as an effective way of safely reaching the experiential system. It is particularly helpful when fantasy is used not only to identify problems but also to include their resolution. This will be discussed in greater detail in the next chapter.

Although there are other emphases in CET-oriented therapies, those I have reported here are sufficient to make my point that CET, although it provides no new procedures, does provide a useful integrative framework for all forms of psychotherapy. Cognitive-experiential therapy also can influence the selection and implementation of a variety of procedures from all orientations in a useful and coherent manner.

RELAPSE IN PSYCHOTHERAPY AND SUGGESTIONS FOR REDUCING IT

According to the learning component of the framework provided by CET, an understanding of relapse can benefit from theory and research regarding spontaneous recovery. Spontaneous recovery refers to the reemergence of a learned response following its extinction. Pavlov (1928) and others attributed extinction to learned inhibition, and they attributed spontaneous recovery to the disinhibition of inhibition that occurs over time. Spontaneous recovery is an adaptive response because it provides for the possibility that the inhibition of a response is no longer necessary.

Relapse and Spontaneous Recovery

Assuming that relapse following therapy is an example of spontaneous recovery, the time for relapse to occur will vary directly with the degree of overlearning. This suggests that the overlearning of a corrective response should increase its resistance to extinction. In other words, a useful procedure for delaying or preventing relapse should be to continue the practice of a corrective belief beyond its initial learning.

Another useful generalization from experimental psychology concerns the use of booster sessions to strengthen a corrective response and reinforce the inhibition of a maladaptive response. It should also be helpful not only to practice corrective responses in real life and in therapeutic sessions, but also to do exercises using imaginary scenarios. The object, according to CET, is to provide sufficient practice in replacing maladaptive with adaptive beliefs until the latter become automatic and therefore indicative of a shift from rational to experiential control.

Other Sources of Relapse

So far, relapse has been discussed with regard to what can be learned from the research and theory on spontaneous recovery. In regarding the occurrence of relapse, other variables, such as treating a secondary belief and failing to treat an underlying primary belief, an absence of need fulfillment, return to an unfriendly environment following psychotherapy, and insufficient positive reinforcement variables are also important.

Failure to Treat an Underlying Primary Belief

The symptom for which a client seeks treatment may concern a secondary, or displaced, source of an underlying problem. Unless the underlying problem is treated, the treatment may either be followed by relapse or be replaced by another symptom. This raises the issue of sympton substitution that was originally considered by psychoanalysts as highly likely but has since been discredited. According to CET, the abandonment of the threat of symptom substitution was premature. Displacement is regarded in CET as a highly common compromise produced by the interaction of the major motives of the two information-processing systems, namely, motivation according to the hedonic principle of the experiential system and motivation according to the reality principle of the rational system. This compromise was well illustrated in research on the ratio bias phenomenon and also by the ubiquitous finding that although most people behave in self-enhancing ways, they behave within acceptable reality constraints. Following this line of reasoning, it may be that symptom substitution is likely to occur if a sufficient period passes after the completion of therapy.

Failure to Provide Adequate Need Fulfillment

Although needs are recognized as important in cognitive therapy, they are not given the emphasis given to beliefs. As a result, irrational beliefs may be corrected without determining whether important unfulfilled needs also exist. Thus, clients may learn to think rationally about their problems, but their lives continue to be unsatisfactory. Under such circumstances, their hopes may be raised and they may take pride in their improved reasoning about their problems. However, in the absence of enduring need fulfillment, the improvement is likely to be transitory. In a case that will be discussed in detail in the next chapter, a client was successfully treated for a life-long depression without a trace of relapse in a period of more than 20 years. In a post-treatment interview many years after her psychotherapy, she was asked to discuss why she thought her treatment had been so successful. She provided several reasons, but the most important one, she said, was that she learned to fulfill her needs in a satisfactory manner so that it completely changed the way she experienced her life.

It is noteworthy that, unlike in CET, there is no list of basic needs underlying the practice of most therapies. Thus, apart from whatever a client indicates about frustration, the therapist has no guidance regarding the importance of need fulfillment and how it can be achieved.

Unfriendly Post-Therapy Environment

According to CET, reinforcement and its opposite, punishment, are the two most important variables that influence changes in experiential beliefs. It follows that an important determinant of resistance to relapse is the post-therapy environment to which a client returns.

A lesson regarding relapse can be learned from an important principle in the psychotherapy of children, in which much depends on the family environment. A child's symptoms do not occur in isolation. They usually occur because of the influence of parents or other significant figures who may unintentionally have a vested interest in a child being distressed or incompetent. This could occur, for example, if a child reminds a parent of a sibling with whom the parent was fiercely competitive. It is therefore often as necessary to treat the parents as it is to treat the child. By the same token, the corrective beliefs and behavior that adult clients acquire in therapy may be treated punitively and the old beliefs rewarded when the clients return to their previous environment. This suggests two solutions if relapse is to be avoided. One solution is to address this issue, either with the client alone or in joint sessions with the other parties.

An Absence of Reinforcement

Reinforcement refers to favorable consequences following a response. As reinforcement strengthens a response, it makes it less vulnerable to relapse. Thus, returning to an environment that is supportive of a corrective response should increase its resistance to relapse.

Reinforcement does not only occur in a family setting. It also occurs intrinsically in the rewards that follow improved beliefs and behavior, as well as from a favorable relationship with a therapist. Note that, to the extent to which this occurs, there is no such procedure as pure cognitive therapy. Rather, because of the influence of the therapeutic relationship, there is always an important experiential component in any therapy. It is noteworthy in this respect that, in the case described as a presumably pure case of cognitive therapy, in which Beck treated a client with anxiety about giving speeches, a broader problem emerged; namely, a fear of disapproval. What better experiential treatment for this problem than having a favorable relationship with an approving and helpful therapist? Although such a therapist may be critical of the client's self-defeating behavior, a good therapist is never disapproving of the client as a person and always responds with positive regard.

The Need for Improved Theory and Research on Relapse

Ellis (1987) performed a valuable service by drawing attention to the high rate of relapse following his cognitive therapy treatments because it spawned a plethora of studies on relapse and procedures for reducing it. In a more recent publication co-authored posthumously with his wife (Ellis & Ellis, 2011), they more optimistically readdressed the issue of relapse and suggested procedures for reducing it. Included were alerting clients to a tendency to relapse and, if and when it occurs, reapplying the procedures learned in therapy. It is noteworthy that Ellis misses the mark in these suggestions by taking an excessively rational-analytic approach and failing to consider sufficiently the experientially determined reasons that relapse occurs.

The rate of relapse in psychotherapy is highly troublesome and will require not only improvements in theory but also further research on how it can be reduced (e.g., Burcusa & Iacono, 2007; Dunner et al., 2007 Richard & Perri, 2010; Shea et al.,1992). Of course, improvements in theory and research are not independent because better theory will provide better research. When conducting such research, it is particularly important that it not only investigate why relapse is so prevalent, but also examine cases in which it has not occurred after an extended post-therapy period.

REFERENCES

Anestis, M. D., Anestis, J. C., & Lilienfeld, S. O. (2011). When it comes to evaluating psychodynamic therapy, the devil is in the details. (2011). *American Psychologist*, *66*, 149–151.

Assagioli, R. (1965). *Psychosynthesis, A manual of principles and techniques*. New York: Hobbs, Doorman, and Co.

Blagys, M. D., & Hilsenroth, M. J. (2000). Distinctive activities of short-term psychodynamic-interpersonal psychotherapy: A review of the comparative psychotherapy process literature. *Clinical Psychology Science and Practice*, 7, 167–188.

Burcusa, S. L., & Iacono, W. G. (2007). Risk for recurrence in depression. *Clinical Psychology Review*, *27*, 959–985.

Dunner, D. L., Blier, P., Keller, M. B., Pollack, M. H., Thase, M. E., & Zajecka, J. M. (2007). Preventing recurrent depression: Long-term treatment for major depressive disorder. *Journal of Clinical Psychiatry*, *68*, 619–630.

Ellis, A. (1987). The impossibility of achieving consistently good mental health. *American Psychologist*, *42*, 364–375.

Ellis, A, & Ellis, D. J. (2011). *Rational emotive behavior therapy: Theories of psychotherapy*. Washington, DC: American Psychological Association.

Ferrucci, P. (1982). *What we may be.* New York: G. P. Putnam Sons.

Gochman, S. I., Allgood, B. A., & Geer, C. R. (1982). A look at today's behavior therapists. *Profession of Psychology*, *13*, 605–609.

McKay, D. (2011). Methods and mechanisms in the efficacy of psychodynamic psychotherapy. *American Psychologist*, *66*, 147–148.

Norcross, J. C., Hedges, M., & Castle, P. H. (2002). Psychologists conducting psychotherapy in2001: A study of the Division 9 membership. Theory, research, practice, training. *Psychotherapy, 39*, 97–102.

Pavlov, I. P. (1928). *Lectures on conditioned reflexes* (translated by W. H. Gannt). New York: Liveright Publishing.

Perls, F. S. (1969). *Gestalt therapy verbatim*. Lafayette, CA: Real People Press.

Richard, C. S., & Perri, M. G. (Eds.). (2010). *Relapse prevention for depression*. Washington, DC: American Psychological Association.

Rogers, C. R. (1951). *Client-centered therapy.* Boston: Houghton Mifflin.

Rogers, C. R. (1961). *On becoming a person.* Oxford, England: Houghton Mifflin.

Rogers, C. R. (1980). *A way of being. Boston: H oughton Mifflin.*

Shea, M. T., Elkin, I., Imber, S. D., Sotsky, S. M., Watkins, J. T., Collins, J. F., Pilkonis, P. A., Beckham, E., Glass, D. R., Dolan, R. T. (1992). Course of depressive symptoms over follow-up: Findings from the National Institute of Mental Health Treatment of Depression Collaborative Research Program. *Archives of General Psychiatry*, *49*, 782–787.

Shedler, J. (2010). The efficacy of psychodynamic psychotherapy. *American Psychologist*, *65*, 98–209.

Shedler, J. (2011). Science or ideology? *American Psychologist*, *66*, 152–154.

Svartberg, M., & Stiles, T. C. (1991). Comparative effects of short-term psychodynamic psychotherapy: A meta-analysis. *Journal of Consulting and Clinical Psychology*, *59*, 704–714.

Thombs, B. D., Jewett, L. R., & Bassel, M. (2011). Is there room for criticism of studies of psychodynamic psychotherapy? *American Psychologist*, *66*, 148–149.

Tryon, W. W., & Tryon, G. S. (2011). No ownership of common factors. *American Psychologist*, *66*, 151–152.

CHAPTER 13

Psychotherapy 3

Communicating with the Experiential System Through the Use of Fantasy

This chapter explores the use of fantasy and imagery to reach the experiential system, using case material to illustrate several procedures. As you may recall, people react to vivid imagery in a similar way to how they react to reality (e.g., Crisp, & Turner, 2009; Dadds, Bovbjerg, Redd, & Cutmore, 1997; Epstein & Pacini, 2001; Kosslyn, Ganis, & Thompson, 2001; Taylor, Pham, Rivkin, & Amor, 1998). Although imagined experience has a weaker effect than real experience, it has several advantages. It is more readily available and safer than real experience, and it can be used not only for vicarious learning, as a substitute for real-life experience, but also for learning about the content and operation of the experiential system. It can also be used to represent real-life events, and it can be used symbolically to reach the deepest levels of the experiential system. It can be used in a directed way, as in systematic desensitization, and it can be used in a free-floating manner, in which it is allowed to follow its own course. It does this, often surprisingly, as if it had a mind of its own.

AN EXAMPLE OF THE USE OF FANTASY AS VICARIOUS EXPERIENCE

The following example illustrates a very simple use of fantasy to explore a person's reactions to an imagined real-life event. This is a very easily applied technique that can be modified as needed to meet the requirements of a wide variety of situations. Because people are often unaware of the schemas and motives in their experiential system that influence their behavior and bias their conscious thinking, the best they can usually do is provide what appears to them to be reasonable explanations for their conscious thoughts and behavior. Since such explanations are often incorrect, it can be useful to employ techniques, such as the use of fantasy, which can put people in touch with their experiential processing. The example that follows is of a person who, under the guidance of a therapist, visualizes an event to learn how he might react to similar events in real life.

Robert exhibited in his behavior an ambivalence about getting married. Recently, the woman he had been going with for several years gave him an ultimatum. She demanded that he either pronounce his intention to marry her or she would leave him. Robert loved her, but he did not feel ready for marriage. He had always assumed he would settle down and raise a family, but somehow whenever he came to the point of committing himself, something went wrong with the relationship, and he and his partner parted ways. At first, Robert attributed the partings to failings in his partners, but, after repeated reenactments, it occurred to him that the problem might lie in himself and his possible ambivalence toward getting married. Since this made no sense to him, he decided to seek the help of a therapist. The therapist instructed Robert about the use of visualization and fantasy, and helped him practice using them. He then asked Robert to vividly imagine coming home to a wife and children after work. When Robert reported that he had the scene vividly in mind, he was asked to attend carefully to his feelings. To his surprise, he felt irritated and burdened when his wife greeted him at the door and the children eagerly began relating their events of the day. The therapist next instructed Robert to imagine an earlier scene in which he had the very same feeling. His mind turned to an image of taking care of his younger siblings when his parents went out for entertainment. He deeply resented having to care for them and not being able to play with his peers. The result was that he learned to dislike interacting with children at the experiential level but had never articulated this at the conscious, rational level. As an adult, although Robert believed in his conscious, rational mind that he wanted to get married and raise a family, in his experiential mind, the thought of being in the company of children produced distressing feelings. He and his therapist discussed whether he should follow his heart (i.e., his automatic experiential processing) or his mind (his conscious rational thinking). To help him to decide what to do, the therapist pointed out that following his heart would entail avoiding marriage and that accepting such a solution would be the path of least resistance. He added that if Robert decided to follow his mind, it would be important for him to work on overcoming his negative feelings toward children. When Robert decided that is what he wanted to do, he was given an exercise to practice in fantasy that consisted of scenes in which Robert engaged in enjoyable activities with children. He was also encouraged to visualize whatever occasions he could remember from his childhood in which he enjoyed being with his siblings. He was given other scenes to imagine, including being pleased with himself for being a more attentive parent to his imaginary children than his parents had been to him.

AN EXAMPLE OF A PSYCHOTHERAPEUTIC PROCEDURE BASED ON COGNITIVE-EXPERIMENTAL THEORY

Because cognitive-experiential theory (CET) is a broadly integrative theory, there is hardly a form of therapy that does not fit under its umbrella. Yet there can be approaches to therapy that are explicitly based on the principles of CET. In one form or another, such approaches employ an integrative approach that includes instruction about the operation of the two systems for processing information, the use of the rational system to correct the experiential system, corrective emotional experiences, and communicating with the experiential system in its own medium.

The following example of such therapy was developed by Lori Katz, who was trained in CET under my supervision as a graduate student. Experimenting with a variety of ways of implementing the principles of CET, she developed her own approach to psychotherapy, which she later termed *holographic reprocessing* (Katz, 2005). She defines experiential holograms as representations in the experiential system of themes of experience that repeatedly manifest themselves in one form or another in relevant contexts in everyday life. Katz refers to them as "holograms" because any component of an experiential hologram that is activated by a situation is assumed to activate the entire hologram. Thus, in a sense, the whole is contained in each of its parts, which is the critical aspect of a hologram. Katz's construct of an experiential hologram is somewhat similar to the construct of a complex in CET because an experiential hologram, like a complex, can be accessed through associations, imagery, and the identification of repetitive behavioral patterns. Moreover, like an experiential hologram, the activation of any component of a complex can trigger the activation of the entire complex because all the networks in a complex are interconnected.

Experiential holograms are reprocessed by an integrative therapy that employs both rational and experiential approaches, with an emphasis placed on communicating with the experiential system in its own medium. Katz describes the stages of her therapy as usually proceeding in the following order: (1) the development of a therapeutic alliance; (2) the establishment of "foundation skills," including self-soothing techniques, breathing exercises, progressive muscle relaxation, and imagining safe havens, which are used as necessary to cope with the stress produced by confronting threatening issues; (3) the identification of "experiential holograms" by using associations, memories, bodily reactions, images, and fantasy productions to connect current maladaptive behavioral patterns to their origins in earlier experiences; (4) the identification of "characteristic responses," which refer to typical patterns of response in reaction to the activation of an experiential hologram; (5) holographic reprocessing, which refers to the use of experiential procedures, such as imagining scenarios in which the source of the hologram is revisited and the problems produced by it are resolved, thereby preparing the way for new kinds of adaptive behavior; and (6) "new behaviors," which refers to the establishment of constructive new ways of behaving in the real world.

The following case material is extracted from a publication by Katz (2001). In her introduction, she states that the procedure she used is but one example of a variety of alternative procedures that she uses flexibly. She notes that she wrote the article in the first person to describe her actual thinking:

> A middle-aged well-dressed woman sat across from me and described feeling a vague sense of depression and malaise. She also mentioned feeling constipated and uncomfortable. She stated this has been occurring since last week and she did not know why.
>
> I asked her to close her eyes, focus on her feelings, and ask herself, "What am I feeling?" She thought for a moment and then said, "I'm feeling nothing really, kind of numb." I hypothesized that her feelings of depression and numbing resulted from an attempt to avoid a different feeling. I also wondered if the avoided feeling is anger because of her symptom of constipation. I let these thoughts cross my mind and asked her to ask herself the same question again. She said, "I don't know. I feel kind of bad, kind of hurt." I asked her where she felt bad and to put her hand there. She indicated that she felt it in her stomach and intestine/bowel area. I said, "The body is a very sensitive instrument and knows exactly how you are feeling. It communicates directly with the unconscious mind. So ask your body if it feels anything else." By asking her about her physical sensations, I bypass an intellectual discussion or lengthy explanation about her feelings. Instead I pursue the associations from her experiential system....
>
> She said, "I'm scared." "Take your time and do what is comfortable for you," I responded.... She took in a deep breadth and then started to rattle off a number of emotions, "hurt, upset, betrayed, lonely...." "Anything else?" I waited.
>
> Finally, she said, "I feel angry." I knew we had hit on the core feeling by the way her whole body responded.... Her posture was more relaxed and her attention was more focused. I acknowledged, "Yes, you feel angry." She repeated, "Yes, I do! I feel really angry!" I could sense she really wanted to let this out, so I encouraged her to express what she felt. I repeated, "Yes, you do!" She burst into a sobbing release of tears. Through her gasps, she kept saying, "I'm so angry!" After she hit the peak of her sobbing release her crying subsided, I asked... "Who did you get particularly angry with last week?"
>
> She then proceeded to tell me the story about her dentist.... She accumulated her finances and had $11,000 to pay for this (her treatment). However, her dentist told her it would cost $14,000, and he refused her request to make payments for the additional $3,000.... She said, "I want to write him a nasty letter or write to his licensing board about his behavior.... You know, it is scary for me to feel so angry." As emotions of fear and anger were activated, I expected them to facilitate the retrieval of situations that evoked similar emotions in the past. I asked

her, "Do you remember a time when it was particularly scary to feel anger?" She said, "Yes, when I was a child. I was abused by my alcoholic father. If I ever talked back to him or expressed my anger, my mother would take me down to the cellar. I was left alone in the cellar." I thought about the words she used to describe her feelings earlier in the session (hurt, upset, betrayed, lonely). I considered that several of these might be associated with this earlier event.... When asked about betrayal, she revealed that she harbors a deep sense of betrayal from her mother. Sometimes her mother was kind to her, and at other times she would physically abuse her.

I asked her if these were similar feelings to how she felt with the dentist.... She stated that she could not express her feelings to the dentist, and this was exactly like being locked up in the cellar. She also felt that he was kind to her during the diagnostics but then ended up betraying her. At this point it becomes clear that her experiential hologram is exposed. The incident with the dentist is the perfect overlay for her experiential hologram of someone betraying, intimidating, and controlling her, which is reminiscent of the feeling of "being locked in the cellar." Her characteristic response is to feel helpless and afraid to express her anger... and finally to suppress her anger and develop somatic symptoms.

Based on the associative principle of the experiential system, I pointed out the connections between her current feelings and those of the emotional experiences of the past. The associations were made through similar feelings, use of words, and relevant images (being locked in the cellar). Also, I was able to point out her characteristic response to her as revealed through her behavioral demonstration in the office, including her fear of expressing her anger and her somatic symptoms.

Now we were ready to transform the hologram. She stated that she felt a little better after talking about her feelings. However, she added that she has done "tons of anger-relief work" and has even "killed her mother in therapy" (metaphorically speaking), only to realize that she still has the same feelings. I reassured her that we were only half way through the therapy. Emotional release by itself does not transform experiential holograms....

I proposed that she imaginally confront her dentist and "rescript" the scene in a more favorable way.... She imagined herself walking through the waiting room and into his office. The dentist was seated at his desk doing some paperwork. She said, "I am angry at you for not allowing me to pay the remainder of my bill in installments." "Tell him what it was like for you," I encouraged. She said, "It felt like you abandoned me, and that makes me very angry." "Go on," I said. She continued, "It felt like I was a child left in the cellar, and I won't let that happen to me anymore." By expressing herself to the dentist, she was able to alter her perception of her relationship with him. Her physiology changed as she spoke. She began to sit more upright in her chair. She appeared more confident and her voice was firm. The involuntary change in her expressive behavior confirmed that she had shifted her reality at the experiential level.

> "Good," I said. Now tell him one thing you have learned as a result of having gone through this experience." She said, "I learned that I can't trust the dentist." I realized I omitted an important part of the statement and corrected myself. "Tell him one *positive* [emphasis in original] thing you have learned. . . . " The purpose of asking about a positive aspect of the experience is to shift the context of a difficult situation into one that is valuable because it facilitates constructive learning. She replied, "I learned that I need to know about payment policies up front." "What else?" I asked. "I learned that I was still afraid to express my anger and I didn't know it," she said. Gentle tears rolled down her face and I handed her a tissue. "I wasn't even aware that I was still acting like that scared little girl." "Anything else you learned?" I asked. "Yes," she said, "I learned that I have a choice. I *can* [emphasis in original] stick up for myself and I will find another dentist that will work for me within my financial parameters."
>
> She stated that she felt relieved and empowered. The next week she reported that she had found a dentist who charged her $11,000 for the entire procedure.

Let us considered what occurred in the therapy sessions in relation to the principles of CET. The therapist utilized several procedures for learning from and influencing the experiential system. She made a point of avoiding prolonged intellectual discussions by focusing on actual experiences. She attended to bodily reactions, encouraged emotional expression, and had the client relate present events to earlier experiences to locate the existence of an experiential hologram. All of these procedures are identified in CET as ways to learn about the operation and content of one's experiential system.

The examination of emotionally significant past experience as a way of locating experiential holograms is consistent with the view in CET that the schematic networks that determine current maladaptive thinking and behavior are generalizations from emotionally significant past experience. For this reason, according to CET, learning about the past is important, a view that is not shared by all therapeutic orientations.

Identifying the characteristic responses of the client when her experiential hologram was activated (which consisted of feelings of helplessness, fear of expressing anger, and psychosomatic reactions) is consistent with the view in CET that people become sensitized by distressing experiences and then react in inflexible, maladaptive, repetitive ways when their sensitivities are triggered.

This case material well illustrates the insufficiency of emotional catharsis. When the client reported that she had engaged in a great deal of emotional catharsis to no avail in previous therapeutic attempts, she was reassured that in the present form of therapy emotional catharsis is not viewed as an end in itself. Rather, its value lies in identifying an experiential hologram and in finding a way to fulfill frustrated needs, including, in her case, the needs to assert herself, feel in control of situations, and maintain self-esteem. This is consistent with the view in CET that adaptive fulfillment of needs in the experiential system is a major goal of psychotherapy.

Holographic reprocessing not only provides practice in resolving problematic situations in fantasy, but it proceeds to a further step of encouraging and reinforcing the same kind of resolution in real life. Thus, in a variety of ways, holographic reprocessing emphasizes communicating with, learning from, and training the experiential system. To do so, it employs procedures from three major ways of learning about and influencing the experiential system; namely, using the rational system to correct the experiential system, providing corrective emotional experiences in fantasy and in reality, and communicating with the experiential system in its own medium, including the use of fantasy, the use of concrete examples, and attending to bodily reactions and emotions.

DEMONSTRATION OF THE POWER OF FANTASY IN A DRAMATIC RECOVERY FROM A LIFE-THREATENING DISEASE

The case material presented here is from an autobiographical account by Alice Epstein (1989), in which she attributes her recovery from terminal cancer to an intensive course of psychotherapy. Of particular interest, the results were available from projective tests given 40 years before the onset of cancer and the beginning of her psychotherapy. The tests suggested a pessimistic attitude and a conflict about attachment. The tests were administered as a requirement in a class in clinical psychology in which I had to test several nonclinical cases. At that time, Alice and I were graduate students who were eventually married. It will be seen that the conflict about attachment was still present during the beginning of therapy and how it was resolved during therapy.

The story of Alice's cancer and its treatment begins in March 1985, when Alice was diagnosed with a hypernephroma in her left kidney. Despite removal of the kidney, the cancer spread to both lungs, which placed her in a terminal stage of the disease. It seemed that no traditional treatment could help her. Her only hope for extending her life beyond a few months was to participate in an experimental program. The likelihood of a prolonged remission, let alone recovery, was less than 4 in 1,000 based on the actuarial data over a two year period. (DeVita, Hellman, & Rosenberg, 1985).

Following her oncologist's advice, Alice made appointments to learn about available experimental programs. Simultaneously, she embarked on an intensive course of psychotherapy. She was treated by two therapists with different but compatible orientations. One was Dr. Dorothy (Didi) Firman, a practitioner of psychosynthesis, and the other was I, her husband, who used procedures guided by CET. Under normal circumstances, I would not treat an acquaintance, let alone someone so intimately related to me as my wife. However, in this situation, we desperately needed rapid and dramatic results, having just been informed that Alice was not likely to live more than three months.

In reading about cancer, I learned to my surprise that there was a presumed syndrome referred to as a *cancer-prone personality*. Although it was controversial, I was struck by the correspondence of the syndrome with Alice's personality. A particularly important part of the syndrome refers to an underlying feeling of despair masked by a happy outward appearance and an eagerness to fulfill the needs of others at the sacrifice of fulfilling one's own needs. I was encouraged by reading about the syndrome because I thought that if psychological factors had contributed to Alice's cancer, there was the possibility that psychological treatment could cure the cancer. I discussed this with Alice, and she agreed to undergo psychotherapy but only if I would be the therapist. I explained to her the difficulties with such an arrangement. We finally reached a compromise. She would immediately begin daily therapy with me, and we would look for an additional therapist. In that way, she could discuss any issues that involved me with another therapist.

After interviewing several therapists, we found the kind of person we were seeking. Alice took an immediate liking to Dr. Firman, who asked us to call her Didi. Didi and I believed we could work comfortably with each other in the arrangement Alice and I proposed to her. As it turned out, we could not have made a better choice.

I had been concerned about complications arising from Alice having two therapists. I certainly did not want to do anything that might interfere with Alice's relationship with her other therapist. This turned out not to be a problem; Didi's approach and mine were compatible, and we both respected what each other was doing. Moreover, Alice coordinated how she used us. I was there to meet with her if she wished on an appointed hour that we set aside on a daily basis on days in which she did not see Didi. Alice used her time with me in any way she thought might be helpful. As therapy progressed, she became increasingly comfortable with Didi, and there was less need for me to serve as a co-therapist. Nevertheless, I kept the appointed time available for Alice whenever she wanted to use it.

It is beyond the scope of this chapter to discuss Alice's therapy in detail. A full account is available in a book she wrote, *Mind, Fantasy and Healing* (A. Epstein, 1989). The book is now out of print but can be obtained for $15.00. which includes postage, by writing to me at the following address: Seymour Epstein, 37 Bay Road, Amherst, MA 01002.

It will suffice to note that Didi and I both used an approach that included three major psychotherapeutic orientations. Sometimes we worked on constructive thinking, sometimes we used cognitive-behavioral procedures, and most often we used procedures that involved communication with the experiential system in its own medium, mainly fantasy. Alice enjoyed working with her fantasies, and she readily became deeply immersed in them.

Although Didi and I used fantasy a great deal, we did so in different ways. Didi used fantasy primarily, but not exclusively, within the framework of psychosynthesis, the orientation in psychotherapy with which she had been trained. I used fantasy in a more general way. In the examples and discussion that follow, communication with the experiential system in the form of fantasy is emphasized because it was the most unique aspect of Alice's therapy and the one that appeared to produce the most dramatic results. It provided important information about the operation of the experiential system, and it was influential in the operation of that system.

Using the Rational System to Correct the Experiential System

Didi and I both used training in constructive thinking. Most often, it consisted of identifying counterproductive thoughts and replacing them with more constructive ones. Through this procedure, Alice learned to fulfill her needs in a direct manner instead of suffering in silence and then feeling resentful. In this and a variety of other ways, she learned to become a better constructive thinker. In this regard, therapy based on CET makes use of a psychoeducational element that has been shown to be an important component in a variety of cognitive therapy (CT) and cognitive-behavioral therapy (CBT) procedures.

Providing an Emotionally Corrective Relationship

Alice very rapidly established a working alliance with her two therapists. She was extremely conscientious and open-minded with regard to exploring any possibility. Although she was determined to do everything she could to defeat the cancer, her primary goal was to become the kind of person she wanted to be. Alice participated as an equal partner with both of her therapists, freely making suggestions about her treatment and trying out procedures on her own initiative. Both Didi and I respected and supported such autonomous behavior. Communication between Alice and her two therapists was very free in both directions. Although we freely made suggestions, Alice was always the final arbiter in determining how we should proceed.

Unconditional positive regard from both of her therapists effectively challenged Alice's belief that she had to please others to be accepted. Of course, the relationship between Alice and me, her husband, was particularly important in this respect. I was well aware that I would be tested and that it was extremely important that I clearly convey that I loved her deeply for the person she was and not for the many things she did to please me. We had a poignant discussion on this issue in the early days of therapy. I told her that

I felt uncomfortable when she went out of her way to do things to please me without considering her own needs. She was not convinced. She said I was just saying that and that if you want people to like you, you have to please them. I disagreed. I said I loved her for who she was, for the way we cared about each other and enjoyed each other's company, and the way we could talk about anything. I added that I would prefer that she not sacrifice her own needs to fulfill mine as it placed a burden on me. Alice burst into tears and said, "We are now fighting. We are disagreeing about something important to me. How can we love each other if we disagree like this?" I expressed surprise that she should have such a strange notion that people who love each other are not supposed to disagree. I told her that disagreeing with her had nothing to do with my love for her. It simply gave me the freedom to be myself without having to worry about our relationship being so insecure that I could not freely express myself. I told her I would be more comfortable if she had the same attitude. She appeared shocked. She said she had been raised to believe that she had to please her mother or she would be rejected. Alice later told me this discussion had a profound effect on her because it seriously challenged her lifelong assumption that she had to please others to be accepted. The incident, of course, is an example of correcting a maladaptive thought in the rational system, as well as of providing an emotionally corrective experience in the experiential system.

Communicating with the Experiential System in Its Own Medium

Here, I illustrate several ways in which fantasy was used in Alice's therapy. In the simplest procedure, Alice imagined destroying the cancer cells using a method she had read about in a book *Getting Well Again* (Simonton, Mathews-Simonton, & Creighton, 1978). She describes her procedure in her book as follows (A. Epstein, 1989, pp. 42–43):

> After sitting quietly for a few moments and trying to relax, I pictured in my mind a scene from a jousting tournament. I would surround a group of cancer cells, black, slimy globs of protoplasm, in a jousting ring. The white cells at first were knights on white horses with long lances who would spear one after another of the slimy things. Later the white cells changed into white polar bears who ate the cancer up. The important part of the visualization is that at its end the participants and observers would all yell, "Hip, hip, hurrah..." for a job well done. I did the visualization four times a day as recommended in the book.

Alice was not so naïve as to believe that her fantasies killed cancer cells. She considered the procedure helpful because it made her feel relaxed and in control rather than feeling distressed and helpless. Nevertheless, the possibility should be considered that the relaxation and feeling of control could have contributed to her immune functioning or other physiological reactions that were helpful in defeating her cancer.

The following is a fantasy that Alice worked on with me early in therapy. Alice had complained about experiencing acute pain where she had been operated on to remove a kidney to which her cancer had metastasized. In the session immediately preceding the fantasy, she had expressed hostility toward her mother for the latter's neglect of her during a period of turmoil in the household when her terminally ill grandmother moved in with the family. Adding to Alice's confusion and anger was the unexpected appearance of her mother nursing a baby, for which Alice was totally unprepared. Her mother had apparently done a good job of hiding her pregnancy. In an attempt to relieve and perhaps learn from the pain, I asked Alice to imagine an animal that represented the pain. This is Alice's description of the fantasy that unfolded:

> Immediately an image of a golden boa constrictor came to mind: it was wound around my body and putting just enough pressure on me to cause the discomfort I was feeling. The snake told me I had no right to intrude into its garden, that I didn't belong there. I, in turn, told the snake that I meant it no harm and asked that it stop hurting me. It retorted that it did not trust me because I was not pure of heart and, like everyone else, I meant to steal its babies for their valuable golden skins.
>
> Despite my denial the serpent did not believe me at all. I begged him to tell me why he thought I was not pure of heart. He replied that I knew the answer and would have to figure it out myself. By now I was physically struggling with the snake, and a feeling of crisis and impasse was developing. I asked if he was hurting me because of my hostility to my mother and others. The snake hissed out that not expressing hostility had nothing to do with not being pure of heart.
>
> My breathing finally began to quiet down, and the pain abated slightly as I left the world of fantasy to once more enter the real world. I thought a little and then said that I believed I understood why I was not pure of heart. And why the snake held me in its grip. I had gone to the pricing session for the League (of Women Voters) book sale not to be helpful but to be with other people. I had not really enjoyed myself but had gone to counter the isolation that I felt. This was the sellout then to my fear, just as I had always sold out to my mother's domination so that I wouldn't have to face the fear of her rejection. The golden snake never returned, and the pain never came back quite the same way because I had learned at least to try to be pure of heart. (A. Epstein, 1989, p. 44)

Since the fantasy of the golden snake was helpful, we decided to use the same technique to try to understand Alice's recent feeling of isolation and discomfort at being alone. The following is her description of the fantasy that emerged when she visualized isolation:

> Visualizing isolation was much more difficult than visualizing pain. After many attempts that we both rejected as trivial, I finally caught the spirit of what I was experiencing. I saw some figures with shrouds, very unclear. Then as they took on a more distinct form, I saw that they were witches standing around a fire. My therapist told me to ask them to come over to talk to us. They were frightening to me in the light of the fire, but they were more horrible as they came closer. They laughed at me and started to poke at me with their sticks. The visualization was so real and their presence was so chilling to me that I burst into tears over the interaction with them.
>
> My therapist told me to ask them what I could do to get rid of the awful fear of isolation. Finally they revealed their price. It was that I make a sacrifice so that they could become beautiful and mingle with other people. When I heard their price I began to tremble. In an almost inaudible voice I whispered, "They want my children so they can turn them into witches like them, but I'll never do it. I'll never give them my children!"
>
> My therapist then told me to destroy them, but I told him that I couldn't possibly do it. He urged me to try to turn my fear to wrath, to try to imagine a creature that could help me. The image that came to me was a white winged horse. He told me to mount the horse and to supply myself with a weapon that would destroy them. I refused to kill them myself, but said that the wings of the horse would fan the flames of their fire, which would turn back on them and destroy them.
>
> There was only one problem with this scenario: the horse and I were one now and I couldn't get airborne. The wings were so heavy that I couldn't flap them hard enough to catch the breeze. The harder I tried, the more I failed and the more the witches laughed at me. My therapist told me that another horse who loved the first horse very much would join her and together they would destroy the witches. The other horse flew above me and made a vacuum into which I could take off. Once in the air, I flew effortlessly and fanned the fire into a huge blaze. The witches ran here and there trying to avoid the flames but in the end they were consumed by the fire.
>
> I practiced the scene over and over again until it became easy, but I never enjoyed it. I liked to fly, but I felt sorry for the witches, no matter how mean they were to me. My therapist felt that it was a mistake to feel sympathy for them because they would take advantage of any mercy that I displayed. He felt they would use any deception and illusion they could to control me. I was not so sure but I did agree with him that I must assume the right to soar into the world and be free of their influence. After the session, my therapist and I discussed the meaning of the images. Although I had begun with the concept of isolation in mind, I knew that the witches related to my mother, particularly the way she

> would poke at me and shame me. They probably represented my fear of isolation if I did not acquiesce to her demands. My therapist added that in destroying the witches I was only destroying the hostile part of our relationship, the witch part of it, and leaving the loving part intact. This was necessary for me to be free, autonomous, and no longer ensnared by fear of abandonment.
>
> The concept that I had a great deal of conflict between the need for association and the need for autonomy was not new. I believed I had to buy affection and that no one would love me if I were myself, i.e., if I attended to my own wants. I knew also that I felt that I had to carry the burden of being responsible for my mother's wellbeing, that she would die at some level if I broke the bond with her. (A. Epstein, 1989, pp. 45–47)

Several aspects of this fantasy warrant discussion. First, the fantasy provides information about important needs and beliefs in the experiential system. It is noteworthy that the only aspect of the situation that reached awareness after Alice's expression of hostility in the previous session was an enduring feeling of loneliness and isolation. It took the fantasy to attach content to the feeling. The content suggested that Alice could not free herself from a destructive attachment to her mother because she feared being alone in the world.

This fantasy not only provided information about Alice's experiential schemas and her conscious awareness of them, it taught me about a mistake I had made when I tried to direct her fantasy. I realized that it was wrong to encourage Alice to kill the witches. After all, it was the expression of hostile feelings to her mother in the previous session that preceded her feeling of isolation. A better solution would have been simply to help her to escape. Later, I tried to compensate for my error by telling Alice that she had killed only the destructive part of her relationship with her mother.

The insight represented in the fantasy about a conflict between autonomy and relatedness was not new to Alice. She had been aware of this conflict long before. In fact, it was evident in the projective tests she had taken more than 40 years ago when she was a graduate student. Since Alice had no new understanding, what then did the fantasy accomplish? It provided a vicarious corrective emotional experience that had a direct effect on her experiential system. To make a therapeutic contribution, the information had to be felt emotionally and processed at the experiential level. Moreover, the fantasy did more than just identify a conflict between autonomy and relatedness; it pointed to a solution. That is, the fantasy indicated that, in order to break the destructive tie with her mother and fulfill her need for autonomy, Alice needed an alternative source of support. She could not simply be left feeling lonely and devoid of any attachment. Only with support by an accepting figure that facilitated her movement toward autonomy was she able finally to believe at the experiential level that it was possible to be both autonomous and loved.

It is noteworthy that, on her own initiative, Alice repeatedly imagined soaring in space and savoring a feeling of unrestricted freedom. Thus, not only did the fantasy reveal a problem and point to its solution, but it provided vicarious reinforcement of autonomy in the form of joyously soaring in the sky. This suggests what may be a generally useful therapeutic procedure; namely, practicing the resolution of a conflict in symbolic form, including vividly experiencing positive reinforcement following the resolution.

This fantasy also provided useful information about the future conduct of Alice's therapy because it informed me of the importance of providing the support that Alice required before she could free herself from the suffocating relationship with her mother. As both her therapist and her husband, I was in a particularly advantageous position to provide such support. In every relevant situation, I made a point in word and deed of demonstrating that I loved her unconditionally and that I supported and admired any attempts she made toward becoming her own person rather than having to please others at the cost of fulfilling her own needs. The love and affection that had always been available to her from her husband, her children, her extended family, and her devoted friends could not penetrate so long as she felt that the price of love was the sacrifice of autonomy and self-esteem. Having developed a life-long pattern of self-denial in order to maintain relationships, she had no way of knowing that self-sacrifice was a hindrance, not a boon, toward establishing mutually satisfactory relationships. Through corrective emotional experiences in real life and in fantasy, Alice was finally able to accept that she could be loved for her own sake.

Didi used fantasy in a variety of ways. She instructed Alice to bring to the first session two spontaneous drawings. Alice drew two stick figures in drab colors. One of the figures was of Alice's mother wrapped in a shroud. The storyline underneath the picture stated, "My mother is reaching out to pull me into the grave with her and I am terrified." Didi asked Alice if she was would be willing to imagine the scene. Alice agreed and, after a period of relaxation, vividly imagined it. She describes what she experienced:

> I was filled with terror; my heart began to beat rapidly and my breadth came in gasps. I tried to resist with all my might. Didi guided me through the visualization and insisted that I tell my mother that I would not go with her. "I will not go," I screamed. "I WILL NOT GO!" Over and over again I shouted it, until I began to believe it myself. After the session was over I was exhausted by the intensity of the emotional experience. (pp. 69–70)

Alice believed that such visualizations were working because within a week the deep feelings of resentment she had toward her mother began to change. "In its place I developed a strong feeling of love for her and a sense that I could tap her love in my struggle to get well. I assume that as I asserted myself against her in my mind, I allowed myself to forgive her in my heart." It is noteworthy that once Alice was able to break the destructive hold of her mother on her, she could feel affection toward her. Thus, it was not simply the emotional release that was therapeutic. More important was the resolution that with Alice's resistance to being controlled by her mother she was able to establish fulfillment of her own need for autonomy. In other words, the fantasy provided a resolution of a problem, not just an outpouring of emotion.

Alice noted that not only did she receive training in self-assertion in such visualizations, but they paved the way for greater assertiveness in real life. She was learning to say "no" to requests by people without feeling guilty.

Of particular interest in this example is what it reveals about the relation between catharsis and need fulfillment. Alice's hostility toward her mother was not resolved by catharsis, but it did play a role in reaching the experiential system. This is important because it can prepare the way for the next step, need fulfillment in fantasy, which in this case was the need for autonomy; that is, for breaking away from her mother's destructive hold on her. Alice had learned in the fantasy that she could resist her mother and therefore no longer needed to fear a suffocating relationship with her. Once she realized she had nothing to fear from the relationship, she could forgive her mother and become her own person. To behaviorally implement this realization was not accomplished in a single session. It was, however, a critical beginning. Consolidation occurred through further fantasy work, through discussions, and through practice in the real world of saying "no."

Didi's most transforming use of fantasy was based on her training in psychosynthesis. As noted in the previous chapter, an important procedure in psychosynthesis is to represent subpersonalities as imaginary figures (Assagioli, 1965; Ferrucci, 1982). It will be recalled that subpersonalities refer to components of a personality represented by figures with their own beliefs, feelings, and behavioral patterns. The aim of the use of subpersonalities in psychosynthesis is to elevate degraded forms of subpersonalities to adaptive counterparts by "taking them up the mountain." The ultimate purpose of the procedure is to integrate the dissident components of a personality into a single unified construction. Much of Alice's book describes her subpersonalities, their progress, and their final integration. It is beyond the scope of this chapter to review all eight of Alice's subpersonalities. For present purposes, it will suffice to describe some episodes that illustrate the transformation of Alice's main subpersonalities.

Alice created "Baby Alice" as her first subpersonality. Baby Alice was a fearful little girl who wears short dresses and lies about her age. Despite hating it, she consents to wearing the dresses and lying because her mother wants her to be judged younger than she is so she can win dancing contests. She does not dare to cross her mother because she believes her mother is always right, although not always honest. Alice pictures Baby Alice as sitting in a corner crying. Her greatest desire is to have a perfect mother.

Didi told Alice to be especially nice to Baby Alice and to promise her that she would always be there to take care of her. Throughout the course of psychotherapy, Baby Alice has a variety of adventures in which she confronts and defeats Alice's inner demons. She eventually becomes the leader and director of the group of the subpersonalities and demands of them that they learn to work harmoniously with each other instead of bickering and sabotaging each other's efforts. Of all the subpersonalities, Baby Alice advances to the highest level of development. By the end of therapy, she is a happy, competent, assertive child who is an excellent constructive thinker. And, as Baby Alice grows psychologically, so does the real Alice. Alice has brought herself up in fantasy in a far better way than her parents had in reality.

Caught up in the fun of creating subpersonalities, Alice, on her own initiative, quickly created a second subpersonality. It was one that represented her difficulty in managing hope. Hope had been problematic all her life because she had adopted a hopeless view about future events as a way of avoiding disappointment. Alice describes her construction of the subpersonality representing hopelessness:

> I sat quietly in my chair with my eyes closed and thought about the word *hope*. *No hope* and *hopelessness* came to mind in rapid succession. Suddenly I envisioned a crab running aimlessly about on a beach, holding its front legs up in the air in a helpless manner. It was the only one of my subpersonalities that was masculine, at least in its original form. His story was as sad as his appearance. He belonged to a little gray-haired lady who spoke sweetly to him and always called him "dear." His desire is to be free, but she tells him that this is impossible because she needs him to cut the woolen threads on a beautiful tapestry she is making. When he tells her of his dream to be free, she makes fun of him. When he asks what he can hope for, she laughs and tells him he can hope to be the flying horse in the tapestry. Every day he hopes to be the flying horse, but every evening he realizes that his hope is foolish and he runs around with his arms in the air bemoaning his fate and continuing to cut the threads for her.
>
> I was very moved emotionally by the creation of this subpersonality.... He was the first one that I took "up the mountain."...We began, as per instruction, in a neutral place, in a meadow; we paused there to get a feel for the place. I always had my subpersonalities engage in certain activities in the meadow so that I could get a good idea of how they might change during the experience of ascent. In my meadow there were lots of flowers. It was an open field with trees on the northern boundary. If I faced south I could see a small mountain. The sun was behind it, so its face was in the shade. The mountain was modest in size, like Barre Mountain, not far from my home. Up the shaded slope is a narrow and rocky trail that begins in easy steps but becomes very steep and difficult as it makes its way through the

rocky ledges. About three quarters of the way up, on the east side of the mountain, there is a ledge that opens out to a view of a river and its valley far below. The final ascent is very difficult and gives one the impression of scaling a cliff. But at the top of the mountain there is a small flat area where the sun is shining.

The crab had little trouble climbing up the mountain, scurrying up ahead of me in a rather frantic way. When I saw that he was going out on the ledge, I became very frightened for him, knowing his desperation and his deep desire to be free. And sure enough, before I could reach him he jumped off in a gleeful manner. When I reached the ledge I expected to see his mutilated body below. But instead I saw a Baltimore oriole flying about and singing beautifully. He never did realize his dream of becoming a flying horse, but as a bird he perched on my shoulder and sang so sweetly that I knew he was happy.

Oriole stayed with the other sub-personalities throughout our other journeys up the mountain and was with us when we all finally learned to fly. I don't recall any dramatic change accompanying this experience, but in retrospect I think I understand what was happening. Oriole, in his crab form, represented my relationship with my mother, who would never really let me fly and for whom I had a deep sense of responsibility. In other words, I knew that I played a very important part in supporting her own unrealistic fantasies. At the same time I knew that I could never satisfy her completely because I was not her little brother who had died at a young age. She often laughed at me, made fun of my maturing body, and teased and goaded me into action by calling me "Mousey." She would take me to school by car and wait with me until the last bell rang. As I walked away she would call after me, "Good-bye, Mousey." Even when I asked her not to do it she would laugh and call all the louder. Hence, my relationship with her was a true trap from which I could see no escape; hence the sense of hopelessness, which was carried over to all my relationships and to my way of being in the world.

Perhaps this exercise freed me in a way that I was not aware of. Perhaps, as well as giving up the goal of a perfect mother, I also gave up the foolish fantasy that things would be better with my mother if I were a boy. The transformation of the helpless crab to the little bird seems quite appropriate also if one recalls Emily Dickinson's description of hope just this way—of a little bird on one's shoulder. So this transformation represents a more mature attitude about hope: I changed it from a sad impossible dream to something within the realm of possibility.

What is it about this fantasy that is therapeutic? There is not a bit of information that is new to Alice. There is something about the information, however, that is new. What she had understood before only intellectually she now incorporated into her experiential system. Most importantly, she experienced emotional reinforcement in the form of positive feelings following the representation of herself as a free and happy female figure. This allowed her to anticipate in her experiential system the positive feelings that awaited her if she freed herself from the destructive relationship with her mother. More generally, she was learning that she did not have to sacrifice her freedom as a condition for acceptance. Thus, she had begun the process of replacing an automatic feeling of fear at the thought of separation with a positive feeling of being free, autonomous, and joyous. In summary, Alice experienced in her experiential system the satisfaction of fulfilling a deeply frustrated need, the need for freedom and autonomy and for being true to her nature rather than believing she had to be what her mother wanted.

There are three additional observations of interest. The first is that Alice replaced the imagery of a flying horse, a symbol for her of masculine freedom. She replaced it with a beautiful bird with a joyous song, a female symbol that also flies and does so with complete happiness for what it is and does.

The second observation is that the fantasy had a life of its own. It was a far cry from a consciously contrived scenario produced logically by the rational system. Rather, it was a spontaneous expression from the experiential system. Alice was not in control of the fantasy. She did not know what was going to happen. She was horrified when the crab jumped off the cliff. She was surprised when instead of the mutilated body she expected to find, the crab had turned into a beautiful Baltimore Oriole that, instead of complaining about its fate, sings a joyous song. The lesson, of course, is that the freedom to be who one is, threatening as it may be, is worth the risk.

The third observation is that the protagonist takes the form of a crab, the very symbol of cancer. When I asked Alice about it, she denied being aware that the crab is a symbol for cancer, and she was surprised and amused when I informed her about it. This is an interesting example of the experiential system being more knowledgeable in some ways than the rational system. Thus, the rational system can learn from the experiential system as well as train it.

Alice had three other main subpersonalities (the few minor ones will not be discussed). Amanda is a builder, strong, competent, practical, and able to cope with any situation. Alice would often repeat to herself, "I am Amanda. I am strong. Kill the cancer! Kill the cancer, kill the cancer! *I am Amanda. I am strong.*"

"Little One" represents Alice's suppressed hostility. Alice describes Little One as "nasty, aggressive, devious, and joyously happy about her evil thoughts and deeds. She throws back her head and laughs a lot. She pushes, kicks, stabs, claws, spits, bites, strangles, beats with a club, punches, etc., and then runs away. She never gets caught. She hates Baby Alice and thinks she is stupid and worthy only of contempt" (A. Epstein, 1989, p. 84). Alice says that despite Little One's contempt for Baby Alice, Alice liked Little One from the beginning. When Little One is taken up the mountain, she is transformed into her elevated form, a powerful, gentle tiger called Bagera. Bagera is very proud of her beautiful coat and, although possessing great power, she uses it only when justified. Bagera is friendly to Baby Alice and lets her ride on her back.

Mickey, is the personification of Alice's jealousy, envy, critical attitude toward others, and dissatisfaction with her own life. Mickey wants to be someone different from whom she is. Alice says Mickey represents her real self, a self that Alice tries very hard to keep hidden from people by presenting a false self while fearing all the time that her true self will be revealed.

Alice describes Mickey as follows:

> She is a jealous little girl with red curly hair who longs to be Shirley Temple. No one likes her because she is critical of what everyone else does. She wants to be admired and liked by her own playmates. But they do not like her because she wants their things and eventually gets them by tricking them. She wants attention from the boys but they do not like her either. When they mention other girls that they do like, she finds fault with them. The boys end up picking on her and throwing things at her. On the way up the mountain she says that the wild flowers are not as beautiful as the ones at home. She gets tired easily and cannot keep up with the others. When she finally reaches the place where Little One turned into a tiger, she turns into a chicken and, as in the children's story, she keeps telling everyone that the sky will fall. (p. 85)

When pondering the significance of this subpersonality, Alice concluded that Mickey was a frightened little girl who was concerned that her true self would be found out. As she thought about Mickey, Alice decided that Mickey was "the skeleton in my closet":

> She represented many secret fears. She reminded me of the fear that I would never amount to anything in the world, that although I always started out ahead of my competitors, in the long run I would always lose out. She was the part of me that feared she would never be satisfied, the part with the unattainable dream. She was the part of me who, before I became ill, feared that Sy could never really love me unless I played the role of the good and accommodating wife. Moreover, since she lived in fear of exposure, she avoided direct confrontation most of all and had to accomplish her goals in a sneaky way. (p. 87)

Alice thought it particularly important to understand this subpersonality better, so she took Mickey up the mountain again. This time, instead of turning into a pathetic creature that runs around hysterically saying the sky will fall, Mickey turns into a monstrous chicken that attacks Alice with the intension of killing her. Alice described the rest of the fantasy as follows:

> In my growing panic there was a terrible new insight: "This is the part of me that wants me dead! How will I stop her?" I somehow sensed that there was some word that she wanted to hear and the word was *forgive*. So I turned to her and screamed, "I forgive you!" To my horror, she did not stop, but turned into a huge vampire bat and came straight for me. I had no choice; I wrestled her down and stabbed her to death. I came out of the visualization shaken but satisfied.

When Alice told Didi about this visualization, Didi asked her to visualize Mickey as a young girl. Alice had an image of Mickey crying because the new baby's crib was going to be put into her room. To cover up her hostility to the new baby, she tries to be very nice to her. She tells everyone that she likes having her sister in her room, but she also jokes about the baby smelling bad and crying too much.

Alice describes Mickey's relationship with the other subpersonalities as hostile. She and Amanda, the builder, are antagonists, and she and Little One hate each other and actually fight. Alice saw little virtue in Mickey and hated her for bringing Alice to this point in her life. Didi urged Alice to try to understand that Mickey was an insecure, frightened child who needed her love. Alice replied that she was unable to do so: "How can I love someone who is trying to kill me?... I hate her!"

At this point, it was six weeks since Alice's cancer had spread to her lungs and five weeks since she had begun psychotherapy. She was not receiving any medical treatment, but she was about to begin an experimental interferon chemotherapy program at the Yale-New Haven clinic. The oncologist said that although the chemotherapy had drastic side effects, it was worth enrolling in the program because it might extend her life for a few months.

As part of the program, x-rays had to be taken immediately before and after treatment. Before administering the first interferon injection, the oncologist compared the new x-rays with the most recent previous x-rays. He could hardly believe what he saw. Instead of increasing in size and spreading, there was no longer any residual cancer in the primary area, and the tumors in the lungs had shrunk. He told us that with such positive results Alice would be an excellent candidate for the experimental program. He then asked if he should give her the first injection. She said that she would like to postpone the decision for a month to see if there would be further progress without any medical treatment. He informed us that he could not do this because it would mean denying other eligible patients the treatment. Besides, he said, he was confident that psychotherapy could not produce such results. He said he would hold a space open for Alice for two weeks, which, although too short a period for any change to occur, would at least give her time to come to her senses and accept the experimental treatment. We thanked him and said we would be back in two weeks, at which time we would make our decision. We hoped beyond reason that there would at least be the slightest indication of improvement, in which case Alice would forego the experimental treatment.

Shortly after our visit to the Yale-New Haven clinic, Alice awakened from a nightmare in which someone was trying to kill her. All during the remainder of the night, she dreamt about being blocked in whatever she tried to do. When she awakened in the morning, she sensed that the dreams had something to do with Mickey and decided that Mickey had to be gotten rid of as there was no sense in retaining a part of herself that wanted her dead. Alice describes what happened when she conjured up an image of Mickey being sent away:

> I saw her standing in a train station, carrying a little suitcase. She was all alone and I was walking away from her, telling her that she couldn't come with me. She sobbed and sobbed, begging to be taken along. I kept walking, but when I turned to look back, the sight of her all alone was more than I could bear. Suddenly I realized that it was she who was in fear of her life and was calling out in pain. As I now was overwhelmed with emotion, I knew that I could not leave her behind because it was she who contained all my emotions. To live without emotions, even the bad ones, was impossible—I might as well be dead. I turned to her and told her to come, that I was going to take her up the mountain once more. . . .
>
> I held Baby Alice in my arms and I had Little One and Mickey by the hand. Amanda walked with us; Oriole was on my shoulder. When we got to the ledge where so many important changes had taken place on other trips, I believed that we should all think about letting go and just float off the cliff. But it didn't happen that way. Instead, Amanda, the builder, changed into a flying horse and we all took off with her. It was wonderful to feel the power of her wings as they slowly beat up and down. Then all at once I realized that we could not only fly, but if we caught the circular currents, we could soar like a hawk. We caught the air current and the warm wind wafted us up higher and higher. It was an incredible experience.
>
> As I came out of the visualization I understood why I could not leave Mickey behind: I desperately needed her energy, her intense motivation, and her emotions. Didi told me that Mickey must change. Now, I, too understood and was ready for her to change. At last I really loved her.

The two weeks were now up, and it was time to return to the Yale-New Haven clinic. Alice was extremely nervous because so much depended on the next set of x-rays. When the physician looked at them, he was even more shocked than he was the first time. The impossible had occurred: the tumors had continued to shrink! The physician again suggested that Alice would be an excellent participant in his study, and he asked if he should now give her the interferon injection. She told him she did not want to do anything that might interfere with the progress that was spontaneously occurring and that she wanted to rely exclusively on psychotherapy so long as she kept on improving with it. He again voiced his skepticism about psychotherapy having anything to do with her improvement and added that every once in a while a spontaneous improvement occurs that no one understands. He then requested permission to keep a duplicate of Alice's x-ray to show to his classes as an example of such a case. We granted him permission. He wished us luck, and we said goodbye.

Although the cancer had shrunk considerably, there was still much work to be done. Alice had by now constructed all her major subpersonalities, she had new insights about her experiential system and, of particular importance, about the part of herself that she believed wanted her dead. Although she had accomplished some degree of integration, as manifested by her subpersonalities acting in a cooperative, cohesive manner when they soared on the wings of Amanda as a flying horse, this was but a single incident, and the subpersonalities soon returned to their bickering. Alice had yet to examine them in greater depth, and Baby Alice had to rework her traumatic experience when her dying grandmother moved into the household and a new baby appeared out of nowhere. Baby Alice also had yet to grow into the competent and confident figure she would eventually become, one who supervised elevating the other subpersonalities to a higher level, taught them to respect each other and function as a cohesive team, and help Baby Alice fulfill her potential.

To tell the rest of the story would take us beyond the scope of this chapter. The interested reader is directed to read Alice's book, in which she describes her psychotherapy from beginning to end (A. Epstein, 1989).

In summary, the rate of Alice's progress was remarkable. In two months of psychotherapy, she had considerably transformed her outlook on life. From a situation of near hopelessness and a chronic feeling of despair, she was enthusiastically engaged in a process that was defeating the cancer. The chronic feeling of despair that she had successfully hidden all her life was no longer present. She felt and looked good. People who did not know about her cancer or psychotherapy spontaneously commented that she looked like a different person, projecting a feeling of calmness and serenity.

It took Alice a little over another year to complete psychotherapy. At that point, she received a diagnosis of "no detectable signs of cancer." She remains free of cancer to the present day, more than 20 years later. The chronic feeling of despair has never returned, and Alice can hardly reconstruct how she thought and felt then because it is so alien to how she thinks and feels now.

A caveat is in order about overgeneralizing from a single case. The case certainly does not suggest that psychological factors are importantly involved in all cases of cancer. It does suggest that there may be something like a "cancer-prone personality" that, if reduced or eliminated, can have an ameliorative effect on the course of cancer. This hypothesis was supported in a study by Lori Katz, who was inspired by Alice's book to conduct a study with me on exceptional recoveries from late-stage cancer in people with cancer-prone personalities (Katz & Epstein, 2005). The hypothesis was supported by finding that the mitigation of a cancer-prone personality was associated with very unusual recoveries from cancer, as indicated by the exceptional cancer-recovered group reporting a greater degree of a cancer-prone personality before their cancer diagnosis and a greater decrease in it after their recovery in comparison to a group with nonremarkable recoveries from cancer, so that the groups no longer differed in their cancer-prone personalities. Similar results were obtained when the exceptional cancer-recovered group was compared to a second control group consisting of unexceptional recoveries from heart disease. A similar hypothesis was supported in a study by Cunningham and Watson (2004).

REFERENCES

Assagioli, R. (1965). *Psychosynthesis: A manual of principles and techniques.* New York: Hobbs, Doorman, and Co.

Crisp, R. J., & Turner, R. N. (2009). Can imagined interactions produce positive perceptions? *American Psychologist, 64,* 231–240.

Cunningham, A. J., & Watson, K. (2004). How psychological therapy may prolong survival in cancer patients: New evidence and a simple theory. *Integrative Cancer Therapies, 3,* 214–229.

Dadds, M. R., Bovbjerg, D. H., Redd, W. H., & Cutmore, T. R. (1997). Imagery in human classical conditioning. *Psychological Bulletin, 122,* 89–103.

DeVita, V. T, Jr., Hellman, S. A., & Rosenberg, S. A. (1985). *Cancer: Principles and practice of oncology.* Philadelphia: J. B. Lippincott.

Epstein, A. H. (1989). *Mind, fantasy, and healing.* New York: Delacorte Press. (Out of print, but available through Alice Epstein, 37 Bay Road, Amherst, MA 01002 for $15.00, which includes postage.)

Epstein, S., & Pacini, R. (2001). The influence of visualization on intuitive and analytical information processing. *Imagination, Cognition, and Personality, 20,* 195–217.

Ferrucci, P. (1982). *What we may be.* New York: Tarcher/Putnam.

Katz, L. (2001). Holographic reprocessing: A cognitive experiential psychotherapy. *Psychotherapy, 38,* 186–197.

Katz, L. S. (2005). *Holographic reprocessing: A cognitive-experiential psychotherapy for the treatment of trauma.* New York: Routledge.

Katz, L. S., & Epstein, S. (2005). The relation of cancer-prone personality to exceptional recovery from cancer: A preliminary study. *Advances, 21,* 1–15.

Kosslyn, S. M., Ganis, G., & Thompson, W. L. (2001). Neural foundations of imagery. *Nature Reviews Neuroscience,* 2, 635–642.

Simonton, O. C., Mathews-Simonton, S., & Creighton, J. L. (1978). *Getting well again.* New York: Bantam Books.

Taylor, S. E., Pham, L. B., Rivkin, I. D., & Amor, D. A. (1998). Harnessing the imagination: Mental simulation, self-regulation, and coping. *American Psychologists, 53,* 429–439.

PART FOUR
Broader Implications

CHAPTER 14
Implications

In this final chapter, I first consider what cognitive-experiential theory (CET) can contribute to theories of personality. I next discuss how CET can resolve four important issues that have been intransigent from other perspectives: (1) why the human species, despite its remarkable intelligence, often thinks unintelligently and behaves destructively, often to its own detriment; (2) intuition, what it is, what it does, and how it does it; (3) religion and, more specifically, why many people believe and accept as literally true clearly unrealistic beliefs; and (4) the continued existence of the human species.

IMPLICATIONS OF COGNITIVE-EXPERIENTIAL THEORY FOR THEORIES OF PERSONALITY

Cognitive-experiential theory is a highly integrative theory of personality that achieves its integration not through a tour de force in which the best elements of each of the grand theories of personality is selected and combined. To do so with theories that are so different would have been impossible. Instead, CET achieves its integration through the expansion of a few fundamental assumptions, such as that everyone automatically constructs an implicit theory of reality by the automatic operation of an associative learning system, referred to as the experiential system.

The implications of CET for theories of personality are that it opens up a new understanding of human behavior via the experiential system, and it allows all psychologists to use the same framework for understanding and discussing human behavior.

The assumption of an experiential system is based on the consideration that humans, like all other higher order animals, adapt to their environments by automatically learning from experience. When *Homo sapiens* began to develop speech, it is inconceivable that the species abandoned an earlier adaptive system that had served it and all other higher order animals extremely well. More reasonably, a conscious, verbal, reasoning system, referred to in CET as a rational system, was added to an already existing automatic, experiential learning system.

The importance of an experiential system cannot be overstated because it is much more than a quick and approximate system for solving everyday problems, as researchers on heuristics have considered it to be. Rather, it is the default system for directing everyday human behavior and, in this way, is superior to the deliberative reasoning of the rational system. Moreover, the experiential system is not even otherwise generally inferior to the rational system. The two systems are simply different adaptive ways of processing information, with the experiential system solving problems by empirically learning from experience and the rational system doing so by reasoning. The systems differ not only in how they process information but in their content. Thus, research has found that the experiential system is more strongly directly related than the rational system to creativity, empathy, intuition, esthetic appreciation, sense of humor, and personal and interpersonal issues, and the rational system is more strongly directly related to solving intellectual problems, adjustment, and impersonal issues.

Since each system operates by different rules and has different attributes, if one wishes to understand human behavior, it is necessary to understand the operation of both systems and how they interact with each other. Cognitive-experiential theory has nothing new to contribute about the operation of the rational system, other than to note its susceptibility to influence by the experiential system. Cognitive-experiential theory has much to say, however, regarding the operation of the experiential system.

It is interesting to consider the role of the experiential system in establishing "truth," in the sense of constructing a sufficiently accurate working model of the world that makes adaptation possible. By doing what feels good and avoiding doing what feels bad, all higher order organisms develop a working model of reality. This is most interesting because feelings are often regarded as leading people astray and are therefore considered an enemy of truth. How can these opposite views of the relation of feelings and truth be reconciled? The answer, according to CET, is by recognizing, that in all higher order animals other than humans, truth is effectively established by feelings because they do not have a rational system that an experiential system can bias. The result is, that despite their brilliance in solving impersonal problems, which fall predominantly in the realm of the rational system, humans often think irrationally when attempting to solve problems regarding personal issues and relationships among individuals and social institutions (including nations) because such problems fall mainly in the domain of the experiential system. Thus, a particularly important implication of the experiential system is that it provides an explanation of why humans, despite their unique capacity for thinking rationally, often think irrationally, a topic discussed in greater detail next.

In conclusion, the experiential system of CET has important implications for understanding human behavior and therefore for theories of personality.

WHY DO HUMANS, DESPITE THEIR REMARKABLE INTELLIGENCE, OFTEN THINK AND BEHAVE UNINTELLIGENTLY?

A particularly important question is why the human species, despite its remarkable intelligence, often behaves unintelligently. Why should a creature that is capable of solving the most difficult problems in science, mathematics, medicine, and technology be unable to solve the conceptually much simpler problem of living with others harmoniously? The human species can fly to the moon, observe the most minute brain processes by way of functional magnetic resonance imaging (fMRI), view objects millions of miles away with telescopes, observe otherwise invisible organisms with microscopes, communicate over great distances on earth and in space, and invent computers. And yet, this same species is unable to solve conceptually much simpler problems that are more important for its happiness and even its survival. In problems concerning individuals, why is divorce so prevalent, why do parents and their children often have antagonistic relationships, and why is dysfunctional parenting so common? In relationships among societies, why have different nations often resorted to warfare to resolve problems? The only way people have changed in this regard is in the improvement of their weapons. Sticks and stones changed to spears, spears to arrows and catapults, then to guns and ordinary bombs, followed by atomic and hydrogen bombs. Presently, only a few nations have these bombs; it is likely that soon there will be more. Where will it end? Given the history of warfare, there is every reason to believe that unless people's thinking and behavior change, it will likely end in atomic and hydrogen warfare and possibly in the end of the human species. So the important question remains: why has a species with as remarkable intelligence as humans, one that has been able to solve the most difficult impersonal problems, been unable to solve its problems regarding harmoniously living with each other?

THE ANSWER TO THE QUESTION OF WHY HUMANS THINK AND BEHAVE IRRATIONALLY

The answer to the question of why humans often think and behave irrationally despite their outstanding intelligence is, according to CET, because of the influence of the experiential system on the rational system. Interestingly, the problem exists mainly with regard to personal issues and interpersonal relationships.

There are several sources for the negative influence of the experiential on the rational system. One concerns the limited cognitive ability of the experiential system, including its inability to think at high levels of abstraction. A second concerns its more rapid operation. A third includes its normal operation outside of awareness. A fourth concerns individual differences in constructive thinking, and a fifth concerns the ability of the experiential system to co-opt the rational system into viewing its experientially induced thinking as rational. Of course, to the extent that people have an intelligent, prosocially operating experiential system, there is less need to control it. Nevertheless, even those with a high level of constructive thinking would benefit from an increased ability to identify and control the influence of their experiential on their rational system. Moreover, it is advantageous for people to be in touch with their experiential system because it is sometimes wiser than their rational system. By being aware of the operation of both systems, it should be possible for people to choose which offers the better solution for a particular problem.

The Importance of Providing Formal Education in Constructive Thinking

Formal education of the rational system is provided to students in the United States for a minimum of 12 years and of their experiential system not at all. Yet the experiential system is more important than the rational system for performance in most jobs, social facility, creativity, and empathy (Epstein, 2001). Thus, even if one were interested only in intellectual performance, it would be important to educate the experiential system because of its influence on the reasoning of the rational system.

It has been found with respect to prosocial behavior that people with higher experiential intelligence, as measured by the Constructive Thinking Inventory (CTI), have more favorable and less prejudicial attitudes toward others than do those with lower experiential intelligence (Epstein, 2001). Accordingly, they are less likely to use their intellectual knowledge destructively. Germany, the most educated and cultured country in the world before the Nazi era, used its advanced technology and training in science nearly to destroy the world. Thus, educating and training the rational system while ignoring the experiential system can have disastrous consequences. In sum, learning to become a better constructive thinker is of great importance because it contributes to the quality of people's lives, including their interpersonal relationships, their reasoning ability, their prosocial attitudes, and their physical and mental well-being.

A procedure for improving constructive thinking has been demonstrated to be effective for college students (Epstein, 1998). Similar procedures could be used to teach constructive thinking at all grade levels, in a manner that effectively addressed the experiential system, perhaps under the title *Science of Mental Behavior*. Such courses could not reasonably be dismissed as mere "frills" with respect to intellectual performance because one of their aims would be to increase the ability to reason logically, objectively, and wisely by favorably influencing the effect of experiential on rational processing. After all, what can be more important in education than learning to reason well in an unbiased manner? An attempt is often made to increase such ability by special courses in which students are taught about the principles of logical reasoning. According to CET, such courses are of limited value because they are directed at educating the rational system, and they fail to consider the influence of experiential on rational processing.

An Example of a Course in Constructive Thinking

A course I taught to college students provides an example of such a course on constructive thinking. There were two components to the course, one directed at the rational system and the other at the experiential system. The one directed at the rational system consisted of lectures and reading assignments in which students learned about CET. Students learned that the implicit beliefs in their experiential systems are automatically acquired from emotionally significant experiences and are triggered in everyday life, usually outside of their awareness, by relevant events. They further learned that by attending to their automatic thoughts and interpretations of events they could identify the experientially derived beliefs that determined how they felt and behaved. They were told that when a distressing thought repeatedly comes to mind, they can cope with it by asking themselves, "What would happen if I did not think that way? How would it affect my feelings and behavior?" When these questions are asked, the usual responses are, "nothing would happen except I would feel better." The students were instructed that it is important to maintain a gentle, tolerant attitude when correcting their thoughts and interpretations and that the corrections do not usually work immediately but improve with practice. With sufficient practice, the corrected responses become habitual. They were told that training their experiential mind should be regarded as a lifetime endeavor in becoming the kind of person they would like to be. In this respect, working on becoming a better constructive thinker can be compared to developing one's body through exercise, but it is even more important as a way of achieving happiness. The students were told that by identifying, controlling, and learning from the influence of their experiential on their rational processing, they could improve their ability to reason logically, objectively, and wisely.

In the second, more important component of the course, students learned about the operation of their experiential systems through self-observation and by responding to specially devised exercises. More specifically, they learned to attend to the automatic thoughts and interpretations that preceded their emotions in everyday life and to substitute more desirable for less desirable responses. Another exercise consisted of responding to prepared scenarios that described evocative events by indicating how, in real life, they would probably behave in such situations based on how they reacted to similar situations in the past. They also inferred the kinds of thoughts and interpretations that could account for their responses. They then substituted for any unsatisfactory reactions more desirable ones.

The most helpful exercise was one in which students reported to the class their most distressing emotion of the week. They described the thought or interpretation that preceded the emotion and how they behaviorally responded. The other members of the class then indicated how they would have reacted in the same situation. The students were often surprised to hear of the variety of responses reported. It became apparent that the responses were highly personally revealing and that some were much more desirable than others. For example, a student who seemed to be depressed much of the time characteristically reported that she would be sad because she would believe it was her fault that an outcome had turned out badly. Most students reported that they would be angry in the same situations because they believed they were treated badly. Among the variety of responses, one student reported she would feel sympathy and try to put the offending person at ease because she believed that someone would have to be very insecure and socially inept to behave so aggressively. It was through experiences like these that students learned in a highly compelling way that interpretations and thoughts matter and that by changing them they could change their feelings and behavior so that they would become more like the person they would ideally like to be.

The course was taught with the aim of improving people's constructive thinking and, accordingly, contribute to their ability to cope with stress; improve their overall well-being; improve their ability to reason logically, objectively, and wisely; and increase their prosocial thinking and behavior.

So far, I have described one approach to improving people's constructive thinking. This is merely a first attempt, and modifications and other procedures should be tried. It should be determined, for example, in what ways procedures can be developed that are most effective with children of different ages.

Why Constructive Thinking Is Associated with Thinking Logically, Objectively, Prosocially, and Wisely

There are several reasons for a positive relation between constructive thinking and thinking logically, objectively, prosocially, and wisely. One is that such thinking is an intrinsic aspect of good constructive thinking, as indicated by the scales of the CTI (Epstein, 2001; Epstein & Meier, 1989). Thus, the CTI includes scales of absence of negative overgeneralization, of positive thinking, of absence of polarized thinking, of absence of distrust, and of absence of intolerance. Second, as good constructive thinkers are better adjusted than others, they are able to reason in a calmer manner uninfluenced by distracting concerns from their experiential systems. Third, good constructive thinkers are more likely than others to be aware of the operation of their experiential systems because its operation is more acceptable to begin with and is therefore more likely to be identified and compensated for when a negative biasing influence occurs. Moreover, as previously noted, because the experiential system is sometimes wiser than the rational system, it is advantageous to be in a position to consider whether to heed or dismiss its promptings. For all these reasons, good constructive thinkers think in a manner that is more logical, objective, prosocial, and wise than do poor constructive thinkers. This conclusion is supported by research in which constructive thinking was related to a wide variety of positive outcomes (Epstein, 2001; Epstein & Meier, 1989).

IMPLICATIONS OF COGNITIVE-EXPERIENTIAL THEORY FOR UNDERSTANDING INTUITION

Although intuition has been of interest since ancient times, there is currently little agreement on what it is, what it does, and how it does it. From the perspective of CET, the answers to these questions are simple and straightforward (Epstein, 2010).

A wide variety of attempts have been made to define intuition, but there is little agreement among them. Many of the definitions are expressed more in terms of what intuition is not rather than in terms of what it is (Abernathy & Hamm, 1995). Thus, intuition is said to be arriving at conclusions in the absence of logical reasoning. The problem is that intuition is a fuzzy construct that cannot be meaningfully identified without indicating how it operates and by identifying its boundary conditions. This problem is dealt with in CET by regarding intuition as a subset of experiential processing. Thus, intuition is considered to operate by exactly the same principles and attributes as the experiential system. The only reason that intuition is not identical with the experiential system is that it has narrower boundary conditions; intuition does not include everything in the realm of experiential processing. For example, intuition does not include irrational fears, religious beliefs, superstitions, and psychomotor coordination (such as catching a ball), although all of these involve operations of the experiential system.

By regarding intuition as a subset of experiential processing, it is possible to answer the questions of what intuition is, what it does, and how it does it (Epstein, 2010). Namely, it is a subset of experiential processing that has more limited boundary conditions. In answer to the question of what it does, it provides information rapidly, automatically, effortlessly, and holistically, often operating outside of awareness. In answer to the question of how it does it, it does so by applying the principles and attributes of experiential processing to solving problems, which allows it empirically to learn from experience, as well as to use the same principles and attributes to respond to completely new situations. Accordingly, people can be intuitively very knowledgeable without knowing why. But intuition can also be wrong. It is only likely to be right to the extent that past associative learning is appropriate for current situations. If there is a poor match between past and present situations, people's intuitive beliefs are likely to be wrong.

In research comparing an intuitive thinking style with a rational thinking style (Norris & Epstein, 2011), neither style was found to be generally superior to the other because each had unique strengths and limitations. A rational thinking style was more strongly associated than an experiential thinking style with academic performance and adjustment, including self-esteem and an absence of depression and anxiety, whereas an experiential thinking style was more strongly associated than a rational thinking style with empathy, creativity, establishing favorable relationships, a good sense of humor, and aesthetic appreciation.

IMPLICATIONS OF COGNITIVE-EXPERIENTIAL THEORY FOR UNDERSTANDING RELIGION

As noted in Chapter 3, the strongest evidence for an experiential system is the universal appeal of religion in all societies and at all periods. Why is it so important and so natural for people to believe in gods and other religious phenomena, including devils, angels, heaven, hell, and miracles that are beyond natural explanation, when such beliefs are highly unrealistic? In the discussion that follows, I emphasize Judea-Christian religious beliefs, but my arguments hold up as well for most other religions.

The Irrationality of Many Religious Beliefs

There is no more fundamental belief in Christianity than Jesus willingly going to his crucifixion to take upon himself the sins of others. The idea of Jesus suffering on the cross is particularly appealing because it inverts the usual process of people giving sacrifices to God and instead becomes God sacrificing for them. Yet, according to secular, judicial law, no one can suffer in place of others to have them absolved of the crimes they have committed.

Many fundamentalists believe that Noah actually saved two animals of each kind on a boat. They do not question how he was able to journey across the world in a very limited amount of time with very limited resources to get polar bears from the North Pole, many varieties of penguins from the South Pole, scorpions from the desert, crocodiles from the Nile, a great many varieties of monkeys from South America, Africa, and India, and millions of varieties of insects from all over the world. Moreover, he would need to transport them back to his boat, to maintain and feed them throughout a great flood, and then to return them to their places of origin.

How can fundamentalist Christians, who may be perfectly intelligent in other respects, believe that the New Testament is the direct word of God when it was verbally passed down over generations and undoubtedly modified in the retelling? Moreover, the Bible that people read is a selection from a larger number of books, many of which were discarded because their content was judged as unacceptable by a human committee convened many years after the books were written. No such evidence that is accepted as the word of God would be accepted in a modern court of law, so why is it accepted by many as such absolute truth that they are willing to live their lives by it and sometimes die for it?

People's religious beliefs are determined mainly by where they were born and into which family. What kind of a God is it who punishes some people and rewards others because of the circumstances of their birth, which they played no role in determining? Certainly, this is neither a rational nor a moral God. There is no need to cite additional examples of the irrationality of many religious beliefs. Clearly, such beliefs are often irrational and are more reasonably regarded as myths than as realistic. Although religious beliefs often make no sense from a rational perspective, many people apparently have no difficulty in believing in them. However, it should also be recognized that people of many faiths recognize religious beliefs as meaningful without taking them as literally true.

Given the Irrationality of Many Religious Beliefs, Why Do Many People Believe Them as Literally True?

Many people's reasoning about religion is so obviously irrational as to make it evident that they must think in some nonrational way that they find more compelling than their logical reasoning. According to CET, this other way is thinking in the manner of the experiential mode, which, as research has shown, can be more compelling than logical reasoning.

Let us consider how the principles and attributes of experiential processing can account for unrealistic religious beliefs. It will be recalled that a major motive of the experiential system is the superordinate hedonic principle, according to which people tend think and behave in ways that make them feel good and tend to avoid thinking and behaving in ways that make them feel bad. Recall that this principle encompasses the feelings generated by all the subordinate basic needs. The hedonic principle can readily explain why many religions propose a wonderful place that good people go to after their death. It can explain why Christians believe that Jesus suffered to relieve people of their sins. It can explain how Noah was able to accomplish his remarkable feats. It can explain why Joshua made the walls of Jericho come tumbling down by the sound of horns and why the Red Sea parted to allow the Israelites but not their Egyptian pursuers safely to pass through an opening in the water. Because the hedonic principle includes the motive to avoid having bad feelings, or at least to have the least bad feelings that circumstances allow, it can also explain why some people believe in a punitive God and being tormented in hell if they behave or believe improperly. Such dire consequences of bad behavior are, in a way, pleasing to people because they support the motivation to believe and behave properly. It also corresponds to their experience: bad things happen in the world, and the belief therefore fulfills the basic subordinate need to maintain a stable and coherent conceptual system that makes sense of the world.

The following attributes of experiential processing can also help to explain why people maintain irrational religious beliefs. The associative principle of the experiential system can explain guilt by association, such as that modern people are guilty for sins carried out by the first human beings and that modern Jews are responsible for some of their forebears having played a role in Jesus's death. Concrete thinking is indicated by the prevalence in various religions of worshiping statues and by using icons as religious symbols. Categorical thinking is indicated by the classification of gods and imaginary figures as either all good or all bad, as in the contrasts between God and the devil and between heaven and hell. The importance of emotions is indicated not only by the emotional states experienced in many religious practices but also by the infusion of feelings into religious practices such as chanting, playing and listening to music, singing, and dancing. The importance of narrative processing is indicated by the stories and myths of religions. The Bible is engaging and experientially compelling because it relates events in terms of parables and stories rather than in the form of abstract lectures. The importance of imagination is indicated by the imaginary figures that play critical roles in most religions, including the existence of gods, angels, devils, and good and bad places, such as heaven and hell. It is also indicated by the popularity of paintings of religious figures and scenes.

According to CET, the relation of imagination to the pursuit of truth is particularly important in understanding why humans regard unrealistic religious figures and events as true. It will be recalled that the experiential system reacts to imaginary figures and events in the same way that it reacts to real experience. Accordingly, people in their experiential systems react to imaginary religious figures and events as if they are real. This helps to explain why the route to truth via the experiential system, which has been highly effective in establishing a working model of the world in nonhuman animals, has often been a source of illusion in humans when applied to imaginary figures and events.

The belief in an imaginary God who lives in the sky and provides unconditional love, protects people from harm, answers their prayers, solves their deepest problems, and provides wise counsel is extremely attractive. Such beliefs can increase a person's feelings of security, self-esteem, confidence, and overall mental and physical well-being (McCullough & Willoughby, 2009). They can also contribute to a person's positive regard for and prosocial behavior toward others.

In other words, there is a fundamental tendency in humans to regard as true those beliefs that make them feel good and that avoid making them feel bad. This is well illustrated in the search for truth by St. Augustine (397/1961), who recounted his search for truth and happiness. He reported that he tried various ways of adjusting to life, including seeking the pleasures of the senses and pursuing various sources of knowledge, including the study of science, mathematics, and astronomy. Only when he turned to God did he find the truth and tranquility he sought. He therefore decided that a satisfactory life can be obtained only through faith. He stated his belief in the superiority of faith over knowledge as a guide to leading one's life as follows: "so a believer . . . who having nothing, yet possesses all things by cleaving unto Thee, whom all things serve, though he know not even the circles of the Great Bear, yet it is folly to doubt but that he is in a better state than one who can measure the heavens, and the number of stars, and poise the elements, yet neglecteth Thee who has made all things in number, weight, and measure" (p. 67).

William James (1902/1961) reported the views of people who had remarkable conversion experiences. They said their religious beliefs and experiences since their conversion had become far more real to them than everyday events. It is interesting that, like Saint Augustine, they reported not only achieving greater tranquility following their conversion, but also discovering a far greater truth than any they had known from a secular perspective. James's interpretation of this relation between happiness and truth is that the most fundamental motive in human behavior is the striving for happiness and that whatever people find works for them to produce happiness they assume is true. Of course, it is true only in the sense that it produces happiness, which is not the truth of science or philosophy. However, as James indicates, most people could not care less about these other truths, which have little bearing on their personal lives.

Of course, not all religions believe in a loving God. How can the belief in a tyrannical God, such as the Incas' belief that they had to present a beating heart to their deity to maintain the stability of their world, be explained by

CET? It can be explained by the influence of the superordinate hedonic principle because of the avoidance of the terrible feelings that would occur if steps to avoid a disaster were not undertaken.

In sum, the reasons that people often regard unrealistic religious beliefs as true are based on the principles and attributes of experiential processing. These principles and attributes include a tendency to regard beliefs that produce good feelings or avoid bad feelings as true, the biasing influence of experiential on rational processing, and the tendency to experience imaginary figures and events as real.

Is Religion Good or Bad?

According to people who are pure rationalists, religious beliefs are bad because it is irrational to believe in imaginary beings and events. To such rationalists, I pose the question of whether they consider the belief in Santa Claus by children bad because it is unrealistic. Many, no doubt, will reasonably answer that belief in Santa Claus is acceptable in children because they will outgrow it. True enough, but it at least establishes the point that, under certain circumstances, unrealistic beliefs can have a positive influence and do no harm. The same point can be made with regard to the use of fantasy in psychotherapy. Imaginary exposure therapy is an effective psychotherapeutic procedure. No doubt, pure rationalists will agree that the use of such fantasy is rational so long as people do not mistake the fantasy for reality. Again, this makes an interesting point; namely, that under certain circumstances it is useful to use fantasy for constructive ends. This raises the question of whether religious myths and other religious beliefs can be beneficial if they are accepted as useful fantasies, as demonstrated by Max Lerner (1990).

That religious beliefs are not rational does not necessarily mean they are bad, as assumed in a number of recent books that have evaluated religion from a rational perspective (e.g., Dawkins, 2008; Harris, 2005; Hitchins, 2007). According to CET, there are valid experiential ways of thinking that operate differently from deliberative, logical reasoning. As noted previously, the experiential system arrives at truth through a combination of empiricism and feelings. However, when applied to fantasy, it arrives at only an illusion of truth. Thus, the problem with religious beliefs as a route to truth is not that they involve a nonrational procedure but that it is applied to imaginary figures and events that are then treated as real.

A further consideration is that deliberative, rational reasoning is often less effective than is generally recognized because it not only may fail in its attempt to be logical, but it is also routinely biased by experiential processing. This is particularly likely to occur when personal concerns or human relationships are involved, which most certainly are involved in religion. Thus, an attempt to replace religious beliefs and practices with a completely scientific, rational approach may not only be extremely difficult to accomplish but may be less compelling for many people than their experiential processing.

Let us next consider what religion has to offer for better and for worse in the contemporary scene as well as in past history.

What in Religion Is Good

The hold of religion on people throughout history has been most impressive. In societies where it has been forcefully suppressed, as in the Soviet Union, it exhibited a remarkable ability to be maintained surreptitiously and to rebound when the restraining forces were removed. Why is religion so important to people? What does it accomplish for them? For many, it is the most important source of their identity, and it provides them with a sense of well-being and an ability to understand and cope with the stresses and vicissitudes of everyday life. Let us take as an example someone who is under great stress, such as a soldier in combat. There is no one to turn to for support other than one's God, who can be depended on if one is a true believer to save one's life and to provide one with the courage to face an ordeal. In fact, if one believes in some form of heaven where an appreciative God will reward valor, this can provide a powerful incentive to fight against all odds in defense of one's homeland or beliefs. Next, let us consider the reaction of a woman to a great personal loss. Someone whom I know well lost her son to a heart attack when he was 18 years old. Unexpected losses that occur before their time are particularly difficult for people to cope with. In this case, the woman's loss seemed beyond anything she could bear. She converted to Catholicism, became very devout, and derived great support from the rituals she engaged in and the signs she believed she received from the spirit of her son, who assured her he was very happy in the afterlife. Such beliefs and experiences brought her great relief and allowed her to regain her equanimity and happiness.

For many people, religious devotion provides a way of being in the world that contributes in important ways to their sense of purpose and to their harmony and peace of mind. People have reported that their lives were transformed for the better by religion from a life of desperation, failure, mental imbalance, or physical illness to a life of happiness, purposefulness, success, and mental and physical well-being (e.g., James, 1902/1961). They noted that they were lost before they turned to God but were saved when they found God.

Religious beliefs are not only extremely helpful for many people; they have often had very positive consequences for society. Several religions advocate helpful behavior and kindness to others, including making donations to the poor. Christianity preaches loving one's neighbors and forgiving and even loving one's enemies. Great works of art, music, sculpture, literature, and architecture have been inspired by religious devotion. Thus, whether considering its contribution to individuals or to society, it must be concluded that religion has been a powerful source of a variety of desirable outcomes.

What in Religion Is Bad

Although there can be no doubt that religion has been the source of great contributions, it has also been the source of extremely destructive behavior. At the individual level, religious beliefs that propose a devil and a hell or its equivalent or a vengeful and punitive God have been a source of dread and anxiety. Such effects are apt to be particularly devastating for impressionable children who may feel continuously threatened by the punishment they anticipate for their minor transgressions or even their aggressive thoughts, particularly if they happen to materialize, as in the death of a sibling. Certain religious beliefs make some people so threatened by evil that they see the work of the devil everywhere, which promotes not only anxiety but also distrust of and aggression toward anyone suspected of being in league with the devil. In their concern about avoiding evil, Puritans reduced their capacity for joy, declaring that some joyous activities, such as dancing, were a path to damnation.

People with certain religious beliefs may be intolerant of others with different religious beliefs, considering them a threat and deserving of punishment, including an inability to enter heaven. This may lead to treating people with other beliefs as infidels who should either be converted or, if necessary, killed. Thus, at the individual level, religious beliefs may be a source of anxiety, distrust, anger, and aggression.

At the societal level, religion throughout history has been a source of violence, exploitation, and mistreatment of others. Religions such as Christianity, despite emphasizing the importance of love and compassion, have not been an exception in this regard. Calling people pagans or savages has been a license to enslave them, usurp their wealth, torture them, and even kill them, and this has been true of other religions as well, including the religion of the early Romans, with their many gods; the religion of the early Jews, who were ordered by their God to kill every living thing in some of the cities they conquered; and the religion of the Spanish Conquistadors, the Crusaders, and the Inquisitors. Even groups that believe in the same God have been violent toward each other because of relatively minor differences, such as a belief in the trinity and whether the messiah has already come or is expected in the future. Christians have persecuted Jews through the ages, holding all of them responsible for the role of a few Jews in the crucifixion of Jesus at a much earlier period.

Antagonism to people of other faiths has been prevalent throughout history. Hindus and Muslims attacked each other when they passed on their way to their new homelands. Violence has also occurred between Christians and Muslims, between American Indian tribes, and between the Incas and their neighbors.

Nor are such horrors that were sanctioned and often instigated by religious authorities a thing of the past. Suicide bombers today kill others with the belief that their God will reward them with numerous virgins in the afterlife. Women are relegated to an inferior status in some religions because it is presumably God's will. By using God as a mediating influence, people subjugate others with a clear conscience because they can say and believe they are simply doing the work of God. Moreover, the disadvantaged not infrequently willingly accept their inferior position because they too have learned to accept it as the will of God.

Religious beliefs sometime represent an inappropriate intrusion into the realm of science. There is an inherent conflict between religious and scientific beliefs because the former are based primarily on processing in the experiential system and the latter on processing in the rational system. The conflict can be satisfactorily resolved only by relegating the two to different realms, the spiritual realm to religious beliefs and the real-world realm to scientific beliefs. Too often in the past, religious beliefs have been used to attempt to explain natural phenomena. A famous example is the reaction of the Roman Catholic Church to Galileo's presentation of evidence in support of Copernicus's view that the sun, not the earth, is the center of the solar system. He was condemned by the church for harboring heretical beliefs, and, but for the support of friends in high places, his sentence could have been burning at the stake rather than permanent house arrest.

Some religious beliefs are only foolish, whereas others, as in the case of Galileo, are serious impediments to the advancement of science. The reason that forks were not used until long after spoons and knives is that it was argued that because God had given people fingers, which were perfectly adequate for the task, it would be a travesty to use forks (Giblin, 1987). An example of a more dangerous belief is when a religious leader convinced American Indians that their God would protect them from the white man's bullets if they engaged in a ghost dance. Many died when their God failed to save them.

Turning to a more modern intrusion of religious beliefs into science, many fundamentalists today do not accept evolution and believe instead in the biblical version of Genesis. They attempt to pass laws that would require the biblical version of creation to be taught as an equally valid theory. This is dangerous as well as foolish because it would promote poor scientific thinking in students, which would have unfavorable ramifications for scientific advancement, including progress in health and human welfare. Moreover, it would put the United States at a scientific disadvantage in competition with other countries. The United States is already at a scientific disadvantage in this respect because it is among the countries with the lowest acceptance of evolutionary theory, with less than 40 percent reporting that they believe evolutionary theory is true (Miller, Scott, & Okamoto, 2006).

It may be concluded that religious beliefs are a mixed blessing that can be used for great harm, as well as for great good. This leads to the question of whether the human species would be better off without religion, as recommended by the authors of several recent books written from a rational perspective (e.g., Dawkins, 2008; Harris, 2005; Hitchins, 2007). However, from the perspective of CET, better solutions are available that can retain what is constructive in religious beliefs without including what is destructive in them. There is a problem with the scientific perspective presented by some authors because it is based on the assumption that rational thinking is the only constructive way to think, which runs counter to the view in CET that humans process information using two adaptive systems.

Would the World Be Better Without Religion?

Some critics of religion argue that people without religion would be more reasonable and therefore behave in more positive and less destructive ways to each other. There are two problems with this view. One is that there is no good reason to believe that if humans gave up their religious beliefs and attempted instead to behave in a completely rational manner, they would be able to do so. It is quite possible that, under the guise of behaving rationally, people would be no less destructive than they have been under the influence of religion, but they would do so for different reasons, which they then would rationalize. In other words, people may be irrationally destructive to each other for reasons other than irrational religious beliefs.

A further problem with the position of replacing an irrational religious belief system with a purely rational one is that the position fails to take into account the experiential system. People cannot be rational by simply consciously attempting to be so because their rationality is biased outside of their awareness by their experiential processing. Thus, to be objectively rational, it is necessary to be aware of and compensate for the biasing influence of the experiential system.

Some Proposals for Retaining the Good Without the Bad in Religion

Religion can be used constructively, without including its destructive aspects, in the following ways: (1) maintaining one's religious beliefs but being tolerant of other beliefs; (2) treating religious beliefs as useful, comforting and even inspirational, but not as necessarily true; and (3) believing in God in the form of an abstract equivalent, as in spirituality, rather than as a deity.

Maintaining one's religious beliefs but being tolerant of other beliefs. The source of a great deal of harm in religious beliefs is the intolerance of other beliefs. Thus, some people believe that only people of their own religion will go to heaven. They may regard others as heretics deserving of punishment, and they are most antagonistic to atheists. An alternative, more kindly and rational view is to maintain one's own religious beliefs without demeaning the beliefs of others. Other people can be regarded as simply having alternative beliefs or false beliefs, but this should be a reason to accept them as they are or feel sorry for them rather than be antagonistic to them. Such an attitude of tolerance for other beliefs should go a long way to reducing the hostility to people with other religious beliefs or to nonbelievers.

Treating religious beliefs as useful, comforting, and even inspirational, but not as necessarily true. People should consider the possibility that religious beliefs can be useful even if they are considered based on imaginary figures and events rather than representing absolute truth. Remember the research with the Bingo players who kept magic charms despite acknowledging that they did not believe they influenced their winnings. Most said they nevertheless would not play Bingo without them. The reason they carried the magic charms with them to Bingo is that they made them feel better. Prayer and talking to God could also operate in the same way. Even if God does not answer a person's prayers, the very act of praying may be rewarding in itself. One does not have to ask for gifts or for wishes to be fulfilled. It may be enough to talk to an imaginary, all-powerful, all-knowing figure who is supportive, understanding, loving, and a very good listener and provider of advice. According to Max Lerner (1990), communicating with such an imaginary figure can be a source of self-understanding and peace of mind. Recall that imagery is a powerful procedure for reaching the experiential system and that it has been used to very good effect in psychotherapy. There is no reason that religious beliefs concerning imaginary beings and events cannot be equally effective.

Max Lerner (1990), journalist, writer, and professor, was not an orthodox religious person and did not believe in a life after death. Yet he coped with three serious threats to his life, two cancers and a heart attack, through deep, soul-searching conversations with an imaginary God. He did so almost every night before falling asleep and at other times when he felt particularly in need of God's help. His imaginary God became emotionally very real to him as he struggled to keep alive despite recognizing that his God was only imaginary. Apparently, the support his imaginary God gave him was so important to him that he said that his imaginary God was more real to him than reality itself. He stated the following: "Anyone who is really sick knows that the presence of God is the realest presence of all, realer than doctors, nurses, procedures, realer even than the support of friends and intimates. . . . That is why I have come to call God 'the great Intervener' for anyone sick, mediating between him and his illness, spurring the self-healer in him" (p. 190).

Belief in spirituality rather than in formal religion. Spirituality differs from religion in that it is usually a private matter and involves no specific dogma and social organization. Its essence is a belief in the importance of what is regarded as spirit rather than matter; a connection with a transcendent power, force, or energy that some refer to as God; and an attachment to the infinite. In other words, it shares some features with religion, such as a feeling of connection with some higher, transcendent reality, but it remains at a highly abstract level without concretizing its beliefs in the form of deities, angels, heaven, and hell. It has both advantages and disadvantages in comparison to formal religions. As an advantage, it avoids the irrationality of many religious beliefs, and it does not lend itself to the promotion of destructive behavior against people with other beliefs. Rather, the emphasis is on loving kindness and unity with the universe. In a study comparing those who identified themselves as spiritual with those who regarded themselves as religious, the former viewed God as more loving, forgiving, and nonjudgmental (Woods & Ironson, 1999). In relation to the broad perspective provided by transcendence and identifying with the universe, spirituality makes people's personal problems appear trivial in comparison. As a disadvantage, spiritual beliefs do not reach the experiential system in as fundamental a manner as religious beliefs, with their rituals and concrete representations. Another disadvantage is that, as a private belief system, spiritual beliefs do not provide as strong social support as organized religion.

Atheism

The most satisfactory solution for a substantial minority of people is completely to reject a belief in religion. They advocate atheism or agnosticism because they value rationality, and religious beliefs are clearly unrealistic and irrational. Although atheists and agnostics are somewhat different, the difference is more one of style than of substance. Atheists deny the existence of a deity and of other imaginary figures, such as angels and devils that are accepted on faith rather than on replicable observation. They believe that the burden of proof lies with those who claim that something exists rather than with those who believe it does not exist until proven otherwise. Agnostics are less extreme, as they say they do not know whether undemonstrated religious figures and events exist. However, like atheists, they do not accept the existence of nondemonstrable religious phenomena. Unlike atheists, agnostics accept the possibility that such phenomena may exist. For the remainder of this discussion, I will not distinguish between the two groups.

Is atheism a viable belief system? Apparently not only do many intelligent, thoughtful people believe it is, but they believe it is the only reasonable way for humans to believe and behave. They regard religion as a primitive belief system that is irrational, unrealistic, and the source of a great deal of destructive behavior. Accordingly, they look forward to a day when humans will think more logically and realistically and abandon their religious beliefs.

According to CET, what is wrong with the scientific approach that atheists endorse is not that it is scientific but that it is not scientific enough. To be appropriately scientific, it would have to recognize the existence of an experiential system that is a source of constructive as well as destructive ways of thinking and behaving with respect to its role in religion. Thus, to be unaware of the experiential system not only prevents an understanding of religion but also avoids an adequate recognition of its contributions. It also prevents addressing the experiential system in ways that facilitate retaining what is good in religion and rejecting the destructive. As noted previously, having an atheistic view is no guarantee that a person will not engage in destructive thinking and behavior based on other aspects of experiential processing. Atheists are no less capable than others of engaging in experientially determined maladaptive behavior and then rationalizing it by attributing it to rational processing.

Implications of Cognitive-Experiential Theory for Human Survival

Einstein said that people have to change their way of thinking if the human species is to avoid nuclear war and the possible destruction of the species (Calaprice, 1996). But how do they change their way of thinking? The first step in learning to think differently is in understanding how we do think. According to CET we think with two minds, experiential and rational, and we think in illogical and destructive ways largely because of the experiential system and its biasing influence on the rational system. It does this in two ways: by its initial influence on people's thinking and by fostering rationalizing in the form of attributing to rational processing what was determined primarily by experiential processing. Interestingly, this does not occur uniformly across domains. Humans are able to use their remarkable intelligence to solve problems concerning inanimate issues but not problems concerning personal and interpersonal issues because inanimate issues fall primarily within the domain of the rational system whereas personal and interpersonal issues, in both individuals and societies, fall primarily within the domain of the experiential system. This can account for why humans have made remarkable contributions in science, mathematics, and technology, but have behaved in a primitive manner when attempting to solve problems concerning personal and interpersonal issues. As noted previously, people fight wars with vastly improved weaponry but continue unabatedly to fight them.

The question remains as to what can be done to solve the problem. The answer, according to CET, lies in the consideration that the problem is in the operation of the experiential system and its influence on the rational system. Thus, the answer is to improve the operation of the experiential system and its influence on the rational system. To do so, people will have to understand that the solution cannot lie in suppressing the experiential system because it is an important source of constructive behavior, as well as of destructive behavior. It is therefore important for people to learn to control the latter and develop the former by using procedures such as those proposed for improving constructive thinking. Yet even more important than inhibiting the expression of maladaptive promptings from the experiential system is training it so that its promptings are constructive in the first place and therefore do not require control.

The experiential system should be regarded as a partner and not as an antagonist to the rational system, so that a harmonious relation can be established between the two. Consistent with this view, it is important for people to recognize that the rational system can learn from as well as train the experiential system. Because the experiential system is an empirical learning system that normally operates outside of awareness, it has its own source of wisdom that can be identified and contribute to the adaptive operation of the rational system.

Two additional reasons exist for improving constructive thinking by training and learning from the experiential system, and these can help people use their intelligence to solve personal and interpersonal problems and therefore live with each other more harmoniously. At higher levels of constructive thinking, people can be expected to experience little interference from disturbing thoughts that can interfere with thinking logically and objectively about personal and interpersonal issues. In addition, given the direct relation found between constructive thinking and establishing favorable interpersonal relationships (Epstein, 2001; Epstein & Meier, 1989), a high level of constructive thinking is likely to be associated with a prosocial attitude toward others.

In conclusion, humans, despite the remarkable intelligence they exhibit in solving impersonal problems, often think unintelligently about personal and interpersonal issues at both the individual and societal level. The reason for this, according to CET, is that personal and interpersonal issues fall primarily within the domain of the experiential system, whereas impersonal issues fall primarily within the domain of the rational system. The solution, according to CET, is to train and learn from the experiential system in an extended formal education period, so that the effect of experiential processing and its influence on rational processing promotes thinking in a manner that is logical, objective, prosocial, and a source of wisdom.

REFERENCES

Abernathy, C. M., & Hamm, R. M. (1995). *Surgical intuition: What it is and how to get it.* Philadelphia, PA: Hanley & Belfus.

Calaprice, A. (1996). *The quotable Einstein.* Princeton, NJ: Princeton University Press.

Dawkins, R. (2008). *The God delusion.* New York: Mariner Books.

Epstein, S. (1998). *Constructive thinking: The key to emotional intelligence.* Westport, Connecticut: Greenwood Publishing.

Epstein, S. (2001). *Constructive Thinking Inventory Manual.* Lutz: FL: Psychological Assessment Resources, Inc.

Epstein, S. (2010). Demystifying intuition: What it is, what it does, and how it does it. *Psychological Inquiry, 21*, 295–312.

Epstein, S., & Meier, P. (1989). Constructive thinking: A broad coping variable with specific components. *Journal of Personality and Social Psychology, 57*, 332–349.

Giblin, J. C. (1987). *From hand to mouth.* New York: Thomas Y. Crowell.

Harris, S. (2005). *The end of faith: Religion, terror, and the future of reason.* New York: Norton.

Hitchins, C. (2007). *God is not great: How religion poisons everything.* New York: Twelve Books.

James, W. (1902/1961). *The varieties of religious experience.* New York: Macmillan Publishing Co.

Lerner, M. (1990). *Wrestling with the angel.* New York: Touchstone.

McCullough, M. E., & Willoughby, L. B. (2009). Religion, self-regulation, and self-control: Associations, explanations, and implications. *Psychological Bulletin, 135*, 69–93.

Miller, J. D., Scott, E. C., & Okamoto, S. (2006). Public acceptance of evolution in 34 countries. *Science, 313.*

Norris, P., & Epstein, S. (2011). An experiential thinking style: Its facets and relations with objective and subjective criterion measures. *Journal of Personality, 79*, 1043–1079.

St. Augustine (397/1961). *The confessions of Saint Augustine.* (Translated by Edward P. Pusey). New York: Collier Macmillan Publishers.

Woods, T. E., & Ironson, H. (1999). Religion and spirituality in the face of illness: How cancer, cardiac, and HIV patients describe their spirituality/religiosity. *Journal of Health Psychology, 4*, 393–412.

INDEX

CPSIA information can be obtained at www.ICGtesting.com
Printed in the USA
BVOW08s0332031115

425380BV00001B/1/P

9 780190 493240